SPITZ

D0936696

SPITZ

An Everyday Modernism: **The Houses of William Wurster**

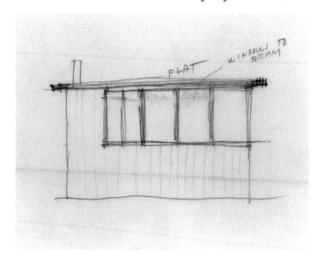

An Everyday Modernism

Edited by Marc Treib

The Houses of William Wurster

with essays by

David Gebhard

Daniel Gregory

Greg Hise

Dorothée Imbert

Alan R. Michelson

Richard C. Peters and
  Caitlin Lempres

Marc Treib

Gwendolyn Wright

San Francisco Museum of Modern Art

University of California Press · Berkeley · Los Angeles · London

An Everyday Modernism: The Houses of William Wurster is published in association with the University of California Press. It accompanies an exhibition organized by the San Francisco Museum of Modern Art, on view from 16 November 1995 to 11 February 1996.

An Everyday Modernism: The Houses of William Wurster is generously supported by the Henry Luce Foundation, Inc., the National Endowment for the Humanities, the National Endowment for the Arts, Frances and John Bowes, and Evelyn and Walter Haas. Additional support has been provided by Ann S. Bowers and Mr. and Mrs. Frank Montgomery Woods.

Library of Congress Cataloging-in-Publication Data:

An everyday modernism : the houses of William Wurster / edited by Marc
    Treib ; with contributions by David Gebhard . . . [et al.].
        p.   cm.
    Exhibition: Nov. 16, 1995–Feb. 11, 1996, at the San Francisco
Museum of Modern Art.
    Includes bibliographical references and index.
    ISBN 0–520–20550–2
    1. Wurster, William Wilson—Exhibitions. I. Treib, Marc.
II. Gebhard, David. III. San Francisco Museum of Modern Art.
NA737. W87A4 1995
728' .37' 092—dc20   95-9410
                                                            CIP

Publications Manager: Kara Kirk
Editor: Janet Wilson
Designer: Robin Weiss
Photography Coordinator: Alexandra Chappell
Indexer: Susan Stone
Text Compositor: Phoebe Bixler

Cover: William Wurster, *King House*, Atherton, 1937 (detail)
Frontispiece: William Wurster, *Harker House*, Mill Valley, 1938 (elevation study, 1937)

9 8 7 6 5 4 3 2 1

Printed in Hong Kong

Contents

Director's Foreword and Acknowledgments

Since its inauguration in 1935, the San Francisco Museum of Modern Art (then called the San Francisco Museum of Art) has been committed to the presentation and interpretation of both historical and new architecture and design. Only two years after it opened, the Museum presented "Contemporary Landscape Architecture," the world's first exhibition of international currents in modern landscape design. The landmark 1940 exhibition, "Space for Living," focused on Telesis, a group of Bay Area architects, landscape architects, industrial designers, and urban planners whose work was the precursor of what we now term environmental design. The 1949 exhibition "Domestic Architecture of the San Francisco Bay Region," which followed in the wake of critic Lewis Mumford's call for regional architecture in his "Skyline" column in *The New Yorker* magazine, prominently featured the work of William Wurster. These exhibitions not only gained recognition for California architecture and design both nationally and internationally but also introduced leading trends in architecture and design to California audiences.

"An Everyday Modernism: The Houses of William Wurster"—the first major exhibition presented by the Department of Architecture and Design during the inaugural year of the Museum's new building—continues this important tradition. And so it is fitting, on the hundredth anniversary of Wurster's birth, that the very institution that first presented his work to the public should undertake a large-scale critical assessment of its scope and importance.

Wurster's architecture is currently not well known to the general public, but he is widely recognized by historians as the foremost proponent of a distinctive Bay Region modernist style, not only through the private architectural practice he established—Wurster, Bernardi and Emmons—but also through his work as a theorist and academic administrator. Although Wurster was based in the region, his influence and ideas extended far beyond the borders of California. As head of two major schools of architecture—first at the Massachusetts Institute of Technology and then at his alma mater, the University of California at Berkeley—Wurster helped shape the ideas of an entire generation of architects and city planners.

An exhibition of this scope, with its interdisciplinary approach and original scholarship, could not have been undertaken without the early and generous support of the Henry Luce Foundation, the National Endowment for the Humanities, and the National Endowment for the Arts. I extend my deepest gratitude to these benefactors, as well as to other major individual donors, for making possible this exhibition, publication, and interpretive programming.

We very much appreciate the enthusiasm, dedication, and scholarship brought to the project by Marc Treib, professor of architecture at the College of Environmental Design, University of California at Berkeley. As guest curator of the exhibition, Professor Treib was intimately involved in almost every aspect of its organization, from serving as editor of this publication and contributing a lengthy essay to undertaking the many conceptual and logistical challenges of the exhibition's organization and installation design.

Special gratitude is extended to the distinguished authors who contributed their scholarship to this publication: David Gebhard, Daniel Gregory, Greg Hise, Dorothée Imbert, Alan R. Michelson, Richard C. Peters and Caitlin King Lempres, and Gwendolyn Wright. We are also deeply obliged to Ms. Imbert for the many hours of research she undertook for both the exhibition and the publication.

The Wurster drawings and papers from the late 1920s to approximately 1950 are held in the Documents Collection of the College of Environmental Design, University of California at Berkeley. We thank Professor Stephen Tobriner and archival assistant Travis Culwell for their help in our research and for making the graphic materials available for the exhibition and this book. Roger Sturtevant's architectural photographs constitute a superb document for understanding the original forms—and architectural intentions—of Wurster's houses, many of which have been changed or even demolished. Senior Curator of Prints and Photography Therese Thau Heyman and Curatorial Specialist Drew Johnson of the Photograph Collection at the Oakland Museum, which holds the Sturtevant negatives, assisted greatly in our endeavors.

Credit goes to Paolo Polledri, former curator of architecture and design at the San Francisco Museum of Modern Art, who initiated this project over five years ago. Gary Garrels, Elise S. Haas chief curator, played an important role in assembling the team to work on the exhibition. Although joining the Museum staff well after the project was launched, Aaron Betsky, curator of architecture and design, made valuable suggestions for the structuring and design of the exhibition.

Publications manager Kara Kirk, editor Janet Wilson, editorial assistant Alexandra Chappell, and designer Robin Weiss added immeasurably to the publication project, especially in light of the geographic distribution of the authors and the complexity of the illustrative materials. We have enjoyed working with our copublisher, the University of California Press, particularly Deborah Kirshman, fine arts editor, whose enthusiastic support of this project has been greatly appreciated.

Special thanks go to former staff member Jeannette Redensek, who was the first to conduct a comprehensive search of the various archives for this exhibition and who also, with Development Department staff members Lori Fogarty and Maggie Russell-Harde, secured the funding to make this project possible. Many other Museum staff members contributed their time and talents to the realization of this exhibition, and I take this opportunity to thank them, particularly Director of Curatorial Affairs Inge-Lise Eckmann, Curatorial Assistant Mark Petr, Exhibitions Manager Barbara Levine, Curator of Education and Public Programs John Weber, Conservators Jill Sterrett Beaudin, Leslie Kruth, and Narelle Jarry; Head Registrar Tina Garfinkel and Assistant Registrar Olga Charyshyn, Operations and Installations Manager Kent Roberts, and Matting and Framing Technician Greg Wilson.

Finally, I would like to offer very special thanks to the lenders to "An Everyday Modernism: The Houses of William Wurster," who have generously made their holdings—original drawings, letters, plans, and photographs—available for this exhibition.

John R. Lane

Introduction

For almost three decades William Wilson Wurster occupied a preeminent position in American residential architecture. His everyday modernism, which tempered national and international architectural trends with a concern for things local, provided a model for living in California and, through coverage in publications, the nation at large. As dean of the schools of architecture at the Massachusetts Institute of Technology and later the University of California at Berkeley, Wurster also exerted a formidable influence on architectural education from the late 1940s through the 1960s. Yet despite this list of impressive achievements, Wurster is no longer well known. Should he be remembered at all today, it is for his 1927 rustic "farmhouse" design for Mrs. Sadie Gregory in Scotts Valley, California.

The year 1995 marks the centenary of William Wurster's birth and provides the impetus for this exhibition. But in many ways the time is ripe to reevaluate Wurster's contribution to California architecture and the role of modernity—and humility—in architectural design. Although the firm of Wurster, Bernardi and Emmons designed projects ranging in scale from foreign consulates and commercial centers to high-rise office buildings and air-force bases, Wurster himself remained committed to residential design. For this reason, we have restricted the scope of the exhibition to houses and their extension as multiple-family housing. Although this purview necessarily circumscribes the demonstrated range of Wurster's accomplishments, it permits a deeper investigation of the residential designs and their social and environmental milieus.

A number of questions have informed the planning of the exhibition. Why, for example, does history pass over a figure so distinguished in the profession and the discourse of his times? To what degree did Wurster's residential work reflect the central architectural ideas of its era, and, conversely, to what degree did these houses engender those living patterns within and around them? Why has not the second Saxton Pope house—an innovative and polished work of 1940—entered the standard histories of modern American architecture? And could it be that Wurster is largely forgotten today because the architectural ideas and features central to his manner have become so common in California houses, both architect-designed and mass market? While no single exhibition can fully answer such questions, we hope that "An Everyday Modernism: The Houses of William Wurster"—bolstered by this publication—will at the very least open the discourse.

The exhibition has been organized on the basis of six subject areas. The first, "Sources and Courses: The Making of an Architecture," presents Wurster's education, apprenticeship, study travels, and early work, tracing his stylistic evolution from a modern revivalist to a regional modernist. "Patterns of Living" compares the architecture of Wurster's many single-family homes with that of his collective-dwelling designs—for example, the Valencia Gardens public housing in San Francisco and the Stern Hall women's dormitory in Berkeley. The wartime defense workers' housing at Chabot Terrace and Carquinez Heights in Vallejo links social concerns with those of "Building Technique," which constitutes the third thematic area. This section establishes the affinity between architectural form and the range of structural and finish materials in Wurster's designs. Central to this section is the second house for Dr. and Mrs. Saxton Pope in Orinda, whose use of industrial elements such as stock chimney flues, corrugated metal sheathing, and concrete block prefigures by some thirty years the "exposed" architecture of the late 1970s. The fourth thematic section, "The Environment," addresses considerations such as landform, climate, locus—rural, coastal, suburban, or urban—and the influence of each on the making of Wurster's architecture.

No architect works in isolation, and we have endeavored to suggest the contributions of Wurster's partners, Theodore Bernardi and Donn Emmons, as well as those of his wife, the planner Catherine Bauer. Landscape architect Thomas Church was also a lifelong participant in the design of the Wurster environment, stressing the concern for human use in creating the contemporary garden. Roger Sturtevant's photographs, many of which appear in the volume, remain our principal photographic record of the houses as they were built. For almost three decades, these three—Wurster, Church, and Sturtevant—each in his own way, each according to his discipline, proselytized as musketeers of modernism in Northern California.

Two segments complete the exhibition. The first, "Regionalism, and Regional Modernism," describes the architectural theater more broadly; the second, "A Wurster Lexicon," seeks to identify the architect's lasting contributions to residential design in California. During the 1930s and 1940s the interrelated trends of modernism, regionalism, and regional modernism engaged practitioners and critics alike. Modernism implied that one could design virtually free from one's locale, as if the prevailing aesthetic zeitgeist dissipated the influence of location, climate, and client. The regionalists, on the other hand, exhibited stronger ties to local traditions than to current social and technical trends. A third group—today termed regional modernists—tried, in various ways, to create an architecture that simultaneously acknowledged its time and place. Houses by Harwell Hamilton Harris, Pietro Belluschi, O'Neil Ford, Gardner Dailey, and Joseph Esherick are among those that closely resembled in concern and ambition the houses of William Wurster.

Although a book lacks the immediacy of the exhibition's original drawings, as well as the impact of enlarged photographs, mock-ups, and scale models, it does allow a study of historical context in greater detail and depth. Here we have sought to establish the degree to which Wurster was typical of his time and in what way he was different, the considerations he addressed, with whom, and for whom. My opening essay outlines the course of William Wurster's life and architectural career—his education, professional training, client group, and stylistic development—and also sketches a composite picture of contemporary American architectural thought and construction during his lifetime. Richard C. Peters and Caitlin King Lempres add a biographical overview, while addressing Wurster's achievements as an educator at MIT and the University of California at Berkeley. Daniel Gregory offers inside views of the deceptively simple Gregory Farmhouse and the social circles in which Wurster moved. Wurster appears as an architect who understood the desires of his clients and successfully translated them into building—a key reason for his continued success in practice.

Dorothée Imbert describes the tight-knit collaboration between Wurster and Thomas Dolliver Church, the formation of the friendship, and the many products of their collaboration. The strong bond between indoors and outdoors so evident in the houses reflected a sensitivity to the California landscape fostered by Wurster's long contact with Church. Throughout his life, Wurster designed for both the meager and the lavish budget. Greg Hise studies the relationship between the "Large Small House" and the minimal dwelling and describes the construction methods by which each was realized. These interests culminated in the prefabrication systems for the defense workers' housing in Vallejo and the Prebilt house of the later 1940s.

David Gebhard surveys the range of professional activities in California during the Wurster decades, covering both the northern and southern parts of the state and the work of both the more traditional and the more modernist architects. Wurster's ideas of community were considerably broadened by his marriage to the noted planner and housing reformer Catherine Bauer, a "partnership" examined in Gwendolyn Wright's essay on the social milieu of the house and social housing.

In an exhibition and publication that feature the single name William Wurster, it would be far too easy to omit the contributions of the architect's partners and staff who brought projects to completion or who served as the principal designers for work listed simply as Wurster, Bernardi and Emmons. Alan Michelson focuses on four houses by Theodore Bernardi and four by Donn Emmons to present their similarities to and differences from the Wurster designs.

It will be obvious to many readers that this book constitutes only the first efforts toward a more comprehensive investigation of California residential architecture from the 1930s through the 1950s. Those who are familiar with Wurster houses—especially those who live in them—will surely question the inclusion or omission of examples in both photographs and text. An exhibition or book produced ten years from now will certainly emphasize different projects for different purposes, for even our judgment today is rooted to its period, our needs, and our values. Under Wurster's name the firm designed several hundred houses, and they constitute only part of the total œuvre by Wurster, Bernardi and Emmons. Thus this exhibition and book, *An Everyday Modernism: The Houses of William Wurster,* must necessarily be considered as a report on a study in progress, not a conclusion.

My rapid education in the work and ideas of William Wurster was greatly enhanced by the gracious assistance of Daniel Gregory, Richard Peters, Donn Emmons, and the many clients, colleagues, owners, and occupants of Wurster houses. Alan Michelson's doctoral dissertation, *Towards a Regional Synthesis: The Suburban and Country Residences of William Wilson Wurster,* an excellent study, provides the most complete listing of projects and sources. Craig Hudson provided valuable information on the location and owners of several houses. In addition, I am grateful to the authors of the essays in this book for meeting very stringent deadlines in order to make publication coincide with the opening of the exhibition without any sacrifice in quality.

Travis Culwell, archival assistant at the Documents Collection of the College of Environmental Design, University of California at Berkeley, spent untold hours reviewing the drawings with us; Jeannette Redensek was the first to research the various archives, providing a critical first introduction to the materials. Curatorial Assistant Mark Petr contributed to both the book and the exhibition in ways too many and too diverse to specify, but to an extent too great to leave unnoticed or unthanked.

George Anastaplos and Greg Tolman constructed the architectural models, a task far more complicated than it may seem at first glance since much of the graphic materials survive in only a fragmentary state. Edward Dyba made new prints from the Sturtevant negatives, which were mounted by Faulkner Color Labs. New architectural photography was undertaken by Richard Barnes, who was also a member of the project team involved in photographically interpreting the Wurster houses today. John Harding, Joel Leivick, Margaret Moulton, and Susan Schwartzenberg produced intriguing views of the spaces in and around the Wurster houses and the people who inhabit them. Due to time constraints, however, these images were not available for the publication.

Of course, I must acknowledge those many individuals and institutions previously cited in the director's foreword; only limited space precludes me from thanking them again. Finally my thanks go to Dorothée Imbert, who in every respect except officially has served as associate curator of the exhibition. As researcher, essayist, designer, Wurster house-visit companion, in-house critic, and general troubleshooter, her contributions have been substantial. Everything might eventually have been completed without her help, but it would not have been done so quickly and so well, nor with equal pleasure.

Note: All houses cited in the text and captions are located in California unless otherwise indicated. Dates given refer to the believed time of occupancy, although individual drawings may be dated as written on them. Given that this is the first major published study on Wurster, there are bound to be some discrepancies owing to gaps in the documentation. In these instances, the authors have attempted to assign reasonable dates to the designs.

I would like to dedicate my efforts to Donn Emmons and to the memory of Theodore Bernardi.

Marc Treib

William Wilson Wurster: The Feeling of Function

Marc Treib

Before returning to Berkeley in the mid-1920s, the young William Wilson Wurster had followed a course both predictable and fruitful. From the University of California at Berkeley he had received a substantial architectural education based on neoclassical norms and developed a network of social contacts for future commissions. From architectural employment in Northern California, he had acquired professional experience and funds sufficient to permit the requisite travel through Europe. There Wurster encountered not only the monuments of European architecture and art but also the humble farms and utility structures in the vernacular traditions. From a year of work in New York he had learned the rudiments of architectural practice and the crucial ability to deal socially with clients. All of these fragments of experience cohered to mold the taste and values of this young architect from Stockton; and all would exert a continuing influence on Wurster's work for the remainder of his long and prolific career.

With financial help from his former boss, William Adams Delano Aldrich,[1] in 1924 Wurster opened his Berkeley office. The Great Earthquake of 1906 had precipitated a minor diaspora for the upper middle class, who departed the dense fabric of urban San Francisco for the peninsula and trans-Bay suburbs. With augmented ferry and rail service, Berkeley, Alameda, and Oakland became increasingly attractive as residential communities at a remove from the hub. Remodelings, additions, and new houses for these communities constituted Wurster's first commissions, graciously aided by a social network that stemmed from several key connections.[2]

Wurster's early residential projects followed the lines of then-prevalent styles and were distinguished neither in their floor plans nor in any spatial or stylistic developments. Taken as a group, they could be characterized as accomplished essays in established genres, whether leaning toward the Spanish Colonial Revival, like the 1928 Kellam House in Santa Barbara (fig. 2), or California Tudor, like the Hawley House in Berkeley of 1929 (fig. 3). While vestigially medieval in its pointed gables and engaged chimneys, the Hawley design also suggested the English Arts and Crafts movement's rediscovery of the cottage—and William Delano's own country house on Long Island (fig. 4). Engaged within the flat plane of the entry, the dramatic triple chimney was the house's central feature. Such a gesture was rare in Wurster's early work; from the earliest projects he seems to have been more concerned with spaces addressed to daily living than with architectural features used for theatrical effect. Period styles prevailed in the Wurster houses for the upper middle class for several years, expressing equally the clients' social aspirations for both a country estate and material comfort in suburbia.

1.
Berry House, Pasatiempo, 1935
William Wurster

2. (top left)
Kellam House, Santa Barbara, 1928
William Wurster
Study of facade from forecourt

3. (right)
Hawley House, Berkeley, 1929
William Wurster
Perspective sketch

4. (bottom left)
Delano House, Syosset, New York, 1915
Delano and Aldrich

From a primarily Beaux-Arts education and an internship at Delano and Aldrich, Wurster acquired a set of planning models that he applied to his early projects, particularly those for larger houses on rural sites. His 1928 country-house design for Clarence Breuner near Sacramento relied on a stately entrance court to announce the grandeur of the residence (figs. 5, 6). This pattern—an entry hall with dining room to one side, bedrooms on the other, and servants' quarters on the upper floor of the service wing—prevailed nationally in dwellings of this scale and standing (fig. 7). The projecting living room—which would remain a central element of Wurster's repertoire—with its two-storied porches, borrowed from accepted prototypes such as Mount Vernon and the plantations of the antebellum South. More importantly, however, the increased perimeter that resulted from this arrangement also acknowledged the role of climate in determining architectural form. The prominence of the room allowed greater air circulation, beneficial in warm weather; the porches offered sheltered outdoor settings that addressed the view. So prevalent was the model of the enclosed courtyard in Wurster's work for this social group that in some projects it seemed to crash head on with his more vernacular sensibilities.

Formation

William Wurster's upbringing in Stockton helped develop a matter-of-fact attitude toward architecture that he would maintain throughout his life. While more formally planned public buildings on the Beaux-Arts model prevailed in his studios at the University of California at Berkeley, the local Bay Area traditions remained a source of inspiration for Wurster's residential designs. John Galen Howard (1864-1931) was still very much in evidence, both in his buildings for the university, including the architecture building itself, and as an educator.[3] Like other architects of his time, Howard seemed to vary considerably in his approach to public and residential buildings, evincing differences that approached stylistic schizophrenia. Howard's residential work, like that of his contemporary Bernard Maybeck, was usually wooden, shingled, and intimate. The public work, in contrast, utilized stucco and stone, symmetry, and more monumental references to Italianate and/or French-inspired buildings. The philosophy underlying each design, however, remained constant. At the dedication for the Hearst Memorial Mining Building on 23 August 1907, Howard declared, in a manner somewhat at odds with its message:

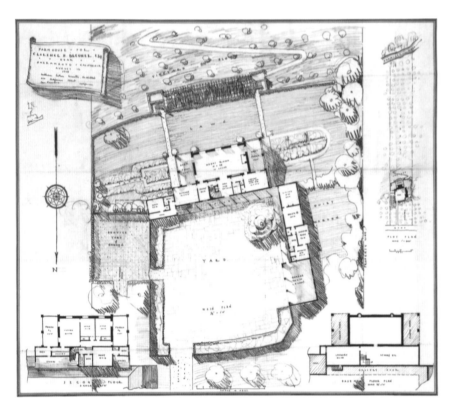

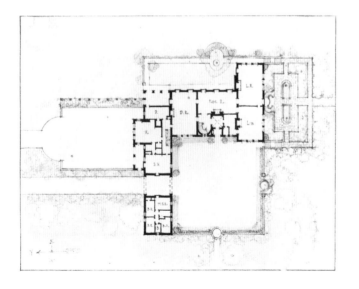

5.
Breuner House, near Sacramento, 1928
William Wurster
Site and floor plans

6.
Breuner House, near Sacramento, 1928
William Wurster
Perspective

7.
Astor House, Port Washington, New York,
1922
Delano and Aldrich
Plan

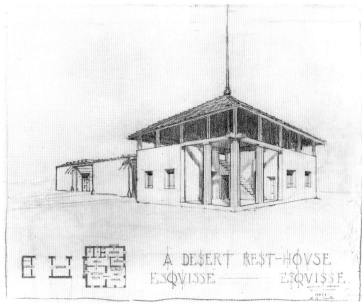

8.
A Public Library, student project,
University of California at Berkeley, 1919
William Wurster

9.
A Desert Rest-House, student project,
University of California at Berkeley, 1917
William Wurster

Our dearest wish has been that it should be able to brave these times and the times to come with a front modest, yet frank—simple, clean, sterling, permanent; beautiful in its own sincere and assured, though reticent way, devoid of anything remotely suggestive of overdoing in the way of ornament or pompous grouping of its parts; its poetic message stripped of verbiage; classic to the core, yet classic of that primitive type which might almost be called archaic, were it not that it is quickened by the breath of modern life.[4]

In many respects, this characterization could have applied equally well to almost all of Wurster's residential architecture.

In his final year of studies at Berkeley, Wurster had produced a public library that seemed to join the blockiness of the San Francisco Public Library with a stack tower in the manner of Bertram Goodhue.[5] As a totality, it was probably the most formal design Wurster ever executed; without question, the labored ink-wash renderings were the most elaborate he ever produced (fig. 8). As he himself later admitted, he had little real talent for drawing. But his school years also produced a charming "Desert Rest-House" that drew upon the exposed beamwork and stuccoed surfaces of turn-of-the-century residential architecture in the Berkeley hills.[6] The vernacular references of the visitors' station demonstrate that even during his student years, the regional and the monumental coexisted in his thoughts and his designs (fig.9).

The concern for social reform given architectural expression by the English Arts and Crafts movement emerged in the United States—transformed—as the Craftsman style. Elbert Hubbard and Gustav Stickley, two of the American movement's leading voices, argued for craft, simplicity, and honesty of materials as the basis for design.[7] The Bay Area's own version of the Arts and Crafts derived from several sources that included the parent Craftsman style, the Californian Mission Revival, and the writings and personality of the Berkeley poet Charles Keeler (1871–1937). Keeler's 1904 book, *The Simple House,* argued that all unessential elements within the dwelling should be discarded. "In the simple home all is quiet in effect," he wrote, "restrained in tone, yet natural and joyous in its frank use of unadorned material. Harmony of line and balance of proportion [are] not obscured by meaningless ornamentation; harmony of color is not marred by violent contrasts."[8]

Architects such as Bernard Maybeck, Ernest Coxhead, Willis Polk, Julia Morgan, and the Swedenborgian minister Joseph Worcester forged an architecture direct in its use of natural materials, minimal in its physical enclosure but maximal in its sense of shelter.[9] Well aware of the benign climate and its

10.
Study for Hillside house, with open passage
from lower to upper garden, no date
Bernard Maybeck

ameliorative powers on both body and soul, and proud of the mythopoetic status of the California landscape as a sort of promised land, the coteries of architects and clients sought an architecture appropriate to the environment and
social milieu of the Bay Area.

Bernard Maybeck (1862–1957) was born in New York to a German immi-
grant family and educated at the École des Beaux-Arts in Paris before relocat-
ing to the Bay Area in 1890.[10] His inventive house compositions accepted few
of the canons of eastern residential architecture and freely twisted the rules of
classical proportions, ornamentation, and detailing. The constituent building
parts remained visible and unpainted, as Keeler had suggested. Houses were
configured to their sites rather than vice-versa. Maybeck's buildings employed
a visible sense of handcraft, although stylistically they might refer equally to
medieval French building and local vernacular structures. In all, Maybeck
manneristically tweaked the accepted habits and freely designed in accord
with the dicta of program, site, and climate.

As a charter member of the Berkeley Hillside Club, formed to preserve the
beauty of the hills from wanton development, Maybeck saw the house as a
refuge from the infrequent inclement weather, and the garden as the center for
living (fig. 10). The club's yearbook for 1906–07 stated: "Hillside Architecture
is Landscape Gardening around a few rooms for use in case of rain." This formulation of the house and garden as an intertwined unit served as Wurster's
ideal throughout his career. Thus, in their regard for the climate, materials, and
site, and in their free interpretation of history and precedent, Maybeck's houses
were the direct precursors of those by William Wurster. It took the young architect a remarkably short time before he, too, discarded the doctrine of period
styles and looked more closely at the vernacular architecture of California
rather than the great houses of Europe and the East Coast.

American residential designers in the 1920s drew on several sources
besides the more formal Beaux-Arts model. Since the 1876 Centennial
Exposition in Philadelphia, architects had eagerly sought a native expression,
a search fueled to some degree by the nationalistic romanticism that surged at
the century's end. The Dutch Colonial Revival—often taking form as a so-called
Cape Cod or "Pennsylvania Dutch" house—became the norm almost nationally after its emergence in the Northeast. Architects such as Royal Barry Wills
proselytized for a domestic architecture that would meet twentieth-century
needs with intangible feelings of place and tradition. In his own work, this
meant styles of a decidedly Colonial Revivalist flavor.

11.
Rogerson House, location unknown, no date
Royal Barry Wills

12.
Rogerson House, location unknown, no date
Royal Barry Wills
Floor plans

As later presented in his books *Houses for Good Living* (1940) and *Better Houses for Budgeteers* (1941), however, Wills outlined a design approach that made the single-family home available to those with limited means.[11] He dismissed size for its own sake and emphasized that "the 'style' of the house should be purely a reflection of the plan's requirements. Form should also follow function, which is something that architects have been talking about for a good many years—and not heeding."[12] This from an avid traditionalist, whose compartmentalized plans contrasted severely with the open spaces of the modernist residences (figs.11, 12). Despite Wills's protests to the contrary, style was indeed an issue, particularly if it was the modern style: "Sloughing off the last hint of antiquarianism and uprooting the rambler roses at the door, the lilac bushes at the corner, they started with a clean slate and made houses which did not look like houses at all, but rather more like shoe-boxes atop one another, the upper ones cantilevered until it hurt."[13]

The influx of modernism and foreign architectural ideas from the early 1920s had cast Wills's revivalism in serious doubt. But the American architects who adopted the modernist stance and broke with tradition never took too literally Le Corbusier's idea of the house as a "machine for living." Virtually every dwelling in the new idiom retained a residual expression of locale and historic architectural precedent. Books published in the early 1940s—for example, James Ford and Katherine Morrow Ford's *The Modern House in America* and George Nelson and Henry Wright's *Tomorrow's House* discussed below—reconceived the single-family dwelling as a structure based on the evolving configuration of the family, developments in technology and fabrication, and the spirit of the times. And yet in their pronouncements for convenience, economy, site planning, and sensible use of materials, the authors—revivalist or modernist—revealed more similarities than differences.

By the end of the 1920s, after very few years in independent practice, William Wurster had already begun to detach himself from historical types. Instead, he tempered the monumental with a renewed appreciation for vernacular architecture and the influential roles of site and climate. During his European travels, Wurster had visited with equal interest the *de rigueur* monuments and vernacular towns and farms of southern France, Spain, and Italy.

This in itself was hardly novel: many modernists, Le Corbusier among them, favored the prismatic masses of anonymous construction and its freedom from the burden of historical styles. But in Wurster's travel writings and subsequent works one senses an empathy with vernacular building for its expression of culture, land, and climate. As he wrote in 1954, "I recall so well how I was equipped with guide books when I first went out to look at the world, and how these were gradually pushed into the background by the history books which told the 'why' of what I was seeing."[14] By the close of the 1920s, this interest in vernacular architecture began to exert itself more strongly in Wurster's work, particularly for those commissions where a sophisticated rusticity was deemed appropriate. The Gregory Farmhouse was the first polished manifestation of these ideas.

The Gregory Farmhouse

Warren and Sadie Gregory had relocated to Berkeley after the 1906 earthquake, occupying a house they commissioned from John Galen Howard in 1903. In addition, the family owned hillside property in Scotts Valley, just north of Santa Cruz, and thought to build a weekend house there. This project, which they termed a "farmhouse," was to be dedicated to informal living beyond the social and physical confines of the city.[15] In 1926 Howard, and later his son Henry, produced schemes for the farmhouse, first by augmenting an existing structure on the site and thereafter by starting from scratch with a completely new building. The Henry Howard scheme—a sprawling design presumably in the Spanish Colonial Revival style—was far more elaborate and formal than the Gregorys desired, and it was left unrealized. On 19 December 1926 Warren Gregory wrote to Wurster soliciting his ideas for the farmhouse; the accumulated Howard drawings were included with the letter. The Gregorys had been impressed with the work of the young Wurster, in particular his use of simple board-and-batten construction in the 1926 Gillespie House in Oakland, which they deemed quite suitable to their needs.[16] In part, drawing upon the *parti* of the second Howard scheme, Wurster produced this, his most celebrated design, which was completed in 1928 (figs. 13, 100–110). It was a simple structure, or series of structures, that fully embodied the values of a monied California society intent on living unostentatiously and close to the land.

Unlike the grandeur of the Howard plan, Wurster's farmhouse was striking in its modesty. Perhaps based on vernacular precedent, perhaps the vestigial remains of the entry court of his early country houses, perhaps just as a cultivated stockade set against the natural hillside, the farm was configured as a court cut from the slope. An existing rammed earth structure provided, literally, the point of departure for the small complex. The principal building was ell-shaped, served by an open gallery, with each space opening directly to a terrace. The planning of the house was so basic and its detailing so frank that it could have been fashioned not by an architect but by a "carpenter endowed with good taste"—a characteristic that always pleased Wurster. The two principal wings of the house were zoned for living and services, although the variety of ages of the many family members and guests suggested dispersing the bedrooms in almost every structure as a buffer against rambunctious youngsters. The buildings were only one room wide throughout in order to provide view, light, and ventilation. The covered corridor lining the inside of the court provided the principal path for circulation, although the rooms were accessible from the interior in a "shotgun" arrangement.

The house was planned as a hillside zone modified for living, its protected court to the north complemented by a linear terrace with a wisteria-covered pergola to the south. A three-quarter circular terrace augmented the interior living spaces to the east, offering a pleasant setting for breakfast and morning

activities. In many ways, the word "setting" seems more appropriate than the words "building," "house," or "terrace"; one sees here for the first time Wurster's synthetic integration of house and site in a completely unassuming manner. Built of whitewashed vertical boards without battens (which would have too strongly animated the wall surfaces), the farmhouse embodied Wurster's (and the clients') belief that houses should lack pretense: "I like to work on direct, honest solutions, avoiding exotic materials, using indigenous things so that there is no affectation and the best is obtained for the money."[17] Only in the treatment of the water tank—elevated above the height necessary for creating sufficient water pressure—did Wurster magnify the mundane need to acquire architectural identity. Adding a third-floor room atop the tank—destined as bunk space for visiting children—Wurster created a tower as the vertical counterpoint to the horizontal ground-hugging extension of the house. This tower, the key element in the architectonic composition, also became the photogenic emblem for the farm and contributed significantly to its nearly instantaneous fame.

The farmhouse graced the July 1930 cover of *Sunset,* while inside it provided the case study for an article entitled "There Must Be Romance in the Home You Build."[18] The following year it received *House Beautiful*'s first-prize award; the accompanying text stressed that the design was based on "the desire for simplicity as an antidote for the complication of city life."[19] From that time on, the house acquired canonical status as a design that straddled the modern and the vernacular. When it was published in *Architecture* in 1935, Wurster could report with satisfaction: "This was a happy job from start to finish, for utmost co-operation lifted it far higher than any one of us could have brought about. Both the actual plan and appearance are not too 'busy' for really simple living."[20]

The celebrity of the farmhouse was crucial in launching Wurster's career as a residential architect. He was the right man at the right place at the right time: fortuitously connected to influential patrons, Wurster had a style and manner that tapped into the spirit of the age and the preferences of his clientele. The collapse of the stock market in 1929 gave way to a decade of depression, and for the most part the architectural profession collapsed with it. Architects and draftsmen joined the ranks of the unemployed across the country and throughout the world. But William Wurster's office never faltered; in fact, it prospered. And it was just during these years of economic hardship that he built a reputation as a solid practitioner and a stylistic leader.

During her college days at the University of Chicago, Sadie Gregory had been an assistant to the noted sociologist Thorstein Veblen, whose book *The Theory of the Leisure Class* (1899) introduced the idea of "conspicuous consumption" into cultural critique. Veblen's was a stinging condemnation of those newly wealthy and anxious to display their gains ostentatiously. While no architectural critic, Veblen included architecture in his social critique, noting that: "The endless variety of fronts presented by the better class of tenements and apartment houses in our cities is an endless variety of architectural distress and suggestions of expensive discomfort. Considered as objects of beauty," he further ventured, "the dead walls of the sides and backs of these structures, left untouched by the hands of the artist, are commonly the best feature of the building."[21] In the wake of such indictments, a segment of the upper classes, emulating the European aristocracy or "old money," more calmly adjusted their lifestyles and possessions in architecture and furnishings. The higher social strata of the Bay Area tended to adopt these precepts and wished to inhabit an architecture at once comfortable yet expressive of social station. Like the "refined poverty" of the sixteenth-century Japanese tea ceremony, or even the "shabby chic" of certain European nobility, Wurster's architecture was far more studied than it first appeared. If simple, it was far

13.
Gregory Farmhouse, Scotts Valley, 1928
William Wurster
Courtyard view

from simplistic. No single element caught the attention of the visitor but quietly contributed to the presence of the whole. And despite its common means of construction, each piece was carefully considered and detailed. The fireplace with its simple surround, the doors made to Wurster's specifications, and the prevalence of half-round molding all achieved simplicity through reduction and condensation, not by inattention. This deceptive simplicity generated numerous anecdotes; most were probably apocryphal but appropriate nonetheless. For example, Catherine Bauer is rumored to have once said, "It doesn't matter how much Bill has to spend on a house, it will always look cheap."[22]

Wurster's appreciation of the vernacular architectures of California and southern Europe, his love of directness and suitability (which should be distinguished from the more purely functional arguments of the European modernists) furnished an architectural idiom that comfortably accommodated the desires of his clients. Given Sadie Gregory's connections with Thorstein Veblen, it is ironic that Wayne Andrews, writing in 1947, categorized Wurster as a Jacobite (after the philosopher William James) rather than a Veblenite, a member of the more stylistically rigorous camp. Andrews cited James's belief that "theories were only instruments, *not answers to enigmas, in which we can rest.* We don't lie back on them,' [James] made plain, 'we move forward, and on occasion, make nature over again by their aid.'"[23] The Jacobites were "warm, casual, pragmatic, willing to take the machine for granted, haunted by the site, and at their best in domestic work." The Veblenites, in turn, tended to be "cool, dogmatic, absolutist, worshippers of the machine, willing to disregard the site and experts at factories, sanitariums and other impersonal buildings."[24] Walter Gropius was a Veblenite par excellence; Maybeck, Harwell Hamilton Harris, and John E. Dinwiddie the corresponding Jacobites. The lack of dogma characteristic of the Jacobites could be summarized in Wurster's quip that he was suspicious of anything that resembled a final answer: "There is always more than one answer."[25]

The Classical, the Vernacular, and Pasatiempo

Wurster's lack of design dogma permitted a considerable range of styles and scales, thwarting attempts at establishing clearly defined stylistic periods. For those of modest means, or those anxious to play down their means, he produced simple shelters of wood; nonsymmetrical, classic but not classical, and planned for climate. For his wealthy clients, on the other hand, he had no hesitation in plotting grand ensembles that looked "back East" to the estates of Newport and country houses on Long Island by Delano and Aldrich. In these great houses, such as the first project for Clarence Breuner discussed above, the architectural planning began with the total site. The sweeping entrance drive was configured to set off the house to advantage and followed in sequence by an entrance courtyard or garden that served as the frontispiece to the house.[26] One then entered a gracious hall and from there proceeded to the living room; often a central courtyard distributed light, allowing a more compact plan.

But Wurster did not appear to be in his element in these great houses, which should have been the cornerstone of his career as a society architect. Although competent exercises in the idiom, they lacked the true flair for the grand seen in the brilliance of William Morris Hunt or McKim, Mead & White. Wurster never seemed to fully exploit monumentality. Instead, he made large projects by amalgamating small-scale elements, each addressing a segment of the family's life. His sympathy always tended toward life within the house rather than the architectural shell that contained it.

This ambivalence between monumental scale and family needs is most clearly represented in the first project (1933) for the George Pope House in

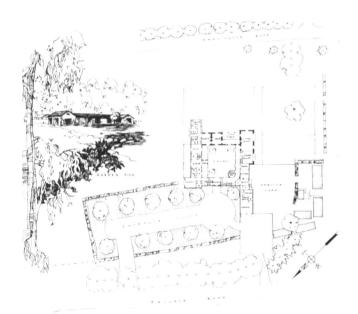

Hillsborough of 1936. The site plan foretold a great house of several stories and majestic dimensions (fig.14). The formal entry garden presaged a monumental facade; from the hall, one viewed the internal courtyard before continuing the promenade to the salon or dining room. The house was zoned for use in a fairly typical manner, segregating the more public rooms from the service areas, and these in turn from the family's living arrangements. A circular nook on the courtyard edge oriented eastward for the morning sun, intended for breakfasts and morning activities.

All preconceptions of a monumental classicism were shattered by the perspective sketch presented to the client. In place of a multistoried building was a single-story wooden structure with a pitched roof of wooden shakes; instead of a neoclassical exterior were vernacular-inspired elevations almost dull in their modesty (fig.15). Quite typically, the project was not realized as first planned. The extensive outdoor spaces, like the internal volumes, were greatly compressed although still formal in character. The house retained the modest architectural style of the first project, but virtually none of the grandiloquence of its plan remained. Perhaps in no other commissions can one read so decidedly the two conflicting aspects of Wurster's architecture at this early stage in his career: the clash between innate leanings derived from childhood and education in California, and architectural ideas gleaned from European travel and employment in a New York office.[27] Gradually, and perhaps ironically, Wurster's predilection would be fed by the emerging prominence of foreign modernist ideas that preached simplicity, regard for function, and a discarding of historical styles.

The first extensive realizations of Wurster's evolving essays in the modern vernacular were found at Pasatiempo, a residential community near the north coast of Monterey Bay. Located not far from Scotts Valley, the site of the Gregory Farmhouse, it was founded in the late 1920s as a golf development not unlike Pebble Beach farther south.[28] Pasatiempo was planned by the Olmsted Brothers of Brookline, Massachusetts, the successor firm to Frederick Law Olmsted, who had pioneered landscape architecture and coordinated site planning in the United States. Marion Hollins, a noted golfer and Pasatiempo's developer, commissioned Clarence Tantau to design the clubhouse as the community's social and recreational center. Given the fall and undulations of the terrain and Hollins's adamant wish to preserve the natural beauty of the landscape, all roads were planned to avoid cutting down trees, while lots were configured to receive sun as well as forest shade. According to Daniel Gregory,

14.
George Pope House, Hillsborough, 1936
William Wurster
Preliminary site and first-floor plan, 1933

15.
George Pope House, Hillsborough, 1936
William Wurster
Aerial perspective of preliminary scheme, 1933

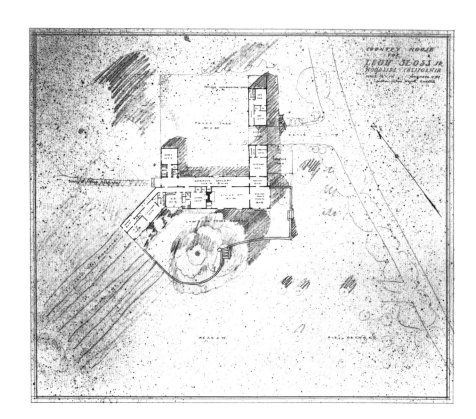

16.
Sloss House, Woodside, 1931
William Wurster
Preliminary site plan, 1930

17.
Sloss House, Woodside, 1931
William Wurster
Entrance to court

18.
Hollins House, Pasatiempo, 1931
William Wurster
Kitchen cave

No tree could be removed to make way for the golf course without [Hollins's] personal permission. She established small parks along the creek beds and in the heavily forested sections . . . [and] drew up a list of protective restrictions which, according to the advertising brochure of 1930, "will go with the land, assuring maintenance to the purchaser of the character of the surroundings as to trees, shrubs and individuality"[29]

To Hollins, the character of the architecture equaled in importance the overall plan of the landscape. Familiar with the elegant simplicity of the nearby Gregory Farmhouse, Hollins commissioned Wurster to design her own house. This led, in turn, to a series of commissions that established the prevailing architectural character of the community. Both Wurster and Hollins were sympathetic to the architecture of Early California. But, as Gregory pointed out, to Wurster and Hollins, Early Californian did not refer to the Mission and Spanish Colonial Revival styles holding sway in Santa Barbara and points south. Instead, Early Californian found its locus in the farm, barn, and shed of the mid-nineteenth century. In his later essay "California Architecture for Living," Wurster cited vernacular monuments such as Fort Winfield Scott in the San Francisco Presidio, the chapel at Fort Ross, and Mariano Vallejo's adobe *rancho* in Petaluma. Of the latter he wrote:

The sense of fitness to site and purpose is impressive. The broad flowing balconies, the protective shadows of wide protecting roofs, the scale of the building and its fine proportions, the distinguished use of crude and simple materials at hand—all reflect intuitive understanding of architectural techniques and objectives with awareness of tradition in the broad sense.[30]

The 1931 Sloss House in Woodside bears a striking affinity, if not direct resemblance, to the Sherwood Ranch near Salinas that Wurster also described in the article: the enclosed courtyard, contrasting textures of materials, and bridged entrance all suggest ideas drawn somewhat overtly—and enthusiastically— from Early Californian (figs. 16, 17).[31]

The Pasatiempo houses reverted to neither rusticity nor romanticism. In place of the weathered shingle was the whitewashed board or masonry wall, its texture minimized to read as a continuous plane. While the verandas of nearby Monterey did appear in several Pasatiempo designs, Wurster's use of such elements derived more from his desire to create buildings in accord with outdoor living than from an interest in historical prototypes per se. These,

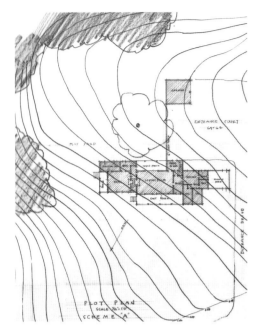

19. Scheme A

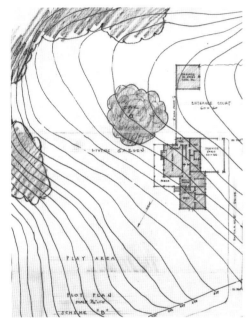

20. Scheme B

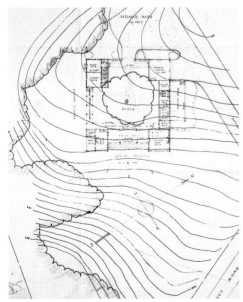

21. Scheme C

Wurster reasoned, could be reinterpreted because they addressed their functions in a simple, matter-of-fact way. Designed exterior spaces—courtyards, patios, and terraces—drew the house into the garden, golf course, or landscape so that the passage between them was effortless.

Hollins's own house of 1931 was one of the first and largest to be built on the site. The structure was stacked compactly in two floors and angled to retain the existing trees, with the entry placed logically uphill. For convenience, the plan also positioned the services uphill, adjoining the dining and living rooms; a separate wing contained the owner's precinct and guest spaces. In this house Wurster introduced the "kitchen cave," an outdoor yet protected room on the lower floor, carved from the downward side of the hill though oriented to the exterior (fig. 18). Although in some respects the cave resembled a porch open to both the view and the weather, it belonged more to the interior than the exterior: a cool room for the warm days of summer or a place to light a fire for those days with fog or nippy temperatures.

The house for Pasatiempo's sponsor firmly established Wurster as the community's "house architect." The archetypal Pasatiempo house, however, was the Butler House of 1935—a project that would solidify many of Wurster's residential planning ideas. For the first presentation to the client, Wurster's office prepared two schemes.[32] Each varied to some degree in its orientation and distribution on the land, although both designs used the massive California live oak on the site as its point of departure. In these early years of practice, it was quite common for Wurster's first design scheme to be more expansive and dispersed, at times almost sprawling across its site. In subsequent revisions, presumably under the pressures of economy and other factors, the house design became smaller and more compact. The progress of the Butler House design, however, went in just the opposite direction.

Scheme A was arranged linearly in two floors, its axis aligned roughly north-south, with the oak to the rear of the house (fig.19). While the principal facade addressed the road to the east, the tree presumably would anchor the center of the family's outdoor activities, providing shade in the heat of summer. Scheme B altered the orientation of the house completely, placing the oak to the south, perhaps to shield the garden facade from direct sunlight (fig. 20). Although the plans of Schemes A and B were similar, Wurster acknowledged the need for augmented air circulation for the living room in Scheme B, projecting the room outward and sheathing it with a porch. Both designs were competent on their own terms and would have fit comfortably within the evolving Pasatiempo mode, but neither appeared to have transcended the limits of its basic layout.

Scheme C followed some months after the first two schemes. This plan, a variant of which was subsequently adopted for construction, radically exploded the spaces of the house into four quadrants and seems to have grabbed the fancy of the client as well as the architect (fig. 21).[33] The overall plan—also uncharacteristic for Wurster—was actually symmetrical. Articulated pavilions anchored the four corners of the house: the garage; the owner's and guests' sleeping rooms; the sons' room and sleeping porch; and the living room. Despite this rigid disposition of elements, however, the resulting architecture was relatively fluid due to the nature of the links between the pavilions. Each of the corners differed to some degree in its orientation and nature of projecting surfaces, and the links between them varied in their degree of enclosure (fig. 22). For example, the servants' rooms and kitchen bound the garage to the living room, while an open porch linked the living room to the sons' room. An arcade joined the remaining two corners.

The central courtyard offered little sense of where to enter the house itself. At the northeast end of the court, the covered porch gave way to a "living porch," which in turn opened to a semicircular "living terrace" beyond the limits of the house (fig. 23). By any standards this was a curious plan, even for

19.
Butler House, Pasatiempo, 1935
William Wurster
Site plan, Scheme A (detail), 1934

20.
Butler House, Pasatiempo, 1935
William Wurster
Site plan, Scheme B (detail), 1934

21.
Butler House, Pasatiempo, 1935
William Wurster
Site plan, Scheme C (detail), 1934

22.
Butler House, Pasatiempo, 1935
William Wurster
View from the golf course

23.
Butler House, Pasatiempo, 1935
William Wurster
Porch

24.
MacKenzie-Field House, Pasatiempo, 1931
William Wurster
View from the golf course

a weekend house; there was no dining room, for example, despite the presence of servants. The plan itself suited a family that wanted to interact with nature almost as monks ritually interact with their cells and cloister. The Butler House quietly coerced its occupants to traverse the outdoors to reach the next interior space; no internal corridors joined the principal rooms. Perhaps no other design would more fully explore the Berkeley Hillside Club notion that the house constituted an enclosed area between two gardens, and that the benign climate of California required little by way of secure enclosure during inclement weather.

Among Wurster's other contributions to Pasatiempo were the Church House and Studio of 1931, the MacKenzie-Field House of 1931, and the Howes-Kaplansky House of 1930. Although none of these designs approached the extreme openness of the later Butler House, each possessed features that would recur in many of Wurster's subsequent designs. His project for landscape architect Thomas Church organized the various rooms linearly, culminating in a studio with a north-facing glazed wall; the living room contained one of the earliest sunken conversation pits. Church's own garden at Pasatiempo epitomized his early balancing of planned footholds of civilized landscape and features of the existing landscape. The remaining photographs by Roger Sturtevant show little of either the formal ingenuity or classical touches characteristic of Church's later landscape designs, many of which accompanied Wurster buildings during their lifelong collaboration. Instead the terraces appear selectively planted rather than comprehensively designed (fig. 117).

The Howes-Kaplansky House, built for Marion Hollins's general business manager, enclosed a central court but lacked the transparency afforded by the pergola and covered porch of the later Butler design. Within the house, Wurster widened the corridor that paralleled the courtyard and provided it with a completely glazed wall. The resulting space was ambiguously defined: more than a corridor and yet less than a discrete room, a space that could be used for play by the children or as a library, since its inner side was lined with books.[34] The house for Pasatiempo's golf-course designer, Alistair MacKenzie, logically faced the links, its living room opening toward the rolling lawns and sand traps (fig. 24). The first plan for the house indecisively pitted a living-room block perpendicularly to the longitudinal alignment of rooms; the whole lacked any formal rigor. The scheme as constructed fitted all the rooms within a single block broken only by an attached screened porch. This served not only as a prominent living space but also as a belvedere from which to view the activity and landscape of the golf course.

Pasatiempo provided William Wurster with a testing ground for his resi-

dential ideas, with almost a dozen houses designed, and many of them built, during the first half of the 1930s. The architectural idiom that evolved was unostentatious in style, simple in construction technique, color (white), and materials, respondent to climate, ideally suited to California living, and reflective of client taste.

Beyond the suburban enclave, Wurster's vocabulary became more rustic. For Mr. and Mrs. Carl L. Voss, Wurster proposed a sophisticated cabin set against a steep hillside in Big Sur (fig. 25). Unlike the blanched surfaces of many previous houses, the wooden sheathing of the 1931 Voss House was left unpainted and exposed both inside and out. The plan was again compact and simply organized on two levels to take advantage of the slope, with a covered porch extending the length of the house and overlooking the ocean. "Small matter in what you live," Wurster wrote, "of great importance what you look at."[35] The 15-by-28-foot "kitchen cave" dominated the lower level and opened to a terrace sheltered by the upper floor (fig. 26). Like the Gregory Farmhouse, the Voss House could easily pass for a vernacular structure. Closer scrutiny, however, revealed that although the mood was informal, no aspect of the design had been treated casually, an observation confirmed by client-architect correspondence.

This rustic villa in Big Sur appeared in publications ranging from American popular and professional magazines with national circulation to architectural journals in France and Sweden.[36] Each admired the directness of the design, its appropriateness to the site, and its suitability to modern life. In the wake of such publicity, numerous would-be clients requested sets of "blueprints" to build a Voss House of their very own. To each, Wurster replied politely, suggesting that his correspondent take the article on the Voss House to a "good" local architect, as one could not build well in a place one didn't know and understand.[37]

At this point—that is, by the mid-1930s—Wurster's career was firmly established. His residential designs had been lauded, published, and premiated, and he was acknowledged as one of the leading architects on the West Coast. As a result, his firm welcomed a continuous stream of commissions. Given the maturity of the work, one can examine its accomplishments and limits, as well as its affinities to other architecture designed in California, in other parts of the United States, and even abroad.

The Influx of Modernism

The terms "modern," "modernism," "functionalism," and "contemporary" are all problematic as categories of architecture. Do they describe a chronological period, a particular style, or merely an attitude toward building?[38] In archi-

25.
Voss House, Big Sur, 1931
William Wurster

26.
Voss House, Big Sur, 1931
William Wurster
Kitchen cave

tecture, the term modernist is usually equated with the so-called Modern Movement, which found its ideological and stylistic bases in the works of Walter Gropius and Ludwig Mies van der Rohe in Germany and Le Corbusier, André Lurçat, and others in France. The 1932 exhibition at the Museum of Modern Art in New York—"The International Style: Architecture since 1922"—popularized the term International Style as the label used for the new architecture. The exhibition's co-curator and essayist, Henry-Russell Hitchcock, defined International Style architecture on the basis of three prominent characteristics: "a stress on volume rather than mass," the use of "regularity rather than axial symmetry," and the proscription of applied ornament.[39] Even at the time the term was proffered, however, many (including the curators) wriggled at the suggestion that the new architecture constituted a style— a term that smacked of historical references—much less that any architecture could be truly international in its application.[40] What the exhibition did accomplish however, was to bring European architecture of the previous decade to the forefront of American architectural debate. In so doing, it seriously undermined the foundations of the historicism and stylistic revivals that had governed American architecture for over half a century.

William Wurster was well aware of the modernist ideas reaching the United States from Europe, however much he might have avoided them. Professional periodicals and books reproduced crisp black-and-white images of prismatic masses and interlocking spaces. Their architects claimed that these structures exploited the new ideas in physics and innovations in building technologies, particularly those afforded by steel and reinforced concrete.

If these European examples remained too distant to be persuasive or too easily dismissed as inappropriate to the California condition, a more proximate body of accomplished and innovative work existed in the Southland. Since the early 1920s, Frank Lloyd Wright, R. M. Schindler, and Richard J. Neutra—the latter two, Austrians first affiliated with the Wright office in Los Angeles—had executed a number of house designs that addressed both climate and new ideas of form and space. Wright's work reflected the forms and ornamental textures of Pre-Columbian Mexican ceremonial architecture. Other more traditional architects such as Wallace Neff and Myron Hunt still grounded their residential design in California's somewhat romanticized Spanish roots. In sharp contrast, Neutra, Schindler, Gregory Ain, and Raphael Soriano designed in an uncompromisingly modernist idiom.

The two houses for *Los Angeles Times* health columnist Philip Lovell alone revealed the progressive gap that divided Wurster from the Austrians.[41] In the 1926 design for the Lovell Beach House in Newport Beach, Schindler used the punctured layers of the reinforced concrete frame to create overlapping spaces that fully mined the constricted dimensions of the corner site (fig. 27). Neutra's Los Angeles Lovell House, completed in 1929, exploited the spatial potentials allowed by the steel structural frame (fig. 28). Planned to utilize the steep slope to develop a dramatic architectural promenade, the house's spaces were revealed sequentially in a modulated cadence: as one descended the staircase, a wall of glass offered an expansive view of the Los Angeles landscape. Despite their varying configurations, both Lovell houses opened walls of windows to the air and featured outdoor areas for sleeping. Although strikingly divorced from their sites by a planar architectural vocabulary, with no reference to California's Hispanic past, both houses addressed the climate and terrain of Southern California. As such, they can fairly be considered regional.

Wurster's Gregory Farmhouse was almost contemporary with the two Lovell houses. In comparison, the Gregory complex was retardataire and romantic, citing historical vernacular precedents rather than invoking a brilliant future assured by the machine. This is a fair assessment if one believes in the idea of *Zeitgeist:* that a single spirit reflects the current age. But this

27.
Lovell Beach House, Newport Beach, 1926
R. M. Schindler

28.
Lovell House, Los Angeles, 1929
Richard J. Neutra

stance also assumes that progress is desirable and that only one selective stylistic stream should constitute the accepted architecture of any given period.

Regionalism, Modernism, and Regional Modernism

Today, on the other hand, many historians and critics look for the adaptation
of national or international ideas to a particular place—and time. Kenneth
Frampton, in his seminal essay "Towards a Critical Regionalism," suggested
that the localizing of an imported idiom constitutes a questioning of the limits of any architectural idea. Thus regional variations—selectively derived and
transmogrified in accordance with local conditions—constitute a critique of
the parent idea. "Architecture," in Frampton's eyes, "can only be sustained
today as a critical practice if it assumes an *arrière-garde* position, that is to say,
one which distances itself equally from the Enlightenment myth of progress
and from a reactionary, unrealistic impulse to return to the architectonic forms
of the preindustrial past."[42] For Wurster, the critique was a form of sensible
domestication rather than a theoretical stance:

> *Architecture does truly mirror change, and changing conditions force upon us
> a recognition of their presence. Architecture, the art and science of building,
> offers solutions that must meet these changing conditions and satisfy them.
> This immediately implies that there is no honesty in attempting to bring into
> being a* blend *of the familiar and the strange. If there is a* blend *it is the result
> of forces, materials, and decisions which are related to basic factors, and is
> not a matter for choice. Failure to recognize this is the cause of much profes-
> sional and lay confusion.*[43]

If these forces for change recognized local conditions, they were inherently
rooted in time. Modernity, for Wurster, was itself an evolving enterprise. "In
reality," he wrote, "I like to think of the word [modern] as meaning 'of today'—
which means it will be different tomorrow—a constant term applying to changing modes and mediums."[44] How can one achieve the modern? Wurster
believed that modernity, like appropriateness, derived from the specifics of the
program and clients, that is, the people, the place and the time: "It was sensible to base the design on the kind of life people wanted, and not on the basis
of theoretical modernism."[45] Was Wurster's residential architecture modernist,
regional, or regional modernist? Was it "critical" in any way?

In 1944 the Museum of Modern Art mounted another major architectural
exhibition, "Built in USA: 1932–1944," with a catalogue edited by Elizabeth
Mock. The purpose of the show was to evaluate building in the United States
since the International Style exhibition as a measure of progress. The war continued, but there was optimism that it was drawing to an end; defense workers' and public housing by architects such as Richard Neutra, Hugh Stubbins,
Burton Cairns and Vernon DeMars, Reginald Johnson—and William Wurster—
figured prominently in the exhibition catalogue. The argument of the intro-
ductory text was by this time quite standard, rehearsing the origins of
functionalism and its metamorphosis from an abstract machine architecture to
a form more humane and appealing to the lay public. Although discussion was
directed toward technological developments such as stressed skin panels and
prefabrication, the ultimate message was that Americans had tamed the foreign
beast. The battle for the modern idiom had been won because the modern
idiom itself had considered the proximate environment and adopted "a human
basis for design."[46]

The resurgence of Frank Lloyd Wright in the late 1930s warranted professional attention. Fallingwater, built in Bear Run, Pennsylvania, in 1936, and a
series of more modest Usonian homes (fig. 29) demonstrated a softer modernism and suggested a viable *American* model to architects wishing to be contemporary. The catalogue's introduction revealed that actually quite little was

29.
Baird House, Amherst, Massachusetts, 1940
Frank Lloyd Wright

30.
Gropius House, Lincoln, Massachusetts,
1938
Walter Gropius with Marcel Breuer
Garden facade

known about what would later be termed the Bay Region style. "The origins [of this style] were certainly mixed, but the result was a flexible native style which could go over into modern architecture without any serious break. Wurster, for example, was producing straightforward, essentially modern houses well before 1932, based on good sense and the California wood tradition rather than on specific theories of design."[47] Wurster was represented by two projects, neither of which were houses, however: the 1942 office building for the Schuckl Canning Company in Sunnyvale and the Valencia Gardens public housing development in San Francisco (1939–43).

In 1940 MoMA architecture curator John McAndrews edited the first of a projected series, *Guide to Modern Architecture: Northeast States,* published by the museum. The intention was to make the public aware of the distinguished modern work already realized in this country. McAndrews cited the "stone and wood barns of Pennsylvania, the trim white farmhouses of Massachusetts, [and] the covered bridges of Maine and Vermont," examples of Yankee ingenuity worthy of study and perhaps emulation.[48] Like his colleague Elizabeth Mock, McAndrews saw Frank Lloyd Wright as the principal American contribution to modern architecture: "[Wright's] sympathetic use of wood, stone, brick, traditional materials avoided by stricter functionalists, has been a refreshing example to many younger men."[49] In the previous decade the number and quality of buildings in the modern idiom had grown substantially, and American architecture could now assume an equal footing with modern work in Europe. Perhaps not too surprisingly, many of the principal players listed in the book were European born.

Senior among them was Walter Gropius, who had emigrated from Germany first to England and then to the United States, assuming the deanship of the Graduate School of Design at Harvard University. The Boston suburb of Lincoln, Massachusetts, contained an enclave of modernist work, with Gropius's own house—designed in collaboration with Marcel Breuer—serving as its flagship. The Gropius House, completed in 1938, amalgamated European and American ideas within a New England setting (fig.30). The house was essentially a wooden-sheathed box whose volumes had been incised to create more complexly configured spaces. The opening of interior spaces tested the tradition of discrete rooms. The internal circulation was peculiar, as visitors entered the living and dining rooms through the study. The house visually rested on fieldstone retaining walls that mediated between architecture and earthen contour, between the natural slope and the constructed terrace. The roof was flat, the walls plain and painted white—a hybrid between a European villa and an American farmhouse of a new order.

Like Gropius, Marcel Breuer also built structures marked by the American condition—not the might of its industries but the dwellings of North America in general and New England in particular: "[I]t was the simple honesty and clarity of the traditional New England wood structure, with its braced frame and fieldstone chimneys that struck him most forcibly."[50] The stark planes and simple prisms of Breuer's European high-modernist period were tempered in the postwar American years by screened living spaces and stone fireplaces. In the Boston area alone, Hugh Stubbins, Carl Koch, Walter Bogner, and G. Holmes Perkins formed an active cadre of architects who naturalized the modernist idiom with building volumes fashioned for living in a climate that demonstrated extremes of both heat and cold, using local materials for walls and floors.

Projects for regional arts, crafts, and architecture thrived throughout the United States during the Depression years. In part their flourishing was due to the geographical circumscription caused by a collapsed economy. In part, it was fostered by New Deal programs to provide employment for artists, writers, craftsmen, and architects. The American guidebook series is perhaps the

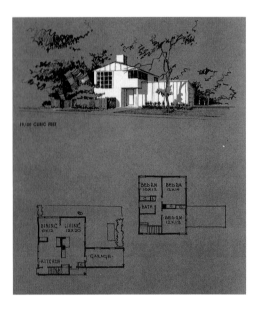

31.
Perspective sketch and floor plans
Royal Barry Wills
Published in **Better Houses for Budgeteers,**
1941

best-known product of the Federal Writers Project;[51] the housing and settlement work for the Farm Security Administration, the Greenbelt town projects, the power production facilities for the Tennessee Valley Authority, and the multitude of designs for the Public Works Administration remain the hallmark architectural contributions. Although these were all national programs, the administration and focus of each project derived from a specific locale.

In the hands of some architects, regionalism was manifested as traditionalism. In New England, Royal Barry Wills's essays in the Dutch Colonial and English Colonial Revival styles produced an archetype that came to dominate residential architecture in the popular as well as the architect-designed markets. Wills's houses tended to be compact, with simple volumes and restrained ornamentation. Like its true colonial predecessors, the door received the architect's greatest attention. The large fireplace marked the center of family life, and the simple plans accommodated shifting needs as the children grew (fig. 31). Wills's *Better Houses for Budgeteers* offered prototypes for the owner-builder, the contractor, and the architect's client, sensible in their spatial planning and cozy in their traditional idiom. He chided both the lilac-dressing of the traditionalist and the skeleton of the modernist, although the latter took the brunt of the beating: "The mirthless addict of advanced ideas which stem from living concepts foreign to your experience or desires. His vibrations are tuned to intellectual theories that leave the ladies' aid definitely uneasy and a little shocked at the stark nudism of this preachment in housebuilding."[52] For Wills, as for so many writers of the 1940s, the successful design boiled down to suitability, utility, beauty, and economy.[53] When Levittowns were constructed in Pennsylvania and New York late in the 1940s, the Cape Cod model that proved exceptionally popular could find its antecedents in the works of Royal Barry Wills.

Perhaps it was the limited resources of the 1930s that conditioned a reexamination of local rather than global conditions. One senses an architectural pulling in, a making do with what conditions allowed rather than an optimism bred on the near-utopianism of the modernist project. In the Southwest architects such as John Gaw Meem in New Mexico literally revived the look, if not the plans, of the historic Hispanic-American dwelling.[54] Meem's Cultney House in Santa Fe (1929) featured the exposed *vigas* (beams), soft plastered walls, and articulated massing of Pueblo-Spanish building (fig. 32). Meem's more elaborate 1932 project for the Simms House, Los Poblanos, in Albuquerque, on the other hand, favored the more refined touches of the Territorial style, although the plan's U-shaped configuration suggested indigenous origins.[55] Only in later and more monumental projects, such as the 1934 Taylor Art Center in Colorado Springs, did Meem produce designs that one might be tempted to call modernistic, if not truly modernist. Meem fabricated a romanticized New Mexican hybrid style that he applied without noticeable hesitation to residences, schools, hostelries, and religious structures of all denominations (despite the Catholic origins of the vocabulary). Ironically perhaps, he shared an essential aspect of what Eliel Saarinen had seen as the "fundamental form of the time."[56] To Meem, however, "[t]his fundamental form is a composite of everything in a people's culture, in their way of thinking and living. It is the real leader of the movement rather than a product of it."[57] Three years later he published "Old Forms for New Buildings" in the November issue of *American Architecture.* Meem appeared pleased and convinced in his revelation that "[s]ome forms are so honest, so completely logical and native to the environment that one finds—to his delight and surprise—that modern problems can be solved and are best solved by the use of forms based on tradition."[58] Obviously, similar concerns, and even similar deductions, did not always lead to the same architectural design ideas.

In the Northwest, architects such as Pietro Belluschi were not so compla-
cent. His architecture of the 1930s and 1940s evidenced a tougher attitude
toward modernity, although the inspiration for form may have derived from
the vernacular wooden shed and the California ranch house popularized by
Clifford May.[59] In its use of exposed siding and its pervasive rusticity,
Belluschi's 1941 Kerr House on the Pacific coast closely paralleled Wurster's
rural work, although Wurster avoided folkloric elements like tree trunks used
as columns (fig. 33). In Belluschi's 1942 house facing Netarts Bay, the plan was
gathered as a U around a central courtyard and, like the Gregory Farmhouse,
paved in round slabs sliced from tree trunks.[60] The use of trellises to extend
the roof line, the exposed wood siding, and the projecting living room all
recalled the elements of a Wurster house. The formal affinities between these
houses by Belluschi and Wurster's Voss and Gregory houses were hardly accidental. Architects along the Pacific coast were then fervently engaged in linking architecture to place, to a place taken almost out of time. Shared interests,
materials, and climate—not to mention the influence of national professional
and popular publications—joined western architects in a common endeavor.

Harwell Hamilton Harris began his independent practice in Los Angeles,
but his long career also included residence and construction in Texas and
North Carolina. His own house in Fellowship Park, Los Angeles, of 1935
revealed yet another influence operating on the West Coast at the time: the
rational flexibility and dignity of Japanese residential architecture (fig. 34). The
hint of things Japanese pervaded both the spatial concept and the detailing of
the house. While a single roof unified the three principal spaces beneath—the
open living room, the kitchen, and the bath—the landscape surrounding the
house virtually precluded seeing the house in a single take. Like the Japanese
practice of "hide-and-reveal," only glimpses were offered the visitor; the large
living room integrated the various fragments of the plan and opened completely to the landscape. The rush matting recalled the *tatami* of Japan; the
approach to free spaces, exposed structure, and tranquillity all suggested that
Harris was familiar with the architecture of the East. "Harmony with the rocks
and foliage was sought," the architect wrote, "so floor, roof, terrace and other
large planes are given uniform pattern and texture." The house was designed
on a three-foot module, giving "a rhythm to the design which is felt even when
it is not consciously perceived, and provides an air of restfulness."[61] Harris's
borrowings were more transformations than literal replicas of Asian architecture, however, and they illustrated the sensibilities shared by Japan and the
western United States without being dependent upon one another.[62]

32.
Cultney House, Santa Fe, New Mexico, 1929
John Gaw Meem
Perspective view

33.
Kerr House, Gearhart, Oregon, 1941
Pietro Belluschi

34.
Harris House, Fellowship Park,
Los Angeles, 1935
Harwell Hamilton Harris
Living room

35.
Haven House, Berkeley, 1941
Harwell Hamilton Harris
End elevation

Harris's most dramatic work of the period was the Haven House in Berkeley of 1941, simple in plan but highly developed in section (fig. 35). Inverted trusses structured the two-story linear block of rooms pulled from the hillside to create a protected court. Exposed at either end of the house, the wooden trusses provided the characteristic double triangle end elevation, a far more forceful expression of structure than Wurster ever allowed. To Harris, view was the key issue: "The house does not frame the view; it projects the beholder into it. The view is no mere segment of something seen through a hole. Instead it is an extension of the sky, the water, and the hills, below and behind one."[63] The passion of the quote reveals the gap between the two architects: Harris strove for poetry; Wurster rested content with prose if used to good effect. Wurster's was the more conservative, and safer, of the two views; we can readily accept—and reward—prose that achieves the rank of poetry, but we condemn poetry that sinks to the level of prose. The Haven House was quintessentially California in its planning, its decks and paved courts, its materials and integration of interior and exterior areas, but Harris achieved the desired effects with a dramatic flair that Wurster could rarely accept in his own work.

Harris was far from timid, and his ideas about regionalism were not limited to local historic architecture. His total oeuvre included works emulating those of the brothers Greene in California, houses that approached those of Neutra or Japan, and even a handful that resembled the simple dwellings of William Wilson Wurster. Harris also demonstrated an interest in theory beyond that of his California contemporary, and he noted that regionalism can take at least two forms:

> *Opposed to the Regionalism of Restriction is another type of regionalism, the Regionalism of Liberation. This is the manifestation of a region that is especially in tune with the emerging thought of the time. We call such a manifestation "regional" only because it has not yet emerged elsewhere. . . . A region may develop ideas. A region may accept ideas. Imagination and intelligence are necessary for both. In California in the late Twenties and Thirties modern European ideas met a still-developing regionalism. In New England, on the other hand, European Modernism met a rigid and restrictive regionalism that at first resisted and then surrendered. New England accepted European Modernism whole because its own regionalism had been reduced to a collection of restrictions.*[64]

Harris's statement remains the most potent contemporary assessment of the relation between the regional and the national or international and implicitly distinguishes between regional and provincial.[65]

Of all Wurster's contemporaries, O'Neil Ford shared the greatest sympathies and closest parallels. Born in 1905, Ford studied manual training at North Texas State Teachers College, but it was his apprenticeship with Texas vernacular-modernist David R. Williams from 1926 to 1932 that provided his formative architectural direction. Williams and Ford soon became involved with an artistic and intellectual circle that produced the *Southwest Review*, whose goal was to "discover and develop a regional culture in the Southwest."[66] Williams's essay "An Indigenous Architecture" described the buildings that he and Ford had visited, sketched, and photographed in their travels:

> *In the many beautiful little houses left scattered over Texas by early settlers, there is full proof that some of our grandfathers and most of our greatgrandfathers possessed the refined taste and culture for which we have been searching abroad. . . . The houses they made were nicely suited to their purpose . . . they seemed to grow out of the ground on which they stood; and they were beautiful because they were simple and natural, and because their builders were honest enough to be satisfied with beauty of line, and simplicity and delicacy of details.*[67]

36.
Bywaters Studio, Bluffview, Texas, 1929
O'Neil Ford

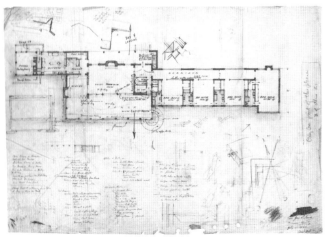

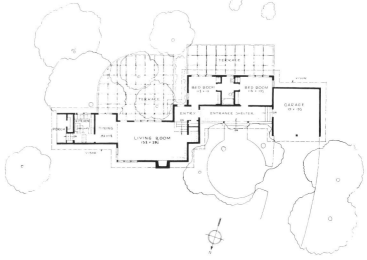

37.
Richardson House, San Jose Island, Texas,
1938
O'Neil Ford with A. B. Swank
Plan

38.
McIntosh House, Los Altos, 1937
William Wurster
Plan

39.
McIntosh House, Los Altos, 1937
William Wurster
Living room

Like Wurster in California, Ford first looked to the vernacular buildings of Texas as the primary source for his architecture, and—ironically perhaps—early works such as the Bywaters Studio in Bluffview (fig. 36) could easily be exchanged for almost any of Wurster's Pasatiempo houses. From publication in *Architectural Forum* and other trade journals, Ford was well aware of Wurster's work of the early 1930s, and in some ways the Californian provided a model for the young Texan.[68]

Influential architectural critic and historian Talbot Hamlin wrote in *Pencil Points* at the close of 1939 that the Southwest was indeed producing viable American architecture by building rather than theorizing. "O'Neil Ford's Texas buildings . . . are as direct and simple in their appearance as the California work. . . . It would seem that we are dealing, not with a mere local and accidental development, but rather with a growing trend, originating perhaps in California and gradually spreading eastward. . . . This spirit pervades the best work." While praising the Texan contribution, Hamlin believed that the impetus lay on the West Coast: "Wurster is of course preeminent. His houses are never the same; each is approached as a fresh problem in the light of its site, its cost, its surroundings."[69]

By 1938 Ford was swayed more forcefully by the modernist urge and, with A. B. Swank, produced a very credible International Style essay in the Richardson House on San Jose Island (figs. 37). The plan of the house bears a striking resemblance to Wurster's McIntosh residence in Los Altos of 1937 (figs. 38, 39). Kitchen and pantry constituted one unit; the living and dining rooms and porch composed the house's central zone; the bedrooms formed a linear wing balancing the volume of the other spaces. Only in the position of their entrances did the Richardson and McIntosh residences significantly differ. But like Wurster—who became a close friend and collaborator after their meeting about 1938—Ford retreated from the extremes of the modern idiom. During the Depression years, Ford had been an active member of the team restoring and re-creating an area of central San Antonio known as La Villita—a project that renewed his interest in vernacular construction. The comfortable and quiet brand of modernism he ultimately forged was well illustrated by the Tinkle House in Dallas, built in 1952 (fig. 40). Neither modernist, historicist, nor vernacular, the house relied on stone and wood for its warmth, while its easy flow of space helped make a small house appear much larger. Two slender columns lost in shadow supported the wooden volume of the library as if floating over Turtle Creek—the singular theatrical gesture in an otherwise restrained effort.[70]

40.
Tinkle House, Dallas, 1952
O'Neil Ford
View from the creek

An Everyday Modernism

Was Wurster slow to accept the new ideas or was he only cautious, not wanting to throw out the baby with the bathwater? The work from the latter half of the 1930s does reveal new influences, perhaps generated by the younger employees in the office, who always exert some pressure on their bosses and influence the manner in which projects develop. Key works of this period also reflect a gradual evolution of the Pasatiempo model reinvigorated with a more clearly stated spatial configuration and sharper construction detailing, albeit without sacrificing the humanistic values that had underlain the earlier designs.

For houses in rural areas, Wurster continued to utilize wood frame construction left unpainted, although each plan varied as dictated by the site and program. For Amelia Jarvie's 1935 rural dwelling near Calistoga, Wurster disposed the house in two wings flaring outward, with the main living level set as a platform against the sloping site (fig. 41). The prevailing symmetry of the scheme belied an asymmetrical and quirkily planned interior. One approached the house expecting a central entrance and a balanced distribution of internal rooms. In reality, the entrance lay right of center, linked to the kitchen and service wing. The central knuckle between the two wings contained the din-

41.
Jarvie House, near Calistoga, 1935
William Wurster

42.
Jarvie House, near Calistoga, 1935
William Wurster
Bedroom with corner windows and
patterned ceiling

ing room—there was no living room per se—leading to several guest suites, each with its own bath. The boards of the bedroom ceilings formed concentric trapezoids, reinforcing the coherence of each room (fig. 42). The Jarvie House, with its mixture of monumentality and rusticity, raked horizontal lines, and unpainted wood sheathing, fully exemplified the modern/traditional dichotomies that continued within Wurster's residential work.

Climate and landscape played a major role in the design of these suburban and rural houses. The 1938 Green "Camp" at the foot of Mount Diablo, for example, assigned each of the family members and their activities to distinct volumes, arranged to disturb only minimally the contours of the land (figs. 43–45). A huge enclosed porch marked the house's architectural focal point and served as the family's social center, a solution also utilized in the Sullivan House in Saratoga of 1939. For the beachfront in Aptos, the Clark House (1937) offered an expansive wooden deck, anchored on both ends by glazed solaria for protection against the wind (figs. 46, 47). The living room, service spaces, and garage shared the first floor with the sun deck, while the sleeping quarters occupied the upper floor. As in the Jarvie House, symmetry prevailed but did not rule, and the diagonal line of the exterior stair to the bedrooms and roof terrace energized the stasis of the building's symmetrical mass.

Of the vacation houses, the unrealized project for the Cowgill Beach House was by far the most progressive (fig. 48). Essentially a translation into wood of Le Corbusier's 1930 Villa Savoye, the Cowgill scheme cleverly assigned the recessed ground floor to dressing and other activities related to the beach. Like the *piano nobile* of the Italian Renaissance palace, the principal living spaces were raised for privacy and view, with all the requisite functional pieces fitting neatly within a crisp rectilinear mass. Like the Villa Savoye, walls enclosed the rooftop terrace areas, providing privacy and architectural cohesion. The Cowgill design was apparently a great favorite with the younger members of the firm, and one could speculate on who was the major player in its design. Theodore Bernardi had joined the firm in 1934, bringing with him more progressive ideas about modernism as well as a more advanced formal vocabulary. Bernardi's proposed renovations for the 1946 Rosekrans House in San Francisco, for example, displayed a sense of fashion that would have been

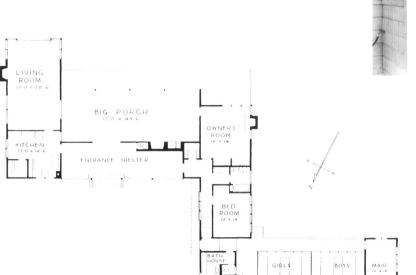

43.
Green "Camp," Mount Diablo, 1938
William Wurster
Central porch

44.
Green "Camp," Mount Diablo, 1938
William Wurster
Plan

45.
Green "Camp," Mount Diablo, 1938
William Wurster
Entry court

46.
Clark Beach House, Aptos, 1937
William Wurster
Beach view

47.
Clark Beach House, Aptos, 1937
William Wurster
Living room

48.
Cowgill Beach House, Aptos, 1935
William Wurster
Aerial perspective

49.
**Alterations to Apartment for Mr. and Mrs.
Rosekrans,** San Francisco, 1946
Wurster, Bernardi and Emmons
Theodore Bernardi, architect
Living Room

50.
Blaisdell House, Watsonville, 1936
William Wurster
Stairwell

anathema to Wurster just a few years earlier (fig. 49). Clearly the office was in a state of transition at the end of the 1930s.

Stridently modernist exercises such as the Blaisdell House in Watsonville of 1936 are rare in Wurster's total oeuvre (fig. 50). The light tones of the stucco surfaces, the transparency of the glass stairwell, and even the disposition of the living room as a distinct volume are by far the exceptions rather than the rule. This hesitancy to use stucco was due partly to Wurster's distaste for materials that tried to imitate others, partly to maintenance problems.[71] For houses in the suburbs, Wurster favored quieter, less unified overall forms. The Timby House in San Carlos (1940), which was selected by Wurster as one of his favorite small houses, employed the dual polarities characteristic of what in the postwar period would be termed the binuclear plan (figs. 51–53).[72] The house, built for a newly married couple and totaling only 1,470 square feet, was divided into two zones. To the left of the entrance—above a garage left open on three sides—were the owners' bedroom and the guest room; the living room and kitchen occupied the other wing. A gallery connected them— Wurster's "room with no name," whose dimensions and lack of assigned use allowed for appropriation from either section of the house. The joining of living room and gallery at an obtuse angle muted the perceived edges of the rooms and provided a feeling of greater extent. Although the lessons of flowing spaces ultimately hark back to Frank Lloyd Wright and European modernists such as Mies van der Rohe, Wurster's use of the interlocking volumes had become his own.

Wurster's mature residential architecture appeared almost effortless in its response to the client's needs, the properties of the site, the various considerations of climate, and the technical constraints of building well. Although he received his share of wealthy clients, particularly in San Francisco, Wurster also designed modest houses for those of more limited means. His distaste for ostentation and his predilection for common-sense solutions to all problems led to an architecture of brilliant planning, making the most out of what the budget and land had to offer. The Jensen House in Berkeley of 1937 has remained an enduring example of Wurster's skill in planning compact dwellings (figs. 54, 55). Disposed on two floors to maximize the minimal land provided by this tight and sloping site, this house of under 1,800 square feet

51.
Timby House, San Carlos, 1940
William Wurster

52.
Timby House, San Carlos, 1940
William Wurster
Plan

53.
Timby House, San Carlos, 1940
William Wurster
Living room / gallery

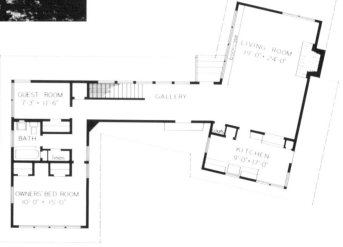

54.
Jensen House, Berkeley, 1937
William Wurster
Garden facade

55.
Jensen House, Berkeley, 1937
William Wurster
Plan

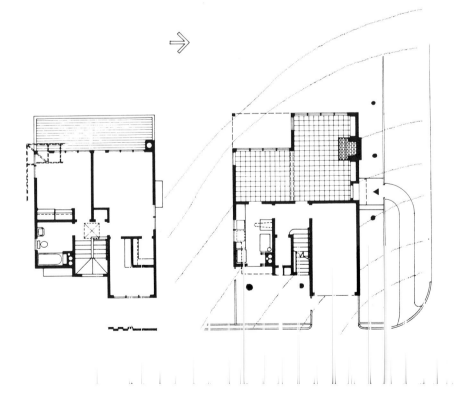

appears much larger than its actual dimensions. An early study of 1936 absorbed the various rooms of the house within an elongated rectangle; only the stair was articulated as a distinct volume. As realized, however, the house was more condensed. The dining and living rooms on the entry level folded into one another and opened to the west. A small terrace extended the interior of the house, as did a deck on the second floor. The whole was integrated within a single prismatic redwood box that has been shaped, excised, and capped with a thin, almost flat roof.

With Thomas and Betsy Church, Wurster returned to Europe in 1937; their travels included Sweden and Finland, for a decade regarded as the locus of a more humane modernism.[73] In Helsinki one beautiful Sunday morning they went for a drive, without a specific destination in mind. They stopped in Munkkiniemi, a suburb of Helsinki, before "a house that we thought was just what we had been dreaming of seeing."[74] As Wurster later described the visit: "I [could] not bear not to know who designed that house." He learned that the architect was Alvar Aalto, with whom the Americans established a friendship that would last until their deaths.[75]

Aalto's own house in Munkkiniemi of 1934, designed with Aino Aalto (fig. 56), like the Villa Mairea built four years later, eschewed the pure modernism of his 1930 Paimio Sanatorium. By that pivotal year architects such as Asplund, Sven Markelius, and Arne Jacobsen in Scandinavia and even Le Corbusier in France had softened their stance on expressing technology and the means of construction. One saw in their works a new regard for the site, a nascent acceptance of historical precedent and even romanticism. In the Aalto house stuccoed prisms prevailed, but to them were "collaged" panels of wooden slats that enclosed the balconies and sheathed segments of the upper floor.

In a similar manner, poles cloaked the studio of the Villa Mairea; unpeeled saplings supported the villa's entrance canopy; its sauna was a sophisticated version of a rustic norm. All these lightened the mass of the masonry walls stuccoed and painted white, energizing the composition through contrast (fig. 57). This freedom in Aalto's work avoided a doctrinaire approach to architectural design; there was a willingness to acknowledge the incidents of program or structure as a means to enrich the design, even if their accommodation vitiated the purity of the architectural style. The structural system for the Villa Mairea, for example, was planned using bearing walls and a regular structural grid. But few of the columns were the same: some were painted black; some were paired and wrapped with rattan; some were covered with slats of wood so that climbing vines could be more easily secured. One could say that from Aalto Wurster received a confirmation that it was possible to be modern without being insensitive to the client and site or the local vernacular. One need not rank architectural purity over the requirements of living. But by the late 1930s Wurster probably needed no such coaxing.

Certain of Wurster's designs bear a striking resemblance to Aalto's work, although they never exactly shared the Finnish architect's vocabulary. The Lyman House in Tiburon (1941), for example, followed the fall of the ground, an approach quite different from Aalto's proclivity to reform the land as a semi-naturalized plinth (figs. 58, 59). Although the V-shaped columns of the Lyman House suggested those of Aalto's 1937 Finnish Pavilion at the Paris Exposition Internationale des Arts et Techniques dans la Vie Moderne and the entrance to the Villa Mairea, such resemblances are isolated and rare. Perhaps the cantilevered bedroom of the Lyman House resembled more closely Frank Lloyd Wright's Usonian projects of the 1930s, particularly the balcony/terrace of the Sturges House of 1938 in Brentwood Heights. Many of the characteristics of Wurster's architecture remained constant, but the actual style of the work continued to evolve, perhaps aided by the rapid production of houses in the Wurster (later Wurster and Bernardi) office.

56.
Aalto House, Munkkiniemi, Helsinki, Finland, 1934
Alvar Aalto and Aino Aalto
Garden facade

57.
Villa Mairea, Noormarkku, Finland, 1938
Alvar Aalto
Detail of the south facade

58.
Lyman House, Tiburon, 1941
William Wurster

59.
Lyman House, Tiburon, 1941
William Wurster

Among the projects produced in the opening years of the 1940s, the most exceptional was the suburban residence for Dr. and Mrs. Saxton Pope in Orinda (1940). In 1932 Wurster designed a first residence for the Pope family in Burlingame (fig. 60). The commission was a joint venture with the local firm of Hall and Proetz, which may explain the rigidity of the plan and the overall formality of its composition. White stuccoed frame or masonry walls contributed to making the first Pope House appear like a box set upon its rocky landscape. Although chronic leaks in the flat roof had troubled Dr. Pope, he returned to Wurster for a second house when he joined the staff of the university hospital in Berkeley. Pope wrote several letters conveying his wishes in excruciating detail, with demands ranging from the overall concept of "play" and "serious" houses to suggestions about building materials. Pope was adamant about one aspect in particular: the roof should not leak![76] In addition, he wanted low-maintenance materials and surface finishes. The house was to be a castle, a retreat from the world, and the garden—for two avid gardeners— was to be the center of the home.

In an unusual move, Pope even provided schematic diagrams for the house, zoning it as a greenhouse and living quarters joined by an oversized atrium, circumscribed and inwardly focused (fig. 61). Just as unusual, the architect accepted these directives as a point of departure for his own design. However, Wurster and Pope differed markedly in their idea of a garden.[77] Wurster held, perhaps due to Thomas Church's tutelage, that the garden was a tended zone proximate to the house. While no misanthrope, Pope wanted a place that kept the surrounding environment at bay. Already at the time of construction, Pope felt the neighboring structures to be intrusive, and he knew the situation could only worsen over time.

The scheme resulting from the Pope–Wurster negotiations was possibly the most interesting residence that Wurster ever produced. He enlarged the atrium to a forty-foot square, far beyond the dimensions of Pope's sketched proposal (figs. 62, 63). In some respects the living areas, service spaces, and garage appeared almost as appendages to the atrium. The first presentation took greater liberties with the clients' requests and veered into the squiggly biomorphism that pervaded landscape and architectural design throughout the late 1930s and 1940s. As realized, however, the amoeba-shaped opening in the atrium roof was regularized as a circle, but set off center within the atrium

60.
Saxton Pope House #1, Burlingame, 1932
William Wurster and Hall and Proetz

61.
Saxton Pope House #2, Orinda, 1940
Saxton Pope
Diagrammatic plan, 1939

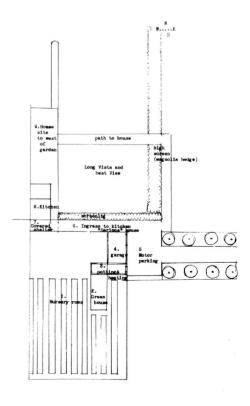

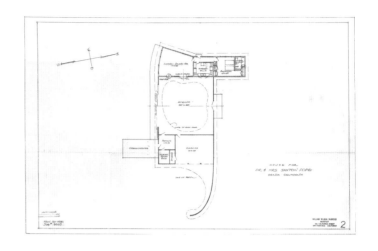

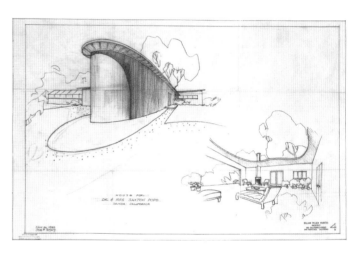

62.
Saxton Pope House #2, Orinda, 1940
William Wurster
Preliminary plan, 1939

63.
Saxton Pope House #2, Orinda, 1940
William Wurster
Preliminary study of the atrium, 1939

64.
Saxton Pope House #2, Orinda, 1940
William Wurster
Exterior view

65.
Saxton Pope House #2, Orinda, 1940
William Wurster
Living room

66. (opposite)
Saxton Pope House #2, Orinda, 1940
William Wurster
Atrium

67.
Valencia Gardens Public Housing,
San Francisco, 1939–42
William Wurster with Thomas Church,
landscape architect

square (fig. 66). Sliding panels allowed the atrium to open to the landscape (fig. 64)

The materials—quite untypically both for Wurster and the times—were corrugated metal sheathing, concrete block (the so-called C-block system), and ceramic tile floors. There would be no major cause for repair if the roof leaked—which it did not—and one senses that the house could almost be cleaned with a hose. Mrs. Pope designed and wove many of the textiles used for pillow coverings and upholstery (fig. 65). Construction of the house lagged far beyond the six months originally scheduled, and the relations between client and architect were quite frayed by the time of occupancy in 1941. But the house that issued from the frequent debates in letters and telephone calls (recorded in numerous office memos) was a masterwork that captured the imagination and the critical acceptance of professional and popular audiences alike. By 1950 the number of architectural visitors to the house had grown so large that the Popes' seclusion was seriously threatened. Dr. Pope wrote to Wurster on 11 September of that year begging him not to send people to see the house, except on certain days when he would be up to it: "Would you do me a favor? Don't send anyone to see the house on weekends from Saturday morning to Monday morning. Privacy is very hard to come by and we need the time to ourselves and our hobbies."[78]

Existing documentation does not conclusively establish the reasons for the success of the house, whether its innovative design derived from frank discussions between Pope and Wurster or from Bernardi and Emmons, both of whom worked on the project. It was a severe blow to both the family and the architectural community when the house was destroyed in 1964 to make way for the freeway that today links Berkeley and Oakland with the suburban communities over the hills.[79]

Wurster regarded his practice as a general physician might regard his or hers. No project was too large or too small to warrant the architect's attention, particularly after designing a family's first residence. In the office files now in the College of Environmental Design's Documents Collection at the University of California at Berkeley, one finds two, three, even four houses designed for the same family or a series of commissions for their relatives. In addition, sketches for small projects such as garages, remodelings, and additions—executed years after the occupation of the house—are not at all uncommon. To Wurster, being an architect implied a trust given the designer by the client. In this sense, accepting a commission implied an obligation to undertake further professional services in the future.

As noted above, one reason for the success of the Wurster office was its ability to address the needs of both wealthy clients and those with modest resources. For the latter, there was the quest for the "large-small house": an economical scheme yielding the greatest amount of quality usable space, even in projects with highly restricted budgets. The invention of such elements as the glazed corridor, the "room without a name," and the linked living-dining space cannot be attributed to Wurster alone, but these architectural strategies allowed him to create houses that felt spacious even if limited in total volume.

In 1939 the Wurster office received the commission for Valencia Gardens, a 246-unit public housing project in San Francisco. It was Wurster's first major excursion into multifamily dwellings, and his largest urban project to that date. For protection against the northwest wind, the building blocks were folded to enclose three garden courtyards and two service courts (fig. 179).[80] The south-facing garden courtyards were designed by Thomas Church and configured as play and social areas. The brick retaining walls that supported the planting beds served as continuous benches for sitting. Plantings of eucalyptus provided pools of shade; box, prostrate juniper, and grass filled out the restrained vegetal palette.

Given the highly restricted budget, the architecture of Valencia Gardens was as severe as a Wurster building would ever get. Slight jogs in the building facades and color—"terra cotta, blue, sand and bright yellow"[81]—prevented the reading of each block as a single entity but did little to energize the long wall planes (fig. 67). In planning the site to maximize light and ventilation and the utility of minimal dwellings, Wurster directly reflected the concern for public well-being that informed European housing of the time, particularly the housing estates in Frankfurt by Ernst May and his collaborators. Wurster's travels had also included social housing projects in Denmark and Sweden.

Given the American dream of the individual house on its own piece of land, however, these ideas for social housing were slow to reach American shores, and took even longer to reach the West Coast. But the Depression and the enormous migrant population that drifted in search of agricultural employment created a tremendous demand for housing, which resulted in the formation of the architectural branch of the Farm Security Administration as a part of the New Deal. Architects such as Vernon DeMars and landscape architects such as Garrett Eckbo were deeply involved in delivering livable housing at extremely low cost, with attractive and socially viable exterior spaces. The Vernon DeMars/Burton Cairns collaboration in 1937 at Yuba City, California, in many ways stood at the forefront of American architectural ideas at the time: uncompromisingly clean with razor-sharp edges, executed in the new materials of asbestos cement and plywood, carefully configured to facilitate ventilation and maintain comfort. Although rock bottom in terms of costs, the FSA projects were highly honored in professional publications and were represented in the Museum of Modern Art's "Built in USA: 1932–1944" exhibition and catalogue.

Wurster also entered into the debate for standardized and prefabricated housing, an interest that may have been stimulated by Alvar Aalto's trials in this area. In the late 1930s Aalto produced a series of design configurations for the Ahlström Company in Finland, whose diversified holdings included sawmills and forest products. True to his values, Aalto did not opt for rigid standardization: instead he formulated a "humanistic standardization," seemingly an oxymoron. But in Aalto's eyes the key to humanism was found in the

scale of the module and the system's flexibility—two concerns that Wurster would share very shortly thereafter.[82] Building norms did not demand exact replication for economy; standardization allowed controlled variation.

With American entry into World War II, in 1942 Wurster, Bernardi, and Ernest Kump received commissions for extensive developments of defense workers' housing in Vallejo. The burgeoning war industries in Northern and Southern California demanded accommodations for the masses of workers entering the state for employment in the war effort. In the San Francisco Bay Area, for example, the tiny town of Hercules exploded as a producer of armaments; the San Francisco shipyards produced a stream of new tonnage almost without cessation; Oakland was reinvigorated as a major supply depot for the Pacific. Situated at the northern extremity of the San Francisco Bay and the mouth of the Sacramento River, Vallejo became a pivotal point for manufacture and shipping. The team of architects that Wurster headed was charged with the production of 5,000 dwelling units to be realized within a very short period of time. For Wurster, the challenge was an opportunity not only to investigate standardization and prefabrication more fully but also to test ideas about community.

In 1939 Wurster had met Catherine Bauer, who had been appointed visiting lecturer in the Department of Social Welfare at the University of California at Berkeley. During the previous decade Bauer had become one of the leading proponents of social housing in the United States. Having studied progressive housing programs throughout Europe—with a particular affinity for the Scandinavian models—Bauer published *Modern Housing* in 1934, which would become the standard work on the subject. The book's introduction noted, "This new housing method recognizes that the integral unit for planning, the economical unit for construction and administration, and the social unit for living, is the complete neighborhood, designed and equipped as such."[83] This idea would inform Wurster's design of collective dwellings. Bauer was also an integral part of several overlapping intellectual and professional circles centered in New York. She was a close friend of Lewis Mumford, whose own more humanistically inclined values tempered an almost utopian socialist idealism. Her sister, Elizabeth (Bauer) Mock (later Kassler), was associate curator in the Department of Architecture and Design at the Museum of Modern Art, certainly the epicenter of the battle for the acceptance of modernism in the Western Hemisphere.[84]

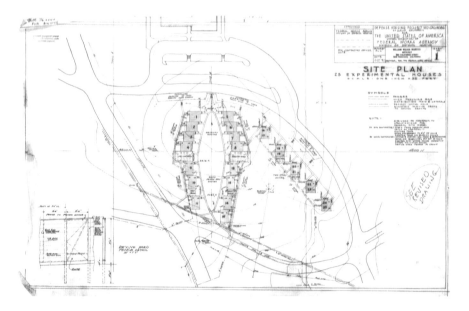

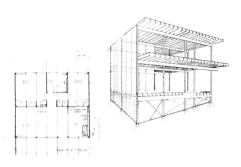

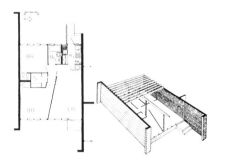

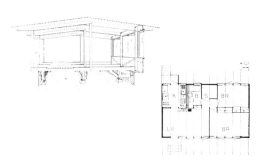

Shortly after their meeting in Berkeley—six months to be precise—Bauer and Wurster married in Seattle. The union would lead Wurster to be concerned with ideas of community in ways that he had never been before; Bauer, for her part, seems to have become more aware of the issues of quality and aesthetics in architecture and housing. Their partnership, both professional and social, was a model in terms of mutual respect, influence, learning, and criticism. For the moment, their worlds were rendered coincident by the war effort. Bauer, who had been a force in New Deal housing legislation and programs, reported on defense-housing schemes in what today would be termed postoccupancy evaluations.

The Wurster teams' designs for two areas of the Vallejo site balanced social issues with the pragmatics of restricted resources (fig. 68). The units were constructed from a standardized-panels system that used the new material of plywood as its principal element. The most innovative parts of the Vallejo project were the experimental units that explored an alternate system of construction. Wurster arranged for two dozen units to utilize structural systems relying on reinforced concrete block, laminated wood, and steel frame, in addition to the more traditional wooden units (fig. 70). The single negotiated restrictions were the overall number of units and the ceiling cost of $2,845 per unit, which matched the cost of construction mandated throughout the project. These experimental units were joined as a group in a staggered diamond pattern that followed the rise and fall of the sloping site, with a common open space between them (fig. 69). Reexamined today, these efforts at prefabrication appear almost primitive and the plan of the site as a whole—destroyed after the war— quite unremarkable. In comparison with contemporary projects such as Richard Neutra's 1942 Channel Heights housing in Los Angeles and certain FSA developments, the Vallejo project appears almost mundane in its simplicity and quiet forms. The architects' achievement was ultimately not in innovative construction, but, perhaps not unsurprisingly, in quickly forming a small, socially viable community where none had stood.

69. (top left)
Experimental units, Carquinez Heights,
Vallejo, 1941
William Wurster
Site plan

70.
Experimental units, Carquinez Heights,
Vallejo, 1941
William Wurster
Axonometric drawing of construction
systems

To the Postwar Era

Even during the war years, the architecture profession turned its attention to the better life that would accompany the return of peace. The modernist camp reframed the question of the house in terms of the act of dwelling. Journals such as *House Beautiful* took issue with Le Corbusier's celebrated dictum that a house was essentially a machine for dwelling, and turned instead to the intangible properties of warmth that houses of traditional form might offer.[85] In *Tomorrow's House,* published in 1945, co-authors George Nelson and Henry Wright instructed future homemakers on "How to Plan Your Post-War Home Now"—the book's subtitle. They chided contemporary families who sought the latest in technological convenience, yet "build houses that were designed originally to conform to the techniques and living requirements of people who were dead two hundred years ago."[86] Their argument cited the *Zeitgeist*—one must live in the spirit of the times: "The great tradition in building is honest building. . . . In designing houses today we have to be ourselves—twentieth century people with our own problems and our own technical facilities. *There is no other way to get a good house.* No other way at all."[87]

The authors' argument did not center on style, however; quite the opposite, it focused on the rational way to plan the house.[88] Natural and artificial lighting, acoustics, flexibility, and storage were prime considerations, as were the social conditions of eating, hygiene, and sleeping and the new spaces needed to accommodate them—spaces such as the "living kitchen." Under the subhead "Work Center–Social Center," Nelson and Wright noted, "The modern kitchen cannot be a small room. It must be a big room—possibly the biggest room in the house."[89] After all, it must address the full gamut of family activities and even accommodate guests in the informal postwar lifestyle. Their pronouncements varied from broad dicta governing approach to the specifics of lamp design to those for storage. Strategies for financing were provided—important considerations for the middle class, for whom the individually designed house was becoming beyond reach. The photographs and drawings were cast only as suggestions; this was not intended as a pattern book.

William Wurster and Wurster and Bernardi were well represented in the book's illustrations; of the California contingent, only Harwell Hamilton Harris received greater coverage. The glazed/screened central porch of Wurster's Sullivan House in Saratoga represented rationally planned space: "Little more costly than an ordinary porch, it provides ample indoor room for games and parties, and made possible a plan in which the balance of the rooms were compact and economical, since further provision for entertainment was unnecessary."[90] Chapter Seven was titled "The Room without a Name," a term often credited to Wurster himself. Nelson and Wright, however, noted that they learned of this idea from several different sources, suggesting that like minds follow similar paths.[91] This space without a specific functional assignment was essentially a sizable room to which were appended alcoves for such activities as study and cooking. In place of numerous small spaces, each with a single function, the new open plan allowed for uses changing over time or according to the presence of various family members. Since the time of the Pasatiempo development, Wurster's houses had included such ambiguous spaces as central to their planning: the kitchen cave, the glazed corridor, and even the room without a name. The houses illustrated in *Tommorow's House* shared a common sensibility: no Dutch Colonials were included, but also missing were the pristine spaces of early European modernism. By the 1940s concern for the locale and its culture, paired with the use of local materials, conditioned the abstraction and severity of the (foreign) parent idea.

The other critical document of the era was *The Modern House in America* by James Ford and Katherine Morrow Ford. The need for such a book was probably stimulated by the output of the Architectural Press in London, which had produced F. S. Yorke's *The Modern House* and *The Modern Flat* in 1934 and 1937 respectively. Like Nelson and Wright, the Fords cited living patterns and contemporary building materials as the central forces behind the new residential architecture. "Analysis and fresh synthesis"—the recurring belief in the palliative power of science—will produce the new dwelling. Just as there have been revolutions in the arts of painting, sculpture, and music, so must there be a corresponding revolution in domestic design: "Modern architecture then seeks not style but substance, not ornament or ostentation but rational simplicity, not standard plans and facade but proficiency in exposition, not fitting the family to the house but the house to the family, not imitation but creation."[92]

Unlike *Tomorrow's House, The Modern House in America* favored work more crisply in the modernist camp; one should note, however, that the Fords' house in Lincoln, Massachusetts, was designed in 1939 by Walter Gropius and Marcel Breuer, both of whom lived nearby. Despite the authors' inherent favoritism, houses with references to local traditions and those that followed in the wake of Frank Lloyd Wright did appear. Southern California prevailed over the north—Richard Neutra's houses dominated the book—and the photographs were weighted toward lively exterior compositions of light and shadow and interior spaces drenched with sunlight. In contrast, the photographs in *Tomorrow's House* appeared almost somber—perhaps a necessary reflection of the wartime economy and printing resources. The Fords included only two of Wurster's designs: the Miller House in Carmel from 1935 and the McIntosh House in Los Altos from two years later. Flexibility and simplicity joined under a single roof were the hallmarks of the Miller design, and the McIntosh's use of exposed concrete-block construction, the permanence and ease of care, and the fluid relationship between inside and outside were exemplary.

One could question why Wurster received so little exposure in *The Modern House*. To some degree, this stemmed from the predilections of the authors, who found in Neutra's architecture more advanced exercises in space and composition. But by the 1940 publication date, questions of the local and the regional had given way once again to viewing international trends and the United States as part of a global arena. Wurster's principal contribution in terms of form had been made over half a decade earlier, and the projects ranging from roughly 1935 to 1945 showed little formal development, with the notable exception of the Saxton Pope House. In many ways, Wurster's maturation as an architect continued as the perfecting of ideas already established; his period of innovation had ended.

Exempt from military service, and justly proud of his recent accomplishments in defense workers' housing, Wurster moved to Cambridge, where he undertook advanced study in city planning at Harvard. Although he would never complete his doctorate, the move east changed the direction of his career. In 1944 he was appointed dean of the School of Architecture at the Massachusetts Institute of Technology; in 1950 he was appointed dean of the School of Architecture at the University of California at Berkeley. From that point on, his efforts were to lie primarily in education, although as Richard Peters and Caitlin Lempres note in their essay in this book, Wurster never actually taught a course. He had risen to a position of leadership, as he put it, assembling the team and running interference for his players.

The Wurster office remained one of the most respected in California and, with Gardner Dailey's, the leading firm in the San Francisco Bay Area.[93] In Wurster's words, the office "was like a series of small offices, each composed of a junior and senior draftsman. Each team had several jobs. One job the senior would do the drafting and the junior would write the specifications—then they would reverse. . . . As I have always thought of the office as a training ground, it gave a fine experience to the men when the time came for them to go on their own."[94] With the 1943 presentation of the firm's work in an *Architectural Forum* portfolio, Wurster included the complete list of his staff employed since 1938—forty of them, including a name of obviously Japanese descent.[95] Realizing that it would be impossible to run an office in San Francisco from a home in Cambridge, Wurster acknowledged the contributions of Theodore Bernardi by accepting him as partner in 1944, renaming the firm Wurster and

Bernardi. A year later a similar valuation of the importance of Donn Emmons, recently returned from military service, resulted in the formation of Wurster, Bernardi and Emmons, which endures to this day.

In 1948 Wurster found himself—perhaps quite unknowingly and surprisingly—in the middle of a theoretical debate that reestablished the criteria by which to evaluate modernism. In his "Skyline" column for 11 October 1947 in *The New Yorker,* Lewis Mumford described the architectural tradition of the Bay Area as one that had utilized modernity without succumbing to modernist dogma. "The modern accent is on living not on the machine. . . . The rigorists placed the mechanical functions of a building above its human functions; they neglected feelings, the sentiments, and the interests of the person who was to occupy it."[96] The dwelling should concern feeling as well as function. With somewhat nationalistic undertones, Mumford dismissed high modernism as "old hat" and instead lauded the architecture of Bernard Maybeck, John Galen Howard, and other members of the first "Bay Region style," a term that Mumford himself seems to have coined. He noted the extent to which their ideas, unlike those of the "rigorists," had been accepted by the public. "That style took root about fifty years ago in Berkeley, California . . . and by now, on the Coast, it is simply taken for granted: no one out there is foolish enough to imagine that there is any other proper way of building in our time."[97] Wurster was the only contemporary architect cited; like Maybeck, he "took good care that [his] houses did not resemble factories or museums."[98] This was their lesson.

The article was followed by Mumford's contribution to the catalogue for the 1949 exhibition "The Domestic Architecture of the San Francisco Bay Region" at the San Francisco Museum of Art. In this essay, Mumford reinforced the ideas first put forward in *The New Yorker,* marking the contributions of architects such as Irving Gill, Ernest Kump, Gardner Dailey, and William Wurster toward an architecture that put people and their locality first. For Mumford, "The main problem of architecture today is to reconcile the universal and the regional, the mechanical and the human, the cosmopolitan and the indigenous."[99] Wurster himself contributed an essay, recalling the pleasure of being in houses by Ernest Coxhead and Willis Polk, although the qualities of their architecture eluded the camera. He described the essence of the informal lifestyle of the Californian: "*Who* you are is not so important as *what* you are"; and he once again noted the influence of climate on local architecture: "The long dry season in California, from May until November, leaves its mark on life and so, in turn, on the design—no need of shelter from summer rains and great need of ground areas covered with gravel or brick, which do not need water."[100]

In his catalogue essay, Gardner Dailey related that the "'Large-Small House' has one very large room, and the balance of the house has been compressed wherever possible to eliminate waste space, long halls, and stairs. The elimination of space has been accomplished by reducing the service section to a one-maid or no-maid unit. The basement has disappeared. The garage, as such, is usually but a roof. Almost all of the houses shown use what has become popularly known as the dual-purpose room."[101]

To an Eastern establishment already under attack during the war for its cadre of [German] émigré architects, the Mumford editorial and its aftermath were a call to arms.[102] In the spring of 1948, Museum of Modern Art Director of Collections Alfred H. Barr, Jr., used the excitement in the air as the point of departure for a symposium at the museum titled "What Is Happening to Modern Architecture?" Lewis Mumford moderated. Although Wurster did not participate, he and his architecture were castigated in absentia. Barr noted: "That there has developed during the past ten years an informal and ingratiating kind of wooden domestic building cannot be denied, but if one studies British, Swiss, and Scandinavian architectural magazines, it is clear that this

SMALL HOUSE FOR
MISSES ALICE & MARIAN BURR
SAN FRANCISCO   CALIFORNIA

MARCH 15, 1940.

71.
Burr House, San Francisco, 1942
William Wurster
Preliminary study

72.
Kenyon Houses, San Francisco, 1937
William Wurster

SECOND FLOOR PLAN   THIRD FLOOR PLAN

BASEMENT PLAN   FIRST FLOOR PLAN

73.
Doble House, San Francisco, 1939
William Wurster
Plan

74.
Doble House, San Francisco, 1939
William Wurster
Perspective study

75. (opposite)
Doble House, San Francisco, 1939
William Wurster
Street facade

style, too, is international." Somewhat deprecatingly he continued: "Indeed, I think we might call this kind of building the International Cottage Style."[103]

Landscape architect Christopher Tunnard tried to intervene, calling for a middle ground between the two extremes. "We have got to look at the buildings that have received the approbation of critics and the buildings which people like," he suggested, "and reconcile public taste and good architectural performance."[104] Mumford's description of the quality of natural materials seems to have piqued Marcel Breuer in particular. In his vituperative and celebrated retort—republished at the end of the catalogue that accompanied his exhibition at the Museum of Modern Art the following year—Breuer chided those who would find humanity in natural materials alone: "If 'human' is considered identical with redwood all over the place, or if it is considered identical with imperfection and imprecision, I am against it; also, if it is considered identical with camouflaging architecture with planting, with nature, with romantic subsidies."[105] Considering the state of Breuer's own residential work at the time, the viciousness of his comments appears quite out of place, if not hypocritical. Even his own house in Lincoln, Massachusetts, which was wood frame—sheathed in tongue-and-groove redwood siding, no less!—employed extensive amounts of natural fieldstone for walls, the central fireplace, and terrace paving.[106]

Breuer also reaffirmed his belief in informal living, although he maintained that it should not suppress the "instinct toward achievement" that propelled the best modernist work. He noted that Le Corbusier's built works were never machines, despite the Swiss-French architect's rhapsodies about mechanization. "His houses," Breuer chided, "are much less machines for living than, for example, the three thousand family housing developments of the West Coast, the same pseudo-prefabricated houses, hill up, hill down, in rigid rows or in rigid curves—though quite redwoody."[107] This pointed reference to Wurster and company's work in Vallejo was not lost on the audience assembled at the museum. In his closing comments, moderator Mumford restated in simple terms what he had first written in his column: "What is the Bay Region Style? Nothing but an example of a form of modern architecture which came into existence with our growth and which is so native that people, when they ask for a building, do not ask for it in any style."[108] One can forgive Mumford his hyperbole, given the somewhat hostile feelings of his audience. But what was the lesson to be learned here if this style was so in tune with its people? "Any local effort," Mumford believed, "if worth anything, is worth reproducing elsewhere; and any universal formula that is worth anything must always be susceptible of being brought home—otherwise it lacks true universality."[109] If viewed on these terms, and perhaps on these terms alone, the redwood, informality, and "camouflaged with planting" of the Bay Region style did constitute a challenge to the hegemony of the International Style as formulated by its fathers.

While no longer at the forefront of architectural development, the residential work of Wurster, Bernardi and Emmons continued to be praised, awarded, and published. Drawing on experience with the defense workers' housing and ideas of community design perhaps drawn from Catherine Bauer, Wurster's office engaged in several noteworthy multifamily projects. Wurster's rental house in San Francisco (1942) for Alice and Marian Burr complemented their twin dwelling, using an enclosed courtyard to join all three units as a single home (fig. 71). For interior designer Nora Kenyon, in 1935 Wurster developed a series of four linked houses that mounted the slope from Bay to Francisco Streets. A wide stair swelled into terraces as it stepped upward (fig. 72). Linking the various levels and house entrances, the common stair both joined and distinguished each house, expressing the singular and the collective aspects of urban dwelling. A linear garden by Thomas Church paralleled the stair and provided greenery for each of the units.

FIRST FLOOR & PLOT PLAN

SECOND FLOOR PLAN

THIRD FLOOR PLAN

76.
Grover House, San Francisco, 1939
William Wurster

77.
Grover House, San Francisco, 1939
William Wurster
Plan

78.
Grover House, San Francisco, 1939
William Wurster
Street facade

San Francisco's disposition as a city on a hill continued to challenge the Wurster office in the postwar period. In the late 1930s Wurster had begun to tackle the thorny problem of the severe slope, a condition made doubly problematic by his preference for making the house suit the hillside rather than vice-versa. To Wurster, the more modernist solution of propping the house on exposed columns was unacceptable. If the house was to suit the hillside, the two must operate as a symbiotic unit rather than as one set in opposition to the other. The compact plan of the 1939 Doble House assigned the street level to a rental unit, the intermediate floor to bedrooms, and the upper level to living spaces (figs. 73–75). In contrast to one Wurster norm, the Doble design maximized garden space by closely linking the facade to the street and eliminating the garage. Of redwood, with apertures freely dispersed and countered by the rungs of the fire escape, this urban facade tantalized and questioned; it provided only vague clues about the building's internal disposition. The plan itself, like so many of Wurster's houses, was undistinguished, especially when compared with the freer internal dispositions of designs by Wright, Le Corbusier, Mies van der Rohe, or even the work of Marcel Breuer in this country.

Given a deeper lot, the Grover House of the same year was disposed in two primary volumes: the street-front pavilion with garage and unfinished living unit above and the principal living pavilion to the rear (figs. 76, 78). A Thomas Church garden, featuring a kidney-shaped plant bed, led to the entry; the south-facing dining room adjoined the garden and kitchen, which, along with the servants' rooms, composed the first floor (fig. 77). The bedrooms were located on the intermediate level, and the third-floor living room offered an unparalleled view of San Francisco Bay. By Wurster's own standards, this was a curious arrangement; the kitchen and dining room were separated from the upper living area, so that serving the latter was somewhat distant. Primacy was given the living room and the connection between dining room and garden.[110] The spiraling curved stair hall became a central element of these houses and the key force linking the various floors spatially as well as functionally.

Wurster rarely conceived the multifloored house as a single, articulated space. Instead, he addressed the particular conditions of the program floor by floor, with services and stairs as the principal elements common to all floors. The Hiken House of 1954 in many ways completed Wurster's formulation of the urban town house and the formality that had crept into his designs beginning in the mid-1940s. From the street, one encounters two symmetrically disposed boxes, cantilevered slightly from the primary building line. The sense of closure and internal focus of the Hiken design contrasted severely with the play of internal and expansive external views of the Coleman House of 1962 in Pacific Heights. From the street, only a quiet and undistinguished two-story facade was visible. The entrance corridor offered a glimpse of the elegant glass-enclosed and planted courtyard, which matched in its restraint the exuberance of the urban panorama seen from the living spaces. At night the courtyard glowed like a lantern, retaining its identity as the center of the composition (fig. 79).

Wurster and Bernardi's own contribution to the *Arts and Architecture* Case Study House program retained its woody integrity in stark contrast to more industrial vernacular projects like the 1948 Eames House or the uncompromising steel frame buildings of Craig Elwood and Pierre Koenig. In describing their project, Case Study House No. 3 of 1945–49 (fig. 180), Wurster and Bernardi stated matter of factly:

> *It seems that nowadays, every house must have a new "system of construction." However our clients will have to get along with good old 2x4's. We do not mean to imply that new materials and prefabrication are impractical. If*

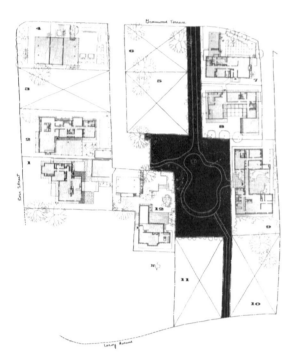

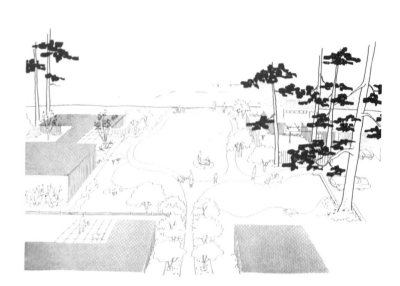

certain standard plans and forms are acceptable, factory production in large
quantities will undoubtedly produce economies. But where the individualized
custom-tailored house is desired, and at the same time the dollar must be
stretched, there is as yet no system that competes with stud construction on a
cost basis.[111]

A large porch—a legacy of the 1930s houses—united the two wings of the
roughly binuclear plan; terraces completely surrounded the house, integrating
indoor-outdoor space as a central part of the design (fig. 154). While the house
as executed (on a different site than first intended) was more compact than the
first project, reducing the openness of the connecting lanai, most of the architects' original intentions were realized.[112]

In 1954 Wurster purchased a two-and-one-half-acre property on Greenwood
Terrace, owned by Sadie Gregory, quite close to where he resided in the latter
days of his Berkeley life. The site was subdivided into twelve lots of varying
sizes and orientations and designed in collaboration with landscape architect
Lawrence Halprin (fig. 80). In some ways, the houses of Greenwood Common
realized the ideas Wurster first proposed in a small brochure for the Revere
Copper and Brass Company published during the war. In this brochure, "Accent
on an Outdoor Room"—the fifteenth in a series commissioned from American
architects for visions of housing after the war—Wurster described the idea of a
"flexible house" that adapts quite easily to the changing nature of the family
(fig. 82). The plan was zoned into messy and presentable areas, both inside the
house and in the garden. In this house, which remained only in very preliminary sketch form, Wurster came as close as he ever did to the open spaces of
Southern California modernist work of Neutra, Schindler, Ain, and Soriano.[113]

Like the "Flexible House," the site planning for Greenwood Common mandated that each of the lots should be just large enough for a house and a private
patio; the remaining land would be pooled for a common park area (fig. 81).
The intention of the architect and landscape architect was to give the residents
three things ordinarily missing in contemporary suburban development: an
outdoor space for residents and children, free of traffic; "one reasonably big
outdoor area instead of 12 unreasonably small lawns"; and "a focal point for
their neighborhood."[114] The project, deemed successful virtually from the day
of occupation, included houses by various architects, including Joseph
Esherick, Harwell Hamilton Harris, and John Funk; there were none by Wurster.

79. (opposite)
Coleman House, San Francisco, 1962
Wurster, Bernardi and Emmons
William Wurster
Interior court at night

80.
Greenwood Common, Berkeley, 1954
Wurster, Bernardi and Emmons
William Wurster with Lawrence Halprin,
landscape architect
Site plan

81.
Greenwood Common, Berkeley, 1954
Wurster, Bernardi and Emmons/William
Wurster with Lawrence Halprin, landscape
architect
Perspective sketch

82.
"Flexible House," ca. 1943
William Wurster
Plan

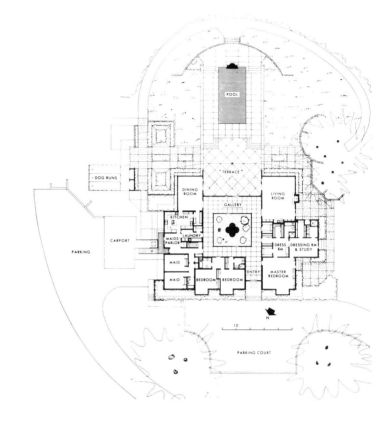

83.
Henderson House, Hillsborough, 1957
Wurster, Bernardi and Emmons
William Wurster with Thomas Church,
landscape architect
Site and plan

84.
Henderson House, Hillsborough, 1957
Wurster, Bernardi and Emmons
William Wurster with Thomas Church,
landscape architect
Garden facade

Like the houses of Greenwood Common, the Henderson House of 1957 addressed the specific aspects of the residential suburb and the linking of interior and exterior spaces. Overlooking a golf course in suburban Hillsborough, the house was configured as a modern classical villa, addressing, for privacy, its own world. From the exterior, the house appeared as a solid, although it was in actuality a square-donut plan, with wide glazed corridors surrounding a minimally planted courtyard animated by a single fountain (fig. 83). The vertical proportions of the design, the windows that directly engage a thin roof overhang, and the palette all suggest the influence of partner Donn Emmons on Wurster's residential sensibility.

The fourteen-foot-high ceilings agreed with the scale of the various rooms, each of which was given a sense of complete enclosure. The move toward more vertical proportions was characteristic of the time. "It is interesting to note that there is a trend against too much horizontality," Gardner Dailey had already noted in 1949; "too much glass in the wrong places; and a happy recognition of the value of the vertical line. The vertical line is a very serene motive."[115] The large-scale porch, the glazed corridor, and the gallery adjoining the terrace had been elements of Wurster's architecture since the early 1930s. The linkage between the interior court and the porch—whose skylights relieved the inherent contrast between shadow and bright areas—and porch and terrace were vintage Wurster, even if the connection was less immediate than in certain earlier works.

The garden, like the courtyard, was designed by Thomas Church; the swimming pool, set perpendicularly to the garden facade of the house, continued the axis established by the courtyard and porch (fig. 84). Somewhat consistently, Church used the pool to provide the armature for the garden, centralizing its most formal element. The layout of spaces flanking the axis and their plantings departed from the symmetry implied by the central feature, softening the transition to more naturalistic plantings on the perimeter of the garden. The Henderson House in many ways culminated Wurster's essays in suburbia. While it is not a small house by any means, it "achieves the stateliness of a large and formal house in what is essentially a small house, containing only the number and kind of rooms suited to the owners' tastes and way of living."[116]

In some rare instances, the site truly dictated the plan and suggested the materials of the house, including in several rarer instances the use of fieldstone. The rocky forested slopes surrounding Lake Tahoe, for example, were probably the origin of the stone walls of the Heller House built in 1950 (figs. 85, 86). The rugged stone walls and steeply pitched roofs of Maybeck's 1903 Wyntoon in Siskiyou County or the 1921 Glen Alpine Springs Resort near Lake Tahoe may have provided Wurster with an architectural precedent. Although the disposition of the spaces within the long rectangular box of the Heller House recalled the open porches of the Green "Camp" and Sullivan houses, the materials and internal planning departed from these earlier precedents. Given the heavy snowfall, steep roofs were in order, animated in this case by the rhythm of dormer windows that punctured the sweep of the corrugated metal roofing. Given that the house was used primarily in winter, the plan understandably focused on a large-scale fireplace.

The house designed for architectural photographer Morley Baer extended the interior openness of the Heller House within massive walls of stone (fig. 87). The strength of the external shell allowed the softness of the interior, painted a uniform white to maximize the sense of space. Situated on a magnificent site overlooking the Pacific, the Baer House was as much a belvedere as an outpost. Completing this trio of related projects was the beach house for the Wurster family, completed in 1962 at Stinson Beach in Marin County (fig. 88). The living wing dominated the two parts of the house, a single vol-

85.
Heller House, Lake Tahoe, 1950
Wurster, Bernardi and Emmons
William Wurster, architect

86.
Heller House, Lake Tahoe, 1950
Wurster, Bernardi and Emmons
William Wurster, architect
Plan

87.
Baer House, Big Sur, 1963
Wurster, Bernardi and Emmons
William Wurster, architect

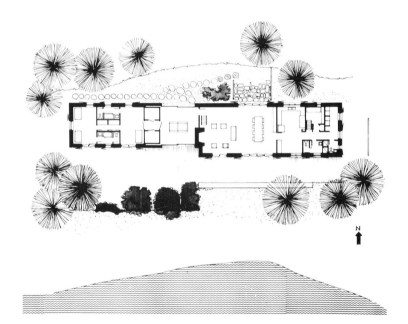

N

(Photo by Morley Baer)

88.
Wurster House, Stinson Beach, 1962
Wurster, Bernardi and Emmons
William Wurster, architect

89.
Wurster House, Stinson Beach, 1962
Wurster, Bernardi and Emmons
William Wurster, architect
"Room with no name"

ume capped by a gently sloping hip roof, with a direct play of shingled wall surfaces against full-height window panels. Wurster biographer Richard Peters captured the accomplishment of this and other Wurster houses of the era: "Overlooking the sand and sea, the room with no name testifies to Wurster's belief that everyday use has symbolic meaning in the making of places"[117] (fig. 89).

While the Wurster, Bernardi and Emmons practice grew to include projects of much larger scope, Wurster himself—perhaps due to his involvement with academic matters at the university—maintained his interest in residential commissions. Working with favored members of the office staff, principal among them Will Rand and Ralph Butterfield, Wurster designed several of his best works toward the end of the 1950s. Of these, the ranch house in Madera for the George Pope family received the most critical acclaim (figs. 90, 91). For a working ranch breeding and training thoroughbred horses in the hot, dry Central Valley, Wurster proposed a singular volume elevated from the ground, surrounded by screened porches and crowned by a tall hip roof of galvanized iron painted red. A grand staircase linked the veranda to a gently raised mound and to the landscape. To mitigate the effects of summer heat, the adobe walls were made two feet thick, and the interior spaces were given high ceilings. A twelve-foot-wide veranda surrounded the full perimeter, offering through ventilation and a view over the valley. Elegant finishes evoked the feeling of the true villa, for example, the refinement of the detailing and the execution of the casework in walnut. The spiral staircase—a favorite feature for Wurster's larger houses—was fashioned from blocks of solid black walnut cut from trees downed on the site (fig. 92).[118] The overall demeanor of the house recalled the continuous verandas and adobe walls of the 1843 Larkin House in Monterey or General Mariano Vallejo's adobe house near Petaluma, but the form of the Pope House seems to have emerged from the architect's response to its particular setting.

Although more visually transparent and rooted to its ground-level plinth, the Nowell House near Stockton of 1951 had earlier explored the idea of the house as a single pavilion (fig. 93). In fact, the Nowell House achieved an openness previously missing in Wurster's dwellings, as if finally acknowledging the possibilities of modernist space. One senses both the interior and exterior as whole entities only subsequently subdivided by rooms assigned to specific tasks. Unlike the early houses, for example, those at Pasatiempo, the house was not the sum of its parts adjusted to the site. Instead, each room felt a part of the next, and each a part of the whole. In both the Pope and Nowell houses the

90. (opposite)
George Pope House, Madera, 1956
Wurster, Bernardi and Emmons
William Wurster, architect

91.
George Pope House, Madera, 1956
Wurster, Bernardi and Emmons
William Wurster, architect
Plan

92.
George Pope House, Madera, 1956
Wurster, Bernardi and Emmons
William Wurster, architect
Spiral staircase

roof predominated, although the roof pitch of the Nowell House was slight, giving the impression of a pavilion or a Japanese umbrella protecting the body from the rain. The broad overhangs of the roof protected the extensive glass areas from the summer sun; the beam structure necessary to carry a double cantilever at the corners was exposed as structural ornamentation (fig. 94). As a totality, the Nowell House exuded a sense of effortlessness, as if it had been sketched quickly, with the architects' rapid grasp of the nuances of program and site, and the architectural response necessary to accommodate them. In this freedom and openness, the Nowell House was probably the closest Wurster, Bernardi and Emmons ever came to matching the transparency of Mies van der Rohe in his 1951 glass Farnsworth House in Plano, Illinois.

These later houses, while varying in the degree of interior openness, their connection to terrace and garden, and the naturalness of their materials, all continued the quest William Wurster had begun in the late 1920s. Looking back over a professional career that spanned four decades, one witnesses Wurster's continued investigation of the California situation in both environmental and social terms. If the early houses more openly cited historical styles, followed by houses that rigorously reinterpreted the vernacular tradition, Wurster's houses from the latter part of the 1930s onward accepted ideas from a new vocabulary drawn from modernist architecture. There was less looking backward to architectural precedent, either high style or vernacular.

In Taoism it is said that "learning is forgetting." Although we apprehend an idea by bringing it to our awareness, we have truly learned only when that idea appears without conscious thought. Like the athlete or swordsman who joins mind and body without thinking, William Wurster assimilated the elements of California residential design to the degree that each house reflected the client and the site more than it did the personality of the architect.

Was Wurster a remarkable architect? If we define remarkable as applying only to an innovative form giver on the order of Frank Lloyd Wright, Le Corbusier, or even Mies van der Rohe, we would honestly have to answer no. Wurster, in many respects, was untypically typical. He embodied the spirit of his age and his region, not as a figure apart from his cultural or economic condition but one who was completely enmeshed in it. He was successful because

93. (opposite)
Nowell House, Stockton, 1951
Wurster, Bernardi and Emmons
William Wurster, architect

94.
Nowell House, Stockton, 1951
Wurster, Bernardi and Emmons
William Wurster, architect
Living room

he understood what architecture was at that moment. He understood what his clients wanted, what was possible within a given budget, on a given site, at a given time. He was competent, thorough, professional. He built with a sense of the joy of living that always kept his work from seeming dull, even if the forms themselves were not exciting. He succeeded on his own terms: "Architecture is not a goal. Architecture is for life and pleasure and work and for people. The picture frame, and not the picture."[119] His was, for the most part, not a utopian vision. His most far-reaching investigations in construction—admittedly minor in the history of industrialized building—were those experiments for the defense workers' housing at Vallejo. And yet even here, if not to the degree castigated by Marcel Breuer, the planning of the community was of considerably less interest than the design of the individual dwellings, realized under the most stringent wartime constraints. Wurster was a personal architect who seemed most at home when designing the home of a client. This was both his accomplishment and his limitation.

In the burgeoning economy of the postwar years, questions of what was regional and local no longer elicited great interest. The Korean and Cold Wars, "containment," McCarthyism and the "Communist threat," nuclear bombs and atomic power, the "ugly American" as the agent of U.S. foreign policy, the rise of the multinational corporation, and expanded media such as cinema and television—all directed attention to the earth as a whole. The quest for a regional architecture fell into obscurity as the profession looked toward the promise of glass and steel rather than the warmth of stone and wood. Certainly architects such as Richard Neutra, Gregory Ain, Raphael Soriano, and Craig Elwood in Southern California, and Joseph Esherick, John Funk, and Roger Lee in the north better encapsulated the drift of the 1960s and 1970s, just as Wurster had captured the spirit of the 1930s and 1940s.

I would suggest that William Wurster's legacy—in addition to his educational contributions at both Berkeley and MIT, of course—does not concern the style or the precise compositions of his dwellings. He bequeathed the view that architecture is part of a greater designed environment, and also left a lexicon of architectonic elements that have been absorbed into the California home of today. Although in some instances we cannot establish with certainty Wurster's invention of any of the features, their widespread popularity can be traced to Wurster's houses of the 1930s and 1940s. The terrace, the direct connection between indoors and outdoors, and the glazed corridor were already critical elements of the Wurster house by the early 1930s; the linked kitchen-dining-living room and the "room without a name" recurred in numerous projects, as did the "kitchen cave" and the heroically scaled porch. An elegant simplicity and honesty paired with a use of balanced lighting—skylights in the kitchen to reduce glare, for example—all quietly introduced features that would be promulgated by popular home magazines and adopted by concerned home builders such as Joseph Eichler.[120]

Wurster's architecture was easily adapted to the mass market because it was, however ambiguously, essentially "middlebrow." Russell Lynes reflected on what he saw as the social stratification of America: "[T]he highbrows are the elite, the middlebrows are the bourgeoisie, and the lowbrows a e *hoi polloi.*"[121] According to Lynes, members of the culture industry tend to be upper middlebrows:

> They are men and women who devote themselves professionally to the dissemination of ideas and cultural artifacts and, not in the least incidentally, make a living along the way. They are cultural do-gooders, and they see their mission clearly and pursue it with determination. Some of them are disappointed highbrows; some of them try to work both sides of the street; nearly all of them straddle the fence between highbrow and middlebrow and enjoy their equivocal position.[122]

This definition fits William Wurster and his architecture quite comfortably, if not precisely. Projects like the Gregory Farmhouse could be—and were—seen as equally elite products from the architect's hand and a homey vernacular.[123]

If today, at first glance, Wurster's architecture appears so ordinary or invisible, it just may be because his lessons and his legacy have been so completely absorbed into the currents of home building throughout the Golden State—and even across the country—and not due alone to the continual march of stylistic development. If today we forget, it may be because we have learned so many of the lessons he tried to teach. In the 1980s we witnessed a renewed interest in things regional, and regionalism as an ethical stance. Taunted by the internationalization and ephemeralization of architecture by print and electronic media, and prompted by Kenneth Frampton's essays on "critical regionalism," we have again begun to question what is appropriate to our place and time. That William Wurster warrants a critical investigation at this time is hardly an accident. A critical regionalism was his product, if not his intention. I tend to doubt that Wurster made any conscious attempt to propagate doctrine or dogma through his architecture. "It is a truly popular architecture," Wurster wrote of the Northern California house. "In a sense that much of the internationalists' work is not, it is an architecture of *everyday use* rather than form or intellectual theory. Viewed as sculpture, it may disappoint, but if in a democratic society architecture is a social art, it may have some validity."[124] He seems to have been more engaged in the pragmatics of the project at hand within a given budget. He had little or no interest in theory, and when he wrote, he tended to develop his ideas using specific examples rather than generalized thoughts. History almost never appeared in his articles, except as vernacular buildings. Although he was, without question, modern, his was a quiet modernism, an everyday modernism.

But despite such self-proclaimed disinterest in architectural speculation, Wurster's houses did critique national and international norms. As we have seen in the example of the 1948 symposium at the Museum of Modern Art, the International Cottage style, as it was pejoratively termed, seemed to threaten those with more industrially minded and progressive ideas. The basic livability, comfort, and attractiveness of the Bay Region house seduced the clients, turning their minds from more "forward-looking" designs. Lewis Mumford ended his editorial on the Bay Region style with this comforting thought: "The good young architects today are familiar enough with the machine and its products and processes to take them for granted, and so they are ready to relax and enjoy themselves a little. That will be the better for all of us."[125] Perhaps William Wilson Wurster's ultimate contribution was to further the architectural campaign to domesticate the machine, to particularize the design of houses, and to bring feeling to function.

Notes

1. William Adams Delano (1874–1940) studied at Yale and Columbia before entering the École des Beaux-Arts in 1900. In 1903, with Chester Holmes Aldrich, he established Delano and Aldrich, whose practice centered on stately houses for families such as the Rockefellers, Astors, and Pratts, designed primarily in the château or neo-Palladian styles. Delano taught at Columbia from 1903 to 1910 and, after the dissolution of the firm, executed the commission for West Point in 1944.

2. In his earlier years of practice, the key connection was Elizabeth (Mrs. Ralph) Ellis, whom Wurster had met through his former boss, William Adams Delano. Mrs. Ellis lived a somewhat bicoastal life, spending part of the year in New York and other times in the Bay Area. Through Mrs. Ellis, Wurster met Sadie Gregory, who would become his patron and lifelong friend. There remain drawings for a number of projects commissioned by her, including a set of small houses in Berkeley and a barn remodeling on Long Island. These drawings are held in the William Wurster Archive, College of Environmental Design Documents Collection at the University of California at Berkeley (hereafter CED Documents Collection).

In college Wurster met Sadie Gregory's son Don, further establishing a close connection with the Gregory family. Warren and Sadie Gregory and Elizabeth Ellis belonged to the same social circle, which added to Wurster's acceptability and brought him numerous commissions.

3. As university architect, Howard was responsible for implementing the campus plan that resulted from the 1897 international competition. During his tenure he designed the 1907 Hearst Memorial Mining Building—acknowledged to be his masterwork—the 1903 Greek Theater, the 1911 Doe Memorial Library, the 1914 Campanile, and the 1906 Architecture Building. See Loren W. Partridge, *John Galen Howard and the Berkeley Campus: Beaux-Arts Architecture in the "Athens of the West"* (Berkeley: Berkeley Architectural Heritage Association, 1978).

4. John Galen Howard, cited in Dave Bohn, *East of These Golden Shores: Architecture of the Earlier Days of Contra Costa and Alameda Counties* (Oakland: Junior League of Oakland/Scrimshaw Press, 1971), p. 117.

5. The San Francisco Public Library was designed in 1916 by George Kelham; the Los Angeles Public Library, by Goodhue and Carleton M. Winslow, dates from 1922–26—later than the Wurster project, but other Goodhue projects had appeared in the professional architectural journals.

6. After the great Berkeley fire of 1923, the highly inflammable wood shingles gave way to stucco as the exterior finish of choice.

7. Hubbard was associated with The Roycrofters of East Aurora, New York, which produced furniture and home furnishings, but he published far more than he designed. His homilies are apparent in this typical quotation taken from his book *Loyalty in Business,* published by The Roycrofters in 1921: "Don't try to eliminate the old fashioned virtues—many have tried it, with indifferent success. No good substitute had been found for simplicity, frankness, sobriety, industry and sincerity" (p. 51). Stickley, on the other hand, was known primarily as a furniture maker who composed chairs and tables of relatively wide slats of wood, often articulated, with exposed joinery and grain. He was also the publisher of *The Craftsman* magazine, which appeared from 1901 to 1916. California Mission style furniture was to some degree a local variant of Stickley's ideas.

8. Charles Keeler, *The Simple House*, 1904 (Santa Barbara: Peregrine Smith, 1979), p. 5.

9. The definitive study of this group is Richard Longstreth, *On the Edge of the World: Four Architects in San Francisco at the Turn of the Century* (New York: Architectural History Foundation, 1983). See also Leslie Freudenheim and Elisabeth Sussman, *Building with Nature: Roots of the San Francisco Bay Region Tradition* (Santa Barbara: Peregrine Smith, 1974).

10. For Bernard Maybeck, see Kenneth Cardwell, *Bernard Maybeck: Artisan, Architect, Artist* (Santa Barbara: Peregrine Smith, 1977); and Sally Woodbridge, *Bernard Maybeck: Visionary Architect* (New York: Abbeville Press, 1992).

11. Royal Barry Wills, *Houses for Good Living* (New York: Architectural Book Publishing Co., 1940), and idem., *Better Houses for Budgeteers* (New York: Architectural Book Publishing Co., 1941).

12. Wills, *Houses for Good Living,* p. 12. Only when collaborating with Hugh Stubbins in the late 1930s did Wills venture into the modern idiom. See Wills, ibid., pp. 70–72, 97–99.

13. Ibid.

14. William Wilson Wurster, "California Architecture for Living," *California Monthly* 44, no. 8 (August 1954), p. 15.

15. The definitive story of the Gregory Farmhouse—told by an insider—is Daniel P. Gregory, "An Indigenous Thing: The Story of William Wurster and the Gregory Farmhouse," *Places* 7, no. 1 (Fall 1990), pp. 78–93. I have relied heavily on this article, in addition to conversations with Dan Gregory, for information on the project. See also Daniel Gregory, "The Nature of Restraint: Wurster and His Circle of Clients," in this volume, pp. 98–113.

16. Gregory, "An Indigenous Thing," pp. 83–84.

17. "Quoting Mr. Wurster," *Architectural Forum* (May 1936), pp. 36–37.

18. William I. Garren, "There Must Be Romance in the Home You Build," *Sunset* 65, no. 1 (July 1930), pp. 22–24, 51.

19. "Our First Prize House," *House Beautiful* 69, no. 3 (March 1931), p. 239.

20. "Farm House of Mrs. Warren Gregory, Santa Cruz Mountains, California," *Architecture* 72, no. 2 (August 1935), p. 91.

21. Thorstein Veblen, *The Theory of the Leisure Class,* 1899 (New York: Penguin Books), 1994, p. 154.

22. Another version goes that "no one can make an $80,000 house look like a $10,000 house like Bill Wurster." And another: "Well, sheet rock is cheaper than Douglas fir plywood, but Douglas fir plywood looks cheaper, so let's use it." Cited by Sally Woodbridge, "From Large-Small House to Large-Large House," in Woodbridge, ed., *Bay Area Houses* (Salt Lake City: Peregrine Smith, 1988), p. 165. The quotations are legion; none have specific attribution.

23. Andrews, *Architecture, Ambition and Americans,* p. 255.

24. Ibid., p. 256.

25. Cited in Andrews, ibid., p. 279.

26. These ideas can be traced at least as far back as the English landscape gardener Humphry Repton. Repton acknowledged the entry court as a necessary evil: "As the gloomy confined view into a quadrangle, or paved court, forms a great contrast to the cheerful landscape of the park, or more distant prospects, it is no wonder that fashion should open the views in every direction; for getting that one side at least of every house must be appropriated to *useful* rather than *ornamental* purposes." *Fragments on the Theory and Practice of Landscape Gardening,* 1816 (New York: Garland, 1982), p. 93.

27. In recounting his early years, Wurster noted that *which* firm you worked for hardly mattered, as long as you acquired experience in a New York office, "for glamour attached itself to any New York experience without any real foundation in fact." William W. Wurster, "Architecture Broadens Its Base," *Journal of the American Institute of Architects* 10, no. 7 (July 1948), p. 30.

28. For an excellent encapsulation of Pasatiempo and its architecture, see Daniel Gregory, "Pasatiempo," in John Chase, *The Sidewalk Companion to Santa Cruz* (Santa Cruz: Paper Vision Press), 1979, pp. 292–309.

29. Ibid., pp. 295–96.

30. Wurster, "California Architecture for Living," p. 14.

31. Like George Frederick Handel, Wurster also took from himself. The addition to the Sloss House proposed two years after the first project clearly drew upon the tower of the Gregory Farmhouse. File 2654, CED Documents Collection.

32. Lucy Butler recalls that the design was developed in at least two stages. That the oak was the central feature of the design, however, is verified both by the drawings and the client's recollection. The tree, alas, died some years later. Lucy H. Butler, "A Pasatiempo Client Recreates the Scene in 1935: Church and Wurster," interviews conducted by Suzanne B. Riess, 27 June 1977, in *Thomas D. Church: Landscape Architect,* vol. 1, Regional Oral History Office, The Bancroft Library, University of California, Berkeley, 1978, p. 143.

33. In a letter to Sadie Gregory, Wurster confessed that after having seeing the twin casinos of the sixteenth-century Villa Lante in Bagnaia, Italy, he had always wanted to design a house along similar lines. The Butler House was the closest he ever came. I wish to thank Daniel Gregory for bringing this letter to my attention.

34. Today we would question the wisdom of this placement of books, since abundant sunlight and ultraviolet rays take their toll on paper.

35. William Wurster, "San Francisco Bay Portfolio," *Magazine of Art* 77, no. 4 (April 1940), p. 301.

36. In late 1937 the Swedish journal *Byggmästaren* published a portfolio of Wurster projects, including the Voss, Thomas Church, and Donald Gregory houses. No critical text accompanied the images. *Architecture d'Aujourd'hui* also published a portfolio of work, drawn from *Architectural Forum*, in the January 1938 issue. The short text distinguished between traditional American house design and a certain new tendency that "weds" the spirit of tradition with the natural environment, using natural materials. The editors viewed Wurster as the representative of this approach (pp. 29–30).

37. In some few instances, where Wurster happened to know local architects—George Nelson in New York, for example—he did refer his correspondents to particular offices.

38. "Contemporary" has been used as a qualifier for both style and time; "modernism" has concerned both style and ideology; "functionalism," on the other hand, has been used to describe building performance as well as style. These categories are too loose and too easily misinterpreted to be truly useful. In Scandinavia, for example, functionalism, or "funkis," is used synonymously with the International Style in particular and most modernism in general. For the most part, all these terms are used somewhat interchangeably.

Edward de Zurko began his study of functionalism with Socrates, emphasizing the antiquity of the idea. He acknowledged that functionalism may be a subjective as well as objective position, opening the discussion to a wide variety of opinions. His main condition for ornament within functionalist thinking was that it "must justify its existence by means of some tangible or practical function. It is not enough that it try merely to delight the eye. It must articulate the structure, symbolize or describe the function of a building, or serve some useful purpose." *Origins of Functionalist Theory* (New York: Columbia University Press, 1957), p. 4. De Zurko also outlined three analogies used by functionalist theorists—the mechanic, the organic, and the ethical—underscoring the broad application of the term. Ibid., p. 9.

Regarding the connection of these ideas to Wurster's architecture, one could rehearse the nineteenth-century sculptor Horatio Greenough's functionalist beliefs: "Beauty is the promise of function made pleasing by a God-given instinct. Action is the presence of function. Character is the record of function. False beauty and embellishment are types of non-performance." Paraphrased by de Zurko, ibid, p. 220.

39. Henry-Russell Hitchcock, *The International Style* (New York: W. W. Norton, 1932), p. 20.

40. Architectural historian John Summerson has written that modern architects, given their condemnation of styles, had only two possible positions: "One was to mix the styles together in the hope that something new would emerge out of the resulting pudding. The other was to choose a style as a starting-point, to believe in it very hard and trust to the future to weave something contemporary out of it." "The Mischievous Analogy," in *Heavenly Mansions* (New York: W. W. Norton, 1963), p. 198. Summerson chided modern architects for trying to engage contemporary life rather than pursuing the formal development of architecture: "[T]he Modern Architect . . . [has] stepped out of his *rôle,* taken a look at the scene around him and then become obsessed with the importance not of architecture, but of the *relation* of architecture to other things." Ibid., p. 197.

41. See David Gebhard, *Rudolph Schindler* (New York: Viking Press, 1971); for Neutra, see Thomas S. Hines, *Richard Neutra and the Search for a Modern Architecture* (New York: Oxford University Press, 1982); for the Lovell projects, see Stephanos Polyzoides, "Sc le ove'l th w Be Ho Lc Angele 19 1 6," *O positi ns*

8 19 , pp. 73

2. ne ar , " rc rit Re ali r : Si I nt f an A hi ec ure f I ta ," i Fc e 'he ti-/ het c J'ss ly n 'o mode 1 Cul ure Po w d, V L.: F 're 98 . 2

3. ia V Wt r, " Tv ietl nt Arc ite ct,' v tte r the on mi ee n at , Aro i an lu Ar ect 948 j. 8.

4. ia Wil Vur " M ha M d n Ar ite t e?," *H ou e nc Garden* 77, no. 4 (April 1940), p. 46.

45. Wurster, "The Twentieth-Century Architect," pp. 8–9.

46. Elizabeth Mock, *Built in USA: 1932–1944* (New York: Museum of Modern Art, 1944), p. 20.

47. Ibid., p. 14.

48. John McAndrews, *Guide to Modern Architecture: Northeast States* (New York: Museum of Modern Art, 1940), p. 13.

49. Ibid.

50. Peter Blake, *Marcel Breuer: Architect and Designer* (New York: Museum of Modern Art, 1949), p. 62.

51. The section on architecture in *The WPA Guide to California* (New York: Hastings House, 1939) discusses contemporary construction as well as historical building. The author clearly distinguishes between those "simple interpretation[s] of the Spanish Colonial type of house," of which the Gregory Farmhouse was an excellent example, and those with affinities to the International Style (pp. 173–74).

52. Royal Barry Wills, *Better Houses for Budgeteers,* p. 6.

53. Ibid., p. 7.

54. For information on Meem, see the most substantive biography, Bainbridge Bunting, *John Gaw Meem: Southwestern Architect* (Albuquerque: University of New Mexico Press, 1983).

55. The Territorial style, which accompanied the American settlement of New Mexico after 1848, was, in fact, the vestiges of the Greek Revival brought to the prairie. Windows received thin attenuated pediments, posts became square with capitals formed of attached molding, and brick replaced adobe on the parapets.

56. Meem had listened to Saarinen's talk at the 1931 meeting of the American Institute of Architects. Bunting, *Meem,* p. 24.

57. Ibid.

58. Quoted in Bunting, *Meem,* p. 24.

59. Although the Gregory Farmhouse was published in *Sunset* in 1930, it was Clifford May who became the darling of the magazine's staff. May's "ranch houses," the first of which was built in 1932, popularized the idiom throughout the state and the country. Virtually all his houses maintained a traditional disposition of rooms, although their interiors became more open, spacious, and "modern" over time. Wurster and May held in common many of the elements of the ranch house: in the early years their plans were quite similar; both stressed the importance of the patio and the porch, which May referred to by its Spanish precedent, the *corredor.* See Editorial Staff of *Sunset* Magazine and Books, *Western Ranch Houses by Cliff May* (Menlo Park, Calif.: Lane Publishing Company), 1958.

60. Unfortunately the houses in the book are identified only by location and year. Jo Stubblebine, ed., *The Northwest Architecture of Pietro Belluschi* (New York: F. W. Dodge Corporation, 1953). In the "Built in USA: 1932–1944" exhibition at the Museum of Modern Art, Belluschi was represented by a 1942 shopping center for war housing at Vancouver, Washington. A comprehensive study of Belluschi's life and work has appeared within the last year: Meredith L. Clausen, *Pietro Belluschi: Modern American Architect* (Cambridge: MIT Press, 1994).

61. Harwell Hamilton Harris, quoted in James Ford and Katherine Morrow Ford, *The Modern House in America* (New York: Architectural Book Publishing Company, 1940), p. 54.

62. In fact, the Southern California houses of Richard Neutra and the residential work of Marcel Breuer were greatly appreciated in Japan and widely emulated in the postwar period, particularly houses by Kiyoshi Seike.

63. Quoted by Andrews, *Architecture, Ambition and Americans,* p. 284. No source given.

64. Harwell Hamilton Harris, "Liberative and Restrictive Regionalism," address to the Northwest Chapter of the American Institute of Architects, Eugene, Oregon, 1954. Quoted in Frampton, "Critical Regionalism," p. 22.

65. I have explored this theme in relation to landscape architecture in "Regionalism in Landscape Architecture and the Modern(ist) California Garden," in *The Regional Garden in the United States,* ed. Therese O'Malley and Marc Treib (Washington, D.C.: Dumbarton Oaks, 1995). One should also bear in mind that the idea of regionalism is itself *dynamic:* due to withering or dispersal and other factors, what is regional today may not automatically be regional tomorrow. For example, architects in 1920s Southern California may have seen Spanish Colonial Revival as regional; today the style (admittedly in a diluted form) is so widespread in mass home building—from California to Minnesota to Florida—that it no longer qualifies as regional.

66. Letter from Henry Nash Smith to the author, cited in Mary Carolyn Hollers George, *O'Neil Ford, Architect* (College Station, Texas: Texas A & M University Press, 1992), p. 22. This is the most comprehensive study of the architect.

67. David R. Williams, "An Indigenous Architecture," *Southwest Review* (Fall 1928), pp. 60–74. Cited in George, *O'Neil Ford, Architect,* p. 22.

68. George presumes that it was Wurster who brought the work of O'Neil Ford to Talbot Hamlin's attention, a connection that resulted in praise and exposure.

69. Talbot Hamlin, "What Makes It American: American Architecture of the Southwest and West," *Pencil Points* (December 1939), pp. 774–75.

70. The plan of the Tinkle House shares an affinity with the "flexible house" scheme that Wurster produced for Revere Copper and Brass Company during the war years.

Wurster also aided Ford in securing what might constitute his largest ongoing project: the buildings for the new Trinity University campus in San Antonio. In 1948 Wurster, then dean at MIT, was summoned by the trustees to be a consultant on the project; still to be determined was whether the style would be traditional or modern. Not surprisingly, Wurster suggested the latter, noting that it would be cheaper and more expedient to build. Given his powers of persuasion and effective, if quiet, manner, he was successful. When he visited the site, he told the trustees: "Don't negate this site. That would be a tragedy. Let its hills design your buildings." Wurster was offered the job but demurred, citing his academic work and participation on the National Capital Park and Planning Commission. He recommended O'Neil Ford. See George, *O'Neil Ford, Architect,* pp. 94–95.

71. "I did some stucco houses too, though. Stucco as it *was* done was an imitation of adobe, you see, and it was rough, with rounded corners, and plaster was used to make believe the walls were this thick, when they really were hollow. This is the thing that got me down. Now when I do plaster I do it so that it looks like what it is, outlined with wood oftentimes; there it is just a plaster panel, which is quite truthful." *William Wilson Wurster, College of Environmental Design, University of California. Campus Planning and Architectural Practice,* (2 vols.), interview by Suzanne B. Riess (Berkeley: University of California, Regional Cultural History Project [now Regional Oral History Office], 1964), p. 272 (hereafter Wurster/Riess Oral History).

72. William Wurster, "My Favorite Small Home," *Our Home,* n.d. (ca. 1942). The binuclear plan—a curious choice of term given the atomic anxiety of the Cold War era—described houses that assigned living, cooking, and service functions to one wing, bedrooms and bathrooms to another. A common entry joined them, the configuration approaching an H in plan.

73. In reviewing American architectural publications, I found a relative paucity of critical examination and presentation of Scandinavian architecture during the 1930s. The high point must have been the Stockholm Exposition of 1930, for which Gunnar Asplund was the chief and coordinating architect. The fair was intended to further the Swedish Society of Arts and Crafts slogan, *"vackra vardags varor"* (beautiful everyday objects), and to provide object lessons in the new architecture. The book *Acceptera* (To Accept), co-authored by Gregor Paulsson, Gunnar Asplund, and Uno Ahren, followed thereafter, a searing polemic for modernism modeled to some degree on Le Corbusier's *Vers une architecture* of 1923.

It was primarily in the field of housing that the Scandinavians were known to excel, finding the middle way between modernism and tradition, capitalism and socialism. Often set within a birch or pine forest, it was an architecture that almost everyone could accept as a model. The work for the Kooperative Förbundet (Swedish Consumers' Cooperative Society), or KF, was particularly lauded, and the Kvarnholm housing outside Stockholm from the mid-1930s by Olof Thunström and the KF Architects' Office acquired nearly mythic status. Given the prominence of Scandinavian housing in Catherine Bauer's 1934 study, *Modern Housing*, and Wurster's interest in the work of Alvar Aalto, it is logical that Scandinavia should figure prominently in their travels. See also John Graham, Jr., *Housing in Scandinavia* (Chapel Hill: University of North Carolina Press, 1940).

74. William Wurster, Wurster/Riess Oral History, p. 92.

75. While dean at MIT, Wurster invited Aalto to teach one term per year just after the war. Through Wurster, Aalto secured the commission to design the Baker House dormitory, which was completed in 1949. After the visit to Finland in 1937, Betsy Church became the first West Coast agent for Aalto's Artek-produced furniture.

76. This directive appears in several of Pope's letters and even in telephone memos taken by the Wurster office staff. Saxton Pope project file, CED Documents Collection.

77. Letter from Saxton Pope to William Wurster, 4 November 1939. Saxton Pope project file, CED Documents Collection.

78. Letter from Saxton Pope to William Wurster, 11 September 1950. Saxton Pope project file, CED Documents Collection.

79. The Popes apparently considered rebuilding the house on another site, but this proved to be impractical. Saxton Pope project file, CED Documents Collection.

80. The resulting buildings, at least in plan, resembled housing blocks that were part of the 1925 Voisin Plan for Paris by Le Corbusier. Given the differences in scale and intention, the resemblance is probably coincidental.

81. Mock, *Built in USA: 1932–1944*, p. 58.

82. Aalto redesigned his AA-system several times, each iteration evolving in accord with the changing conditions effected by reconstruction after the 1939 attack on Finland by Soviet forces. Aalto's studies actually began by examining American prototypes; in 1940 he lectured at MIT on "Housing Problems in Finland and the Reconstruction Program," and subsequently headed a research unit on standardized housing at the school. See Pekka Korvenmaa, "The Finnish Wooden House Transformed: American Prefabrication, War-time Housing and Alvar Aalto," *Construction History*, vol. 6, 1990, pp. 47–61; and Göran Schildt, *Alvar Aalto: The Mature Years* (New York: Rizzoli International, 1991), pp. 32–40.

83. Catherine Bauer, *Modern Housing* (Boston: Houghton Mifflin, 1934), p. xv.

84. Ibid., p. 7. Elizabeth Bauer Mock Kassler played an influential role in proselytizing for modernism in the United States. After majoring in English at Vassar and graduating in 1932, she became one of Frank Lloyd Wright's first fellows at Taliesin. There she met her first husband, Rudolph Mock, and spent the next few years living in Switzerland (Conversation with the author, 14 May 1994, Lexington, Massachusetts). During her tenure at the Museum of Modern Art, where she remained until 1946, she organized "Built in USA: 1932–1944," and also co-curated the exhibition "What Is Modern Architecture?" (1942). She wrote *If You Want to Build a House* (1946), *The Architecture of Bridges* (1949), and *Modern Gardens in the Landscape* (1964)—all published by the Museum of Modern Art. Other publications include co-authoring the revised edition of J. M. Richards, *Introduction to Modern Architecture* (New York: Penguin Books, 1947).

85. Frank Lloyd Wright, as an American and an architect who relied on natural materials, would come to figure prominently in their articles.

86. George Nelson and Henry Wright, *Tomorrow's House* (New York: Simon & Schuster, 1945), p. 1.

87. Ibid., p. 7.

88. Modernist landscape architect Christopher Tunnard, writing during the war years, stated that "the right style for the twentieth century is no style at all." See "Modern Gardens for Modern Homes: Reflections on Current Trends in Landscape Design," *Landscape Architecture* (January 1942).

89. Nelson and Wright, *Tomorrow's House*, p. 72

90. Ibid., caption to illustrations 68–69, p. 67.

91. Ibid., pp. 76–78.

92. Ford and Ford, *The Modern House in America*, p. 11.

93. One anonymous anecdote described Wurster as "a poor man's Gardner Dailey."

94. "William Wilson Wurster," *Architectural Forum* (July 1943), p. 46.

95. This despite the executive order authorizing the internment of all Japanese Americans and the anti-Japanese sentiment that was rampant on the West Coast. Ibid.

96. Lewis Mumford, "The Skyline: The Status Quo," *The New Yorker,* 11 October 1947, pp. 106, 109. Reprinted in *Museum of Modern Art Bulletin* (Spring 1948), p. 4.

97. Ibid.

98. Ibid.

99. Lewis Mumford, "The Architecture of the Bay Region," in *Domestic Architecture of the San Francisco Bay Region* (San Francisco: San Francisco Museum of Art, 1949), n.p.

100. William Wurster, "A Personal View," in *Domestic Architecture of the San Francisco Bay Region,* n.p.

101. Gardner Dailey, "The Post-War House," in *Domestic Architecture of the San Francisco Bay Region,* n.p.

102. In "Mr. Moses Dissects the 'Long-Haired Planners,'" New York City construction coordinator Robert Moses attacked foreign planners and their ideas—Walter Gropius, Erich Mendelsohn, and Eliel Saarinen, among others—as well as Frank Lloyd Wright and Lewis Mumford. He argued for hands-on pragmatics rather than theory, as well as an unquestioning patriotism. Originally published in the *New York Times Magazine,* 25 June 1944; reprinted in Joan Ockman, *Architecture Culture 1943–1968* (New York: Rizzoli International, 1993), pp. 55–63.

103. Barr also noted that despite his stylistic predilections at the residential scale, when even Wurster designed larger buildings, such as his project for the United Nations, he also resorted to the International Style. Alfred H. Barr, Jr., "Opening Remarks," *Museum of Modern Art Bulletin* (Spring 1948), pp. 6–7. Wurster, Bernardi, and Ernest Born shared the credits for the project when it was published, but according to Donn Emmons, the project was entirely Born's. Conversation with the author, 2 February 1995, Sausalito.

104. Christopher Tunnard, ibid., p. 14.

105. Marcel Breuer, ibid, p. 15.

106. Peter Blake, who wrote the text for the Museum of Modern Art catalogue, described Breuer and Gropius's 1940 design for the Chamberlain Cottage in Weyland, Massachusetts: "Like some of the earlier houses, the Weyland cottage defies nature; but unlike those earlier houses, it is not a brittle product of industrialism. Its 'human-contact' surfaces are warm in color and soft in texture, fully satisfying the demands of 'human nature.'" Breuer did stop short of putting "redwood all over the place," however. *Marcel Breuer: Architect and Designer* (New York: Museum of Modern Art, 1949), p. 72.

107. Ibid.

108. Lewis Mumford, ibid., p. 18.

109. Ibid.

110. This disposition of floors appears in several of Wurster's San Francisco houses, including the Sibbett House of 1941.

111. "Case Study House No. 3," *Arts and Architecture* 62, no. 6 (June 1945), p. 38.

112. Elizabeth Smith, ed., *Blueprints for Modern Living: History and Legacy of the Case Study Houses* (Los Angeles: Museum of Contemporary Art, 1989) p. 45.

113. I thank Joan Ockman for bringing the Wurster project to my attention.

114. "By-Pass Land in House and Home (February 1955) p. 109-10.

115. Gardner Dailey, "The Post-War House," n.p.

116. "Two Houses; A Formal House in an Informal Setting," *Architectural Record* 127, no. 4 (April 1960, p. 80.

117. Richard C. Peters, "William Wilson Wurster: An Architect of Houses," in Woodbridge, ed., *Bay Area Houses,* p. 152.

118. Ralph Butterfield, conversation with the author, 16 August 1994, San Francisco.

119. William Wurster, "Competition for U.S. Chancery Building, London," *Architectural Record* 119 (April 1956), p. 222.

120. The prototypes for Eichler homes were designed by the San Francisco firm of Anshen and Allen. For background on the home-building market, see Ned Eichler, *The Merchant Builders* (Cambridge: MIT Press, 1982) and Edward Eichler and Marshall Kaplan, *The Community Builders* (Berkeley: University of California Press, 1967).

121. Russell Lynes, *The Tastemakers: The Shaping of American Popular Taste,* 1949 (New York: Dover, 1980), p. 310.

122. Ibid., p. 320.

123. In fact, Wurster's houses were seldom as middlebrow as ranch houses by Cliff May. To the mass market, Wurster's attention to idea, space, and form cast him more as a high-brow designer. Seen in terms of the profession, however, the populism of his work and his disregard for theory made him appear quite middlebrow.

124. Quoted in John Burchard and Albert Bush-Brown, *The Architecture of America: A Social and Cultural History* (Boston: Little, Brown, 1961), p. 465.

125. Mumford, "The Skyline," pp. 106, 109. Reprinted in Ockman, *Architecture Culture 1943–1968,* p. 109.

An Architectural Life

Richard C. Peters and Caitlin King Lempres

illiam Wilson Wurster perceived a special character in the geography and social framework of the region stretching from the west coast of San Francisco to the north, south, east, and inland for a radius of about a hundred miles. As a native son, he felt called upon to express the region's physical nature in his architecture. This appreciation of the region's qualities did not differ significantly from the general concerns of architects everywhere; site and climate, in addition to the personal needs of the client, condition the design approach of all thoughtful architects. However, it was Wurster's particular interpretation of these factors and his deep concern that differentiated him from his contemporaries.

William Wurster was born in Stockton, California, in 1895. His family encouraged him to observe, read, and draw, but he often admitted in his later years that his was "more an intellectual than a drawing gift." As a child, he had a close relationship with his father, a banker. On bank holidays and weekends the elder Wurster would take his son to observe the life of the town in order to find out how it functioned. As Wurster later recalled, "I went to a newspaper and they would cast my name in a slug of lead, I went to the Stockton Iron Works and they made a casting of a mold to show me how you cast iron, to the firehouse, to show me how the horses went to a fire. . . . There wasn't a thing you could name that he hadn't taken me to see."[2]

During his high school years Wurster worked in the office of Edgar B. Brown, an Englishman who designed the Stockton Hotel and was one of the city's most influential architects. There the youth drew plans, made measured drawings, did the blueprinting—"anything that was done by an office boy." This early training whetted his interest in architecture. Because his father's education had been curtailed, Wurster's parents felt strongly that their son should attend a university. They advised him to attend the architecture school at the University of California at Berkeley because it was headed by John Galen Howard, who had trained at the École des Beaux-Arts in Paris. Wurster enrolled at the university in 1913 and received his architectural education from such notable teachers as Warren Perry (later dean from 1927 to 1950) and William Hays. Although Howard never criticized his work, Wurster acknowledged that the dean's Beaux-Arts spirit pervaded all aspects of school life.

Wurster joined the Sigma Chi fraternity for which he later expressed gratitude. "They further bolted me into reality and learned how to get on with people and to express myself not undogmatically. For an oversensitive child it was very good to have the edges blunted just a bit, because it made me a stronger person in the end."[3] A physical ailment kept him from voluntary mil-

itary service in World War I, so he studied naval architecture and joined the merchant marine in 1918. After a year's tour of duty in the South Pacific, he returned to the university and graduated with honors in architecture in 1919.

Wurster briefly apprenticed in the office of John Reid, Jr., a San Francisco architect whose practice consisted mostly of school buildings. In 1920 he became the architectural designer for Charles Dean, an architect on the staff of the water-treatment facility of the city of Sacramento and worked for two years designing the Sacramento filtration plant. At the same time he moonlighted on independent commissions, designing several small residences. He became a registered architect in the state of California in April 1922.

Having saved $4,000, Wurster decided in 1922 to embark on a "grand tour" of Europe to complete his classical education. "I went thinking I would go into Spain to get bits and pieces of architecture which I could understand," he later stated, "but instead of that I threw away all of the guide books, more or less, and tried to get hold of social books of the time when these buildings were done, [to learn] what caused them to be done in such a way, rather than just seeing the evidence of them. It changed my whole point of view from one of eclectic skill to much more an attempt at fundamental knowledge."[4] His travel diary of that time reveals many insights gained on his trip.

In Paris Wurster shared an apartment with friends from San Francisco, Eldridge (Ted) and Jeanette Spencer.[5] The Spencers were studying—he at the École des Beaux-Arts and she at the Louvre—and they helped introduce Wurster to the exciting world of young American intellectuals traveling and studying in Europe. Many of the young architects he met during this time became major teachers in architectural schools and ateliers throughout the United States.[6]

Wurster's European travels broadened him intellectually, socially, and architecturally. He encountered major works of art and architecture that he had previously known only through such books as Sir Bannister Fletcher's *History of Architecture on the Comparative Method*. His descriptions of the buildings, places, people, art, and music constitute a vivid commentary on his experiences and reflect his personal preferences.[7] There is no mention, for example, of the works of Le Corbusier, and in Paris he abhorred "the architectural horror of the art nouveau." He viewed the Grand Salon art exhibition of 1923 and thought the Futurist paintings were "vulgar in their conception of the nude form." On a trip to Barcelona he wrote of the Sagrada Familia (Church of the Holy Family) by Antonio Gaudí: "It is truly a strange creation that has resulted in architecture calculated to startle rather than for beauty to please." Of the Villa d'Este he wrote: "I am filled with awe at the wonders of man's planning, when combined with nature's creations. This tying together of the works of man and nature is a noble thing and here is the place to study it."[8]

In England Wurster had the great fortune to tour the Letchworth and Welwyn garden cities with the man responsible for their creation, Ebenezer Howard, and wrote, "I am truly so happy, for I know my work will be better for having seen these garden cities. . . . I fully believe the garden city idea has come to stay."[9] At the same time he expressed strong appreciation for the unexpectedly simple rural architecture of France, Italy, and Spain: "They all seem to suit the place, the climate and the way of life of the people."[10] It would be presumptuous to suggest that these images and ideas had a literal impact on Wurster's work. However, it is clear that his observations often contain the seeds of architectural considerations that would later be manifested in his work.

Returning to the United States in 1923, Wurster went to New York with the intention of spending a year there. He had originally arranged to work with McKim, Mead & White, but upon the advice of his former professors chose instead to join the office of Delano and Aldrich.[11] William Adams Delano and Chester Holmes Aldrich had designed such notable works as the John D. Rockefeller estate at Pocantico Hills in Westchester County and, on Long Island, Otto Kahn's château at Cold Spring Harbor and the Georgian-style James Burden House at Syossett (which received the Architectural League gold medal in 1920). In addition to these and many other private residences for wealthy clients, the office did extensive work for private clubs and schools in Manhattan.

While at the Delano and Aldrich office, Wurster developed what would become a lifelong friendship with Delano, who in 1924 lent him the money necessary to open his own office in Berkeley. Delano also introduced him to Elizabeth Warder Ellis, a Long Island socialite who also maintained a residence in Berkeley. She and her good friend Mrs. Warren Gregory would become the great patrons of Wurster's early work. Along with these introductions and the exposure to a very different scale and style of living than he had known in California, Wurster gained experience during his short stay in Delano's office that would later serve as the model for his own practice.

In 1924 Wurster returned to the Bay Area and opened his own practice in the Hotel Whitecotton in downtown Berkeley. In 1926 he moved to the Newhall Building in San Francisco, where the office grew into one of the most successful practices on the West Coast.

Wurster's earliest work offered simplicity and restraint in form, a direct expression of materials, a careful regard for the climate, and economy of construction. This architectural approach appealed to those who could afford to build during the Depression. Contrary to the lavish habits of the 1920s, and typical of the conservative Northern California ethic, those with wealth sought to build houses that were not ostentatious, yet maintained the level of comfort to which they were accustomed.

These ideals, which can be seen throughout Wurster's entire career, appear even in his earliest buildings—a series of suburban houses designed in the stylistically correct architecture of the day. Popular architectural practice reflects what trade journals publish, which during this period was revivalist architecture in a variety of styles. Examples of Wurster's earliest commissions include the Mediterranean Hagar House (1927) and the French Regency Smith House (1927) in Berkeley and the Spanish Colonial Kellam House in Santa Barbara (1928). The Gillespie House, a small cottage in the hills of Oakland, built of whitewashed redwood board and batten, was the least stylized of Wurster's earliest projects. The vernacular of this house appealed to Mrs. Warren Gregory, who asked him to develop this language further in a manner appropriate to the specific requirements of a farmhouse/weekend retreat for her family.

The design of the Gregory Farmhouse (1928), located in the Santa Cruz Mountains, further evolved the concept of efficient, gracious spaces that respond appropriately to site conditions without regard to style. Wurster's particular architectural language, as well as his guiding principles, gained wide exposure when the project was published after winning *House Beautiful*'s Small House Award in 1931. National publicity served to firmly establish his reputation as an architect of simple, relaxed houses in what others would describe as a "modern" style that embodied the spirit of a region.

The Gregory Farmhouse was followed by a portfolio of work at the new vacation community of Pasatiempo, which further refined Wurster's architectural expression. Marion Hollins, the internationally known golfer, who was a friend of Mrs. Gregory and Mrs. Ellis, retained Wurster and Clarence Tantau as project architects. Wurster brought in the young landscape architect Thomas Church (who later became a national figure in this field) to design the golf-club estates and gardens. The eight houses that Wurster designed are clear examples of his philosophy of living and the relationship of a building to the land. The Hollins House (1931) winds among an existing grove of oak trees on a steep ravine, and the Butler House (1935) places four pavilions, connected by living porches, around an oak tree.

Concurrent with the development of Pasatiempo in the 1930s, Wurster had numerous other commissions that reinforced his importance on the architectural scene. Three that represent the body of work from this period are the Voss House (1931) in Big Sur, with its large kitchen cave and simple living spaces; the Church House (1931), located in Pasatiempo, which gave clear articulation to the most important space in the house, Church's studio; and the Clark House (1937) in Aptos, a beach house with large wind-protected alcoves that formally articulated life at the edge of the ocean. Although inexpensive materials and simple detailing were used in all of these houses, and layouts and forms were simple and direct, they succeeded in being architecturally quite sophisticated.

As Wurster's reputation grew, his practice expanded to include significant nonresidential commissions. His designs continued to be efficient and graciously proportioned, yet appeared almost commonplace to the uninitiated eye. Materials suitable and readily available were used for construction, typically locally milled redwood or masonry. Wurster's typical building details furthered standard trade practices, with only slight variations to shift the perception of scale or use: for example, eave rafters tapered to reduce the profile of the roof; siding extended above stud walls to become second-floor rooms. Wurster also continued to seek an appropriate response to site and client. "When I am given a hillside," he said, "I do not yearn for a meadow."[12] His notable residences from this period include a townhouse for Chase Grover in San Francisco (1939), which despite its urban narrow lot had a sunny, private central courtyard; a suburban house for Saxton Pope in Orinda (1940), built of steel and concrete block around an atrium; and a country house for Allen Chickering in Woodside (1941), with a great "room with no name." Wurster also designed the "modernist" stucco Stern Dormitory for women at the University of California at Berkeley (1938); a lodge in "ski shack" style for Sugar Bowl ski resort, Placer County (1940); and headquarters for the Schuckl Canning Company, Sunnyvale (1942), sheathed in redwood plywood.

The early Wurster office was the training ground for several generations of architects. Their work was the product of teams, not one-man design efforts. This operating style continued when Wurster joined forces with longtime friends and employees Theodore Bernardi and later Donn Emmons to establish the firm of Wurster, Bernardi and Emmons in 1945.[13]

Wurster believed that the training of younger architects should introduce them to the full range of professional responsibilities. They should meet clients, participate in conferences, sketch preliminary drawings, complete working drawings and specifications, and supervise construction. He did not believe in assigning them only "stair details." "When there are many jobs in the office, teams can be formed—two men or more—to each job, and several jobs per team. One member of the team always sat in at all conferences I had with the client. This saved my time, in not repeating the matters for the draftsmen, helped him learn the procedure, conveyed the temper of the job directly to the drafting room and gave the client a friend in the office with whom he could talk or leave a message when I was not there. The man rotated various phases of the job. . . . This freed the practice of design from the dead hand of caution, routine and skepticism which makes new ideas shrivel before they develop strength."[14] Recalling his experiences with the firm of Delano and Aldrich, Wurster established regular visits for the office staff to completed buildings. He always wanted the office to provide this great variety of experiences while he maintained his "finger on the pulse of things."[15]

Wurster did not believe in specialization. He never turned down a com-

mission, whether it was a company headquarters or a kitchen remodeling. "Once you take a job there should be no limit in what you should do for it, and you should do it so it gives satisfaction. When something begins to go wrong, that is the very time you should give more to it."[16] From the late 1940s to the 1960s, "Bill" Wurster (as he was commonly known) and his firm continued to produce work exemplifying a simple, direct approach to design that blended with the environment and satisfied human needs. But to some, like Frank Lloyd Wright, "Redwood Bill" was a "shanty builder."

Among the firm's numerous projects exemplifying the ideals of simple regional architecture was the Heller House (1950), on the shore of Lake Tahoe. Appropriately constructed of local granite boulders, it is an overgrown version of the typical summer cabins in the area.[17] The Center for Advanced Study in the Behavioral Sciences (1954) in Palo Alto is perhaps the most successful of all the nonresidential commissions, conclusively marrying building to site. In these and many other designs, the choice of a simple, direct solution does not waver; the buildings rarely can be described as grand, even though they represent notable institutions and endeavors.[18]

Wurster never advocated any particular school of thought; his was an architecture of understatement, not dogma. This was important because young architects looked to Wurster for direction and inspiration to counter the stylish and eclectic work being produced in that era. This rejection of dogma was also reflected in the way he dealt with problems in architectural education. Faculty members who received one of those famous one- or two-sentence letters signed "Bill" knew that he always expressed his opinion in the fewest possible words. Like his architecture, it was direct and to the point.

In 1937 Wurster went to Europe again, this time with his close friends and collaborators, Thomas and Elizabeth Church.[19] The focus of the trip was

97.
Left to right: Alvar Aalto, Robert Woods Kennedy, and William Wurster in the late 1940s

Scandinavia to see the works of such architects as Kay Fisker, Gunnar Asplund, and, most importantly, Alvar Aalto, whom they met while standing in front of his house in awe of its simple beauty.[20]

In early 1940 Wurster met Catherine Bauer, the planner and author of the seminal book *Modern Housing,* published in 1934. After a whirlwind courtship, they were married in 1940, and Wurster became immersed in the world of urban planning. In 1943, after completing five thousand houses for defense workers in Vallejo, Wurster decided to take some time off to reflect. Unable to enter the armed forces because of his age, he decided to take a year off "to read." As he put it, "I didn't want to go on just being a successful architect, but I wanted to get an insight into her [Catherine's] world."[21] He received a Wheelwright fellowship from Harvard University, and in 1943 moved to Cambridge to begin his studies toward a doctorate in urban planning under John M. Gaus, professor of government and a scholar in the field of regional planning.

During this period Wurster was invited to teach at Yale University by Everett V. Meeks, dean of the School of Fine Arts. He commuted from Cambridge to New Haven as a lecturer and design critic for one semester. In 1944 he was invited by James R. Killian, then vice president of the Massachusetts Institute of Technology, and later president, to become dean of what is today known as the School of Architecture and Planning. Wurster accepted the position, thinking that if "he could do all the work in one month at MIT he could go away the other eleven" to work in his office on the West Coast.[22] On the contrary, a constant parade of drawings went back and forth from coast to coast, while Wurster totally committed himself to revamping the architecture and planning programs and developing a new school at MIT. In the meantime, Catherine began teaching at Harvard; their daughter, Sadie, was born in 1945. Their house became a mecca for architectural visitors, scholars, and students of architecture.[23]

The new school at MIT, like his first office, was not a one-man show. He was not a mentor; he was a facilitator. Unlike Harvard, which had brought Walter Gropius to head the Graduate School of Design six years earlier, Wurster had no dogma to espouse, no idealistic singular position; if anything, his interest in achieving ends in modest ways was the basis of his approach. Understanding the need for a variety of opinions, he avoided having a faculty that was single-minded. He was instrumental in working with the faculty to separate planning from architecture and established MIT's School of Planning, which became one of the foremost programs in the country.

Wurster believed that "the staff and the subjects were as a stream which is flowing by the students for them to dip into, each as his talents allow."[24] Technology must touch the humanities, and the basis for architectural study is not just the isolated building but its relationship to people, the community, and all other buildings. His concerns changed the school dramatically from the elite confinement of the Beaux-Arts system to one that related architecture to the broad range of educational opportunities available at the institute. Like Joseph Hudnut, dean of Harvard's Graduate School of Design, Wurster believed that architecture is first a social art, which implies that it cannot be solely the self-expression of the architect; it is a part of the life of all those who use it or look at it. To be successful in the fullest sense, architecture should be beautiful, and when that pinnacle is achieved, it is fine art. "The frame for living is not life itself," Wurster wrote, "so do the thing which leaves room for the growth of the occupant without his scraping his knuckles against your arbitrary decisions with each change in his development."[25] To realize this goal, he believed that the school must recognize social research, economics, geography, and political science as part of the educational experience. "We must have knowledge of the rules under which we live and in the way and process by which these may be modified."[26]

For Wurster, architectural education was a process, not a drawing on a sheet of paper. He had great disdain for the then prevalent system of "sending drawings to New York for judgement" in the competitions of the Beaux-Arts Institute of Design, and stated: "How can you show a process of education in this way?" Thus he instituted a system that avoided the master-studio organization. Each student was assigned two or more critics by Lawrence Anderson, then in charge of the architecture school; according to Wurster, this enabled the student "to taste the chaos which will be his when he meets the world."

Under Wurster's direction, the process of finding the solution to a problem undertaken in the studio was revolutionized. "The process," he explained, "is the jury meeting when the student presents his problem. It is an open jury with all the students present. This does diminish the mystery and glamour, but it is a sounder process and the whole event is viewed by students and staff alike as integral with the educational process."[27] As Lawrence Anderson recalled:

> It seems incredible, but when WWW [as Anderson called him] came to MIT we were still conducting our juries "in camera" without the students and then one person would be designated to give a public critique. Bill thought this was silly and he immediately had the students appear to explain their work and to defend it. This was for him necessary so they would learn how to deal with negative reaction. I think Bill was a pioneer in this, which became so much a part of the school process. At the time, it transformed the relation between students and teachers. It exposed the biases and inadequacies of jury members and made everyone aware of the need to justify himself publicly.[28]

Wurster was a pragmatic maverick in education. He saw to it that architectural studies reflected real-life situations. He believed that architects should not presume leadership unless they were equipped with more than just techniques of the profession. To this end he worked to liberalize and broaden the educational base and stressed diversity, not as an end in itself but as the opportunity for students to see the world around them. He never wavered from the belief that schools should have contact with reality.[29]

In 1948 Wurster was appointed to the National Capital Park and Planning Commission and became a close friend and adviser to President Harry S Truman. He was chairman of this commission until 1950, when he resigned as dean at MIT and returned to Berkeley to become dean of the School of Architecture at his alma mater. It was his friend Jack Kent, who had received a master's degree in city planning from MIT and was director of planning in

San Francisco, who backed Wurster for the deanship.[30] Before embarking on his eastern sojourn, Wurster had planned to return to California and teach at the university when he completed his Harvard degree, but MIT hired him first. Now he wanted to return to the West and "have the University of California school be one of the leaders in doing things less in the shadow of the past."[31] Wurster replaced his former teacher, Warren Perry. Berkeley was still a mirror of the Beaux-Arts system. In its place Wurster built an institution of international stature, the present College of Environmental Design.

In only two years, from 1951 to 1953, the School of Architecture, with its four-year curriculum, was completely revamped into a college under Wurster's guidance. The College of Architecture was established, with a five-year program; new faculty members with "different slants" were appointed to formulate the educational objectives.[32] During those tumultuous years Wurster proved himself a "good administrator running fences for good teachers."[33] Perhaps that might explain in some small way why he had the knack for bringing together such extraordinary teachers. He admitted, "I don't pretend to be a great teacher myself, but I know good teaching when I see it, and I can try desperately to make a surround for good teachers so they can do their work unimpeded."[34]

Wurster never actually taught a single course, but he knew what should be taught and found the best faculty to do the job. With a vision of what beginning design students should experience, he introduced three courses that he considered the best of their kind in the country. The first two he viewed as "aptitude tests which dealt with space and perception." As the basic design courses, "they do not do plans as such but focus on what to observe and not to observe and how to portray this in simple mechanical ways." Or, as he put it simply, "Focus on the forest and not just on the tree."[35] The third course, intended to counterbalance the concentration on creative aspects of design education, was formulated to provide "vistas into fields which have an important effect on architecture."[36]

Wurster was not a revolutionary, but he did believe in "controlled chaos, where there is no master school where one person sets the dominant note, the dogma of the school."[37] "The school," he insisted, "wouldn't present a united face to everything as if it were a feat accomplished, but present a very rough face, with many cracks in it."[38] He realized that students didn't necessarily like this approach because they would much rather have answers, but he was convinced that many years after they graduated they would come back and say, "Oh, it was good that we had these disagreements and all these different people."[39]

Wurster would carry his message far beyond Berkeley. In 1957 he and his family embarked on a round-the-world trip that disseminated his ideas internationally. It was an opportunity to put forth his belief that regional characteristics should be reflected in the man-made environment. He lectured extensively on architecture and planning and met with professional colleagues in many countries. Upon returning to California, he began implementing his long-held dream to amalgamate into one administrative unit the three separate departments: Landscape Architecture, City and Regional Planning, and Architecture. This was not done without some dissatisfaction both in the faculty and the profession. In the end, however, Wurster prevailed, and his firmly held belief in this educational unity became a reality.

Wurster was appointed the first dean of the College of Environmental Design in 1959. From his viewpoint, there was no mystique in the term "environmental design"; he saw it as the appropriate designation since each of the professions had a common interest in the complex tasks of organizing and designing the physical environment for human needs. Wurster said, "It becomes necessary to be not only the master of one profession, but also to have

98.
Left to right: partners Donn Emmons,
Theodore Bernardi, and William Wurster
in the late 1950s

real perception of the other disciplines in order to know how these may be integrated with one's own to produce a harmonious result."[40] For him, each profession's broadened and deepened responsibilities demanded mutual contact and understanding. Since the three professions were linked in so many ways, it was appropriate to bring them into a unified college; however, the primary responsibility for formulating and coordinating departmental programs was left in the hands of individual faculties. One of the results of this regrouping was the establishment of joint degree programs taught by faculty with appointments shared by departments.[41]

Wurster argued that an inquiring mind was the most important attribute a person could have. He often said, "I do not teach facts, but teach as a process of arriving at facts."[42] Students should work under teachers who were currently meeting the contemporary requirements of professional practice. Both full-time teachers and part-time lecturers were expected to be actively involved in research or architectural work.

Education, if it is to be healthy, he stated, "must be attacked with expressed doubts and enthusiasms and the changes which result should be ever-fluctuating."[43] In this regard, he emphasized that the school was for students, and the staff should not become a "haven for timid spirits." He referred to a student's time in school, and later in practice, as the "architectural life" and considered education in architecture as a ten-year cycle—five years in school and another five in an office, culminating in assuming mature leadership in the profession. Wurster was not eager to make the architect a "special creature, but a creature of the world," and thus the curriculum was not as important as the goal it was to serve. He knew that this education must be directed toward both skill and content, "that you don't want all education to be dessert." As a result, the force of his leadership was always directed toward defining a depth and breadth of program that would ensure that students took full advantage of the rich, full life of the university.

Another integral part of Wurster's contribution to the university was his role as supervising architect of the Campus Planning Committee. Similar to his tenure at MIT, he was instrumental in formulating a building policy for the long-range development plan of the Berkeley campus. His appointment provided the opportunity for promoting members of the faculty to design univer-

99.
Catherine, William, and Sadie Wurster, 1960

sity buildings or consult on the campus building programs. As a consequence, in 1966 the College of Environmental Design moved into a new building designed by three members of the faculty: Joseph Esherick, Vernon DeMars, and Donald Olsen. Wurster Hall, named jointly after Bill and Catherine, was his pride and joy. He delighted in telling the story that he "wanted it to look like a ruin that no Regent would like. . . . It's absolutely unfinished, rough, uncouth and brilliantly strong. This is the way architecture is best done. . . . What I wanted was a rough building, not a sweet building. . . . The Regents like cutie-pie and slick things."[44]

Before the new building was completed, Wurster's fortunes changed. In 1963, because of Parkinson's disease, he retired as dean of his beloved college.[45] Catherine Wurster's tragic death from a fall while hiking in 1964 was a terrible blow. Wurster's stamina was remarkable in the face of such adversity, and his spirit never wavered. Despite his handicap, he continued to participate in as many activities as his physical condition would permit.

Wurster was elected a Fellow of the American Institute of Architects, the American Academy of Arts and Science, and the Royal Academy of Fine Arts of Denmark. He was also a member of the Akademie der Kunst of Germany and a corresponding member of the Royal Institute of British Architects. The honorary degree of Doctor of Laws was conferred on him in 1964 by the University of California, and in 1969 the American Institute of Architects awarded him its highest honor, the Gold Medal.

Wurster was unique in his dedication to the belief that architecture "must be measured by its meaning for people" and must be concerned with the everyday things that shape their physical and pychological needs. He believed that architects must be involved with the total environment, and that architecture gained its importance not from the isolated building but from its relation to the people, the community, the site, and other buildings.

Wurster died in 1973, an honored and loved man whose vision, leadership, and deep concern for human values in architecture have been an enduring influence.

Notes

This essay is an expanded version of an article by Richard C. Peters, "WW Wurster," in the *Journal of Architectural Education* 33, no. 2 (November 1979).

1. *William Wilson Wurster: College of Environmental Design, University of California, Campus Planning and Architectural Practice,* interview by Suzanne B. Riess (Berkeley: University of California, Regional Cultural History Project [now Regional Oral History Office], 1964), p. 270 (hereafter Wurster/Riess Oral History).

2. Ibid., p. 4.

3. Ibid., p. 12.

4. Ibid., p. 53.

5. Eldridge Spencer later became a noted San Francisco architect, and his wife, Jeanette, a painter. Jeanette Spencer painted the famous murals at Yosemite's Awahnee Hotel.

6. Among those whom Wurster met during his 1922–23 tour of Europe were Shirley Morgan of Princeton University, Lionel "Spike" Pries of the University of Washington, and George Licht of the Atelier Licht in New York. In Europe Wurster was constantly exposed to new ways of thinking about architecture and education. Later reflecting on his visits to Oxford and Cambridge, he wrote, "The tutorial system is a fine one, after all education does not consist of going to lectures and mirroring the thoughts of the professor back at him. . . . All students take identically the same preliminary work. That must mean they do not give them the concrete facts to work on, but rather, the general ideas." William Wurster, diary, 1923–24.

7. Wurster traveled from May 1922 to May 1923. He bicycled through France and also visited Switzerland, Italy, Spain, Portugal, Belgium, Germany, the Netherlands, England, and North Africa.

8. William Wurster, diary, 1923–24.

9. Ebenezer Howard wrote *The Garden Cities of Tomorrow* (Faber & Faber, 1902). Based on the theories presented in this book, Unwin and Parker designed the cities of Letchworth and Welwyn.

10. William Wurster, diary, 1923–24.

11. During his tenure in the Delano and Aldrich office, Wurster continued his studies by competing in design competitions of the Beaux-Arts Institute, New York, and studying at the Atelier Licht.

12. William Wurster. "Architectural Education," *AIA Journal* 9, no. 1 (January 1948), p. 36.

13. Wurster and Bernardi first formed a partnership in 1944, the year after Wurster went to study at Harvard.

14. William Wurster, "Design in Practice," speech at Ann Arbor, Mich., 5 February 1945.

15. Ibid.

16. William Wurster, Wurster/Riess Oral History, p. 71.

17. Bernard Maybeck's project in Eldorado County for the Glen Alpine Springs Resort (1921), which combined natural materials and industrial products, can be seen as an influence on the architecture of the Heller House. Other important residential commissions by Wurster, Bernardi and Emmons during this period include the Walter House, San Francisco (1950); the George Pope House, Madera (1956–58); the Henderson House, Hillsborough (1957); the Salz House, San Francisco (1953); and the Coleman House, San Francisco (1962).

18. Some of the other important nonresidential projects during this period include

Woodlake Apartments, San Mateo (1964); Golden Gateway housing, San Francisco (1965); Cowell College, University of California at Santa Cruz (1965); Ghirardelli Square, San Francisco (1967); and world headquarters of the Bank of America, San Francisco (1970).

19. Wurster and Church had become friends during their work together at Pasatiempo. By 1937 Church was the most influential landscape architect on the West Coast.

20. Wurster's meeting with Alvar Aalto in 1937 developed into a long friendship that ultimately brought Aalto to the United States to teach at MIT when Wurster was dean there. It was on this trip to Europe that Wurster was first exposed to Le Corbusier's work, visiting his Salvation Army Building in Paris.

21. William Wurster, Wurster/Riess Oral History, p. 105.

22. Ibid., p. 109.

23. During Wurster's tenure as dean at MIT he brought to the school Gyorgy Kepes, Richard Filipowski, Henry-Russell Hitchcock, Ralph Rapson, Carl Koch, Robert Woods Kennedy, Vernon DeMars, Lloyd Rodwin, and Kevin Lynch.

24. William Wurster, lecture at the Architectural League, New York City, 6 November 1947.

25. William Wurster, "The Twentieth Century Architect," written for the Committee on Education, American Institute of Architects, 1948.

26. William Wurster, "New Directions in Architectural Education," lecture at the Association of Collegiate Schools of Architecture regional meeting, Atlanta, Georgia, 1946.

27. Ibid.

28. Letter from Lawrence Anderson to Richard Peters, January 1979.

29. Another of Wurster's important contributions at MIT was his influence on the campus building program. He arranged for his close friend Alvar Aalto to be a visiting professor at the School of Architecture each fall from 1946 to 1948. During this time Wurster was intrumental in convincing the MIT Corporation to select Aalto to design the now famous Everett Moore Baker Residence Hall, which was completed in 1948. This building, coupled with Anderson and Beckwith's Alumni Swimming Pool of 1940, signaled a break with the traditional pattern of architectural development of the campus and was the impetus for Wurster's efforts to have members of the faculty and other important architects design buildings there. Eastgate faculty housing, completed in 1949 and known simply as "100" (100 Memorial Drive), was one such opportunity. Wurster was consultant to the faculty design group he formed, including Carl Koch, William Brown, Ralph Rapson, Vernon DeMars, and Robert Woods Kennedy. The MIT campus would ultimately include buildings by Eero Saarinen, I. M. Pei, Walter Netsch, Eduardo Catalano, Pietro Belluschi, Edward Durell Stone, the Architects' Collaborative, Marvin Goody, and John Clancy.

30. Their friendship went back to the late 1930s when Jack Kent, Vernon DeMars, Francis Violich, Corwin Mocine, and Garrett Eckbo—later to become important members of the Berkeley faculty—belonged to the Telesis group in San Francisco, an organization dedicated to improving the quality of life and architecture in the Bay Area. Wurster, although not a member, was one of its strongest advocates and supporters.

31. William Wurster, Wurster/Riess Oral History, p. 115.

32. Charles Eames, the internationally known designer; Jesse Reichek, a distinguished painter; and Philip Theil, who studied with Kepes at MIT, developed the basic design program for the first two years in the College of Architecture. James Prestini, sculptor; Joseph Esherick, architect; James Ackerman, historian; Rai Okamoto, planner; and Donald Olsen, architect, among others, joined the faculty, which also included architects Eric Mendelsohn, Ernest Born, and Vernon DeMars.

33. William Wurster, "Interview with Wurster on the Occasion of His Retirement," *San Francisco Chronicle,* 3 June 1963, p. 11.

34. William Wurster, Wurster/Riess Oral History, p. 149.

35. Ibid., p. 168.

36. Ibid., p. 172. Such notable Berkeley scholars as Stephen Pepper, philosophy; Ira Cross, economics; Sherman Maisell, business administration; and Eugene "Bud" Burdick, political science, taught in this course with College of Architecture faculty members Catherine Bauer, Francis Violich, Jack Kent, Leland Vaughn, Donald Foley, Walter Steilberg, and Winfield Wellington.

37. William Wurster, Wurster/Riess Oral History, p. 143.

38. Ibid., p. 144.

39. Ibid., p. 145.

40. William Wurster, "The University and the Environmental Design Professions," lecture at Berkeley, October 1959.

41. In architecture, as in the other departments, new faculty members were part of this exciting transition. Many became leading architects, heads of schools, and teachers in other architecture departments. Among those on the faculty during the formative years of the college (1958 to 1965) were Gustavo da Roza, Ezra Ehrenkrantz, Norma Evenson, John Fisher, Rory Fonnseca, Sami Hassid, Steve Jacobs, Spiro Kostof, Donald Koberg, Roslyn Lindheim, Bill Liskamm, Donlyn Lyndon, Gerald McCue, Charles Moore, Carlos Pellicia, Richard Peters, Patrick Quinn, Amos Rapaport, Horst Rittel, Henry Sanoff, and Claude Stoller. International figures such as Ernesto Rogers, Steen Eiler Rasmussen, Wilhelm Wohlert, Sven Markelius, Nikolaus Pevsner, Alvar Aalto, and British historian Frank Jenkins, to name but a few, were all part of this adventure.

42. William Wurster, "The University and the Environmental Design Professions."

43. Ibid.

44. William Wurster, Wurster/Riess Oral History, pp. 175–77.

45. Martin Meyerson was appointed new dean of the college and, with two other nationally renowned planners, William Wheaton and John Dyckman, set the new leadership of the college. John Burchard, a former colleague of Wurster's as dean of humanities at MIT, joined the faculty and became acting dean during the 1964 Free Speech movement when Meyerson became acting chancellor at Berkeley.

The Nature of Restraint: Wurster and His Circle

Daniel Gregory

A few weeks before Frank Lloyd Wright died, he telephoned Bill Wurster and said: "Well, Bill, we don't see enough of each other—not that I like anything you do, but I like you, and we ought to get together and talk architecture." Bill replied, "We certainly should. What about right now?" Wright said: "No. I'm on my way someplace. But I just wanted to say hello." With Wurster, Wright was ever the beguiling provocateur. He referred to Wurster as "that shack architect" and attempted to get a rise out of him whenever they met. "Well, Bill," he said another time, "your roofs leak, too. They tell me that after the first rains sometimes you don't come into the office for a day or two."[1] Architecture critic Allan Temko recalls a mid-1950s lecture at the University of California at Berkeley in which Wright opened his speech—after having been introduced by Wurster, who was by then dean of the School of Architecture—with the incendiary statement: "Three words describe what is wrong with Bay Area architecture: William Wilson Wurster."[2] Wurster fumed in silence.

It's not difficult to see why Wright disdained Wurster's architecture. It was too simple, regional, and ephemeral for one who strove for originality, grand sculptural gestures, and a sense of permanence in every commission. Modesty was not a quality Wright admired in an architect. Though Wurster's work embodied such Wrightian principles as continuity between indoor and outdoor space, careful siting, and a dedication to expressing the nature of materials, it did so with restraint. Wurster arrived at his modernity by a process of simplification, not by inventing wholly new shapes and forms. His houses were modern in their functional approach to clients' needs, but they did not loudly proclaim their individuality. He believed that architects "should design up from the log cabin, instead of trying to compress the mansion."[3] Indeed, plainness is a characteristic of his work. Wright implied as much when he told longtime Wurster client Harriet Henderson, after touring her Hillsborough house built in 1933, "Bill Wurster is like a plug horse—good for the family. I'm difficult. I'm a thoroughbred."[4]

At the time of Wright's visit with Mrs. Henderson, in the early 1950s, he was completing a dramatic copper-roofed, stone and glass house for her mother, Mrs. Clinton Walker, by the ocean at Carmel. In Wright's eyes it was a case of the daughter being more conservative than the mother. The hip-roofed, two-story Henderson House had a rusticated Georgian flavor, with cream-colored walls, corner quoins, and double-hung windows all made of redwood, whereas the Walker House resembled an abstract extension of its rocky beachside site. Ironically, Wurster's great friend, landscape architect Thomas Church, planned the planting for both houses.

100.
Sadie Gregory in front of the tower at the
Gregory Farmhouse, Scotts Valley, 1953

Once Wright died, Wurster could afford to be amused by most of Wright's reactions to his work, but it is clear that his admiration for Wright's architecture did not extend to the great man's ego. Indeed, there could be no more diametrically opposite architectural personalities: Wright was the consummate individualist, rule-breaker, opponent of the American Institute of Architects, and founder of his own architectural school, whereas Wurster was the patient seeker of consensus and accommodation, the card-carrying member of the AIA who helped redefine existing schools of architecture at MIT and the University of California at Berkeley.

Wurster took pleasure in designing houses that looked straightforward yet artful enough to make you think they belonged where they were. If a house looked shacklike, so much the better. In a 1936 interview he explained: "I like to work on direct, honest solutions, avoiding exotic materials, using indigenous things so that there is no affectation and the best is obtained for the money."[5] He believed in what he called "the importance of the everyday thing, that is, that art doesn't necessarily consist of remote things by dead persons, art consists of lively things done with objects you use every day."[6]

The Appearance of Simplicity

So what is the nature of architectural understatement, or restraint, in Wurster's work, and how did it develop? It is a story not just about Wurster but also about the Wurster milieu at the beginning of his career. I think the farmhouse he designed for my grandmother Mrs. Warren Gregory, known as Sadie, offers some answers. Completed in the spring of 1928, the Gregory Farmhouse received wide publicity and helped launch Wurster's career. The history of its design is a study in evolutionary simplicity.

On the morning of 12 October 1927 Wurster happened to meet Sadie Gregory at the corner of Hearst and LeConte in Berkeley. They exchanged greetings and then he spent the rest of the day working on the drawings for her new summer house. That evening after dinner he presented his ideas to her in San Francisco at the Russian Hill home of her eldest son and daughter-in-law, Don and Josephine Gregory. Bill knew Don from college at the University of California at Berkeley. They were celebrating Sadie's fifty-seventh birthday. Her husband, San Francisco corporate attorney Warren Gregory, had died of a heart attack the previous February at the age of sixty-three, just after hiring Bill to begin work on the farmhouse. Now, after a seven-month hiatus, it was time to begin again. She looked over Wurster's simple, almost childlike colored-pencil drawing of the south elevation—showing the living room wing in front and the separate water tower-bedroom structure behind it—and said: "Yes, that's it. When do we start?"[7] (fig. 101).

Situated on an isolated ridge in the densely forested Santa Cruz Mountains, the house resembles a miniature frontier stockade—a toy Fort Gregory—glowing white against the dark, druidic green of the surrounding forest. The road descends a small hill to a dirt parking area beside the front gate. Everything is visible at once. In the foreground is the wall made of hollow-tile blocks and the central, diagonally braced wood gates flung wide. Behind the wall and to the left stands the sheer, three-story water tower, like an enlarged milk carton, with a thick mud-walled one-story structure at its base. The tower's only visible windows are tiny slits at the top—one on each face—reinforcing the structure's defensive stance. A little farther back and to the right is the unassuming L-shaped house proper, its gable ends and covered walkways forming two sides of a courtyard. Whitewashed vertical boards—without battens—double-hung windows, porch overhangs, and shingle roofs combine to form a structure of seemingly indigenous simplicity (fig. 102).

From the beginning, Wurster described the house as a return to fundamentals: "My first glimpse of the site before building the house showed what

101.
Gregory Farmhouse, Scotts Valley, 1928
William Wurster
Color pencil sketch of south elevation,
12 October 1927

102.
Gregory Farmhouse, Scotts Valley, 1928
William Wurster
West facade, ca. 1930

103.
Gregory Farmhouse, Scotts Valley, 1928
William Wurster
Living room, ca. 1930

possibilities lay before me as a designer. There was a garage (now made into the owner's bedroom) of rammed earth (pise de terre), large madrones and red-woods protecting it at the north, a vineyard on the south slope of the spur with an old apple orchard below that. . . . This farm is a place of peace and rest—of realities rather than the formalities of life, so a resolve was formed to make it simple and direct—no substitutes of any kind—to keep it free from any dis-torted or overstudied look. This quality was helped by the arriving at the plans and preliminaries in one day of work. The place is locked when the Owners are not there so it was to have a finished look even though there be no garden. And so we have a house of carpenter architecture—no wood beams or posts larger than absolutely necessary—an arid California yard with the protecting walls about."[8]

Wurster's design made a virtue of economy. He wrote that "there was a definite attempt to keep the building free from so-called 'decoration'—relying for interest upon the proportioning of the necessary elements."[9] Take the liv-ing room as an example. After passing through the front gate, you walk to the front door at the rear of the forecourt: it's on the right, at the inner corner of the L, where two covered brick walkways intersect. The big door is in a long, blank, north-facing facade. Open it and you enter the large white rectangular living and dining room with a fireplace on the right and a long refectory table on the left. There is no entry hall: the forecourt functions as an outdoor foyer (figure 103).

The room is almost stark: no moldings; plain white twelve-inch-wide boards cover the walls and the flat, rafter-supported ceiling; three simple dou-ble-hung windows are set low in the wall to reinforce a connection to the ground outside. Built-in brick seats flank the fireplace—also painted white—and behind the seat on the left and extending under one window is what the

104.
Gregory Farmhouse, Scotts Valley, 1928
William Wurster
Construction photograph, 1927

Gregorys called the "hike e"—the Hawaiian term for a pillow-covered bed used as a sofa. The only ornamental element is in the novel treatment of the floor: rough-sawn fir two-by-twelves are laid in a basket-weave pattern. Here the rustic and the urbane meet to form a sort of wilderness parquet. Opposite the front door is an identical door that opens to the south terrace. On hot summer days when both doors are open, the living room becomes a cool breezeway. The whiteness, vertical board walls, horizontal board ceiling, and textured floor give the room a kind of barnyard modernity. It is economy with elegance, like a denim work shirt that has been carefully starched and ironed.

The farmhouse provided a vivid complement to the Gregory residence on Greenwood Terrace in Berkeley, which also exemplified a brand of rustic simplicity. Designed by their close friend John Galen Howard, the university's campus architect, this two-story, gabled, Shingle style house stretched along the side of a hill north of the campus. Begun as a summer bungalow in 1904 when Warren and Sadie lived in San Francisco, the house became their permanent residence after the earthquake and fire of 1906, and it was expanded several times as the family grew. Their fourth and last child, born in 1912, was named John Howard, after the architect.

The Greenwood Terrace house resembled a shingled barn. Casual, heavy, large, and dark, it rambled through a stand of pine trees—an opening was even cut in an overhang to accommodate one of the trees—on a parcel of land that included a stable, a tennis court, and a field used for touch football. Unpainted redwood boards and battens covered interior walls; the living room contained a massive fireplace made of unpainted clinker brick, and a library and a formal dining room were also included. The farmhouse, on the other hand, took this expansive simplicity into a new realm verging on the ascetic. It exemplified a stripped-down, unornamented, more-from-less approach to house design

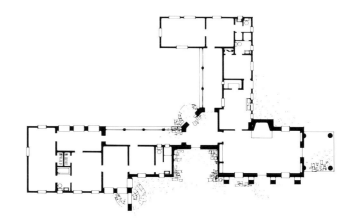

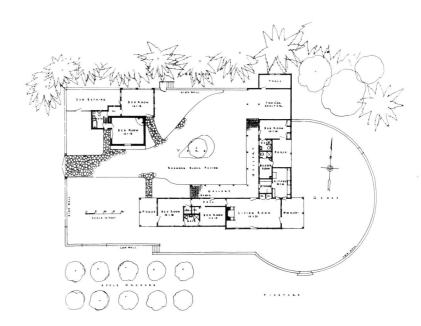

105.
Gregory Farmhouse, Scott's Valley, 1926
Henry Howard
Early plan

106.
Gregory Farmhouse, Scotts Valley, 1928
William Wurster
Plan, 1927

107.
Gregory Farmhouse, Scotts Valley, 1928
William Wurster
Elevation of tower group, 1927

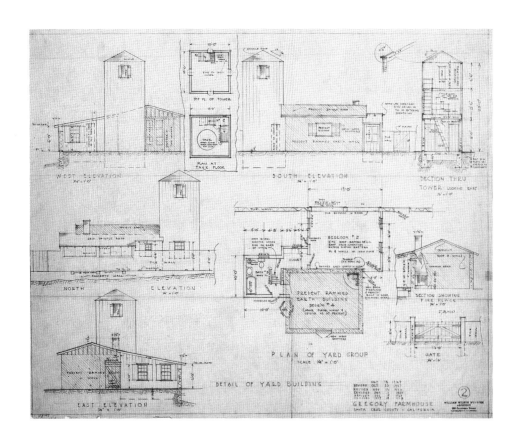

that would become increasingly attractive to Bay Region clients during the Depression. In the words of architect Donn Emmons, who became one of Wurster's partners after the war, Bill "developed great skill in making use of simple detailing and devices that added little to cost (i.e. high ceilings) but added much to quality of space."[10]

With six bedrooms and four bathrooms—not counting the "lookout" at the top of the tower, used as a bedroom by the Gregorys' youngest child, John, known as Jack—it was not a particularly small or modest house. But without conventional stylistic effects, such as thick plaster walls or tile roofs, it seemed assertive and modest at the same time (fig. 104). The fact that the house was to be used only during the warmest months of the year made it, of course, a good deal easier to be so simple. (The thin board walls, outdoor orientation, and dirt terraces made it a very cold, damp, and muddy house during the winter.)

The Mechanics of Simplicity

The desire for simplicity had come originally from Warren, who wrote Bill that "we want this house to be a simple one which can be closed when we are away, but which nevertheless will have a maximum of comfort when we are there."[11] It had not been easy for the Gregorys to get to this point. Warren and Sadie had already rejected two other schemes for the same site, as well as a plan to remodel an existing Gothic Revival farmhouse elsewhere on the Santa Cruz property, all from the Howard firm.[12] The second Howard scheme, initialed by John Galen Howard's architect son Henry, embraced the Spanish Colonial Revival style. With its tile roofs, stucco walls, and ornamental grillwork, it was more elaborate than their Berkeley house.

Born in 1864, Warren was the son of an Ohio farmer who moved to California in 1850 and found enough gold to stake his purchase of land on the slopes of Mount Diablo in Contra Costa County, where he established a working ranch. Warren grew up in the Victorian farmhouse that his parents built on the ranch. After graduating from the University of California at Berkeley in 1887, he studied at Hastings College of Law in San Francisco and then went into practice, helping to found the firm that became Chickering & Gregory. The success of his law practice made it possible to build a kind of family compound on Greenwood Terrace, including a house for his sister, Frances, commissioned from Bernard Maybeck, and a house for the John Galen Howard family (which Howard designed and then rented from Warren). Warren's compound-building activity was about to begin again in the Santa Cruz Mountains. He sent Wurster all the accumulated Howard plans to review and then waited to see what he would do. But then Warren died of a heart attack.

So Sadie took over, and to Sadie simplicity was even more important than it had been to Warren. An only child, she had grown up with her schoolteacher mother in Oakland. Money was always tight. Her father separated from her mother when Sadie was seven years old and helped support them only sporadically from Kauai, where he was a federal judge. Nevertheless, she graduated with honors from the University of California at Berkeley in 1893 and then, at her mother's urging, pursued a Ph.D. in political economics at the University of Chicago before breaking off her studies, after a brief teaching stint at Wellesley, to marry Warren. At Chicago she worked with Thorstein Veblen, author of *The Theory of the Leisure Class,* and in later years she kept a photograph of him on her dressing table.[13] Marriage to a successful attorney had made her a woman of means, yet she frowned upon signs of "conspicuous consumption"—though pangs of guilt did not keep her from enjoying first-class travel to Europe or belonging to an elegant San Francisco women's club.

The task of studying the Howard drawings became a kind of postgraduate studio assignment for Wurster. He reviewed the sheaf of plans with Warren and Sadie's request for simplicity ringing in his ears. His solution was to combine

108.
Cover of **Sunset** magazine featuring the
Gregory Farmhouse, July 1930

elements from different schemes and pare everything down to essentials (figs. 105–107). It was literally "restraint in action." He preserved the L-shaped outline of the second Howard plan but removed the ornamental Spanish tile roofs, plaster walls, wrought-iron grilles, and the formal vaulted entrance hall. Concentrating on the idea that the house would be used as a weekend camp— stimulated by a Howard plan for a rustic, freestanding, shed-roofed bedroom wing—Wurster made sure that every major room in his design opened to the outdoors. The living room opens to the outdoors on three sides, and most bedrooms open to porches or covered walkways or both. There is even a porch off the east end of the living room to be used for outdoor dining. Wurster fundamentally changed the Howard plan, making it his own by abstracting it, removing its stylistic associations, and giving form to the idea of the house as a walled compound in the wilderness. His gate, walls, and tower made a ceremonial event of arrival after the day-long drive from Berkeley. He created an understated house with an overstated entrance, or what might be called "conspicuous simplicity."

Regional Romance

Instead of turning to a high-style idiom like the Spanish Colonial Revival, Wurster found inspiration in vernacular sources. Like John Galen Howard before him, Wurster had studied California adobe architecture, especially the early nineteenth-century buildings of Monterey with their signature verandas, shingled roofs, and walled "yards." He certainly knew the handsomely proportioned double-decker porches of the Larkin House (1835–37), designed by Thomas O. Larkin, and he might well have seen the Sherwood Ranch (1824–60, designer unknown), also in Monterey County, which consisted of adobe and wooden buildings helping to enclose a partially walled courtyard, with a gable-roofed archway at one end.[14] The wooden agricultural buildings around his native Stockton in the Central Valley would have been another source of simplicity. Wurster's composition is ranchlike and abstract, casual and emphatic at the same time. It was the perfect, somewhat contradictory solution for the somewhat contradictory client.

It stood apart from the many Tudor, Neoclassical, and Spanish Colonial Revival houses being published at the time. Professional architectural journals and popular shelter magazines alike loved its romantic simplicity. *Pencil Points* editor Kenneth Reid wrote: "Forms natural to materials and uses undistorted by any faint suggestion of 'artiness,' give this house the charm of honesty that might have been produced by a carpenter endowed with good taste."[15] *Sunset* magazine published it under the headline "There Must Be Romance in the Home You Build," and included a painting of the courtyard on its cover, complete with a figure in chaps, charmingly, if clumsily, underscoring the western ranch-house theme (fig. 108).[16] *House Beautiful* wrote, "Obviously a copy of no other house, it is a straightforward attempt to solve a specific problem, which it does in the most direct manner. The result is not only convenience of plan but charm of composition in no small degree."[17]

The design expressed a pragmatic, even modern, approach to function without assuming radical new shapes and forms. It looked fresh and familar at the same time. Bay Region architect Joseph Esherick recalls seeing articles about the house while still a student at the University of Pennsylvania in 1935. What impressed him most strongly was "the clarity and discipline of the plan of both the house and the beautifully simple garden. The sharp, clear definition of the house and garden separated from the entrance and a low garden wall had the greatest impact."[18] Wurster's design won him an honor award from the Northern California Chapter of the American Institute of Architects in 1929 and the $500 first prize in *House Beautiful*'s Small House Competition of 1931.

109.
Fourth of July Parade at the Gregory
Farmhouse, 1953

110.
William Wurster at the Gregory Farmhouse,
ca. 1953

Over the years the house has achieved an almost mythic status as one of Wurster's seminal works. Architectural historian Sally Woodbridge summed up the reaction of many when she wrote that in the farmhouse Wurster "took the body of Modern architecture and gave it a regional soul."[19] The house struck a chord with architects, editors, and architectural historians because it seemed to capture the promise of California life. Indeed, it was a house where Alvar Aalto—who visited it with Wurster in 1939—felt right at home. A photograph by Thomas Church shows Aalto sleeping off a multi-martini lunch on a bench on the south terrace. Rooted in nature and responsive to climate and tradition, the farmhouse nonetheless seemed progressive, original, and free of cant. Its very ambiguity made it memorable. As one visitor remarked after touring the house in the 1970s, at a time when the house had just undergone a meticulous restoration by Sadie's daughter Elizabeth Gregory Kent, "It must have been quite a place, *once.*"

A Collective Enthusiasm

The building process had a therapeutic aspect for the recently bereaved Gregory family. The house became both a realization of Warren's dream and the confirmation of Sadie's resolve to rebuild her life. And its construction provided a delightful distraction. Family and friends enthusiastically offered advice and encouragement. The idea of making the water tower a distinctive three stories instead of the strictly functional two needed for gravity flow came from one of Sadie's closest friends, Elizabeth Ellis (Mrs. Ralph Ellis), who divided her time between her Jericho, Long Island, estate known as The Puddles, and Berkeley.[20] She had met Bill while he was working for the firm of Delano and Aldrich in New York in 1926 and had encouraged Warren and Sadie to hire the young Wurster. A wealthy, strong-willed, politically liberal woman whose husband had a seat on the New York Stock Exchange, Ellis came to Berkeley to be near her ornithologist son and ultimately rented the Gregorys' Greenwood Terrace house after Sadie moved back to San Francisco to be near her grandchildren. According to Ellis's niece Elizabeth Rublee, she referred to herself as "midwife to *The New Republic*" because its founders, including

Walter Lippmann, used to meet in her living room.[21]

One idea that did not work was the use of unpeeled madrone saplings as beams for the living-room ceiling. This would have been a picturesque homage to Warren and Sadie's friend Joseph Worcester, the influential Swedenborgian minister whose San Francisco church had madrone log beams in the nave, which came from the Santa Cruz Mountains. Collectively Don, Josephine, Sadie, Elizabeth, and Bill decided the logs looked hideous. Sadie herself contributed the idea of built-in brick seats flanking the fireplace.[22] Bill alluded to the participatory aspect of the design when he wrote: "This was a happy job from start to finish, for utmost cooperation lifted it far higher than any one of us could have brought about."[23]

The family's excitement about the design continued well after the house was completed. In 1929 the sculptor Bob Howard—another of John Galen Howard's sons, who had grown up with Don—made a home movie in which the house had the starring role. Called *Futility,* it told the story of two families, the Goodwins and the Devlins, who fought over buried gold. In the key scene the Devlin scion, played by Bob, strangles Josephine Gregory alias Goodwin in the courtyard in order to steal the treasure map, is discovered and then chased over the roofs and up to the top of the tower. After a fight with Don, Bob's body—a dummy—hurtles to the ground.

Sadie and a Widening Circle of Clients

The farmhouse launched an abiding friendship between Bill and Sadie; she treated him like an adopted son, and he ultimately named his only child after her. The house became Bill's magnetic north, providing a reference point in his professional and personal life. He returned to it whenever he could, participating in Gregory family rituals on the Fourth of July and Thanksgiving and sometimes simply staying overnight on his way to job sites in the area. He told Sadie what the house meant to him on several occasions, notably in an undated letter:

> *Dear Mrs. Gregory:*
>
> *Fresh from the joy of the Farm I want to write to you. Saturday night as I drove in from the road a great spirit of rest and contentment came over me and I realized anew how much the house and your friendship and your hospitality mean to me. In the morning it was great to see the trees and the plowed grape land— and to lie in the sun. It was hard to leave—so much so that on the way home I couldn't pass without again stopping in. The place never seemed more beautiful—there was a haze about the distant hills and woods—Thank you for allowing me to have a participation in this joy.[24]*

Sadie drafted a reply that showed a mother's affection and pride:

> *Dear Bill:*
>
> *There is a quality in your note to me about the farm which makes me want to answer it. Forgive my teasing you about it the other night. Of course the joy of the place is just that—that the people I love shall feel about it as you do. May I say, that to have you find joy and peace in it makes me very happy. I think it is a child of your heart—as it is of mine—too, I like to believe we are linked by a mutual affection. So, Bill dear, as you go on in prosperity and fame, remember that, as long as I live, it is your house too as well as mine.[25]*

Bill always sent Sadie a birthday note, in which he often recalled working on the sketches for the farmhouse on her birthday in 1927. He also sent her articles on his work and copies of his speeches. After Bill's marriage, his wife, Catherine Bauer, became an equally close friend to Sadie. In 1952 Sadie sold Bill and Catherine her Greenwood Terrace in Berkeley. Bill had wanted to live in it ever since he attended a musicale there with Mrs. Ellis one Sunday in

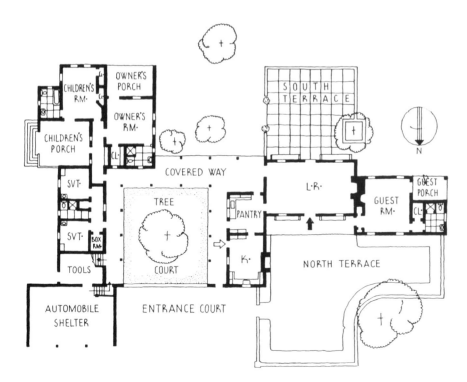

111.
Donald Gregory House, Scotts Valley, 1932
William Wurster
Plan

1924. Informal, woodsy, and spacious, it had been a meeting ground for artists and academics, and Bill wanted it to be such a place again. The transaction became another expression of Sadie's Veblenesque nature. The appraiser told Bill that the land was very valuable, but the old house was worth practically nothing. Bill gave the appraisal to Don, who took the proposal to Sadie "and she looked at it with her glasses and she said, 'Isn't that wonderful! We'll *give* Bill the house.'"[26]

Bill's career had gotten off to a promising start well before the Gregory commission, but the completion of the farmhouse gave it an additional boost as he became an integral part of the extensive Gregory-Howard-Ellis network of friends and relatives. It was a close-knit world that included landscape architect Thomas Church and his wife, Betsy, who had grown up knowing the Gregorys in Berkeley, as well as assorted doctors, lawyers, and business executives from San Francisco, Marin County, the Peninsula, and the East Bay.

The farmhouse commission led directly to others both within the Gregory family and beyond their circle. Josephine and Don, a partner in the Chickering & Gregory law firm, hired Bill to design another, more expansive courtyard house on an adjacent knoll in 1932. Thomas Church designed the landscape plan. Sadie had given her daughter-in-law the land as a birthday present in a note that said, with characteristic understatement, "Three acres, with love and affection." This house extended the design vocabulary established with the farmhouse: white vertical board walls without battens, shutters, gabled shingle roofs, and partially covered outdoor areas, but in an even more relaxed architectural ramble (fig. 111).

It is really two separate, roughly L-shaped houses linked by a covered walkway that wraps around three sides of a central pedestrian courtyard. The east wing is anchored by a three-stall garage and contains a workshop, storeroom, bedrooms, bathrooms, and a sleeping porch. The west wing contains the living-dining room, kitchen, and pantry, as well as additional bedrooms and bathrooms. Like the farmhouse, this design enthusiastically embraced the outdoor life. It also boasted an outdoor dining porch, treated here as part of the walkway between the two wings. Two spacious terraces on opposite sides of

the living room form the functional heart of the design. A sun-splashed brick terrace on the south was used for gatherings during the day and for the occasional afternoon siesta; the shadier pea-gravel terrace on the north—which also served as the front entrance and sported a built-in brick barbecue on the rear wall of the kitchen—became the site of the summer's eve ritual of cocktails before dinner. It was here that Don, dressed in a plaid shirt, cotton tie, tweed jacket, and khaki pants, and Joe, wearing a faded Hawaiian palaka shirt and a jean skirt, would entertain family and friends with a graceful, offhand, slightly shabby elegance. On the bench outside the big living-room door there was always a large basket full of books, like an immense tray of hors d'oeuvres for the imagination. Inside, the living-dining room resembled the one in Sadie's house, down to the "hike e" placed at one side of the big brick fireplace. However, some details differed: the floor was terra-cotta tile and the rafters were hidden, which, with the flat ceiling, gave the white-painted room more of the feeling of an abstract volume (fig. 112).

Don and Josephine's close friends Wellington and Harriet Henderson hired Bill to design their more formal house in Hillsborough, as previously noted. After the war, the Churches bought an old farm adjoining the Gregory property and used it as their summer house, drawing the two families even closer. Connections between family and friends became more complex as the years wore on. Sadie's older daughter, Elizabeth, married Sherman Kent, a Yale professor of history and son of the California senator and conservationist William Kent, who donated Mount Tamalpais and Muir Woods to the state. Sherman's sister, sculptor Adaline Kent, married John Galen Howard's son Bob, also a sculptor, and Bob's sister Janette married Josephine Gregory's brother, Ralph Wallace. All of these individuals became intimate friends of Bill's, and they all gathered at the Gregory Farmhouse with Bill and the Churches for weekends and family celebrations. Even architect Henry Howard got a second chance when Janette and Ralph Wallace asked him to design their summer house on another parcel not far from the Donald Gregory House.

And so it went, the work and the relationships expanding from the farmhouse like ripples from a pebble cast into a pond. In 1937 Donald and Josephine Gregory, the Wellington Hendersons, and several other investors, including Walt Disney, developed the Sugar Bowl ski area and hired Bill to design the lodge. He designed a number of ski chalets there as well. After the war, Sadie's son-in-law Everett Griffin and his wife Nona (his first wife, Sadie's younger daughter Jean, had died of hepatitis) remodeled the old Gothic Revival farmhouse at the Gregory Farm, with the help of Thomas Church, who added a large deck. In 1957 they hired Bill to design a handsome concrete-floored, board-and-batten-sided courtyard house at Stinson Beach. After a long and active life, Sadie died in 1959 at the age of eighty-nine.

Finally, in 1963, Sadie's youngest son, Jack, and his wife, Evey (my parents), hired Bill to design the last house in the Gregory compound, on a leveled hilltop site with a view of Monterey Bay (fig. 113). It stands near a small existing wood frame house that the Gregorys had rebuilt in 1949 and opens to a dirt-and-grass play area, that helps to frame it. Church sketched the site plan while enjoying a glass of bourbon and water with Jack and Evey on the porch of their existing house. For his final Gregory design, Bill returned to the early California vernacular and designed an utterly simple, steel-reinforced adobe rectangle with a gabled shingle roof that extends to cover long porches on two sides. Like his much grander George Pope Ranch House of 1956, it recalls the Mariano Vallejo adobe at Petaluma. It is a small house, with only a living-dining room, galley kitchen, two bedrooms, and one bath; unlike the other Gregory houses, it was meant for year-round living. Still, every space opens directly to a porch. There are only five actual windows—double-hung, naturally. All the other openings are elegantly proportioned glass doors. Indeed,

112. (opposite)
Donald Gregory House, Scotts Valley, 1932
William Wurster
Living room

113.
John H. Gregory House, Scotts Valley, 1963
William Wurster

along the front or southeast-facing porch facade, the repeating rhythm of redwood-and-glass doors, unpainted adobe wall, porch posts, and boardwalk gives the house its elemental character. It is a Wurster-designed pony-express station, an unassuming archetype. The use of adobe bricks brought Bill full circle, back to the mud-walled structure that had been the preexisting part of the Gregory Farmhouse. He returned to it and made it his own.

Bill's commissions were generally for people who just wanted good houses that took advantage of Northern California's benign climate and beautiful natural settings. As Donn Emmons wrote, "His clients were mostly families who could afford to build and were socially relaxed and with little interest in display."[27] Restraint was what they wanted, and restraint was what he gave them. The understated approach became a process of clarifying or framing the life to be lived in his houses, but it was clarity with a twist. That twist is the contradictory nature that many of his best houses express. One visitor to the farmhouse gently asked, "So where is the architecture?" It is a question Frank Lloyd Wright might have posed. Another guest, on the same day, said: "I feel I have taken a sentimental journey to a place I never knew."[28] Perhaps both are right.

Notes

1. *William Wilson Wurster, College of Environmental Design, University of California, Campus Planning and Architectural Practice,* interview by Suzanne B. Riess (Berkeley: University of California, Regional Cultural History Project [now Regional Oral History Office], 1964), pp. 101–02 (hereafter Wurster/Riess Oral History).

2. Allan Temko, interview by the author, 27 November 1994.

3. Quoted in Richard C. Peters, "William Wilson Wurster, An Architect of Houses," in Sally B. Woodbridge, ed., *Bay Area Houses,* (Salt Lake City: Peregrine Smith, 1988), p. 124.

4. Mrs. Wellington Henderson, interview by the author, 6 November 1994.

5. "Quoting Mr. Wurster," *Architectural Forum* 64 (May 1936), pp. 36–37.

6. William Wilson Wurster, Wurster/Riess Oral History, p. 59.

7. William Wurster, letter to Mrs. Warren Gregory, 12 October 1949. Collection of the author.

8. William Wurster, "Farmhouse in the Santa Cruz Mountains, William Wilson Wurster, Architect" typescript, William Wurster Archive, College of Environmental Design Documents Collection, at the University of California at Berkeley (hereafter CED Documents Collection).

9. "Farmhouse for Mrs. Warren Gregory," typescript, CED Documents Collection.

10. Donn Emmons, letter to the author, 6 February 1991.

11. Warren Gregory, letter to Bill Wurster, 19 December 1926. William Wurster Papers, CED Documents Collection.

12. A more extensive discussion of the Howard plans and the genesis of the Wurster design may be found in my "An Indigenous Thing: The Story of William Wurster and the Gregory Farmhouse," *Places* 7, no. 1 (Fall 1990), pp. 78-93.

13. Lucy Sprague Mitchell, *Two Lives: The Story of Wesley Claire Mitchell and Myself* (New York: Simon & Schuster, 1953), pp. 152–3.

14. According to Wurster's biographer, Richard C. Peters, Wurster toured Monterey adobes in 1926.

15. Kenneth Reid, "The Architect and the House: William Wurster of California," *Pencil Points* 19 (August 1938), pp. 472–74.

16. "There Must Be Romance in the Home You Build," *Sunset* 65, no. 1 (July 1930), p. 22.

17. Editorial, *House Beautiful* 69 (March 1931), p. 237.

18. Joseph Esherick, "Image and Reality," *Places* 7, no. 1 (Fall 1990), p. 86.

19. Sally Woodbridge, "From the Large-Small House to the Large-Large House," in Woodbridge, ed., *Bay Area Houses,* p. 157.

20. Donald and Josephine Gregory, interview by the author, 15 September 1989.

21. Elizabeth Rublee, interview by the author, 21 January 1995.

22. Donald and Josephine Gregory, interview by the author, 15 September 1989.

23. "Farmhouse for Mrs. Warren Gregory," *Architecture* (August 1935), p. 91.

24. Bill Wurster, letter to Sadie Gregory, n.d. Collection of the author.

25. Sadie Gregory, letter to Bill Wurster, written on the back of letter from Bill Wurster to Sadie Gregory. Collection of the author.

26. William Wilson Wurster, Wurster/Riess Oral History, p. 254.

27. Donn Emmons, letter to the author, 6 February 1991.

28. Two guests made these remarks to the author in the fall of 1980.

Of Gardens and Houses as Places to Live:
Thomas Church and William Wurster

Dorothée Imbert

William Wurster designed a house and studio for landscape architect Thomas Church and his wife, Elizabeth, in 1930 (fig. 115). Situated at Pasatiempo, near Santa Cruz, the house expressed "simplicity, purity of design, poverty of embellishment and turn[ed] away from imitation," thus "truly liv[ing] up to the tradition of California."[1] As a collaboration between architect and landscape architect, the design and siting of the house manifested a stylistic sobriety that characterized both Wurster and Church.

Following the contour of the land, the plan roughly formed an elongated T oriented north to south; the East Entrance Garden responded to the West Living Terrace overlooking a ravine (fig. 116). The interior was suited to "simple country living," with built-in furniture, no hall or dining room, a kitchen spacious enough for entertaining, a conversation pit before the fireplace, and a north-facing skylit space for the studio.[2] Similarly the outdoors offered informal spaces that drew on the beauties of the existing vegetation rather than on any elaborate planting scheme (fig. 117). A row of trees screened the brick court and flower borders from the road, and the rear terrace faced a landscape left natural—a copse-thick arroyo whose banks were covered with wild azaleas.[3]

The Church House design received an award from the American Institute of Architects and was published extensively both in the United States and abroad. However, the true measure of its success was perhaps best expressed in correspondence between the owners of the house and its architect.[4] On 18 March 1931, Thomas Church wrote:

> *Dear Bill:*
>
> *I can no longer resist putting in writing how complete we both feel in our Santa Cruz house. Living in it for a week has made us deeply grateful to you for as nearly perfect a house as we could ever want. We feel that, all the way through, your thought has been clear and your decisions right, and we wish to be known as appreciative and enthusiastic clients. We are so sure that you are fast beginning to fill a definite need in California architecture that we consider ourselves fortunate to have got our house while you are still doing jobs among the ten thousands. . . . Our final wish is that you come to see us often and consider the house yours—as indeed it is.[5]*

The cohesion between the Church project and its site revealed Wurster's vision of the house as a backdrop for the life within and the garden without. Stressing the unity of architecture and landscape architecture, albeit insisting on their specificity, Wurster later described the two disciplines as being "separated only as to materials and technique, not as to basic approach."[6] Thus the siting of a house resulted from a discussion between architect and landscape

114.
Martin Garden, Aptos, 1948
Thomas Church

architect that evaluated orientation, topography, vegetation, views, and connections to utilities.

Unlike Wurster, who had already received recognition for the Gregory Farmhouse (1928) in Scotts Valley, Church was still a novice when he started work at Pasatiempo. He was then officially employed by Oakland landscape architect Floyd Mick,[7] armed only with degrees from the University of California at Berkeley and Harvard, some brief teaching experience, and internships in several landscape offices.[8]

The Pasatiempo Country Club and Estates were based on a plan by the Boston landscape firm of the Olmsted brothers. The site covered six hundred acres and included an eighteen-hole golf course, nine miles of roads, a clubhouse, tennis courts, open spaces, six miles of bridle paths, and house lots of various sizes.[9] Upon returning from his honeymoon trip to northern Mexico in 1930, Thomas Church met with Marion Hollins, the developer of Pasatiempo, who offered him the opportunity to serve as the project's supervising landscape architect. In addition to overseeing the subdivision of lots and overall road planning, Church designed several individual gardens. Living on site for approximately eighteen months and collaborating with both William Wurster and Clarence Tantau, Church was thus able to develop a private practice in the midst of the Depression.

Pasatiempo was laid out on rolling terrain planted with native vegetation—California live oaks, redwoods, madrones, Douglas firs, manzanitas, California poppies, lupines, and yerba buena—whose delicate balance could easily be disturbed by the modifications of grading and drainage patterns. Church functioned as keeper of the existing vegetation and as consultant on the siting of houses and driveways. Like his own garden, all his designs at Pasatiempo appeared as subtle extensions of the houses into the landscape. Thus the gardens for the Howes and Hollins houses, both by Wurster, sought "simplicity and color rather than a formal effect."[10] Church merely complemented the Pasatiempo Guest House, by Clarence Tantau, with a brick terrace that expanded the living areas into the shade of a large California live oak (fig. 118).[11] Similarly, he co-signed the site plan of Wurster's Berry House, but did little more than utilize an existing oak to shelter the terrace and balcony.

Wurster and Church also collaborated on the Pasatiempo house and garden for Lucy and Vincent Butler, which became one of the architect's most significant early projects. Wurster proposed three schemes, whose centers of gravity revolved around a mature oak. In Scheme C, which was executed in a modified form, Wurster centered the picturesque tree within a courtyard, thereby recapturing the native vegetation through an architectural frame (fig. 120).[12] To accommodate the outdoor orientation of the Butlers' lifestyle, Wurster planned a progression from indoors, or enclosed space, to outdoors.

From the domesticated vegetation of the courtyard, one moved through the Living Porch onto the Living Terrace overflowing into the natural landscape, where one could contemplate the distant views toward the southeast. Church joined house to site by adapting its natural qualities for greater use and effect. Mrs. Butler recollected Church's intention to keep "the field empty and the woods around the house rough, [with] just enough planting to make it civilized."[13] The courtyard design featured a bifurcated path traversing islands of planting, while preservation measures were taken to ensure the survival of the live oak (fig. 121). Church had the tree braced and filled with cement to reinforce its structure, and to protect the roots from excessive moisture, he installed an elaborate drainage system.[14] The goal was low-maintenance landscape—a logical decision for a weekend residence. Little earth was moved, as the central court followed the natural contours; the terrace was paved with brick, the paths with gravel, the service yard and driveway with macadam. Only a hint

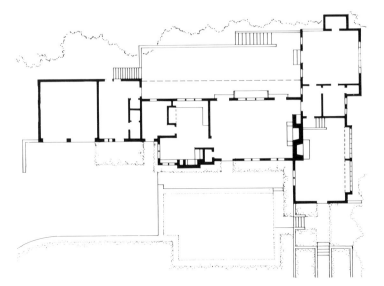

115.
Left to right: William Wurster, Elizabeth Church, Thomas Church, and Carlos (Marion Hollins's dog), Pasatiempo, ca. 1930

116.
Church House, Pasatiempo, 1931
William Wurster
Plan

117.
Church House and Garden, Pasatiempo, 1931
William Wurster with Thomas Church, landscape architect
Front lawn and entrance court

of lawn, a few potted flowers, vegetable beds, and hedges necessitated the efforts of a gardener.

At Pasatiempo, Church acted as the modern equivalent of an "improver," the role Humphry Repton notably played in late-eighteenth-century England. A landscape conjurer, Repton displaced buildings, dug lakes, and transplanted groves. More modestly, Church surveyed the land for the optimal siting of the house and assessed the surroundings for the most beneficial view and use. For the Butlers, he pruned the trees in the canyon not only to reveal views but also to increase the sculptural qualities of branch structures. In *Gardens Are for People* (1955), Church included two illustrations of the Butler design, each showing a different view of the live oaks. In the first, the house receded behind the interior plantings of the central court; in the second, the lines of the covered passageway framed the exterior vegetation (fig. 119). The caption read:

> Look carefully at your trees to be sure you have developed all they have to give you. Their beauty is not in foliage alone but in their shape and branching and in the relation of their structure to their foliage. It's pleasant and very exciting to look up into a tree and through a tree, as well as at it.[15]

Departing from the secluded microcosm of the Moorish paradise garden or the Hispanic patio, the Butler House and Garden achieved an almost uninterrupted confluence of building, interior open space, and natural surroundings. The juncture between the realm of the landscape architect and that of the architect appeared seamless. In the centripetal paradise garden, architecture served as both a barrier excluding the wilderness and a shelter that focused on the domesticated nature within its walls. Instead, the Butler House functioned as an envelope that merely suggested, rather than imposed, the limits between interior and exterior. The living porch served as a membrane between bedroom and living room and court and natural landscape. The courtyard functioned as a lens that refracted and reflected nature back onto itself and onto architecture.

The unity of the Butler House and Garden was perhaps closer to early twentieth-century Bay Area architecture than to any Spanish precedent. The Berkeley Hillside Club had stated in 1902 that an architecture adapted to the Northern California climate required "roofs to shed rain but not snow" and "windows to let in all the sunlight possible, not to keep out the heat."[16] Wurster's and Church's blending of indoors and outdoors could ultimately be more aptly compared to Bernard Maybeck's house and garden for James Fagan, erected in Woodside in 1920 (fig. 122). Maybeck extended the landscape into the building with a narrow court stretched between the wings of the sleeping and living spaces. The formality of the terrace and planting—a hybrid of English cottage garden and Italianate styles—differed radically from the loosely defined boundaries of the Butler House. But the trellis of the Fagan "garden" covered with wisteria and grapevines functioned as a vegetal ceiling in much the same way that the canopy of the oak formed a vault of branches and leaves over the Butler courtyard. Church not only stylistically modernized Maybeck's approach, he also adjusted its impact on the landscape. As Dianne Harris has demonstrated, Maybeck conceived his gardens in relation to, and totally dependent upon, their architectural framework.[17] Church, on the other hand, treated the house and its inhabitants as points of departure for garden design, which in its turn grew into the landscape.

Pasatiempo promoted a relaxed lifestyle. William Wurster's modest houses and Thomas Church's designed connections to the native landscape would provide lasting models for a regional modernist architecture and a low-maintenance garden—alternatives to the International Style and either its naturalistic or ultraformal response. The functionalist current underlying Church's approach, regardless of style, may be traced to the formative years of his childhood and to the thesis he submitted to Harvard in 1927.

118.
Guest House and Terrace, Pasatiempo, 1929
Clarence Tantau with Thomas Church,
landscape architect

119.
Butler House and Garden, Pasatiempo, 1935
William Wurster with Thomas Church,
landscape architect
View through the covered passage looking
southwest

120.
Butler House, Pasatiempo, 1935
William Wurster
Axonometric drawing

121.
Butler House and Garden, Pasatiempo, 1935
William Wurster with Thomas Church,
landscape architect
Central court with California live oak,
looking southeast

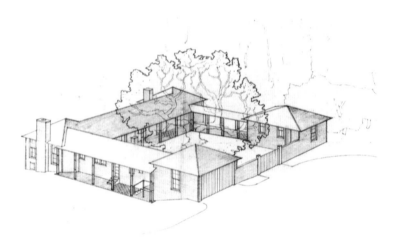

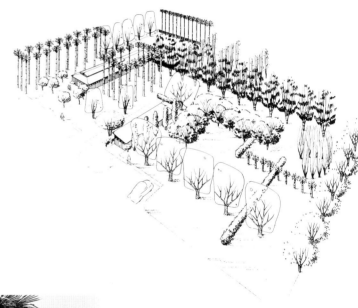

122.
Fagan House, Woodside, 1920
Bernard Maybeck
Court between the building wings

123.
Farm Security Administration Community Center, near Weslaco, Texas, 1939
Garrett Eckbo

124.
Lloyd Garden, Beverly Hills, 1925–29
A. E. Hanson
Harold Lloyd in front of the water cascade,
ca. 1931

Thomas Dolliver Church was born in Boston in 1902. He and his sister were taken by their mother to Ohio and later to California's Ojai Valley. Unlike Santa Barbara, where easterners sought to re-create Italianate Edens, Ojai (then named Nordhoff) was the destination for people escaping tuberculosis who sought a dry, sunny climate and year-round outdoor life.[18] Instead of advertising purely scenographic and grand estates to lure visitors, the Ojai Valley boasted a landscape in which beauty was overlaid with utility—a landscape of ranches and simple architecture that promoted a casual, sportive lifestyle set against a background of citrus orchards.[19]

After studying at Berkeley and Harvard and acquiring what Betsy Church termed a "bird's-eye view" of Europe in his travels through Italy, France, and Spain, Church wrote his master's thesis, "A Study of Mediterranean Gardens and Their Adaptability to California Conditions," in 1927.[20] Drawing parallels between the climate, topography, vegetation, and countryside of each region, Church asserted that "California has much to learn from Italy in the way of moderation and restraint." But it was the utilitarian aspects of the Italian garden that particularly attracted his attention—the simple pools and terraces, the pergola of humble origin supporting grapevines or providing shade over the terraced lemon groves. Perhaps Church's vision for the future of California was announced in his comparing it to Renaissance Italy: "[I]n both there is a class of people with the wealth to demand comfort and luxury, and the intelligence to demand beauty—a combination that wherever found in the history of the world has resulted in the planning of beautiful gardens. . . . That it will happen in California is in the way of being a prophecy."[21]

From the beginning of his practice at Pasatiempo to the late 1970s, Church devoted his attention predominantly to the private sector of landscape design. Although he was occasionally involved in the planning of large projects such as Wurster's Vallejo defense housing (1942), his contribution to the social landscape never equaled that of Garrett Eckbo.[22] Eckbo established plans and guidelines for trailer camps, housing, and parks for migrant workers for the Farm Security Administration (fig. 123). In contrast, Church remained within the bounds of the residential garden in order to maintain control over the design process and the scale of his office. With tongue in cheek, he would later state, "I'm asked once in a while how I feel about minority groups and I say I'm very sympathetic to their problems. The minority group that I really feel very sorry for is the very rich. And if I can just help them get their lives straightened out then I will have done something for a minority group."[23] Ironically it was the restraint demanded by the Depression years and the ensuing simplicity of postwar life that shaped many aspects of Church's modern California residential landscape. Gardeners were the first "help" to disappear, recalled Elizabeth Church, and naturally maintenance became a central issue in garden design. The economic problems of the Depression years were felt by both architects and landscape architects. At the same time that A. E. Hanson, the garden designer of the rich and famous, abandoned his lucrative practice after the 1929 crash, Church began to develop his own.[24]

Hanson borrowed heavily from Italian and Spanish sources, compressing time and space in his gardens in Southern California.[25] The estate of the movie actor Harold Lloyd in Beverley Hills featured a "Villa d'Este pool," a "Villa Medici fountain," and a Palladian pavilion (fig. 124); the pools and benches of the Young Garden in Pasadena offered twice-removed references to the Moorish garden, modeled on twentieth-century designs.[26] Hanson and Church followed a similar itinerary in their nearly concurrent European travels, and both absorbed lessons from the villas of Italy and the tiled courtyards and enclosed gardens of Spain. But while Church was also eclectic in his references, he was more modest in his vision, avoiding the mere sampling of historical styles and focusing instead on the functional aspect of garden structures.

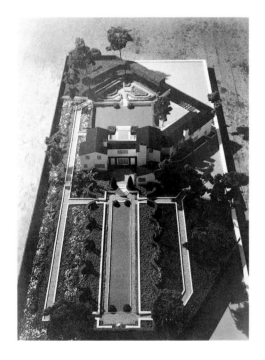

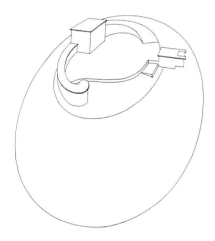

125.
George Pope House and Garden,
Hillsborough, 1936
William Wurster with Thomas Church,
landscape architect
Model presented at the 1937 "Contemporary
Landscape Architecture" exhibition at the
San Francisco Museum of Art

126.
"Holiday" project for a country house
on a lake, 1937
William Wurster with Thomas Church,
landscape architect
Presented at the 1937 "Contemporary
Landscape Architecture" exhibition at the
San Francisco Museum of Art

Imported elements such as quatrefoil pools, boxwood knot gardens, and cast-iron Danish streetlights recurred occasionally in Church's designs, but he never sought to reflect wealth ostentatiously, as did Hanson in his landscape design for a movie cardinal's Palazzo Farnese. In "A Study of Mediterranean Gardens," Church distilled the essence of all Italian gardens into a balance of scale, evergreens, stonework, and water, which became equally pertinent to *his* design method. "The pleasure of living out of doors, the need of shade and the conservation of water," he concluded, were "all problems which the California gardener must meet and answer"—points that also announced his evolving attitude toward garden design. Church looked toward the heritages of southern Spain and early California to extract a modern model for an "economic" garden.

"The Andalusian way is worth studying," he wrote, for its parsimonious use of water because in California "it costs more to water the garden than to heat the house."[27] Like the Spanish garden, which featured a restrained range of plants—orange tree, cypress, and myrtle—Church exploited a very limited palette of vegetation. Interpreting the Moorish model, he framed evergreens with a man-made structure—paving, fence, or pergola. Planting large specimens and relying on a mineral structure, he created gardens that were not only ready to use but also ready to be photographed. He often improvised the planting scheme *in situ*, after the brickwork, deck, and pool were constructed, relying essentially on the live oak, pittosporum, olive tree, boxwood, and a spare use of lawn and flowers.

It is difficult to define stylistic periods within Church's career, as he followed no single formal trend at any given time. He indulged his clients' taste, as Wurster did, and their stylistic divagations were often paired. Thus Church's design complemented Wurster's first Henderson House in Hillsborough (1933), executed in a "more or less French château type done in 12-inch board siding . . . painted white and with a shingle roof,"[28] with a design that he described as "borrow[ing] line and simplicity of layout from the French formal gardens but . . . reduced in size to fit modern living."[29] He ornamented the entrance court with boxwood tracery, planted a rose garden adjacent to the dining terrace, and framed the lawn with hedges of pruned yew and pittosporum.[30] He played the formal frame of boxwood parterres against the convoluted branches of an existing oak tree. The sunken terrace—with a canopy of leaves and paved with brick—transformed this more casual space into the focal point of an overall symmetrical and formal garden. Apart from the hedges requiring intensive labor, the Henderson Garden announced the principles that would underlie Church designs: an evergreen structure for year-round visual effect and a mineral outline to reinforce the spatial patterns.[31]

Similarly, the stately plan Wurster conceived for Mr. and Mrs. George Pope, Jr., in 1935—complete with a children's dining-room and quarters for servants and nurse—inspired a two-part formal garden by Church with stretches of lawn framed by low walls and pruned shrubs (fig. 125). The contrived serpentine hedges, the neatly outlined compartments of greenery, and perennial borders were nonetheless described as being easy to maintain.[32] In fact, despite their formal pattern, Church saw these parterres as simpler versions of French antecedents. "On a modest scale, they are suitable to our half-a-day-a-week (or less) gardening help. . . . Bi-annual pruning will maintain their form and good looks. Usually of evergreen materials . . . they are suitable to our local climatic conditions."[33]

The catalogue accompanying the exhibition "Contemporary Landscape Architecture" at the San Francisco Museum of Art in 1937 prominently featured a model of the Pope House and its garden. The exhibition presented modern expressions of landscape architecture as well as historical sources to emphasize the continuity in the development of garden art. Such designs as

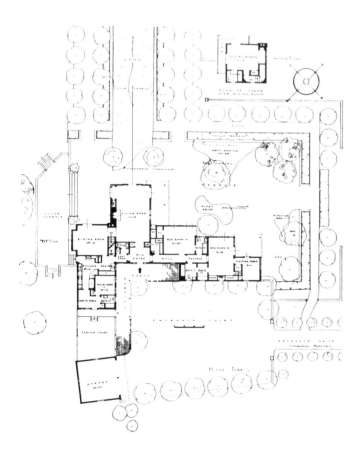

127.
Clark Garden, Woodside, 1937
Hervey Parke Clark with Thomas Church,
landscape architect
Plan

the Pope Garden and that for Everett Griffin, also by Church, championed a formalism that appeared closer to historical precedents than to any contemporary incarnation. In contrast to these classical visions were Church's urban garden, whose simple yet dynamic design complemented a house by Ernest Born, and his collaboration with Wurster on the whimsical project titled "Holiday" (fig. 126). This design was described as "suggest[ing] possibilities [for] a pavilion and beach in some mirage, with thought released from actualities and need." The elusive drawing and model belied any accusations that Wurster and Church were overly pragmatic.[34]

Church held a central position in the 1937 show, serving as the representative of both a simplified French-inspired formal tradition and a new functionalist trend that answered "the house 'to live in'" with "a garden 'to live in'"—to quote Grace Morley, director of the museum and the exhibition's curator.[35]

The San Francisco exhibition—first of its kind internationally—was intended to have as strong an impact on landscape architecture as the 1932 New York exhibition of American modern architecture had achieved in that field.[36] The 1937 landscape show reflected a mitigated view of contemporary design, intent on demonstrating "to the public how the modern garden—small or large—can be useful and inexpensive as well as colorful and in good taste."[37] Despite promoting the elusive benefits of a product combining function and charm, the exhibition presented landscape and architecture on a rare equal footing. Architects and landscape architects submitted models of their work, and the catalogue included articles by Henry-Russell Hitchcock, Fletcher Steele, and Richard Neutra. The exhibition achieved its goal, bringing recognition to the field of landscape architecture, particularly to Bay Area garden designers.

Also displayed was Church's transitional design for the architect Hervey Parke Clark. In this Woodside garden—realized in 1937 and modified over time—Church expressed a confluence of stylistic tendencies (fig. 127). The

overall layout followed an arrangement of *allées* and green rooms whose simple formalism evoked the work of contemporary landscape figures such as
Fletcher Steele and André Vera, the French author, garden designer, and leading proponent of classical modernism.[38] Against this candid structure of outdoor rooms, Church placed amoeba-shaped islands of festuca floating on
compacted gravel. He described the composition as "simple [and] straight-for-
ward" and "well related to the house, with maintenance costs reduced to a
minimum. . . . All plants [were] chosen to resist drought and to look well the
year-round."[39] Apart from an *allée* of Lombardy poplars—a species usually
requiring deep watering—the planting scheme needed little help and only rare
pruning. Specifications included olive trees, *Pittosporum undulatum,* oaks,
and plane trees, whereas he labeled the remaining plantings simply "gray
ground cover," "bunch grass," and "planting bed." The "subtle shades of gray"
of the vegetation were intended to complement Mrs. Clark's interior-design
palette, while the terraces and courtyards were each structured as an outdoor
equivalent to each room of the house. Church ultimately constricted his plan
to an excessive formalism, despite the simplicity of the spaces. Thus the axis
framed by a double *allée* of olive trees planted in forced perspective contradicted the direction of the views indicated on the plan.[40]

Church cited the past in several later projects, such as the Keator Garden
in Hillsborough (1941), whose boxwood festoon and rose garden mingled a
retardataire formalism with the rusticity of annual plantings. Similarly, the
1942 Bradley Garden, also in Hillsborough, featured a medley of styles that
appeared to ignore any temporal continuity. There the dynamism of the zigzag-
ging raised planters complemented, or contradicted, the symmetry and formalism of an ivy parterre punctuated by topiary boxwood.

The variation in stylistic patterns within different periods of Church's
career tended to derive from a confluence of factors, such as the preferences of
the client, topography, means, and the employees assisting on the project. To
Church, theory was as irrelevant to his practice as any defined style: "arbitrary
shapes—amoebas, zigzags, etc.—used without reason or apparent forethought,
can be disastrous and become constant irritants in the scheme."[41] The unusual
shapes and materials used in his garden for the 1939 San Francisco World's
Fair perhaps reflected, as Michael Laurie pointed out, the influence of Church's
voyage to Finland and his contact with Alvar Aalto. But they also acknowledged the input of Robert Royston, then working in the office.[42]

Church superimposed an understanding of planning and functionalism on
the lessons drawn from his Beaux-Arts education and historical European gardens. Regardless of style, all his designs were developed in relation to site and
use. Church saw these garden forms as borrowing "the best from these two
schools of thought: the formal and the informal—the symmetrical and the picturesque—the geometric and the natural—the classic and the romantic." The
garden *was* a work of art, but the vocabulary that shaped the functional structure mattered little.

In 1948 the San Francisco Museum of Art mounted a second landscape
architecture exhibition, "Landscape Design." The first show had stressed the
historical precedents of modern gardens, but the second looked toward contemporary art and æsthetics. The catalogue's preface, written by Assistant
Director Richard Freeman, outlined the changes that had occurred in garden
design during the intervening decade: "The first exhibition with its plans and
models represented hopes. The present one now represents a partial fulfillment of those hopes together with fresh new plans for the future.[43] Stephen
Pepper, professor of philosophy and æsthetics at Berkeley, wrote the
"Introduction to Garden Design." Distinguishing between pictorial formalism
and the shaping of gardens, the author saw "the purely visual elements of line,
plane, shape, volume and mass tak[ing] on the values of the functional ele-

ments," and, as a result, "function fuses with the purely spatial elements." With this "fusion of function and plastic space," Pepper continued, "a garden is no longer essentially a visual prospect. . . . It is a usable thing that extends out of a house; it is practically part of the house. And yet at the same time it shares something of the spontaneity and freedom of imaginative spatial composition characteristic of painting—particularly of abstract painting."[44] In fact, Church structured his Martin and Donnell gardens on almost purely functional terms—benches for sunbathing protected from the wind and a terrace paved with tan concrete to avoid glare—but created pictorial entities whose occult dynamism came closer to painting than to landscape architecture.

Just as William Wurster's catalogue essay, "The Unity of Architecture and Landscape Architecture," brought the landscape into an architectural focus, garden design appeared to have evolved once again into a self-sustained art form. The garden's spatial construct may have grown from the house, but it did not depend on architecture. Art came to the foreground in the essay by sculptor Claire Falkenstein, who described her collaboration with landscape architects.[45] Garrett Eckbo, inspired by modern art, layered and dilated space in an apparent diffraction of perspective. He also used architectural structures in his gardens but did not confuse architecture with landscape architecture. Stressing the spatial qualities of vegetation and their potential as sculptural elements, he established parameters—selection, arrangement, and maintenance—for the plants in the new landscape.[46]

The 1948 exhibition not only reoriented landscape architecture toward art, it also broadened the scale of inquiry from residential garden design to planning and housing. Christopher Tunnard, author of the seminal book *Gardens in the Modern Landscape,*[47] shifted his attention to open spaces in his catalogue essay, "Landscape Design and City Planning." No traces of the past, no traces of gardens "in the style of," remained in the show. Instead, it featured landscape planning by Eckbo, Royston, and Williams for the Ladera Housing Cooperative and Church's courtyards for Valencia Gardens.

Almost confirming Eckbo's view of him as "the last great traditional, and the first great modern designer,"[48] Church appeared in the exhibition catalogue as both a representative of the landscape establishment and as a player at the forefront of garden design. The garden for Everett Turner in Modesto (1942), which accompanied Wurster's house, still represented a landscape that complemented, and was dependent on, architecture. The Martin and the Donnell projects radically departed from this approach.

In 1948 Church created several gardens on the beach at Aptos, all variations on a theme. The designs were to be compact, inexpensive, and informal, requiring very little gardening; they were planted essentially with native beach grasses and ice plant.[49] For Ernest Meyer and Charles Kuhn, Church created an expansive wooden deck from which he cut a circle to be filed with sand (fig. 128). The geometric design underlined by crisp shadows was severed from sky, sea, and beach—floating in the landscape like the deck of an ocean liner—secluded from wind and public gaze, yet connecting with all the elements. Similarly, the sand enclave and deck for Mr. and Mrs. Mark Elworthy, although less formal in its angled and somewhat awkward geometries, provided a prelude to the beach below and the sea beyond.

The garden for Mr. and Mrs. Charles Martin combined the elegance of the Meyer-Kuhn design with the dynamism of the Elworthy lines; moreover, the plan wholly engaged the house, which was designed by Hervey Parke Clark (fig. 129). All the rooms, arranged in a U, faced the central sand area and opened onto the deck. Church played the curves of the sand island and the sensuous undulations of its texture against the crispness of the deck and the zigzag lines of the sunbathing bench. Because the wooden floorboards formed a checkerboard pattern set at a forty-five-degree angle to the house, the garden

appeared as the perfect complement to, yet independent from, the architecture. Church described the Martin House and Garden as intended to "sleep, feed and sunbathe eight people with little effort," and the lines of the garden as "restless and flowing, like the sea."[50] Wrapped by a wave of vegetation that formed a plinth to the sea and the horizon, the deck and sand area were protected from the public beach below (fig. 114). But as the grasses and sand in the distance appear to extend the garden, Church manipulated the perspective, appropriating the landscape through *shakkei*[51] and moving the beach into the garden.

The garden Church designed with Lawrence Halprin for Mr. and Mrs. Dewey Donnell in Sonoma that same year also achieved an exquisite balance among garden, architecture, and the greater landscape. Although it was a two-part composition, the terrace and pool, paired with the lanai and guest house, deserve, and have received, closer attention (fig. 130). The two structures, designed by architects George Rockrise and Germano Milono (a Wurster employee), anchored the fan-shaped platform opening onto a thirty-mile panoramic view of the San Francisco Bay area.

Placed on a knoll on the Donnell Ranch, the pool and terrace plateau appeared to float over the wetlands, creek, and bay. Both the extension of the terrace into the air—with the cantilevered deck—and the alien nature of its forms removed the design from its surroundings, bringing it closer to the sky than to the alluvial landscape below (fig. 131). The pool functioned as a light and cloud reflector; its amoeba shape, supposedly inspired by the meandering creek in the distance, conferred on the terrace a sophistication that was underlined by the contrast between its areas of manicured lawn and the adjacent native rocks and natural grasses below.

Church's optical juxtaposition of the Donnell pool and the distant bay recalled the play between the Martin sandbox and the beach in the background. The Sonoma project differed from its Aptos contemporary, however, by focusing on its abstraction—revolving around the pool's sculpture—and severance from nature. The Donnell terrace looked out toward the landscape but remained detached from it. Architecture also receded; the guest house behind a tree and the lanai dissolved in the transparency of glass. Photographs almost always looked outward from the building. The existing live oaks framing the view remained at the edge of the garden; neither here nor there, they added to the ethereal quality of the space.

Ironically Church described the Donnell project almost exclusively in functional terms, with the trees "offering wind protection and shade," while the pool "was designed to provide adequate space for all water activities . . . [with] a shallow area for children near the recreation room, 60 feet of unobstructed swimming, and a deep section for diving." Even the sculptured island by Adaline Kent—whose abstract convolutions evoked an oversized concrete piece of jewelry by Margaret de Patta rather than Kent's more figurative works—was evaluated in terms of use: "It separates the swimming and play areas and is a center of fun for divers and underwater experts who swim through a hole in the base. Like most islands these days, it's crowded with sun-bathers."[52] The lanai was complete with a fireplace for cooler days and a soda fountain for the children; when the two glass walls slid open, the structure became part of the terrace on which "three people are not lost . . . nor are a hundred crowded."[53]

Church's almost mundane description may reveal his favoring of function over form. No stylistic predilection colors his account in *Gardens Are for People;* use, maintenance, and client's preference mandate form. The spatial sophistication of the Martin project and particularly the Donnell pool and terrace ultimately relies on more than innovative shapes. Their strength—which surpasses that of any urban project, no matter how dynamic its design—derives from the connection between the garden and the greater landscape. Church

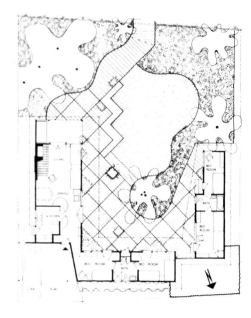

128. (opposite)
Meyer-Kuhn Garden, Aptos, 1948
Thomas Church
Sun deck with sandbox

129.
Martin House and Garden, Aptos, 1948
Hervey Parke Clark with Thomas Church,
landscape architect
Plan

130.
Donnell Garden, Sonoma, 1948
Thomas Church and Lawrence Halprin
Plan

131.
Donnell Garden, Sonoma, 1948
Thomas Church and Lawrence Halprin

fully understood this connection, entitling a chapter of *Gardens Are for People* "How to Enjoy Land You Don't Own."[54]

Thus he captured the background scenery for the Packard Garden in Los Altos (1945), using a strong horizontal wall that served as a plinth to the hill behind, directing the gaze toward the apricot orchard and seemingly shortening its distance from the front lawn.[55] For Dr. and Mrs. Robert Bush (1954), Church left the view unobstructed and perceptually extended the semi-rural Palo Alto garden into the adjoining flowing meadows and woods, captioning the site plan "They Own This—They See This" (fig. 132). Agreeing with Humphry Repton's view of cattle as objects of improvement, he borrowed the cows of nearby pastures, from whose grazing habits he protected the unfenced lawn by edging the property with a ha-ha (sunken fence).[56] Ever the pragmatist, Church based the reason for this extension of view not on aesthetic or sensorial grounds—the feeling of elation experienced in front of grand scenery—but on economics. Concluding these project descriptions, he wrote: "Someone else is maintaining [the neighboring property] and paying the taxes; you're enjoying it. . . . Someone else feeds and milks the cows. The Bushes look at them."[57]

Church constantly redefined the modern garden by focusing on functional rather than stylistic issues. His essay for the catalogue *Landscape Design* was titled "Transition: 1937–1948," referring to the time period between the first and second landscape architecture exhibitions. Giving little consideration, however, to the formal transformation that gardens had undergone during the eleven-year interval, instead he enumerated the social, economic, and functional changes that now shaped the new designs. In Church's view, "the landscape architect no longer [had] a choice between a functional or esthetic approach. Like it or not, the functions of the house have spilled out into the garden and must be provided for." Such modifications in American life called for new provisions in the garden. For instance, one built storage structures there to compensate for the attic and basement that had disappeared. The modern baby required a sandbox visible from both living room and kitchen, being "no longer dressed in white and taken around the block in perambulator for an airing," but "tossed, almost naked, into the sunniest spot in the back yard." The center of gravity of the house had altogether moved outward. Tea in the parlor had given way to cocktails on the terrace, which needed direct access to the pantry and a large enough expanse so "guests [wouldn't] back into the flower beds, but small enough so it [wouldn't] look like a parking lot." Despite its reduced scale, the garden also accommodated activities such as swimming, badminton, and croquet; if necessary, the lawn could double for croquet and the driveway for badminton. In addition to the service yard, one had to plan a garden service area, no matter how low maintenance the design, with tool closet, potting bench, and mulch pile. In other words, concluded Church, the space around the house is "made to produce living space, play space and work space."[58]

Ultimately Church exerted an influence on the profession of landscape architecture, not because of any particular project but rather the quality of his entire body of work.[59] He marketed the image of the modern California garden in numerous trade journals and shelter publications such as *Pencil Points, Architectural Forum, House Beautiful,* and *Sunset.* Perhaps most significant was Church's central role in producing the next generation of designers. As Theodore Bernardi, Wurster's partner, recalled: "I don't think of anybody being his competitor until he brought up his own tribe of competitors."[60] Several of the projects displayed in the 1948 catalogue *Landscape Design* were designed by once, or current, employees or collaborators of Thomas Church, such as Robert Royston, Lawrence Halprin, June Meehan, and Douglas Baylis.

Over a number of years, the professions of landscape architects and archi-

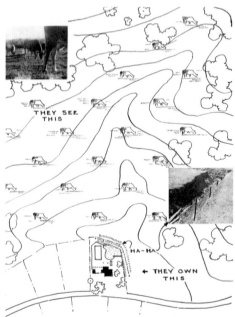

132.
Bush Garden, Palo Alto, 1954
Thomas Church
Conceptual site plan with ha-ha and pasture beyond
Published in **Gardens Are for People,** 1955

133.
Henderson House and Garden,
Hillsborough, 1957
Wurster, Bernardi, and Emmons
William Wurster with Thomas Church,
landscape architect
View from the veranda toward the pool

tects underwent osmosis. The former acted in accord with siting and architectural considerations, and the latter designed the house in relation to the
exterior spaces. Thus Elizabeth Mock, architecture and design curator at the
Museum of Modern Art, devoted a significant portion of *If You Want to Build
a House* to the design of surroundings, advising:

> *Think in terms of sun, view, domestic privacy and outdoor living. The land
> should be as carefully planned as the house itself. The two problems are really
> one and the same, as house and garden together constitute the living space.
> Questions of utility, space, light and upkeep are as important in the one as in
> the other, and the modern landscape architect works very much like the archi-
> tect in his choice and arrangement of materials.[61]*

In 1932 Church had opened his office in San Francisco on a floor below
William Wurster; for several decades their practices were interdependent.[62]
Although Church worked with other Bay Area architects, such as Gardner
Dailey, Hervey Parke Clark, and Ernest Born, Wurster apparently relied extensively, if not exclusively, on Church's expertise for landscape design well into
the 1940s.[63] Neither traditionalist nor modernist, Church was a "transitionist"
with a variety of modes. Ironically, it was his more classical strain that seemed
to appeal to Wurster, who, according to Royston, "felt that Tommy was really
a modern landscape architect. . . . Tommy's work *did* develop a kind of timeless
quality. His little recognizable details were subordinate to the spatial
qualities."[64]

Church and Wurster's collaboration on the second Henderson House (1957)
proved as effortless and harmonious as that of the early Pasatiempo projects.
Despite the formalism of the overall scheme and the sophistication of materials and details, the Henderson Garden responded simply to the plan of the
house as if architecture and landscape had been drawn by a single hand. While
Church had designed only the garden for the first Henderson project, he played
a more active role in the siting of the second house. As the lot was "solid with
trees," he reversed the approach taken at Pasatiempo, clearing the land instead
of designing around the existing vegetation.[65]

Church's plan for the garden reflected the skewed symmetry of the house.

The formal pool terminated the axis of light spaces formed by the glass court and the skylit veranda: elevated, it reflected sunlight during the day and glowed at night (fig. 133). Church paved the internal court with gravel, ornamented the center with a quatrefoil pool, and anchored the corners with orange trees and a mature Italian cypress, subtly disrupting the symmetrical balance of the space. In spite of apparent differences with the Henderson project, Church had come full circle from his Butler design. In place of the native live oaks that formed the point of departure of the Pasatiempo house, the existing vegetation served to frame the crisp lines of the Henderson House and Garden. Both projects, however, expressed the uninterrupted flow between architecture and landscape, and both designs recaptured nature—whether in a controlled or picturesque form—within the architecture.

In a 1938 article, "Of Houses as Places to Live," Talbot Hamlin praised the work of William Wurster for illustrating a "humanized" approach to designing a house. Both simple and flexible, Wurster's plans graciously accommodated the changes in living patterns that had occurred in the early twentieth century.[66] Similarly, Church addressed these changes in "gardens as places to live." As Wurster opened up his houses with "caves" and "living porches" (fig. 134), Church extended the architecture into the garden with decks and arbors and into the greater landscape with selective pruning and the technique of borrowed scenery. Landscape architect and planner Francis Violich saw Church as rising above the "competent exterior decorator" as he worked closely with the architect throughout the design process.[67] The collaboration between Wurster and Church ranged from the siting of the house to the design of brick patterns in diminutive terraces to the landscape planning of Federal Public Housing Authority projects. Church's graduate education as a planner may account for his ability to evaluate the relationship between architecture and landscape. But then again this facility may simply be due to human understanding, both of the client and of the architect.

In *Gardens Are for People,* Church quoted Sir George Sitwell, author of *On the Making of Gardens,* whom he had met on his 1926–27 voyage to Italy:

> *It may be argued further that real beauty is neither in garden nor landscape, but in the relation of both to the individual, that what we are seeking is not only a scenic setting for pool and fountain and parterre, but a background for life.[68]*

Both Church and Wurster avoided theory and formalism to create gardens and architecture that sought simplicity in the fulfillment of function. Because clients came first and styles varied accordingly, no project was typical, but all consistently responded to site and human factors.

Eventually, with landscape architecture no longer an exclusive accessory to architecture, Church gained great prominence, and the ties between him and Wurster loosened.[69] But their later collaborations revealed the same mutual understanding and respect as did early ones. In spite of its sophistication, the second Henderson House of 1959 expressed the refined balance of architecture and garden that was evident in their first collaborative projects in Pasatiempo. Thus their association ended as it had begun. Prescient of the architect and landscape architect's lifelong friendship and complementary professional skills, Elizabeth Church had written in 1932: "Certainly there could be no grander feeling than mine—that Tommy's complete admiration and mine for everything that you do might find an echo in you."[70]

And it did.

134.
Turner House and Terrace, Modesto, 1941.
William Wurster with Thomas Church,
landscape architect

Notes

For Elizabeth Church

1. "Homes Recall Simplicity of Mission Days: California Tradition Preserved in Architecture at Pasatiempo," *San Francisco Chronicle,* 4 June 1932, p. 7.

2. See the description of the house provided by Wurster's office for publication. Church File, William Wurster Archive, College of Environmental Design Documents Collection at the University of California at Berkeley (hereafter CED Documents Collection.). In her recollection of the design process, Elizabeth Church described the layout of the house as a product of the combined efforts of Wurster, Thomas Church, and herself. See Elizabeth Church, "A Life by the Side of Thomas Church," interviews by Suzanne B. Riess, 30 December 1975 and 20 April 1977, in *Thomas D. Church, Landscape Architect,* vol. 2 (Berkeley: University of California, Regional Oral History Office, The Bancroft Library, 1978), pp. 382–83, 399, 405–06.

3. Ibid. See also Elizabeth Church, "Pasatiempo," *California Arts and Architecture* 39, no. 6 (June 1931), p. 42.

4. William Wurster received an Honor Award from the American Institute of Architects in the category "Small houses under seven rooms" for the Church House and the Howes House, also at Pasatiempo. See *San Francisco Chronicle,* 4 June 1932. Publications that featured the Church House and Studio included *California Arts and Architecture, Architectural Record, Architectural Forum, Sunset, Homes of the West, Pencil Points, Redwood Association Bulletin,* and *La Maison* (Brussels).

5. Shortly thereafter, Elizabeth Church also wrote to Wurster: "No flaw—no crack in its rare charm—have we discovered in our house. We are so deeply grateful to you that it will take years of praise to make it properly known. . . . Our cup most certainly runneth over." Appreciation was unanimous, and far reaching; the Church House would grace the cover of a Belgian architectural magazine as late as 1955. In 1948 Catharine Griffen, who had purchased the Pasatiempo house earlier, also lauded its simplicity and warmth in a letter to Wurster: "I love my little white house, and enjoy living in it. Of course you planned it for the Churches, but the fact remains that it fits me like a glove—fits my personality and fits my needs. The house has endeared itself to me during all these years I have lived in it—14 now—it is so intimate and comfortable and so closely tied to the garden." Letter from Catharine Griffen to William Wurster, 8 February 1948. All three letters are in the Church File, William Wurster Archive, CED Documents Collection.

6. William Wilson Wurster, "The Unity of Architecture and Landscape Architecture," in *Landscape Design* (San Francisco: San Francisco Museum of Art and Association of Landscape Architects, San Francisco Region, 1948), p. 7

7. In a letter to William Wurster, Oakland-based landscape architect Floyd Mick accused Church of conducting negotiations with Mick's clients and prospective clients while still receiving a salary from him. Wurster replied: "The Santa Cruz work was brought to your organization because of my friendship and admiration for Mr. Church. Mr. Church immediately explained that it would go through your office, as he was working for you. . . . An offer was made directly to Mr. Church, which came, I feel sure, as a great surprise to us both. It was clearly a proposal from my clients based upon their need of having someone on the ground and their feeling that Mr. Church was the man for such a position." Letter from Floyd Mick to William Wurster, 4 August 1930, and reply from William Wurster to Floyd Mick, 8 August 1930. Church File, William Wurster Archive, CED Documents Collection.

8. Church received an A.B. from the Division of Landscape Gardening and Floriculture in the College of Agriculture at Berkeley in 1923 and was admitted to the master's degree program in City Planning and Landscape Architecture at Harvard in 1924. He worked as an intern with John Nolen City Planners and the landscape architecture office of Stiles & Van Kleek, both in Boston. Awarded a Sheldon Traveling Fellowship from Harvard University, he spent 1926–27 in Italy, France, and Spain. In 1928–29 he was an assistant professor at Ohio State University and in 1929–30 a lecturer at Berkeley. He established his own office in 1931.

9. Elizabeth Church, "Pasatiempo," p. 54.

10. Ibid.

11. See Margaret Olthof Goldsmith, *Designs for Outdoor Living* (New York: George W. Stewart 1941), pp. 322–23.

12. Schemes A and B were designed on 30 January 1934 and Scheme C on 30 March 1934; the latter was revised into its final form in May 1935. See Wurster Archives, file 2732, CED Documents Collection.

13. Lucy H. Butler, "A Pasatiempo Client Recreates the Scene in 1935: Church and Wurster," interview by Suzanne B. Riess, 27 June 1977, in *Thomas D. Church, Landscape Architect*, vol. 1, p. 143.

14. In spite of these preventive measures, excessive water eventually caused the death of the oak, according to Mrs. Butler, in "A Pasatiempo Client Recreates the Scene in 1935," p. 140.

15. Thomas Church, *Gardens Are for People* (New York: Reinhold), 1955, pp. 3, 48.

16. Quoted in Kenneth H. Cardwell, *Bernard Maybeck: Artisan, Architect, Artist* (Santa Barbara: Peregrine Smith, 1977), p. 57.

17. Dianne Harris, "Making Gardens in the Athens of the West: Bernard Maybeck and the San Francisco Bay Region Tradition in Landscape and Garden Design," in *The Regional Garden in the United States,* ed. Therese O'Malley and Marc Treib (Washington, D.C.: Dumbarton Oaks, 1995), pp. 43–68.

18. Ojai was originally named Nordhoff in honor of the *New York Herald* columnist Charles Nordhoff. Next to this rustic village was the Thacher School, a preparatory school founded by Sherman Thacher in 1888, which was attended by the sons of the wealthy. Church, who went to the Nordhoff public school, later collaborated on several projects with Adaline Kent, niece of Sherman Thacher, and consulted on a landscape project for his school.

19. Church's grandfather, a retired judge on the Ohio Supreme Court named Wilson, apparently cultivated extensive terraces of citrus varieties on his Ojai property, where Thomas and Margaret Church grew up. See Elizabeth Church, "A Life by the Side of Thomas Church," p. 447. In 1916 E. D. Libbey, owner of a 500-acre estate and Spanish-style castle, persuaded the community to rename Nordhoff as Ojai and to recast the buildings in a Hispanic style. By then "the climate was advertised; resort hotels sprang up; retired men of means came here and took up ranching; ranchers took up culture, businessmen took up tourists; and architectural development was rapid." See *The WPA Guide to California* (New York: Hastings House, 1939; reprint, New York: Pantheon, 1984), pp. 471–72.

20. Elizabeth Church, "A Life by the Side of Thomas Church," p. 378.

21. Church, "A Study of Mediterranean Gardens and Their Adaptability to California Conditions," M.S. thesis, Harvard University, 1927, n.p.

22. "[Church] did a few public housing projects, but I don't think it was because he had a social consciousness or felt a great desire to do them." Geraldine Knight Scott, "A Landscape Architect Discusses Training Since 1926 and Changes in the Profession," interview by Suzanne B. Riess, 3 February 1977, in *Thomas D. Church, Landscape Architect,* vol. 1, p. 27. Church served as landscape architect for a number of defense-housing projects, including Happy Camp, California, 1943; Victory Housing Project, San Francisco, 1944 (with Hutchinson and Bernardi); and Parker Homes, Sacramento, 1943 (with Wurster). See Defense Housing Files, Wurster Archives, CED Documents Collection.

23. Church, discussion with the Northern California Chapter of the American Society of Landscape Architects, 9 February 1971, Transcript courtesy of Michael Laurie, reprinted in *Thomas D. Church, Landscape Architect,* vol. 2, p. 759.

24. Hanson did realize a garden in 1932 for Mr. and Mrs. Daniel Murphy in Los Angeles. Although by that time he had already moved into the field of land planning and development, he worked on the Murphy estate with Lutah Maria Riggs, a Montecito architect. See A. E. Hanson, *An Arcadian Landscape: The California Gardens of A. E. Hanson, 1920–1932,* ed. David Gebhard and Sheila Lynds (Los Angeles: Hennessey & Ingalls, 1985); and David Gebhard, *Lutah Maria Riggs: A Woman in Architecture, 1921–1980* (Santa Barbara: Capra Press/Santa Barbara Museum of Art, 1992).

25. Among Hanson's garden designs were those for Harold Lloyd in Beverly Hills (1925–29), Kirk Johnson in Montecito (1928–29), and Archibald Young in Pasadena (1929). See Hanson, *An Arcadian Landscape.*

26. The models for these were located in Spain and designed by Jean-Claude-Nicolas Forestier: the garden for the Casa del Rey Moro in Ronda (1912) and the Parque de María Luisa in Seville (1914). Hanson praised both designs in his account of a European voyage taken in 1927–28. See Hanson, *An Arcadian Landscape,* pp. 9–12; and Dorothée Imbert, "J.C.N. Forestier: Plants and Planning," in *The Modernist Garden in France* (New Haven: Yale University Press, 1993), pp. 11–25.

27. Church, "A Study of Mediterranean Gardens," n.p.

28. Harriet Henderson, "A Hillsborough Client Recalls Two Gardens, 1934, 1954," interview by Suzanne B. Riess, 8 June 1976, in *Thomas D. Church, Landscape Architect,* vol. 1, p. 114.

29. Church, *Gardens Are for People,* p. 85.

30. Wurster had designed an earlier house, in 1930, for Harriet and Wellington Henderson, also to be situated in Hillsborough. Lockwood de Forest, Jr., the Santa Barbara landscape architect, had planned the grounds with formal spaces as well as naturalistic areas heavily planted and traversed by meandering paths. Both site plan and sketch for a pergola are in the CED Documents Collection. Mrs. Henderson recalled Wurster's early scheme as being in the "Monterey-Colonial" Style. See Henderson, "A Hillsborough Client Recalls," p. 114.

31. Church apparently served only as the garden designer; he had nothing to do with the siting of the house, as it had already been built when he was consulted. See Henderson, "A Hillsborough Client Recalls," p. 115.

32. *Contemporary Landscape Architecture,* (San Francisco: San Francisco Museum of Art, 1937), model 9, p. 34.

33. Church, "Make It Geometric," in *Your Private World* (San Francisco: Chronicle Books, 1969), p. 22.

34. "Holiday" is illustrated on the first page of *Contemporary Landscape Architecture;* the description of the model is on p. 34.

35. Grace L. McCann Morley, "Foreword," *Contemporary Landscape Architecture,* p. 13.

36. "Fitting the Garden to the House: Exhibit in San Francisco Shows the Best in Gardens," *Christian Science Monitor,* 17 February 1937. "Modern Architecture: International Exhibition" was organized by the Museum of Modern Art in New York in 1932.

37. "Fitting the Garden to the House."

38. André Vera was most active and prolific between the 1910s and 1930s. The gardens he realized with his brother Paul were extensively published, and his books—*Le nouveau jardin* (1912) and *Les jardins* (1919), among others—were reviewed internationally. See Dorothée Imbert, "André Vera; Paul Vera; Jean-Charles Moreux: Modernity and Tradition," in *The Modernist Garden in France,* pp. 71–107.

39. See "Country house and garden. Residence of Mr. and Mrs. Hervey Parke Clark, Woodside, California," in *Contemporary Landscape Architecture,* p. 33.

40. Church subsequently altered the garden he designed for architect Hervey Parke Clark in Woodside in 1937. The shapes described were implemented around 1940. For a description of the various stages of the garden's history, see Pam-Anela Messenger, "1936: Woodside, California," in "The Art of Thomas Dolliver Church." Unpublished master's thesis, Department of Landscape Architecture, University of California at Berkeley, 19 June 1976, pp. 45–69.

41. Church, *Gardens Are for People,* p. 104.

42. See Michael Laurie, "Thomas Church, California Gardens and Public Landscapes," in *Modern Landscape Architecture: A Critical Review,* ed. Marc Treib (Cambridge: MIT Press, 1993), p. 171. Robert Royston recalled working on the garden for the fair; although he acknowledged a turning point in Church's design approach after his 1937 trip to Finland, Royston saw him as a "transitionist [who] came from a knowledge of what the

book said, derivative of the Renaissance." See Robert Royston, "A Landscape Architect Considers Changes in Practices since his Church Apprenticeship," interview by Suzanne B. Riess, 11 March 1976, in *Thomas D. Church, Landscape Architect,* vol. 1, p. 217.

43. Richard B. Freeman, "Preface: Landscape Architecture," in *Landscape Design* (San Francisco: San Francisco Museum of Art, 1948), p. 3.

44. Stephen C. Pepper, "Introduction to Garden Design," in *Landscape Design,* p. 50.

45. Claire Falkenstein, "Sculpture in Relation to Landscape Architecture," in *Landscape Design,* p. 9.

46. Garrett Eckbo, "The Esthetics of Planting," in *Landscape Design,* pp. 17–18. Eckbo subsequently developed his arguments in "Anti-Gravity Materials: Plants and Planting," in his *Landscape for Living* (New York: F. W. Dodge, 1950), pp. 93–115.

47. Christopher Tunnard wrote *Gardens in the Modern Landscape* in 1938. After he moved to America and joined the faculty of the Yale Department of City Planning, a second edition was published, augmented with examples of modern American gardens. All the projects illustrated in this portfolio were his own, except for Frank Lloyd Wright's Taliesin West (no landscape architect cited) and Thomas Church's 1939 World's Fair Garden. See *Gardens in the Modern Landscape,* 2nd. ed. (London: Architectural Press; New York: Charles Scribner's Sons, 1948), p. 172.

48. Garrett Eckbo, cited by Laurie, "Thomas Church, California Gardens and Public Landscapes," p. 172.

49. See Church, "Beach Gardens," in *Gardens Are for People,* pp. 129–35.

50. Ibid., p. 131.

51. *Shakkei* (from the Japanese) captures through framing and mimesis a distant vista as part of the garden. See Marc Treib and Ron Herman, *A Guide to the Gardens of Kyoto* (Tokyo: Shufunotomo, 1980).

52. Church, "A Free-Form Pool Is at Home in This Natural Setting," *Gardens Are for People,* pp. 227–28.

53. Ibid.

54. Ibid., pp. 28–31.

55. Ibid., p. 29, and Church, "Architectural Pattern Can Take the Place of Flowers," *House Beautiful* 90, no 1 (January 1948), p. 41. Church also designed a garden for Mr. and Mrs. William Stark of Fresno (1950), which looked out on the tree-studded prospect of the adjacent golf course so that it seemed part of their own property.

56. Church, *Gardens Are for People,* pp. 30–31. Humphry Repton observed: "Both [boats on the water and cattle on the lawns] are real objects of improvement, and give animation to the scene; indeed . . . a large lawn without cattle is one of the melancholy appendages of solitary grandeur observable in the pleasure-grounds of the past century." *Sketches and Hints on Landscape Gardening* (1794); reprinted by J. C. Loudon, in *The Landscape Gardening and Landscape Architecture of the Late Humphry Repton, Esq.* (1840; reprint, Westmead, Farnborough, England: Gregg International, 1969), pp. 81–82.

57. Church, *Gardens Are for People,* pp. 28–31.

58. Church, "Transition: 1937–1948," in *Landscape Design,* pp. 14–15.

59. "As far as I am concerned Tommy made a tremendous contribution to the profession, not really in the avant-garde of design, but in the consistency of good work." Robert Royston, "A Landscape Architect Considers Changes," p. 222.

60. Theodore Bernardi, "Two Architects and a Photographer Recall the Hard Work and the Good Times with Church and Wurster, 1930s, 1940s," interview by Suzanne B. Riess, 19 April 1977, in *Thomas D. Church, Landscape Architect,* vol. 1, p. 97.

61. Elizabeth Mock, *If You Want to Build a House* (New York: Museum of Modern Art, 1946), p. 81.

62. Apparently employees also moved from one office to the other. Lawrence Halprin first contacted Wurster before being hired by Church, and Germano Milono, who worked as an architect for Church on several projects, was originally employed by Wurster.

63. After 1950, when Wurster returned to San Francisco from his sojourn at MIT and moved his office, the collaboration with Church became more occasional. Wurster seemed to rely on younger landscape architects, such as Lawrence Halprin, in sympathy for his partners Theodore Bernardi and Donn Emmons. Conversation with Donn Emmons, 20 December 1994, Sausalito. Halprin collaborated with Wurster, Bernardi and Emmons on Greenwood Common, Berkeley (1950), and Woodlake, San Mateo (1965), among other projects.

64. Royston, "A Landscape Architect Considers Changes," p. 221.

65. Mrs. Henderson recalled that Church selected the lot and placed the house and the driveway. "A Hillsborough Client Recalls," pp. 119–20.

66. Talbot Faulkner Hamlin, "Of Houses as Places to Live," *Pencil Points* 19, no. 8 (August 1938), pp. 487–89.

67. Francis Violich, "A Professor of City Planning and Landscape Architecture Considers where the Professions have moved since the 1930s," interview by Suzanne B. Riess, 21 January 1976, in *Thomas D. Church, Landscape Architect,* vol. 1, p. 51.

68. Sir George Sitwell, *On the Making of Gardens* (1909; reprint, New York and London: Charles Scribner's Sons/Gerald Duckworth, 1951), pp. 26–27. Quoted by Thomas Church, in *Gardens Are for People,* p. 3.

69. Although Church accorded prominent credit to architects, designers, photographers, and contractors in *Gardens Are for People,* all architectural traces had disappeared from his second book, *Your Private World* (1969).

70. Elizabeth Church to William Wurster, ca. 1932. CED Documents Collection.

Building Design as Social Art:
The Public Architecture of William Wurster, 1935–1950

Greg Hise

Greg Hise

Let us accept a minimum by way of basic needs with the hope that we will really build up from the simple, rather than down from the complex and outmoded. . . . [This requires] a fine balance which will come only with the most realistic adjustments of cost, space, materials, construction, mechanical features—and yes, even neighborhoods.

—WILLIAM WURSTER 1946[1]

What is modern housing? Modern housing is a collective effort to create habitable domestic environments within the framework of an integrated community.

—LEWIS MUMFORD 1934[2]

135.
Prebilt House prototype, San Anselmo, 1945
Wurster and Bernardi with Ernest Kump
Assembling the "arch-ribs" (detail)

These epigraphs underscore two themes essential for understanding William Wurster's architecture: the minimum house and modern community planning. Although we tend to think of Wurster as a designer of housing for clients with means, over time he engaged in what we might term social housing, that is, an effort to address issues of availability and affordability, as well as what he termed the "environment that surrounds and controls our buildings . . . the frame in which we live and work."[3] In concert with many of his professional colleagues, Wurster was interested in transforming home-building into a modern industry fine-tuned for the quantity production of efficient dwellings. For Wurster, the design of these small units, typically under 1,000 square feet, provided an opportunity to refine a rational plan with multifunctional spaces. Although precedents for these experiments can be traced to better-known European studies and prototypes, there were concomitant and correlative investigations in the United States. California, Wurster's principal milieu, was an important locale. Here self-builders, tradespeople, and developers raised popular house types such as the bungalow and mail-order kits. And California's speculative homebuilders, many of whom headed comparatively large firms, given national norms, devised important innovations in construction practices and community planning.[4]

During the 1920s, concern with rising costs and declining ownership rates heightened interest in identifying and codifying a standard minimum house. The Depression and consequent building interregnum intensified these efforts. Californian Herbert Hoover carried the small-house ideal to Washington, D.C., in 1921. As secretary of commerce and later president, he formulated, endorsed, and enacted policy and programs designed to encourage residential construction, extend home ownership, and set neighborhood standards. The latter included the design of infrastructure systems, street layouts, lot patterns, and access to amenities and services; in other words, progressive land-use planning. At the same time, technicians employed by organizations and agencies such as the Pierce Foundation and later the National Housing Agency and American Public Health Association were conducting empirical research, analyzing users in situ. From this data they set spatial standards, principally minimum requirements, and lobbied builders and buyers to substitute pantries and eating nooks for "wasteful" basements and dining rooms. The parallels to Wurster's "room with no name" are apparent. Catherine Bauer was active in these investigations as a participant and occasional critic.[5]

When introducing himself and his practice at a Washington, D.C., meeting of prefabricators in 1941, Wurster chose the virtues of small scale as a distin-

guishing factor. "I have been doing in the main small houses . . . [and] have always had a great interest in securing the most for the money and in doing small things because I feel that even though inexpensive, the essence of a little thing can be the best of its kind. . . . [Y]ou should seek out the virtues inherent in what you are doing, showing no modesty about it, and then go ahead and make something good out of what is your problem."[6]

Wurster designed minimum dwellings for private clients, including the Dondo and Harker houses and the Shaw vacation house, but he also developed prototypes for exhibitions, magazines, department stores, and material manufacturers. For example, in 1938 *Life* magazine approached Wurster regarding its housing program coordinated by *Architectural Forum* editor Howard Meyers. The program's objective, as explained to the architect, was to alert potential home buyers to recent technical progress in housing, as well as to the Federal Housing Administration's (FHA) recent financial innovations. The housing problem, they assured Wurster, was "neither one of need nor opportunity, but of public knowledge."[7] The magazine publisher offered Wurster $350 for his design and documentation: a perspective illustrating unit siting and garden, dimensioned quarter-inch plans, material and equipment specifications, and brief notes outlining features that met the client's specific needs.

Meyers injected realism into the program by selecting families from four different regions—Philadelphia, Atlanta, Minneapolis, and Los Angeles—with annual incomes varying from $2,000 to $10,000. To enhance reader interest, *Life* matched each family with two architects; one would design a modern house, the other traditional. Meyers paired Wurster with Los Angeles architect H. Roy Kelley and assigned them the Calverts, a Southland couple whose $3,000 annual income afforded them a detached, three-bedroom, one-bath rental in the West Adams district, with a garage and small yard for their three-year-old son, Dinky. The Calverts dreamed of a two-bedroom house with a den convertible to a guest room, a rustic living room and dinette, an all-electric kitchen with breakfast nook, and a darkroom for Paul Calvert, a *Los Angeles Times* photographer.

Architectural Forum documented the architects' design process in "*Life* Houses." Initially Wurster sketched out a 960-square-foot, two-story cube. He set this aside for a linear and then a U-shaped, courtyard plan. The latter, a regional type with deep historical roots, allowed him to capture maximum space at minimal cost. In plan, the entry and living room linked a kitchen and service wing with the bedrooms and bath (figs. 175, 176). Wurster placed the den and a sun deck over the garage and dining area.

Kelley produced a compact plan "following the traditional character of houses developed by the early settlers in California who came from New England." The architect's historicism did not deter the Calverts, who preferred Kelley's "subtle and harmonious blend of Spanish and New England Colonial" (figs. 173, 174). As for Wurster's modern house, *Forum* reported that Mrs. Calvert rejected it "at first glance."[8] *Life*'s readers responded more favorably when the design appeared in a twenty-two-page "Housing Portfolio." Program staff tracked requests for plans and specifications and forwarded these to Wurster. Interest came from all regions of the country, including an inquiry from Kaufmann Stores and a builder, both in Pittsburgh who proposed a hipped-roof version to meet climatic conditions. Wurster declined graciously. *Life* also sold "full color" models. Fred Van Dam, a Santa Monica pharmacist, purchased a model of Wurster's design and displayed it at his store. He wrote to the architect, informing him of his clients' "favorable comments" and his intention to build. Appreciative letters from building-product firms and suppliers clutter the project files.[9]

Wurster valued and consistently tapped producers' and tradespeople's experiential knowledge. Formal collaboration with manufacturers and suppliers underscored his attention to construction processes and building techniques. For example, when Edward L. Soule, head of Soule Steel Company, a San Francisco-based fabricator of iron and steel products, approached Wurster concerning his interest in manufacturing sectional housing, the architect recognized an opportunity to develop a small, low-cost prototype and to explore site planning multiple, quantity-produced units. At the time, the Soule Company was supplying the Farm Security Administration (FSA) with modular shelters for migrant agricultural workers in California's Central Valley. At these sites a crew of six assembled five panels into a finished unit in ten minutes.[10] The FSA contract alerted Soule to the benefits of combining quantity production and housing.

In November 1937 the Wurster office produced schematic studies for a "Unit Steel House." At first the plan of these one-bedroom dwellings, approximately 750 square feet in size, took the form of a modified shotgun, with a linear progression of rooms and direct connection from one to the next. Design drawings show units sited on 50-by-100-foot lots, set back twenty-five feet from the street and tight to a side property line. Ironically, or perhaps in response to these sketches, Soule sent Wurster a copy of Albert Farwell Bemis's *The Evolving House* and a unit plan based on Bemis's four-foot modular measure. In a cover letter Soule presented his rationale. First, Bemis's system aligned with his firm's preferred stud (two feet on center) and truss spacing (four-foot centers). More importantly, a four-foot module might "lead to economy in the house layout" and make possible a "flow through the warehouse. . . . If we can coordinate architecture and line production methods, I think we are tending toward the answer for low-cost production."[11]

Two weeks later Soule sent Wurster a memo "on a subject which has received your consideration . . . facing residences in a tract toward the *rear* of the lot and accentuating the gardens there." The manufacturer set out "this rather *radical* subject" as a series of design strategies: placing the garage, kitchen, and dinette or dining room on the street and the living room and bedrooms toward a rear garden [emphasis in original]. Soule posited both social and technical benefits. These included improved security and safety as well as reduced service runs and a shorter driveway.[12]

Revised drawings incorporated Soule's recommendations. Wurster devised a 28-by-28-foot, one-bedroom unit with a living room and dinette, galley kitchen and breakfast nook, a utility and service room, and a generous entry porch, or "shelter" (fig. 136). This basic house type, Scheme A, became the basis for a series of iterations; a two-bedroom version, Scheme B, was sited against the opposing lot line. A plot plan with fourteen units illustrates one solution to the challenge of creating variety and visual interest from repetitive units (fig. 137). Here Wurster proposed alternative unit siting, plan rotation, variations in roof types, and alternative locations for garages to enliven what could have been a homogeneous tract. Of course plan rotation compromised Soule's preference for placing the living room and bedrooms to the rear for access to a private yard and garden.[13]

Wurster's approach was consistent with strategies first popularized by large-scale builders such as David Bohannon in the Bay Area, Walter H. Leimert, active in Oakland and Los Angeles, and Southland developers Fritz B. Burns and Fred W. Marlow, entrepreneurs who successfully consolidated land subdivision, construction, and sales into a single organization. These builders applied progressive land-planning principles drawn from England's garden suburbs, particularly Raymond Unwin and Barry Parker's streetscape designs for Letchworth, by way of Radburn, New Jersey, and the American regionalists, most notably Clarence Stein, Henry Wright, and the Regional Planning Association of America.

Following passage of the 1934 Housing Act, the FHA's Land Planning

136.
Unit Steel House, 1937
William Wurster
Revised plans and elevations

137.
Unit Steel House, 1937
William Wurster
Site plan

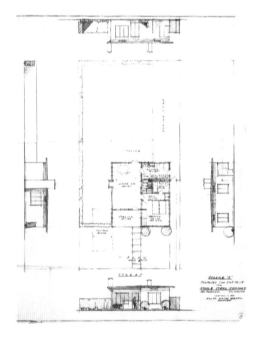

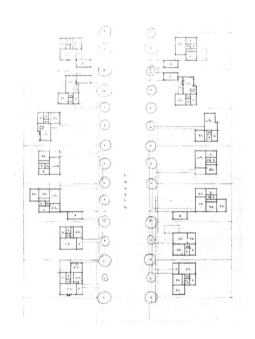

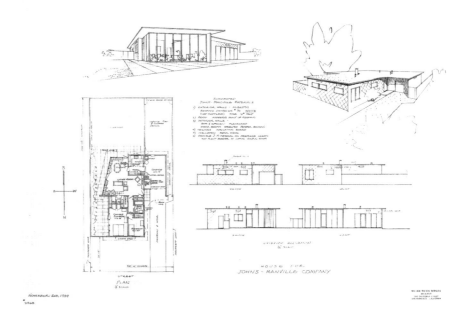

138.
House for Johns-Manville Company, 1939
William Wurster
Plan and elevations

Division endorsed these design practices. The Administration's mortgage-insurance program virtually guaranteed its technical bulletins would become a blueprint for neighborhood- or community-scale projects. For example, *Planning Neighborhoods for Small Houses* contrasted examples of "good" and "bad" site planning. The former included diagrams illustrating dwelling set-backs calculated to evince picturesque curves along straight streets. Wurster's contribution to this ongoing investigation was the plotting of a formal, cadenced building line, a gesture designed to introduce a relatively expansive mid-block opening.[14]

In addition to his interest in the quantity production of small single-family units placed in speculative tracts, Soule continued investigating compact housing for migrant workers and engaged Wurster in this effort. The architect, clearly intrigued by the challenge, wrote Soule in February 1938, informing him that "we feel there is a great field for a fifteen-foot square (225-square-foot) unit with kitchen, bath, and heater room all installed, to be turned on edge and transported by truck for all sorts of summer camp work."[15] Although nothing came of this specific proposal, Wurster had subsequent opportunities to examine minimum housing and community planning.

In 1939 Randolph Evans, a New York architect associated with Johns-Manville's Housing Guild, queried Wurster concerning a minimum house highlighting the company's building products. The guild offered $150 for a set of sketches. Wurster accepted enthusiastically, expressing admiration for "what [Johns-Manville] is doing for the cause of modest houses."[16] Evans supplied the architect with plans for a hypothetical unit, spelling out the design parameters in terms of rooms, dimensions, and lot size. Three days later Wurster received a telegraph with revised requirements, along with a terse, four-word explanation: "Changes due to war."

An undated, hard-line plan and elevations show a planar, 880-square-foot unit with an angled, glass-walled living and dining "space" and an exterior clad in white asbestos shingles (fig. 138). In mid-October Evans alerted Wurster that despite Johns-Manville's interest in adding a "modern house" to its 1940 program, these plans were a "selling medium" for products; therefore, "we must stick to the styles which are in greatest demand throughout the country. There is no great demand for the ultra-modern style in the lower price brackets at the present time." The company also questioned whether contractors in "outlying sections of the country" were equipped to apply built-up roofing, this despite the fact that Wurster had specified a Manville product. In relaying

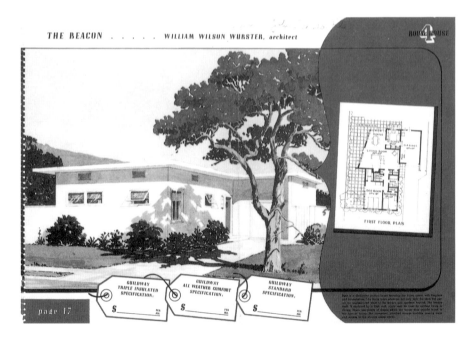

139.
"Four-Room House" prototype, 1940
William Wurster
Featured in the Johns-Manville Company's
Housing Guild's small-house catalogue

this message, Evans underscored his support for the design and suggested that one of the program's objectives was to stimulate the imaginations of prospective homebuilders and buyers, "and your scheme does just that."[17]

Eventually Evans secured approval for a flat roof, but Johns-Manville insisted the living room be squared off and a new exterior finish selected. Wurster responded defiantly, questioning whether "my name [should be] under such an emasculated affair," while arguing that the living-room shape and exterior shingles were "absolutely imperative." The latter, he believed, were essential for design "honesty"; Johns-Manville's #70 shingle "fills the bill perfectly and does not become confused with fake shingles."[18]

The Wurster prototype, a "Four-Room House," appeared as "The Beacon" in the Housing Guild's 1940 small-house catalogue (fig. 139). Reflecting on the collaboration in a letter to Johns-Manville, Wurster underscored his affinity for the guild's program, which "is close to my interest[.] [T]his office has made every effort to bridge the gap between the small job and the large work which falls more easily into the Architect's office." Then Wurster went on to challenge the guild on two substantive issues. First he criticized the brochure's focus on products, which suggested that new materials and equipment alone could improve living conditions. More significant perhaps was Wurster's critique of the presentation, which implied that housing, in terms of both production and use, was equivalent to the motor car, a position he considered an oversimplification.[19]

Catherine Bauer shared this perspective and had formulated a more stringent critique. In an unpublished review of *Housing America,* a *Fortune* magazine compendium published in 1932, she challenged the commonly held assumption that factory-based prefabrication could meet the current crisis in housing inventory and affordability. Bauer used the editors' bias for a new "big industry" to make her point: "[T]he very reason the dwelling business has been so backward is the fact that mechanization has so little to do with it. Shelter is inseparable from problems of land, government, and income distribution." In her view, *Fortune's* editors understood housing solely as an inefficiently produced commodity. Their solution, a factory-fabricated dwelling set up on individual lots by individual entrepreneurs and sold through the same "indefensible Own Your Own Home propaganda," succeeded simply in shifting production from contractors to the "more nauseous cunning of high-pressured national [firms engaged in] cosmetic advertising."[20] Wurster and Bauer feared that stories detailing housing "built in a day" would lull people into a false complacency regarding the depth of need and the breadth of the response necessary for solutions.

Their concern reveals the degree to which pundits, the press, and the public had linked housing progress with mass production. During the interwar years technicians, design professionals, and entrepreneurs shared an abiding fascination with factory-assembled dwellings and panelized housing, which they imagined propelling building into the modern era. Contemporary observers from many fields believed "Homes built like Fords" could eliminate waste and inefficiency, reduce final costs, and improve housing conditions for society's less fortunate. In truth, these commentators were enamored of Ford's vertically and horizontally linked corporation, which encompassed not only belt-line manufacturing but also marketing and merchandising through a network of licensed dealers and maintenance.[21] Wurster and Bauer, on the other hand, preached the gospel of quantity production, reducing costs through large-scale operations and rationalized building practices. They advocated design and planning that anticipated savings through a judicious siting of units and systems, component standardization and pre-assembly, and the on-site application of jigs and other techniques adapted from belt-line processes.[22]

Increasingly during the late 1930s and then almost exclusively from 1941 onward, the federal government enlisted designers, homebuilders, and quantity production for the World War II homefront effort. Because defense-related employment and economic opportunity were not distributed evenly across the country, constructing, equipping, and operating an "Arsenal for Democracy" required a mobilization of workers to production plants. Federal expenditures guided this migratory stream. To save time and money, the Defense Council channeled prime contracts to firms with existing plant and the capacity to expand. The South and West received a disproportionate share of jobs and job seekers. The President's Committee on Congested Production Areas (CCPA) tracked population growth in fifteen designated centers throughout the war; Pacific Coast cities set the pace. California industries secured over ten percent of the production-contract total. Here wartime manufacturing centered on shipbuilding and aircraft firms located in metropolitan areas.[23]

While almost everyone rejoiced to see lines forming at factory gates rather than at soup kitchens, city administrators faced challenging boomtown conditions, as newcomers overwhelmed existing infrastructure and services.[24] In the 26 March 1941 edition, *PM* magazine reported, "No Housing in California for New Defense Migrants." An October 1941 *Oakland Tribune* article, "Migration to California at New Peak: Job Seekers Coming for Defense Work Greatest Influx Yet," spoke to the magnitude of migration as well as public perception. The author drew parallels to the "mad rush of gold miners in 1849" and the more recent influx of agricultural laborers. Catherine Bauer, speaking as vice-president of the California Housing and Planning Association, reminded her "Town Meeting of the Air" radio audience that the state's population had increased twelve percent in two years. This translated into 800,000 newcomers, an increase that "makes the once famous *Grapes of Wrath* problem look like a picnic. . . . And hundreds of thousands more are still needed."[25]

In Bay Area communities such as Vallejo (200 percent increase, 1940–43) and Richmond (250 percent increase, 1940–43), the sheer number of incoming war workers taxed existing accommodations beyond their capacity, creating an urban equivalent of the better-known Depression-era "Hoovervilles." The USO-Travelers Aid Service found Richmond defense workers and their families living in converted storefronts, theaters, trailers, garages, automobiles, and chicken coops.[26]

While newcomers and long-term residents endured shortages and hardship, defense contractors and a military dependent on the timely production of matériel perceived poor housing and the lack of community services as a grave threat.[27] To address this emergency, Congress approved the Lanham Act in October 1940. The legislation, with amendments, appropriated $1.3 billion for war-worker housing in areas where acute shortages impeded the defense effort. In the San Francisco Bay Area, the Federal Works Agency (FWA) oversaw a program of temporary housing, trailers, and demountable dormitory units. In March 1941 a local civil defense official identified the urgent need for community-scale projects, noting that "whole new towns are springing up, a thousand houses at a clip, where yesterday were empty fields and where today there are no provisions for sewers, playgrounds, fire and police protection, hospital facilities, and all other local services."[28]

At first the federal response was decentralized, and multiple agencies received projects. Following its successful design and construction of rural settlements—in cases such as Woodville, virtual new towns—the defense housing coordinator drafted the San Francisco FSA office (Region IX) to produce temporary housing for war workers in the Bay Area and San Diego. At Vallejo the agency completed housing for 3,200 Navy Yard workers in forty demountable dormitories and 157 cabins.[29]

In his notes for a 1942 office tour Wurster singled out the FSA, which "is doing the most brilliant work there is in architecture." Elaborating on this assessment in an article, "Architecture Broadens Its Base," Wurster described the Depression's effects on architects and architectural practice, arguing in a mock exclamatory tone that in the 1930s "architects *chose* to work for the Government . . . [and] we had the FSA migrant camps in California, designed with real brilliance by [Burton] Cairns and [Vernon] DeMars. Minimum shelter for human beings became 'architecture.' The design of buildings emerged as a social art, and I hope it will never be placed exclusively on the luxury shelf again" [emphasis in original].[30]

Catherine Bauer also praised the FSA, noting the "economy, good sense, and technical brilliance" of its community design. According to Bauer, if the defense emergency mandated stopgap housing, it should be assigned to the Farm Security Administration. Other agencies did not fare as well in her assessment. She lambasted the Public Buildings Administration (PBA) in a 1941 postoccupancy evaluation that the Federal Works Agency commissioned for Linda Vista, a PBA project in San Diego. Bauer faulted the "politically powerful old-line agency" for its lack of both housing experience and "concern for either the immediate or long-term implications" for existing communities. Her analysis followed a comprehensive survey, with attention to demographics, site planning and community facilities, maintenance and management, and unit design. "Inside the city limits of San Diego," she concluded, "the PBA planned 3,000 dwellings for a nice piece of desert they optioned, several miles from any existing utilities or schools, without consulting local officials. An unbuildable site-plan was prepared in Washington, DC. Needless to say, the whole thing is still in deadlock in spite of the city's dire need."[31] Here Bauer rehearsed a familiar brief in favor of local decision making, design, and control, which she understood as essential for crafting successful housing policy and programs. She lobbied stridently for hiring design professionals whose knowledge of conditions ranging from climate to culture would provide considerable advantage over stock plans.

Through her interviews with Linda Vista tenants, Bauer found a universal concern about the dearth of shops and basic services. Around San Diego she uncovered a consensus regarding the need for commercial buildings in the project, a perspective shared even by "conservative realtors." Next on the list were school buildings, community space, and health facilities.[32] Prior to this assignment, Bauer had examined retail operations as a component of community planning. With the architect and planner Clarence Stein, she undertook a pioneering study at Radburn to determine the number and kind of commercial establishments required for 10,000 persons—the garden suburb's projected population at buildout. Bauer and Stein established guidelines for determining the total amounts a given population would spend on particular goods and the number of stores necessary to handle the probable volume of business.[33] Knowledge of these investigations must have informed Wurster's subsequent site planning for large-scale defense projects in Vallejo and Sacramento.

In 1940 the FWA received authorization for 1,677 demountable units to house civilian workers employed at the Navy's Mare Island facility. Mare Island was an important shipbuilding center located across the channel from Vallejo, a town of 30,000 that billed itself as the "Naval Capital of the West." One year prior to authorization, 6,000 employees were producing cruisers and destroyers. Within two years, that number reached 23,000. Fifty percent of the work force resided in Vallejo, many in cramped, overcrowded conditions; the remainder commuted from as far away as Oakland and Santa Rosa.[34]

Once the project received authorization, the FWA assigned site selection to its Planning Section, while a separate division, the Construction Section, solicited bids from prefabricators. Barrett & Hilp, a San Francisco firm, was awarded a contract to supply 992 units based on Albert Farwell Bemis's Precision-Built system using stress-skin homosote panels. Robert McCarthy teamed with W. S. Watkins & Sons to erect 690 plywood units. It was at this point—after choosing a windswept, hilly, 260-acre site, hiring two contractors, and approving plans for freestanding units with pitched roofs and fenestration on all four sides—that the FWA engaged Wurster as architect and engineer for CAL-4086, or Carquinez Heights.

Given his demonstrated expertise and interest in minimum housing, community planning, and construction practices, his public profile, and his connections, Wurster must have been an obvious candidate for federal agencies engaged in war housing. Following site analysis, and drawing on his knowledge of war workers' needs, Wurster requested a series of modifications. In terms of physical planning, he decided to align unit multiples along a north-south axis across the grain of the steeply sloping hillside (fig. 140). This strategy turned the row housing into windbreaks that blocked onshore westerly winds and fog, maximized opportunities for sunny exposures, and provided one outdoor space, albeit small, for each unit. And by stepping the rows across the slopes Wurster provided the majority of units with views out to the Carquinez Straits and San Pablo Bay. Although the objectives were different, reflecting local conditions, the formal principles were remarkably similar to German *Zeilenbau* planning at housing estates such as Berlin's Bad Durrenberg district (1930), attributed to Alexander Klein, or Ernst May's Westhausen, a satellite suburb from 1929.

Recognizing that tenants would be "busy workers," Wurster argued against land and lawns around each structure, which would require regular watering and maintenance and become a "burden rather than a pleasure." He also pressed for demountable housing. Projections that employment at Mare Island would drop dramatically when the war ended informed his preference. Sectional construction would permit units to be relocated for other uses. When the FWA approved demountable units, the design challenge, according to Wurster, became how to "relate standard units to each other, to roads and paths, and to a dramatically steep and rolling terrain." A central concern, given plans for postwar removal and resale, was limiting grading and "scar[ring] the hills as little as possible. An absolute minimum of earth was moved. Instead of cutting shelves, each house was dropped into place. . . . [P]osts and [redwood] skirts accommodated the slope"[35] (fig. 141).

By introducing row housing Wurster modified the unit design, eliminating pitched roofs and fenestration on all sides in favor of flat roofs and windows on the long, east-west facade. Both builders set up shops for quantity

140.
Row housing, Carquinez Heights, Vallejo, 1941
William Wurster

141.
Homosote-panel units, Carquinez Heights,
Vallejo, 1941
William Wurster
(note redwood skirts)

production of standard units. Barrett & Hilp fabricated floor, roof, and wall panels on site. The flat-roof design simplified the construction process since the same jigs could be used for both floor and roof sections. The stress-skin wall panels had homosote nailed and glued on a lightweight wooden frame. This single sheet provided structural integrity, insulation, and the interior and exterior finish. Sections were fabricated in order of use, which demanded a high level of coordination and organization. Once a unit's piers were poured and floor panels in place, the walls were put up and tied in thirty minutes. After tradespeople fixed plumbing subassemblies, workmen, assisted by a crane, set the roof panels, and the unit was complete.

Sized framing and sheeting for the 690 plywood units completed by McCarthy were shipped to the site from Watkins's plant in Reno, Nevada. At a staging area three blocks from the building site, workmen made final cuts for fenestration before glue up. Rail cars carried finished sections on a spur line the company ran to the site. Once in place, the plywood units received an exterior varnish. Wurster chose a bold palette—sand, barn red, green, blue, and yellow—which he described as "gay but durable," for the homosote units.[36]

In his article describing the project and process, Wurster emphasized the "discipline of speed and economy."[37] Applying this criterion, Carquinez Heights should be considered successful; despite rains and unfavorable conditions, Barrett & Hilp and McCarthy completed the project in seventy-three days, an average of twenty-three units a day. In addition, both construction systems produced units consistent with the FWA's mandate for cost reductions through "streamlined architecture." At the prefabrication summit in Washington, D.C., Director of Defense Housing Clark Foreman argued against simply eliminating decoration and endorsed Wurster's position that large-scale operations and unit repetition should be viewed as a virtue. In his presentation Wurster made a direct reference to English squares, where the "uniformity of parts adds up to a pleasing whole." And he sharply criticized the application of nonessential elements and the introduction of minor variations.[38]

At this point in the war housing program the FWA was encouraging experimentation with new systems and enlisting firms that had not previously secured contracts. To further these objectives, the agency expanded the scope of work at Carquinez Heights and funded the design and construction of twenty-five "experimental" units. The only guidelines were a $2,845 ceiling per unit set by Congress and established defense-housing spatial and equipment standards. True quantity production could not be achieved at this scale, a shortcoming project manager Fred Langhorst outlined in "A New Approach to Large Scale Housing," especially since the firm elected to test a range of construction systems for comparative study. While cognizant of the limitations inherent in the unit count, Wurster and his associates apparently relished the opportunity the FWA experiment afforded.[39]

Eventually the design team settled on three systems, which they termed skeleton, frame bent, and masonry. According to Langhorst, minimizing load-bearing partitions and supports in order to maximize the flexibility of interior space was the primary criterion for selection. For example, the ten two-story, wood skeleton-frame units combined posts and beams on four-foot centers with standard, prefabricated infill panels (fig. 142). The entire east and west walls consisted of alternating fixed and casement windows milled and preassembled before placement. Inside, a single partition divided each unit into two zones, a large living-kitchen space and two bedrooms with bath. There were only three interior doors; each opened to the ceiling, a move intended to enhance spatial overlays in these 670-square-foot dwellings (fig. 143).

Three columns fixed to a roof truss and connected to a floor joist formed the basic structure in the seven frame-bent units (fig. 144). Craftsmen fabricated these subassemblies on site from interchangeable parts and then hoisted them into place, twelve per dwelling. Set at three-foot centers, these standard structural elements became the ribs on which workmen secured flooring, roofing, sash, and siding. Exterior cladding and interior finishes included Douglas fir plywood panels and sheets, redwood, and Douglas fir boards (fig. 145). To expand upon the knowledge garnered from the eight masonry units, the designers specified four types: brick, Basalite block, Haydite block, and hollow tile (fig. 146). Along with a center beam carried on three posts, these raked, reinforced masonry party walls carried the single-slope roof. Nonbearing plywood partitions, set at an angle, parceled out the interior space in these minimum units. The design team sited the masonry and frame-bent units in a diamond pattern (fig. 70); community buildings were proposed for the common interior court.

Although the Wurster office, the FWA, and the architectural press referred to these units as "experimental," none of these systems were new, nor could they be considered innovative when compared with prior or concurrent developments. For example, the federal government, through the Department of Agriculture's Forest Products Laboratory, had been engaged in similar studies since the 1920s. However, two factors make Carquinez Heights noteworthy. The first, simply, was having a nationally known architect involved. The second was an implicit understanding that the experimental units at Vallejo, along with investigations at other locales, were laying the foundation for a broadly anticipated increase in housing production in the immediate postwar era. Langhorst spoke to this point directly: "If either housing of the unit dwelling type or the cost benefits of the mass-produced house is to be wholly desirable in the future, it is important that as full a measure of growth as possible be fostered. Experimentation is needed and new ideas must be given a chance."[40]

142.
"Experimental" housing, Carquinez Heights, Vallejo, 1941
William Wurster
Skeleton-frame units

143.
"Experimental" housing, Carquinez
Heights, Vallejo, 1941
William Wurster
Skeleton-frame units, interior view

144.
"Experimental" housing, Carquinez
Heights, Vallejo, 1941
William Wurster
Frame-bent units

145.
"Experimental" housing, Carquinez
Heights, Vallejo, 1941
William Wurster
Frame-bent units, interior view

146.
"Experimental" housing, Carquinez
Heights, Vallejo, 1941
William Wurster
Masonry units

Although some commentators criticized Carquinez Heights as an eyesore and the units as dull and repetitious, others found virtue in the project.[41] When introducing Wurster at the Washington conference on prefabrication, Clark Foreman cited unsolicited testimonies from architects and planners who considered the project a "brilliant piece of housing design." Reflecting on his recent experience, Wurster underscored a familiar maxim when he counseled those in attendance that success in large-scale projects demanded a synthesis of two kinds of thinking: the universal and the particular. In this case Wurster found value in blending standardized production and construction practices with local knowledge concerning site conditions and patterns of behavior or cultural preferences.[42]

Wurster's increasing commitment to community-scale projects and large-scale operations must have informed his decision to undertake design and engineering at Chabot Terrace in association with architects Franklin and Kump and Thomas Church. Here Wurster played a role in setting the scope of the project, persuading the National Housing Agency (NHA), the FWA's successor, to consolidate a series of smaller housing allocations into a single, 3,000-unit cluster four miles north of Vallejo's ten-block business district. His rationale was both contextual and pragmatic. Wurster recognized the benefits of interspersing units throughout an existing locale so as not to overwhelm the setting. In Vallejo, however, he found the prewar settlement so small that the "tail would wag the dog, with no gain." In his view, realizing scale economies and efficient infrastructure provision also favored consolidation. Although services had to be extended to the 127-acre site, once in place the proposed superblock planning would permit a reduction in water, gas, and sewer runs and limit street improvements. And Wurster recognized that siting these units contiguously would allow the design team to redefine the NHA-mandated "emergency strips"—open areas required for protection from possible bombing or fire—and turn these into recreational amenities.[43]

The Office of the Defense Housing Coordinator approved Chabot Terrace in April 1942. An escalating demand for civilian housing adjacent to Mare Island's shipyard made time the critical factor. The NHA's schedule called for construction to begin in June and completion by September. To meet these deadlines, Wurster designed a single, demountable rowhouse type, and the NHA let contracts to multiple firms.[44] When the *San Francisco Chronicle* announced Chabot Terrace's imminent opening in mid-September 1942, the reporter assigned to the story noted that tenant selection for all 3,000 units was already complete. For the next two years, more than 10,000 residents, approximately forty percent of Vallejo's wartime influx, called Chabot Terrace home. Although residential demographics cannot be attributed directly to Wurster's design, it is worth noting that Chabot Terrace was a rarity among defense housing projects: a City of Vallejo Housing Authority survey completed in 1944 revealed that African-American tenants constituted approximately twelve percent of the population.[45]

In his design for the Chabot Terrace commercial center Wurster applied his long-standing interest in crafting space that users could modify and adapt as needs changed over time (fig. 147). The Major Commercial Building, seventy-two feet deep and four hundred feet long, was a post-and-beam shell infilled with four- by-twelve-foot preassembled and demountable wall and roof panels. Vertical tongue-and-groove and plywood served as the exterior and interior finishes. Tenants could divide and subdivide the resulting space simply by rearranging movable interior partitions. As originally drawn and configured, a market occupied one-third of the structure. Ancillary services included dry goods and hardware, a drugstore with soda fountain, women's and men's clothing, a beauty parlor and barber, a restaurant with lunch counter, and a bakery. Wurster envisioned the Major Commercial Building and the Management-Maintenance Building forming an integrated civic center.

Since children numbered almost half of Chabot Terrace's residents at any given time, the design team proposed an intermediate and two elementary schools. The reach of Clarence Perry's neighborhood unit is evident in the site plan. Buildings for the elementary students were placed approximately one-half mile apart on either side of the site's center line. Their overlapping catchment areas, designed following Perry's formula, meant that every child lived within one-half mile of a school. The junior high, scheduled to have an associated clinic, was midway between the two elementary schools. This physical centrality reflected Wurster's stated intention to have the "social life of the project center around the three schools." Budget constraints intervened, however, and the intermediate school and clinic were not constructed.[46]

At Parker Homes, a 332-unit collaboration with Charles F. Dean, Wurster addressed many of the site planning, unit design, and construction shortcomings that had compromised previous defense housing efforts. This project, for the civilian work force at U.S. Federal Airport in Sacramento, was designed with permanent housing, since employment projections indicated continued growth in the postwar period. Given this, the FWA secured a site within an existing residential district. Here the design team, which included landscape architect Thomas Church, carefully sited streets and prefabricated single- and multifamily dwellings forty-five degrees off the north-south axis to provide better exposure to winter sun and to capture prevailing summer breezes. Church's landscape plan called for front lawns accented by regularly spaced street trees (fig. 148). Stepped massing and cantilevered carports enlivened the uniform building setback. Cul-de-sacs, chosen for increased safety from street traffic, were lined with larger, three-bedroom family units. In his article "Architecture Broadens Its Base" Wurster made explicit the garden-suburb connection: "Beginning with Radburn, we have principles advanced to bring about land use which acknowledges the cul-de-sac and quiet gardens. We track this effort down through the Resettlement Administration and greenbelt towns to the site plans of war housing projects. Today the experimentation is bearing fruit."[47]

A majority of the Parker Homes units were the standard four-room-plus-bath, minimum house placed with their ridge lines paralleling the street. These approximately seven-hundred-square-foot dwellings were finished with Douglas fir plywood on the exterior and interior. Wurster experimented with a variation on this type of plan, dubbed the "house in the air" (fig. 149). The

147.
Commercial Center, Chabot Terrace, Vallejo, 1942
William Wurster

148.
Parker Homes, Sacramento, 1943
William Wurster with Charles Dean
Front yards and street

149.
Parker Homes, Sacramento, 1943
William Wurster with Charles Dean
"House in the air"

150.
Prebilt House prototype, San Anselmo, 1945
Wurster and Bernardi with Ernest Kump

151.
Prebilt House prototype, 1945
Wurster and Bernardi with Ernest Kump
Delivery of prototype

idea was to create simple, "loft-like" spaces that could be divided and subdivided as needed. In an *Architectural Forum* article "Flexible Space," he criticized other defense housing, which he viewed as "expansible plans [which]
propose adding space." On the other hand, "houses in the air" were raised
eight feet above finished grade on four-by-six-inch posts. The space below provided a sheltered carport; a large plywood-sheathed storage area anchored the
house to the site. Wurster imagined this area doubling as a rumpus room for
children. Preliminary estimates assigned these units lower construction costs;
comparative as-built figures were never calculated. A community building
housed management and maintenance as well as kindergarten space, a kitchen
sized to accommodate demonstrations and home economics classes, and
a multipurpose social room.[48]

The decision to build within an existing residential district posed a challenge for Robert McCarthy, whose bid for quantity production using on-site
prefabrication beat out contractors who proposed conventional, stick-built construction. To compensate for a shortage of production space, McCarthy set up
a staging area just off site where craftspeople precut lumber, preassembled windows and doors, and sized materials for mechanical systems. Workers fabricated standard components that were than stockpiled for shipment to the site
"only a few hours in advance of the time they would be needed."[49]

Wartime advances in materials, construction practices, and community
planning led many to believe that one of the defense emergency's legacies
would be housing produced like aircraft or liberty ships. In fact, when scout-
ing the postwar economic landscape, manufacturers such as Donald Douglas
and Henry Kaiser did investigate the feasibility of converting their operations
and producing housing. The Wurster office kept a file of articles clipped from
Bay Area papers, such as "Houses Mass-Built Like Wartime Ships, Planes"
(San Francisco News); "Couple Solve Housing Problem—in 35 Minutes" *(San
Francisco Chronicle);* and a photo essay illustrating an "In-a-Jiffy" house under
construction *(Berkeley Daily Gazette).* Material shortages, rising prices, and
consumer uncertainty stifled the majority of these operations.

In an article titled "Building Now: How You Can Meet the 50 Percent Rise
in Building Costs," Wurster cautioned readers against succumbing to the
seduction of industrialized housing and the profusion of appliances and gadgets. He encouraged potential home buyers to stick with basic needs and simplicity. "In all our thinking let us take 1,000-square-feet as the base for any
permanent family residence. . . . I know from experience that it is fun building to a minimum and I feel sure it is a national duty to do so."[50] Wurster rec-

152.
Prebilt House prototype, San Anselmo, 1945
Wurster and Bernardi with Ernest Kump
Assembling the "arch-ribs"

153.
Prebilt House prototype, 1945–46
Wurster and Bernardi with Ernest Kump
Interior view

ognized that people expected those "real improvements . . . yet if these can only come with the elimination of space I shout: Beware."[51] In these articles Wurster pressed his case for "unspecialized" and "uncompartmentalized" space, which he deemed appropriate, given Americans' increasing informality, as reflected in fashion, foodways, and cultural patterns. To meet these requirements he counseled readers that "where the site allows it, a one-level floor plan is best. I mean that the basement area which is needed to make the house functional is brought onto the main floor, and the attic also." He questioned whether bedrooms should remain "condemned to sleeping and dressing only" and singled out the dining room as the "most conspicuous waste of space."[52]

In terms of construction practice, Wurster favored only those innovations that furthered these objectives. In an article timed for the initial phases of postwar homebuilding he urged returning veterans and other potential buyers to "accept new materials and construction methods if they help us accomplish cost reductions. We eagerly await any reduction in cost brought about by imaginative production methods which give real meaning to the word 'prefabrication,' a meaning only realized if the saving reaches consumers." Here Wurster restated a familiar maxim; he was interested principally in providing the maximum shelter area for the dollar.[53]

Although the Carquinez Heights experimental units did not become prototypes for postwar housing, principles drawn from these investigations did inform small house projects in the postwar years. The Prebilt House, a collaboration between the Wurster office and Ernest Kump, drew on the latter's school design for Chabot Terrace. There Kump and Mark Falk, a structural engineer, used the latest synthetic resins, a product of wartime developments, for a system of laminated plywood arches they called "arch-ribs."[54]

Wurster and Bernardi had found Kump's schools "handsome" but, more importantly, "childishly simple to erect. Once the foundations are in place, no rulers or saws were used on the job. The only tools required are a hammer and screwdriver."[55] This assessment is consistent with Wurster's expressed interest in innovation that would translate into cost reductions rather than novelty.

Like other promoters of postwar housing, Standard Engineering Corporation, which had purchased the Prebilt production facility from Kump, decided to complete a model house, based on the architects' design, along Sir Francis Drake Boulevard in San Anselmo (figs. 150, 151). For the official opening the participants engineered a gala event. Local and branch banks orchestrated publicity, inviting potential home buyers to this "revolutionary new type home ready for your inspection here in Marin County." On 10 March 1945, San Anselmo's mayor, along with mayors from surrounding Marin communities, joined Bay Area housing officials, subdividers and homebuilders, and curious home seekers who flocked to the event.[56]

The San Anselmo prototype used laminated ribs on four-foot centers as the frame for a 1,056-square-foot, two-bedroom, one-bath unit sited on a 60-by-100-foot lot. Thomas Church's landscape plan called for an enclosed "outdoor living room" accessible from the entrance and service porches. Reports in the architectural press stressed the construction system and plan flexibility, suggesting that interested buyers could set up the ribs and panels as a weathertight shell, while interior room layout and subsequent rearrangement could be determined by need and ability to pay (fig. 152).[57] Like the wartime demountables and experimental prefabricated dwellings, the Prebilt model featured interior plywood finishes as well as glazed wallboard in the kitchen, bath, and service area and, perhaps most provocative, given its location, a corrugated asbestos panel fence (fig. 153).

Wurster's genius for promotion and willingness to participate in mass-market forums allowed popular dissemination to proceed apace. When Richard Pratt, architectural editor for *Ladies' Home Journal,* organized an exhibit in 1945 and published articles featuring "Homes for Tomorrow," he requested prototypes from nine architectural firms; four Bay Area architects, including Wurster and Bernardi, made the list. In a memo spelling out the program's objectives, Pratt defined the "modern manufactured house." Topping his criteria were the off-site production of framing sections, panels, and utility units, and dwellings designed for the techniques, materials, and methods "inherent in this age in which we live." According to the *Journal*'s retail merchandising editor, these units would be targeted at families composed of two adults and two to four children, with annual incomes between $2,000 and $3,000. Wurster and Bernardi contributed the Prebilt House.[58]

In San Francisco the Emporium department store set up a special exhibition room and displayed the *Ladies' Home Journal* models on stands that afforded visitors a "window-eye view." The Prebilt house, renamed "Right Off the Line," appeared on the first page of the accompanying brochure. Copywriters claimed: "You wouldn't guess it, but here is a house that can be completely put together in a matter of hours." They extolled the virtues of a "mass-production assembly line" that allowed buyers to purchase only the ribs and panels necessary for a unit of "any size or shape you want."[59] The Wurster office also produced drawings of a full-scale mock-up for display at Macy's, San Francisco. Then in September 1945 the *Ladies' Home Journal* published Pratt's account of the Prebilt House. Here the editor extolled the design as "easy to look at, easy to live in, and easy to own," emphasizing the advantages of a structural framework that provided flexibility, roominess, and convenience at a price below "yesterday's conventional construction."[60]

Wurster did not share the copywriters' interest in mass production and would have responded unfavorably to the implicit analogy with automobile manufacturing. However, the Prebilt House highlights the firm's ongoing investigations into low-cost, minimum house types and advanced construction practices as well as a continued interest in popular, mass-market housing. A similar set of objectives informed other postwar projects, and it is instructive to consider these themes in an alternative setting.

For editor John Entenza's self-consciously high-style *Arts and Architecture,* Wurster and Bernardi produced a decidedly lowbrow dwelling for a family of four do-it-yourselfers (fig. 154). Case Study House No. 3 employed a flexibly planned, semi-enclosed courtyard as the hinge in an H plan. This "garden room," or lanai, was intended as an entry, indoor patio, and informal

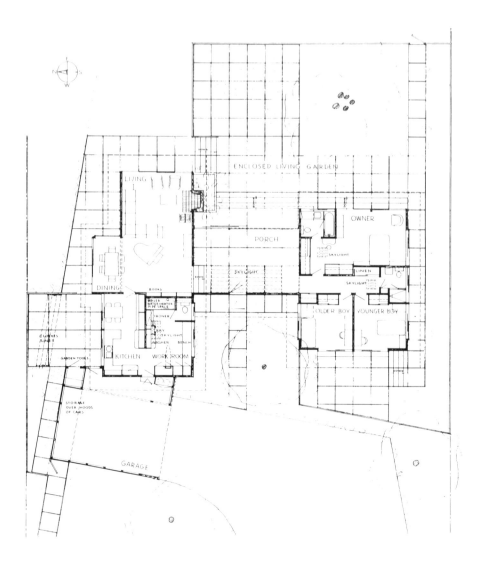

154.
Case Study House No. 3, 1945
Wurster and Bernardi
Plan

dining area. The designers zoned opposing public and private wings, one for service and entertainment, the other for sleeping and study.[61]

Even though they structured the plan with a four-foot module, Wurster and Bernardi purposefully excised any trace of this on the drawings. They also made a declarative statement for stud wall construction, thereby incriminating colleagues who believed that every house deserved a new "system of construction."[62] As they drew it, the key distinction was between designs that only appeared to be standardized or assembled from stock materials and components and their own work, constructed from readily available materials according to methods time-tested for economy and performance. Case Study House No. 3 shared other features common to Wurster's earlier house projects. For example, Douglas fir plywood interior walls were detailed with flush joints and finished "natural." Schematic designs showed ceilings with fiberboard squares or sheets chosen for their "soft look" and insulating qualities. Even the relatively new materials and appliances specified for this prototype, such as aluminum siding and a prefabricated Kaiser kitchen unit, had been designed for quantity production and a popular market.

In many respects, the firm's Case Study House was pragmatic and pedestrian, in keeping with Wurster's understanding of standardization, which emphasized simplicity and the repetition of materials and details without "a lot of elaboration."[63] Ironically, despite a dearth of critical interest in Wurster and Bernardi's contribution, their design came closer to meeting John Entenza's stated objective than many of the more admired and celebrated "prototypes."

Although successful in terms of formal innovations, these were, not surprisingly, less adaptable for quantity production at a cost consistent with the purchasing power of the intended mass market. Case Study House No. 3, on the other hand, was less innovative but more amenable to replication.

In an *Arts and Architecture* article describing the house and their approach to the project, Wurster and Bernardi scorned architects who would design housing for any location equipped only with a site survey. In a tone bordering on self-parody they pressed their case for an alternative method: intimate knowledge of local conditions, "heart-to-heart" client talks, and interpersonal "communion." "Any other process," they argued, "tends to make a house either overly conventional or overly intellectual." This assessment of design methods offers a metric we can use to situate Wurster, his office, and its output in their contemporary milieu.[64]

Viewed from the perspective of sanctioned, high-style Architecture, Wurster and his associates occupied a somewhat incongruous position, simultaneously central and marginal to the aesthetic, formal, and functional debates that bound professional discourse. Although Wurster sought and received professional recognition, it came with qualifications and was relatively short-lived. Throughout his career he was considered to be between the poles of the intellectual and the conventional, the avant-garde and the prosaic. However, viewed from our vantage point there is much to admire in Wurster's conscious blurring of the distinction between Architecture and building, or high style and popular. In practice, these boundaries—a conceit crafted by design professionals and maintained by architectural historians—were and continue to be far more porous than the simple dichotomy would suggest.[65]

Like most professionals, architects draw from multiple sources and answer to multiple constituencies. This was particularly true in California during the interwar years. Here talented members of a vital design community recognized their distance from centers that sanctioned and understood this as both blessing and curse. Their isolation and simultaneous engagement in a rich local and regional culture encouraged an extraordinary interplay between those who designed buildings and those who put them together. Vernon DeMars reconstructed the California building world when discussing his much admired designs for the Farm Security Administration. In a single drawing he ascribed debts to both Le Corbusier for formal attributes and Southern California's speculative homebuilders from whom the FSA staff cribbed their structural system. Joseph Esherick sketched out these lines of learning among contractors, material manufacturers, fabricators, and designers, using the example of mill draftsmen employed by multiple firms who generated and disseminated construction details. This exchange of technical expertise contributed to the creation of a knowledge base shared throughout the Bay Area.[66] Like many of his regional colleagues, Wurster included his clients, the users, in this process.

In other words, assessing Wurster and his architecture requires us to look beyond individual buildings. What impresses from this vantage point is the breadth of his interests and his commitment to what we would call a multidisciplinary endeavor. We can consider this on a range of scales, from individual dwellings to multifamily clusters with associated infrastructure planning, out to the neighborhood and complete community. During the period under consideration in this essay, Wurster undertook his East Coast sojourn and graduate studies. At MIT he worked with Frederick Adams, director of a "field station" devoted to analyzing urban redevelopment proposals—a project run jointly with the American Public Health Association's Committee on the Hygiene of Housing, the Albert Farwell Bemis Foundation, and Boston's City Planning Board. Participants paid special attention to urban districts with sound building stock but "obsolete" neighborhood patterns and prepared schematic designs and cost estimates for reconfiguring street systems, as well as providing parks, playgrounds, and other community facilities.[67]

Wurster was active in these investigations. Even here, however, he was not unique. At the time there were parallel studies and professional clusters in other metropolitan regions, including Telesis in the Bay Area and Los Angeles. But Wurster clearly had a gift for synthesis and galvanizing people and ideas for action. With hindsight we can locate in these endeavors the foundation for the College of Environmental Design, arguably Wurster's most significant legacy.[68]

Notes

Jeannette Redensek (San Francisco Museum of Modern Art) provided invaluable research assistance, as did Cynthia Wordell and Travis Culwell (College of Environmental Design Documents Collection at the University of California, Berkeley). At the University of Southern California, Stephen Flusty and Clarence Eng tracked down articles. Marc Treib critiqued an earlier version of this essay.

1. William Wurster, "From Log Cabin to Modern House: An Architect Urges a Return to Simple Fundamentals in Planning Our New Homes," *New York Times Magazine,* 20 January 1946, pp. 10, 53.

2. Lewis Mumford, "The Social Imperatives in Housing," in Carol Aronovici, ed., *America Can't Have Housing* (New York: Museum of Modern Art, 1934), p. 15.

3. Wurster, "Architecture Broadens Its Base," *AIA Journal* (July 1948), p. 36.

4. Ibid. For California homebuilding innovations, see Greg Hise, "Home Building and Industrial Decentralization in Los Angeles: The Roots of the Postwar Urban Region," *Journal of Urban History* 19, no. 2 (February 1993), pp. 95–125; Anne Bloomfield, "The Real Estate Associates: A Land and Housing Developer of the 1870s in San Francisco," *Journal of the Society of Architectural Historians* 37, no. 1 (March 1978), pp. 13–33; Richard Walker, "Landscape and City Life: Four Ecologies of Residence in the San Francisco Bay Area," *Ecumene* 2, no. 1 (Winter 1995), pp. 33–64; Marc E. Weiss, *The Rise of the Community Builders: The American Real Estate Industry and Urban Land Planning* (New York: Columbia University Press, 1987).

5. See, for example, the American Public Health Association, Committee on the Hygiene of Housing, *Basic Principles of Healthful Housing* (New York: The Committee, 1939); Jane Callaghan and Catherine Palmer, *Measuring Space and Motion* (New York: Pierce Foundation, 1944); Robert T. Jones, "Omitting the Cellar to Cut Building Costs," *Small Home* (January–February, 1926); and Alexander Klein, "Judging the Small Home," *Architectural Forum* 55, no. 2, part 1 (August 1931), pp. 166–96.

6. Division of Defense Housing, *Meeting of Manufacturers of Prefabricated Housing with Division of Defense Housing, Nov. 10th and 11th, 1941* (Washington, D.C.: Government Printing Office, 1941), p. 143.

7. *Life* to Wurster, 21 September 1938, William Wurster Archive, College of Environmental Design Documents Collection at the University of California, Berkeley (hereafter CED Documents Collection), file 2547.

8. "*Life* Houses," *Architectural Forum* (November 1938), p. 330. According to this report, Mrs. Calvert thought Wurster's design "uncomfortable from the outside." She also questioned the courtyard plan, which increased the distance she had to travel when cleaning. Mr. Calvert was more sympathetic. In a letter sent on *Los Angeles Times* stationery he suggested that the selection process had been difficult and congratulated the architect on the darkroom location, which he describes as a "honey." Calvert to Wurster, 27 September 1938, file 2547, CED Documents Collection.

9. Van Dam to Wurster, 23 October 1938, file 2547, CED Documents Collection.

10. Farm Security Administration Contract and Construction Docket Files, 1929–46, Farmers Home Administration, Record Group 96, National Archives–Pacific Sierra Branch, Box 10.

11. Soule to Wurster, 13 November 1937, file 3782, CED Documents Collection. To reinforce his point, Soule directed the architect to the November 1937 issue of *Architectural Forum*, which showcased Bemis's principles. See Albert Farwell Bemis, *The Evolving House, Volume Three, Rational Design* (Cambridge: MIT Press, 1936).

12. James Reed to Wurster, 29 November 1937, file 3782, CED Documents Collection.

13. During the war Soule Steel licensed a demountable metal shelter from Tennessee Coal, Iron, and Railroad Company, a subsidiary of U.S. Steel, and adapted it to meet federal defense-housing standards. Following a $150 million plant expansion, Soule began bidding on projects throughout California, including one of Wurster's in Vallejo. Letter from Mr. Dawson (Soule Steel Co.) to Rudolph Forster, 19 May 1941, in the Franklin Delano Roosevelt Papers, Franklin Delano Roosevelt Library, folder FDR OF4240a.

14. United States Federal Housing Administration, *Planning Neighborhoods for Small Houses, Technical Bulletin* #5 (Washington, D.C.: Government Printing Office, 1 July 1936).

15. Wurster to Soule, 23 February 1938, file 3782, CED Documents Collection.

16. Wurster to Evans, 5 September 1939, file 2526, CED Documents Collection.

17. Evans to Wurster, 19 October 1939, file 2526, CED Documents Collection.

18. Wurster to Evans, 8 November 1939. In a subsequent letter Wurster asked Evans if he had ever seen Bernard Maybeck's Christian Science church in Berkeley "with your wonderful diagonal shingles on the wall," 17 November 1939, file 2526, CED Documents Collection.

19. Wurster to Johns-Manville Company, 21 December 1939, file 2526, CED Documents Collection.

20. Catherine Bauer, "When Is a House not a House?" (n.d.), Catherine Bauer Wurster Papers, Bancroft Library, carton 3 (hereafter CBW Papers). In a 1946 speech to the California Women's Club, Bauer warned against the "recurring romance of prefabrication, the idea of ordering [house] parts at the corner hardware store" and assembling them, CBW Papers, carton 1.

21. Howard T. Fisher's General Houses, Inc., is representative. Fisher, a Chicago architect, intended to "Fordize" the building industry. "Sees Future Homes Bought like Autos," *New York Times,* 25 May 1932, and "Fordized Housing Plan of New Group," ibid., 23 June 1932. For another contemporary account, see *Fortune* magazine's six-part series republished as *Housing America* (New York: Harcourt, Brace, 1932).

22. Greg Hise, "The Roots of the Postwar Urban Region: Mass Housing and Community Planning in California, 1920–1950," Ph.D diss., University of California, Berkeley, 1992, chaps. 2 and 3.

23. United States Congress, *Hearings Before the Select Committee Investigating National Defense Migration* (Washington, D.C.: Government Printing Office, 1941–42), better known as the Tolan Committee. For interpretive accounts, see Carey McWilliams, *Southern California: An Island on the Land* (Salt Lake City: Peregrine Smith, 1990); Roger Lotchin, *Fortress California, 1910–1961: From Warfare to Welfare* (New York: Oxford University Press, 1992); and Gerald Nash, *The American West Transformed: The Impact of the Second World War* (Bloomington: Indiana University Press, 1985).

24. See, for example, "From Line-up to Job at Busy Aircraft Factories," *Los Angeles Times,* 12 November 1939, part 2, 1.

25. *New York Times,* 29 October and 1 December 1941; *Oakland Tribune,* 27 October 1941, 1. Bauer's transcript appeared in *Architect and Engineer* (October 1942), p. 33.

26. Richard H. Foster, Jr., "Wartime Trailer Housing in the San Francisco Bay Area," *Geographical Review* 70, no. 3 (July 1980), pp. 276–90.

27. On 18 December 1941 the *New York Daily News* reported "Housing Lack Called Arms Output Obstacle." Testifying before the Senate Military Affairs Subcommittee on Manpower, Marshall Beaman, industrial relations director for North American Aviation, stated: "An alarming number of job terminations may be attributed to housing dissatisfaction." *Los Angeles Evening Herald and Express,* 27 April 1943.

28. California State Planning Board, "Hearing on the Establishment of a San Francisco Bay Regional Planning District, March 28, 1941" (Sacramento: California State Planning Board, 1941), p. 35.

29. Drawing on their experience designing and managing community projects, the FSA staff included an administrative center with restaurant and social services. Budget constraints canceled the center, leaving tenants only a small lobby in each dorm for socializing. Later the FSA would supply demountable dorms and a cafeteria building at Carquinez Heights. Sally Carrighar, "Dormitories in Transition," *Architect and Engineer* (February 1943), pp. 15–25; Hise, "The Roots of the Postwar Urban Region," chap. 3.

30. Office memo in Daniel Gregory's possession. William Wurster, *AIA Journal* (July 1948), p. 31.

31. Catherine Bauer, "Special Report to the Federal Works Agency on Three Defense Housing Projects" (27 January 1942), CBW Papers, carton 3, and "Housing Wavers: Backward or Forward" (n.d.), CBW Papers, carton 2. In a memo of 12 November 1941, "On the Experience of California with Defense Housing Agencies and Recommendations Therefrom," Bauer cast Linda Vista as a "barbaric assault" on San Diego, and the PBA as "post office architects" incapable of divining the intricacies of house design and site and community planning. CBW Papers, carton 10.

32. Tenants also lodged complaints about a lack of parking and voiced a preference for detached housing. In her report Bauer notes that 10,000 residents resorted to a salvaged construction shack for their Linda Vista Sunday School.

33. Clarence S. Stein and Catherine Bauer, "Store Buildings and Neighborhood Shopping Centers," *Architectural Record* 75 (February 1934), pp. 174–87. See also "Appendix A: Calculation of Store Frontage," in Clarence Arthur Perry, *Housing for the Machine Age* (New York: Russell Sage Foundation, 1939), pp. 225–28.

34. Solano County Chamber of Commerce, *Solano County Greets You* (1939); H. W. Jewitt and Z. E. Bells, "Analysis and Appraisal: Commercial in FWA Emergency Housing Project, Cal. 4086 at Vallejo, CA," 20 January 1942, Vallejo Museum.

35. William Wurster, "Carquinez Heights," *California Arts and Architecture* 58 (November 1941), p. 34. Wurster noted with dismay that site and budget constraints militated against access roads and covered parking adjacent to individual units. Here, he felt, he had not "live[d] up to my knowledge of this part of the country . . . where people are more proud of their car than anything else."

36. Ibid., p. 34.

37. Ibid. p. 34.

38. Division of Defense Housing, *Meeting of Manufacturers,* pp. 170–71.

39. Fred Langhorst, "A New Approach to Large Scale Housing: The Office of William Wilson Wurster Attacks the Problem of Mass Housing," *California Arts and Architecture* 59 (April 1942), pp. 27–31.

40. Ibid., pp. 28. In his revised introduction to "Mass Production and Housing," prepared for a 1945 republication in *City Development,* Lewis Mumford cited Wurster's experimental site-fabricated houses, which proved cheaper per unit than factory fabrication, to underscore his point that prefabrication could not solve the housing problem.

41. Henry Luce, editorial in *Time* (13 April 1942); "Vallejo War Housing," *California Arts and Architecture* 59 (December 1942), pp. 22–25.

42. Division of Defense Housing, *Meeting of Manufacturers,* p. 142.

43. The *San Francisco Chronicle* reported on 28 March 1941 the condemnation of a 127-acre parcel on Sears Road and Napa Bay for housing; "Chabot Terrace: Public and Commercial Structures," *Pencil Points* 25 (October 1944), p. 80.

44. Plywood Structures, a Los Angeles-based prefabricator, produced the majority of the units. Robert McCarthy, who had worked with Wurster previously at Carquinez Heights, erected 1,700 units.

45. *San Francisco Chronicle,* 14 September 1942, Housing Authority of the City of Vallejo, survey in the John Ihlder Papers, Franklin Delano Roosevelt Library, box 103, Housing Authority of the City of Vallejo.

46. On the neighborhood unit, see Wurster's discussion of his redesign for a section of Cambridge, Mass., according to these principles for Frederick Adams (MIT) and Alvin Hansen (Harvard) in "Toward Urban Redevelopment," *Architect and Engineer* (July 1944), pp. 25–28. The article originated in a San Francisco Planning and Housing Association lecture at the San Francisco Museum of Art, 31 May 1944.

47. Wurster, "Architecture Broadens Its Base," p. 35.

48. Wurster, "Flexible Space," *Architectural Forum* (September 1942), p. 140.

49. "Planned for Prefabrication," *Architectural Record* (January 1944), pp. 79–84.

50. Wurster, "Building Now," *House and Garden* 89, no. 5 (May 1946), pp. 74–77.

51. Wurster, "From Log Cabin to Modern House," p. 10.

52. Ibid.; Wurster, "When Is a Small House Large?" *House and Garden* 92 no. 2 (August 1947), pp. 72–75.

53. Wurster, "From Log Cabin to Modern House," p. 10. When administrator Nathan Straus published "USHA Cuts Costs by Eliminating All Frills and Gadgets" in the *Washington Evening Star,* he could have had Wurster in mind. Straus cited more than a dozen savings the agency had instituted in order to achieve simple, economical, and comfortable dwellings at minimum costs, a process he termed "degadgeting." Among the strategies adopted were the elimination of basements, attics, and dining rooms, a reduction in interior and exterior trim, cement as a finish floor surface, and the use of simple yet durable hardware. *Washington Evening Star,* 25 May 1940, in Straus Scrapbook, Franklin Delano Roosevelt Library.

54. During the war Kump had set up a production facility in association with Falk, but soon sold the factory to Standard Engineering Corporation while retaining patent rights to the structural system.

55. Letter from Wurster and Bernardi to the Federal Public Housing Administration, 11 December 1945. CED Documents Collection.

56. "Standard Engineering Corporation Shows New Type Manufactured Home at San Anselmo Preview," *Daily Pacific Builder,* 13 March 1945, p. 1. The banks supplied a survey that asked respondents whether they liked the Prebilt's "informal California style," the graceful sweep of the arches, and the combined kitchen and dinette. More focused questions probed ownership status, timing of possible house construction, and loan requirements.

57. "Prefabrication for Flexible Planning," *Architectural Record* (August 1945), pp. 96–98; "Unit No. 1 of the 'Prebilt' House," *Architectural Record* (September 1945), pp. 82–85.

58. Pratt memo to Wurster and Bernardi, 11 December 1945, file 4526, CED Documents Collection.

59. "Exhibit Gives Ideas for House You Are Planning," *San Francisco News* (1945), p. 12; The Emporium, "Homes for Tomorrow from Ladies' Home Journal" (1945), both in file 4526, CED Documents Collection.

60. "Right off the Line," *Ladies' Home Journal* 62 no. 9 (September 1945), p. 155. Although Prebilt units never came "off the line," they did have a life beyond domestic advertisements, displays, and a single model unit. In 1945 France's minister of reconstruction and town planning organized a housing exhibition, and Paul Nelson, the American liaison, contacted Kump, who arranged for the shipping and assembling of a Prebilt prototype. Pierce Williams to Kump, 22 September 1945, file 4526, CED Documents Collection.

61. See "Case Study House No. 3," *Arts and Architecture* 62 (June 1945); "Case Study House No. 3 Interiors," *Arts and Architecture* 62 (July 1945); "Case Study House No. 3," *Arts and Architecture* 66 (March 1949); Marcia Lee, "Utility Use of Aluminum in Attractive Residence, Mandeville Canyon, Los Angeles County," *Architect and Engineer* (January 1951). For a more recent assessment, see Elizabeth Smith, ed., *Blueprints for Modern Living: History and Legacy of the Case Study Houses* (Los Angeles: Museum of Contemporary Art, 1989).

62. *Arts and Architecture* 62 (June 1945), p. 30.

63. Ralph Butterfield (principal, Wurster, Bernardi and Emmons), interview by Paolo Polledri, Summer/Fall 1993, p. 3, transcript from San Francisco Museum of Modern Art.

64. *Arts and Architecture* 62 (June 1945), p. 26.

65. On this point, see Dell Upton, "Pattern Books and Professionalism: Aspects of the Transformation of Domestic Architecture in America, 1800–1860," *Winterthur Portfolio* 19, no. 2–3 (Summer/Autumn 1984), pp. 107–50; and idem, "The Traditional House and Its Enemies," *TDSR* 1 (1990), pp. 71–84.

66. Vernon DeMars, interview by the author, 18 October 1988; Joseph Esherick, "Bill Wurster," in R. Thomas Hille, *Inside the Large Small House: The Residential Design Legacy of William W. Wurster* (Ann Arbor, 1994; reprinted New York: Princeton Architectural Press, 1995).

67. "Urban Redevelopment Field Station Established at MIT," *The American City* (February 1945), p. 5.

68. See, for example, Roger Montgomery, "William Wilson Wurster and the College of Environmental Design," *CED News* 13, no. 1 (Fall 1994), pp. 4–6.

William Wurster and His California Contemporaries:
The Idea of Regionalism and Soft Modernism

David Gebhard

During the years 1937 through 1942 the architectural journal *Pencil Points* published a series of articles entitled "The Architect and the House."[1] The third architect presented in the series, in 1938, was the forty-three-year-old San Francisco architect William W. Wurster.[2] Kenneth Reid, managing editor of the magazine and author of the piece on Wurster, discussed the fast-growing reputation of this young architect: "Editors of magazines featuring residential architectural work have been discerning enough to select photographs and plans of his houses for publication as rapidly as they were available."[3]

Reid suggested several reasons for Wurster's success. Looking into Wurster's education, he noted that the architect had attended the University of California at Berkeley, where he had pursued a strict Beaux-Arts course of study administered by John Galen Howard. After completing this program and taking the traditional trip to Europe, Wurster went to work in the New York office of Delano and Aldrich, both graduates of the École des Beaux-Arts. Their designs, especially for their well-known suburban and country houses, reflect this influence.[4]

Wurster's experience in the Delano and Aldrich office, as Reid indicated, was crucial to his professional development. During his year in the office the young architect absorbed two basic ideas: the overriding importance of proportion in design and the possibility of realizing twentieth-century modernity through various architectural images. "In architecture," Aldrich noted in 1929, "more than half the fundamentals are proportion, the shaping of space and the disposition of voids and solids. Laymen should know that is what makes architecture, and not superficial details."[5] As to the question of modernity, Aldrich asserted, "By all means let us meet modern problems in a straightforward way, but let us not forget that in order to say new things it is not necessary for us to invent a new language."[6]

In his article Reid suggested several other reasons why Wurster had so quickly become a successful and much publicized architect. He characterized Wurster's buildings as expressing "the art of building beautifully—not just differently" and, through their reticence, expressing a "livable charm."[7] In his discussion of the 1928 Gregory Farmhouse near Santa Cruz (fig. 13), Reid illustrated what he felt Wurster had learned from Delano and Aldrich: "Forms natural to materials and uses, undistorted by any suggestion of 'artiness,' give this house the charm of honesty that might have been produced by a carpenter endowed with good taste."[8]

156.
Osthoff House, San Marino, 1924
George Washington Smith

157. (opposite top)
Bourne House, Pasadena, 1927
Wallace Neff

158. (opposite center)
Morgan House, "La Quinita," Indio, 1934
Gordon Kaufmann

159. (opposite bottom)
Power House, Brentwood, 1939
Paul Williams

From the mid-1930s, Wurster's reputation continued to grow, both within California and nationally. He was spoken of as an important member of the new, younger contingent of West Coast architects who were producing a "warm" regional version of modernism. The May 1936 issue of *Architectural Forum* presented an interview with Wurster, accompanied by extensive illustrations of four of his houses.[9] "In 1938 he was selected by *Life* magazine as one of America's "Famous Architects" and commissioned to design one in its series of "*Life* Houses."[10] For this project, he posed as a woodsy modernist. The following year he assumed the guise of a traditionalist in his version of a California ranch house, one of a group of exhibition houses designed for San Francisco's 1939 Golden Gate International Exposition.[11]

Wurster's move to the East Coast, his marriage to Catherine Bauer, and the deanship at MIT certainly helped to solidify his popular and professional reputation. Along with several other exponents of the Bay Region tradition—Gardner A. Dailey, John Funk, and the landscape architect Thomas D. Church—he was represented in the exhibition "Built in USA: 1932–1944," organized by Elizabeth Mock at the Museum of Modern Art in New York in 1944.[12] A year earlier, *Architectural Forum* had again devoted its lead article to eight of Wurster's buildings. In the immediate post-World War II years his houses continued to be widely published in professional architectural journals and shelter magazines.[13]

In 1947 Lewis Mumford placed Wurster in a class with Bernard Maybeck as architects who "took care that their houses did not resemble factories or museums."[14] Wurster found himself increasingly cast as a woodsy West Coast regionalist. At the famous 1948 symposium "What Is Happening to Modern Architecture?" held at New York's Museum of Modern Art, Wurster's work was described by Alfred H. Barr, Jr., as an example of the "International Cottage Style," while Peter Blake commented, "I think of the Bay Region Style as lots of fun . . . but I don't think it has much to do with what we should be trying to do today."[15]

In his 1947 book, *Architecture, Ambition and Americans,* Wayne Andrews took up the battle between the soft- and hard-line modernists (he, of course, was an avid exponent of soft modernism, as was Lewis Mumford).[16] Andrews divided his good guys (the regionalists) and bad guys (International Style modernists) into two camps that he labeled "Veblenites" and "Jacobites." He characterized Wurster, along with John Ekin Dinwiddie and Harwell H. Harris, as "one of the leading Jacobites of our time."[17]

The principal apologists of high-art modernism, Sigfried Giedion and Henry-Russell Hitchcock, generally dealt with the embarrassing question of Wurster and other exponents of regionalism and soft modernism by ignoring them. In most instances, when the eastern establishment critics discussed Wurster—as John Burchard and Albert Bush-Brown did in their 1961 book, *The Architecture of America*—he was dismissed as an unfortunate romantic who was still designing picturesque buildings in the post-World War II period.[18]

Since the late 1960s, history's view of Wurster's work has only occasionally improved. Vincent Scully made a passing reference to him and the Bay Region tradition in his 1969 book, *American Architecture and Urbanism*.[19] Leland M. Roth, in his *Concise History of American Architecture*, wrote warmly of Wurster, Bernardi and Emmons's reinterpretation of forms of the past in the firm's Ghirardelli Square project (1964) in San Francisco.[20] However, other contemporary histories of modern architecture, such as those by William J. R. Curtis and Kenneth Frampton, either completely ignored Wurster and California's version of soft modernism or presented him as someone behind the times.[21]

Wurster and His California Contemporaries: Clarence Tantau and Gardner Dailey

From Wurster's entry into the architectural scene in the late 1920s until the early 1960s, he gracefully and easily took over whatever was fashionable at the moment. Not, it should be noted, the latest fashion of the avant-garde modernist but what was accepted by most architects and certainly by the middle and upper-middle classes. He was not a major innovator, as were R. M. Schindler and Richard J. Neutra in the twenties and thirties in Southern California. Nor could it be said that he really pioneered any new spatial concepts, use of new materials, or new structural forms. Nonetheless, like a small group of his California contemporaries, Wurster was viewed as being in the forefront, whether his design was a simplified and abstract version of a traditional image or a form that read as modern.

In many ways, Wurster's place in the California architectural scene matches that of a number of other gifted traditionalists of the twenties and thirties. The names of George Washington Smith (fig. 156), Reginald D. Johnson, Wallace Neff (fig. 157), Gordon Kaufmann (fig. 158), Paul Williams (fig. 159), H. Roy Kelley, and Lutah Maria Riggs immediately come to mind.[22] While each of them continued to make reference to historic prototypes, they all went through a continuous process of "modernizing" their designs. But—and this "but" is important—all of these gifted traditionalists (in contrast to Wurster) strove to create works of high art. By the beginning of the 1930s and into the 1940s, these and other California traditionalists sought to create a series of images that could be perceived as both traditional and modern. Just as one may speak of soft modernism, one may also speak of soft traditionalism.

The one element separating much of Wurster's work from that of other California traditionalists has to do with his self-conscious effort to produce buildings that up front would not openly read as Architecture. Wurster succeeded by indirection; his buildings subtly obscure the presence of the architect as artist.

Two of Wurster's early contemporaries who exhibited a similar approach to design in Northern California were Clarence A. Tantau (1885–1943) and Gardner A. Dailey (1895–1967). Being a generation older than Wurster, Tantau had a well-established practice in San Francisco by the teens. Like his Southern California compatriot, George Washington Smith, Tantau's forte was

160.
Armsby Ranch House, Carmel Valley,
1928–29
Clarence Tantau

161.
Converse House, Carmel, 1933
William Wurster

162.
Manning House, Palo Alto, 1929
Gardner Dailey

an ability to create impressive abstractions of Spanish and Mexican historic types, for which he became most widely known. However, he could work with ease in any number of historic modes, from the English Tudor and French Norman to the English Georgian. His rustic stone 1928–29 Armsby Ranch House in Carmel Valley (fig. 160) is similar in many ways to Wurster's Gregory Farmhouse of 1928, although there is one salient difference: it openly advertised the hand of the architect far more than did Wurster's rural farmhouse.

In the late 1920s, Tantau participated with Wurster in designing buildings for the Pasatiempo Estates, near Santa Cruz. Like Wurster, he looked back to California's architecture of the 1830s and 1840s for his sources.[23] His Guest House at Pasatiempo of 1925 (fig. 118), with its two-story porch, is pure Monterey Revival. In contrast to Wurster's work at Pasatiempo, Tantau's buildings transform the earlier vernacular into urbane designed artifacts.

In tandem with Wurster, Tantau shifted his ground appreciably during the Depression years. Much of his work of the mid-1930s reflected an interest in the soft modern, coupled with elements derived from the Anglo-Colonial Revival. Tantau's 1936 project for a country residence came close to matching Wurster's Converse House in Carmel (1933) in its commitment to gentle modernism via a low horizontal single volume with a carefully disposed pattern of windows and doors (fig. 161).[24]

Comparing Tantau's two model houses for the Golden Gate International Exposition of 1939 with Wurster's model houses, one can see how easily Wurster could produce buildings in either vernacular traditionalism or soft modernism, depending on the client's preference.[25] In contrast to Wurster's lightly modernized California ranch houses, Tantau's model houses were insistently popular moderne (not high-art modern), with their flat cantilevered roofs and horizontal banded walls. Going a step further at the end of the 1930s and early 1940s, Tantau was even able to maneuver several late designs into the machine-image Streamline Moderne—something Wurster was never interested in doing.

Certainly the one figure who was in direct competition with Wurster throughout his career was Gardner A. Dailey. They both had studied under John Galen Howard, and both had established their practices in the mid-1920s. Like Wurster, Dailey tended to justify his woodsy architecture by references to the historic past of Northern California. But Dailey's historic past tended to be found in the work of the first exponents of the Bay Region tradition—Willis Polk, Bernard Maybeck, Louis Christian Mullgardt, and Bruce Porter—rather than, as in Wurster's case, the nineteenth-century vernacular architecture of California.[26]

Dailey's early designs of the 1920s were closer to those of Tantau than of Wurster. Reminiscent of both Tantau and George Washington Smith were Dailey's thick-walled sculptural Andalusian villa for Dean S. Arnold at Hillsborough (1926–27) and his Allied Arts Guild Building in Menlo Park (1928–29).[27] By the end of the decade, like Tantau and Wurster, he had turned to California's Monterey tradition. His 1929 Manning House in Palo Alto, like the historic Castro adobe in San Juan Bautista (1840–41), presents a cantilevered porch on one side and a two-story porch on the other (fig. 162). In strong contrast to Wurster's versions of this regional historic style, such as his 1934 Randall House in Santa Cruz (fig. 163), Dailey's Manning House, with its painted brick exterior, refined bay windows, and interior details, leaves no doubt that a sophisticated architect has produced this upper-middle-class country house.[28]

Throughout the 1930s Dailey continued to produce residences based upon historic precedent, usually versions of the single or two-story Monterey or the California ranch house, made more fashionable to Anglo clients by references to the Anglo-Colonial Revival and the Regency tradition of England. These

163.
Randall House, Santa Cruz, 1934
William Wurster

164.
Lowe House, Woodside, 1936
Gardner Dailey

165. (opposite)
Yerba Buena Clubhouse, Golden Gate
International Exposition,
San Francisco, 1939
William Wurster

designs often received awards from the American Institute of Architects and prizes from shelter magazines such as *House Beautiful* and *House and Garden.*[29] Versions of the modern and moderne entered Dailey's work by the mid-1930s. His Coral Casino on the beach at Montecito (1937) is a suave, sophisticated version of the Regency Revival, while his small weekend house for William Lowe, Jr., at Woodside (1936) marked a full commitment to the then popular Streamline Moderne (fig. 164).[30]

The differences in approach between Wurster and Dailey are evident in the buildings they designed for the Golden Gate International Exposition of 1939. Wurster's task was to produce the Yerba Buena Clubhouse, erected for a women's club (fig. 165). Capturing the intention of this design, Eugene Neuhaus wrote: "It achieves an ingratiating appearance, gay and appealing. Its walled courtyard, the lattice-covered walls [à la Bernard Maybeck] which carry vines, lends it the character of a secluded suburban residence."[31] Dailey's task was quite different; he was commissioned to create a pavilion representing Brazil. Like Wurster, he sheathed his wood frame building in plywood, but the image was that of the popular moderne, formal and elegant.[32]

The imagery employed in Dailey's 1939 model house in Berkeley was, like the Lowe House, low-keyed Streamline Moderne. His *Good Housekeeping* model house for the 1939 Golden Gate International Exposition combined a low horizontal modern volume with the informal extended plan of the California ranch house.[33] Through the early 1940s, Dailey continued to clad his designs with detailing that sometimes read as modern, other times as popular moderne.

Though not among the initial group of architects selected, as was Wurster, Dailey was engaged to design one of the houses in *Life*'s second series.[34] For his small wood-clad dwelling, he provided three different roof treatments, ranging from gable and hipped-roof schemes to a flat-roofed design. Commenting on the style of the house, the editors of *Architectural Forum* wrote that "the architect brings an idiom all his own, and at the same time peculiarly American. Neither 'Modern' or 'Traditional.' "[35] In contrast, Wurster's entry in the *Life* series was meant to be perceived as modern, but since it openly shed the appearance of an architect-designed house, it ended up being labeled "shack" modern.[36]

In 1941 houses designed by Dailey were included in a number of exhibitions in San Francisco and New York. The projects he chose to exhibit were generally representative of his woodsy Bay Region style houses or, in contrast, his refined versions of the California ranch house. A group of his soft-modern designs were also included in various exhibitions and published extensively.

The scheme so often encountered in the work of Dailey and Wurster—horizontal redwood-sheathed volumes, fenestrated by white horizontal bands of painted casement windows—can be observed in Dailey's design for the combined office and dwelling of Bernard Berliner in San Francisco (1938).[37] In the hillside Owens House in Sausalito (1939), across the bay from San Francisco, Dailey opened up the two principal two-story facades so that only glass and structure were apparent (fig. 155).[38]

During World War II Dailey and Wurster completed two nondomestic projects that were high points in their respective careers. From the moment it was finished and photographed, Wurster's Schuckl Canning Company Building in Sunnyvale (1942) was continually illustrated and written about as the ideal example of the second Bay Region tradition.[39] Here, indeed, the International Style of the thirties was domesticated, easygoing and pragmatically logical. The building exhibited the hallmarks of the modern style: sections of the building supported by pilotis (in this case, thin metal columns; no drama as in Le Corbusier), banded horizontal windows, projecting bands of sun screens, and even the inevitable roof deck for dining and recreation.

Dailey's project was the U.S. Merchant Marine Cadet School at Coyote Point, San Mateo (1942).[40] His simple redwood-sheathed structures were beautifully sited within an existing grove of eucalyptus trees (fig. 166). The buildings and their connecting covered links responded in a natural fashion to the contours of the site. As the editors of *Architectural Forum* commented, "In the Maritime School, the 'California School' is used with consummate skill to meet a rigidly restricted building program."[41]

These two buildings illustrate the close linkage and perhaps interchange between these two exponents of the second Bay Region tradition. Wurster's Schuckl Building (fig. 167), with its thin lacelike wood members embracing glass, is similar to Dailey's Owens House, while Dailey's maritime buildings are akin not only to his own domestic work but also to that of Wurster. Both the Schuckl Building and the Merchant Marine School were included in the Museum of Modern Art's 1944 exhibition and were frequently illustrated in popular and professional articles on contemporary American architecture during these years.[42]

In later histories of American architecture, Dailey's Merchant Marine School was described as one of the few "beacons in the murk [of architecture of these years]," and Wurster's Schuckl Building was, according to Wayne Andrews, "likely to be remembered as one of the incomparable business buildings of the twentieth century.'[43]

During the war years, architects and editors of architectural magazines used architectural sketches and drawings to project what they hoped would represent the postwar scene. The editors of *Architectural Forum* devoted the September 1942 issue to this subject. Among the participants were Dailey (in this instance associated with Joseph Esherick) and Wurster. Dailey and Esherick proposed a prefabricated simple gabled-roof dwelling with a low mechanical box (labeled "Mechanical Nurses") connected to the house via a long tube. The two architects wrote that this house "could be flown any place [their sketch of the dwelling shows an accompanying streamlined car and an airplane], put up by unskilled labor in a matter of hours, and it will suit any climate and condition. It will be as American as a hot dog and the jeep, and it should be recognizable anywhere."[44] Although their text read as futuristic, the actual house, with its broad overhanging low-pitched roof and extended deck, was pure second Bay Region tradition.

Wurster's entry was a two-story single volume whose basic premise was "Flexible Space."[45] Although the structure had two stories, it was essentially a single-floor house. The lower level was devoted to an "auto shelter" and a "social hall." The upper floor could be divided in a number of different ways

166.
U.S. Merchant Marine Cadet School,
San Mateo, 1942
Gardner Dailey

167.
Schuckl Canning Company, Sunnyvale, 1942
William Wurster

to accommodate a family of from two to five people. Wurster presented his house via cutaway isometric drawings. No elevational views were presented to indicate the building's appearance, but close study of his drawings indicates that the house would have been similar to several of his pre–World War II minimal houses.

Although the appreciable difference in size makes it somewhat difficult to compare these two projects, they are in fact quite similar, although once again the smaller Dailey and Esherick project advertised the hand of a designer. In Wurster's project the designer's hand is only present in the details.

In the postwar years, from 1945 until Dailey's death in 1967, Dailey's and Wurster's designs continued to have more similarities than differences. It might perhaps be argued that some of Dailey's domestic designs, compared with those of Wurster, were more openly traditional, and that occasionally he incorporated elements such as low-pitched gabled volumes and details inspired by Japanese architecture. Most of Dailey's designs conveyed a feeling of formality, although this was of a relaxed kind. Dailey's exterior and interior detailing made reference to traditional fine cabinet work, whereas Wurster's designs generally bespoke the on-site carpenter. Both architects continued to utilize elements of the International Style after 1945: Wurster in his collaboration with Skidmore, Owings & Merrill in the Bank of America Building in San Francisco (1970–71), and Dailey with Walter T. Steilberg in the American Red Cross Building in San Francisco (1948).

When Henry-Russell Hitchcock and Arthur Drexler mounted an exhibition of American architecture in 1952 at the Museum of Modern Art in New York, they deemed the Bay Region tradition as no longer warranting serious consideration.[46] Wurster was not included, and Dailey was represented by his poured-concrete Red Cross Building.[47]

In James Ford and Katherine Morrow Ford's 1940 book, *The Modern House in America*, Dailey is quoted as saying: "In smaller residential houses American 'Modern' is expressed mostly in wood, following the Colonial and Victorian tradition. This vocabulary of painted wood and stucco over wood frame—almost never found in Europe—seems to me to be the unique contribution of America in the development of modern."[48] Although Wurster and Dailey occasionally diverged in their architecture, their source—the commonplace—was the same.

The Younger Bay Region Architects

A second figure who had emerged by 1941 as a spokesperson for the Bay Region tradition was John Ekin Dinwiddie (1902–1959).[49] In 1940 *House and Garden* posed the question "Tell Me, What Is Modern Architecture?" The editors paired two doctrinaire modernists—Walter Gropius and Marcel Breuer—against two soft modernists—William Wurster and John Ekin Dinwiddie.[50] Dinwiddie rejected the classic International Style, primarily because it was a self-conscious development out of early twentieth-century abstract and non-objective painting and sculpture. He observed, "There is a new generation behind the new architecture, but this new generation is not just hunting for new fashion. . . . There are new needs of an informal and healthier life which must be served."[51] Although Dinwiddie expressed reservations about traditional architectural images, he wrote, "We have done many houses with a Colonial feeling, American farmhouse types, etc., which we consider successful, but which bear little relation to any established style."[52]

During the thirties Dinwiddie actively participated in, and won awards in, numerous regional and national competitions. The designs he submitted to the shelter magazines tended to use traditional imagery—the Colonial or the California ranch house.[53] But by the early 1930s he was producing popular moderne designs, such as his General Electric Model Home, which was built in Berkeley in 1938.[54] Although Dinwiddie generally expressed reservations about the International Style, he came close to incorporating its imagery in the 1939 Bagley House in San Francisco (fig. 168), and especially in his Wilson Medical Building in Berkeley (1938–39).[55]

By the end of the 1930s he adopted the vocabulary of the woodsy Bay Region tradition, although, like Wurster and Dailey, he continued to design traditional houses.[56] His 1939 redwood-sheathed Cole House in Oakland lightly meanders over its site, creating a wonderful interplay between inside and outside. Interior space projected outward to a garden designed by Garrett Eckbo. More closely allied to the informal "shack" vocabulary of the Bay Region tradition was the Smith House in Menlo Park (ca. 1939) and a small town house in San Francisco (ca. 1942).[57]

Surprisingly Dinwiddie was not included in Elizabeth Mock's 1944 exhibition at the Museum of Modern Art, although he was represented in the 1949 exhibition "Domestic Architecture of the San Francisco Bay Region" at the San Francisco Museum of Art.[58] Perhaps Mock found his range of imagery disturbingly too broad. Compared with the work of Wurster, and even Dailey, Dinwiddie's buildings strongly projected the presence of the designer.

Another Bay Region figure missing from the Museum of Modern Art exhibition was Hervey Parke Clark (1899–1982), although he was included in the San Francisco exhibition.[59] Clark was certainly more committed to the woodsy Bay Region tradition than was Dinwiddie. Although hardly shacklike à la Wurster, his 1941 de Bivort House in Berkeley (fig. 169) played off formal modernist details and fenestration against a shed roof that certainly conveyed a sense of the ordinary.[60] In its refined form and detailing, Clark's beach cottage in Aptos for Charles O. Martin (1945–47), with a garden by Thomas Church, was much closer to Dailey than to Wurster.

168.
Bagley House, San Francisco, 1939
John Ekin Dinwiddie

169.
De Bivort House, Berkeley, 1941
Hervey Parke Clark

170.
Heckendorf House, Modesto, 1939
John Funk

By 1940 these already established Bay Region architects were joined by a younger contingent that included John Funk (b. 1908), Clarence W. Mayhew (b. 1907), Mario Corbett (b. 1900), Francis Joseph McCarthy (1910–1965), Michael Goodman (1903–1991), and Vernon DeMars (b. 1908).[61] All of them produced buildings before World War II—usually small to modest-size houses—that were regarded at the time as being part of the Bay Region tradition. Funk had worked in Wurster's office before opening his own practice in 1939.

From the moment it was completed, Funk's Heckendorf House in Modesto (1939) became the talisman of California's soft modernism (fig. 170). Featured on the cover of the catalogue accompanying the 1944 Museum of Modern Art exhibition, the house was published repeatedly in shelter magazines and architectural journals.[62] The design appeared beguilingly simple in its site layout, plan, and detailing. The house itself was a single elongated rectangle whose south wall consisted of a long bank of glass doors opening onto a walled outdoor living space that intervened between the street and the house. To one side of the wood-walled garden was the entrance walkway and the garage.

"This brilliant design by one of the younger San Francisco architects," wrote the editors of *Architectural Forum*, "presents new and tangible evidence of California's leadership in the field of modern domestic architecture."[63] As with most houses in the Bay Region tradition, it utilized redwood boards for the exterior and white pine plywood for the interior walls. The thin, flat, projecting roof plane and long garden wall of glass and French doors made the house modern, but not insistently so. The delicate detailing brought it closer to the Southern California soft modernism of Harwell H. Harris than to the work of either Wurster or Dailey.

Clarence W. Mayhew's reputation as an exponent of the Bay Region tradition rests, as does Funk's, on one house. In Mayhew's case, it is the often illustrated 1937 Manor House at Soule Tract, Contra Costa County (fig. 171).[64] California's ability to wed indoors and outdoors was beautifully captured in the solarium, with its glass roof, sliding glass walls, and the adjacent sliding glass walls of the living room. This house was a realization of flexible indoor/outdoor space, so often discussed by the exponents of modernism but never achieved in such a lyric fashion. "In general," Mayhew wrote, "the house has a Japanese character in both plan and elevation. Although I did not copy any Japanese details, I did copy the underlying principle."[65]

What is surprising about Mayhew's Manor House is that, with the exception of the solarium, the basic form of the house comes close to being a

171.
Manor House, Soule Tract,
Contra Costa County, 1937
Clarence W. Mayhew

172.
Tryon House, Berkeley, 1936
Michael Goodman

California ranch house that could have been produced by any number of California architects or designer/builders. Mayhew's other houses of the pre- and postwar period were generally well thought out and gracious designs, but they never repeated this singular tour de force.

Two other figures also considered exponents of the Bay Region tradition were Michael Goodman and Francis Joseph McCarthy. Unadorned redwood- or plywood-sheathed boxes are the images that come to mind for Goodman's houses (though he, like others of his generation, designed watered-down versions of the International Style as well as the low-lying California ranch house).[66] Goodman was perfectly capable of designing houses with traditional scale and proportions, but his strongest work seems to have been committed to the awkward and at times the ungainly. His Crandell House in Oakland (1936) projected various redwood-sheathed wings off a central volume covered by a very low-pitched shed roof.[67]

Goodman's L-shaped Tryon House in Berkeley (1936) aggressively broadcast its sheathing in plywood by covering the horizontal and vertical joints with battens (fig. 172).[68] The proportions were intentionally ungainly, a feature accentuated by the shed roof. Surprisingly, Goodman's use of plywood and "unsophisticated" proportions still ended up conveying the sense of an architect-designed building.

Francis Joseph McCarthy began his independent practice in San Francisco in 1938. One of his first published houses was the steep hillside residence for H. A. McPherson in San Francisco (1938).[69] In this and other houses McCarthy came close to producing a refined piece of furniture, somewhat similar to the work of Harwell H. Harris. There were, however, intentional disturbing notes; in the case of the McPherson House, the ungainly garage with its shed roof intervened between the house and the road.

In the years just before World War II, several young designers took up and continued the Bay Region tradition. As previously noted, Joseph Esherick (b. 1914) was associated with Gardner Dailey from 1938 to 1943. Esherick established his own firm in 1945 and quickly became, along with Wurster and Dailey, one of the chief figures of the postwar Bay Region tradition. In substance, Esherick's buildings—finely designed and detailed—were closer to those of his mentor, Gardner Dailey, than to Wurster's. An article on Esherick in the January 1952 issue of *House and Home* noted that Dailey's qualities of "meticulous attention to 'composition,' grace and distinction" had been passed on to those who had worked in his office, including Esherick.[70] If one were to suggest a point of similarity between his work and that of other architects, it would be with such Northwest regionalists as Pietro Belluschi, John Yeon, or Paul Thiry.

Other designers whose names are closely associated with the Bay Region tradition during those years were Ernest Born, Mario Corbett, and Vernon DeMars.[71] All three found a place in the 1949 seminal exhibition at the San Francisco Museum of Art, "Domestic Architecture of the San Francisco Bay Region."[72] DeMars was represented in the 1944 Museum of Modern Art exhibition by his two farm workers' communities, located near Woodville, California (1941), and at Chandler, Arizona (1936–37), while Corbett's stone and wood Thomsen House in Vina (1952) was the only Bay Region dwelling included in the 1952 Museum of Modern Art exhibition organized by Henry-Russell Hitchcock and Arthur Drexler.[73]

Born and Corbett, as products of the period revivalism of the twenties, played the field in terms of architectural images, ranging from the California ranch house and the Colonial Revival to redwood-sheathed boxes. Characteristic of these was Corbett's Perry House in Menlo Park (1941).[74] The house itself was an almost square box, accompanied by another two-story box housing the garage and study. Over both boxes was a simple shed roof covered with

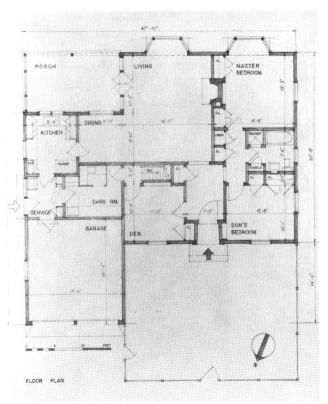

173.
Life House, 1938
H. Roy Kelley
Rendering

174.
Life House, 1938
H. Roy Kelley
Plan

rolled asphalt roofing. The editor of *Architectural Record* remarked upon the commonplace nature of structure and sheathing, although it should be noted that this had more to do with image than fact. If one's ideal was a low-cost house, redwood sheathing, interior plywood walls, exposed ceiling rafters, and vertical studs between the windows certainly did not constitute the cheapest approach.

Southern California Contemporaries

The out-and-out demanding modern image was not the main characteristic of the Bay Region before 1945. High-art modernism's center in California—or for that matter the United States—was Los Angeles. Here, in the 1930s the older established practitioners, R. M. Schindler and Richard J. Neutra, were joined by Paul Laszlo, J. R. Davidson, and the younger Raphael Soriano and Gregory Ain. Both Neutra and Schindler had designed a few houses in the Bay Region in the 1930s, but there is no indication that these houses or their other much published work had any direct impact in and around San Francisco. While most of the exponents of the Bay Region tradition tried their hand at the International Style, their work always came out as soft, accommodating moderne rather than modern.

The Southern California figures who came to share with their Bay Area compatriots a preference for comfortable woodsy modernism were Harwell H. Harris, at times Lloyd Wright, Gordon Drake, and, above all, H. Roy Kelley. Harris's strong but suggestively easygoing designs in wood or stucco always ended up being delicate, beautifully conceived pieces of sculpture. They certainly had little to do with the image of the commonplace—the central theme underlying the architecture of the second Bay Region tradition. In its dramatic forms, Harris's Haven House in Berkeley (1941) had more in common with Frank Lloyd Wright's Sturges House in Brentwood (1939) than any design by Wurster. Lloyd Wright's version of the woodsy California ranch house, such as his Griffith House in Canoga Park (1936), combined the traditional California image with that of his renowned father's Usonian Homes then being developed.[75]

In a number of ways, the Southern California figure who was the closest

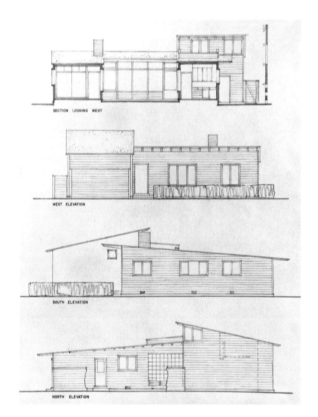

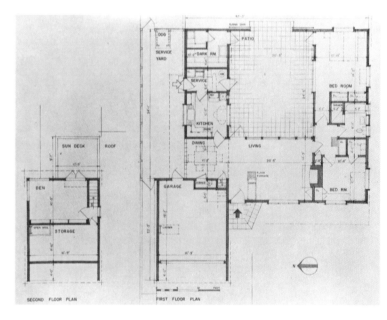

to Wurster was H. Roy Kelley (1893–1989).[76] Kelley's Beaux-Arts educational background was similar to that of Wurster, and he, too, opened his practice (in Los Angeles) in the mid-1920s. Like his northern contemporary, Kelley displayed an adroit ability to maneuver the various popular architectural images of the time: Monterey Revival, the California ranch house, the Anglo-Colonial, and English and French types.[77] He also turned to a form of soft, woodsy modernism in the late 1930s and continued in this vein in the decades after World War II. In its refinement of details and proportions, his redwood-sheathed Bagshaw House in Beverly Hills (1938) echoed both Dailey and Wurster.

In the 1938 series of *Life* houses, the pairing of Wurster as the modernist in opposition to Kelley the traditionalist was at best arbitrary; the roles could just as easily have been reversed.[78] Each designer fulfilled his assigned task: Kelley provided his Los Angeles clients with an Anglicized version of the California ranch house (figs. 173, 174), and Wurster seems to have gone out of his way to design an ungainly, awkward assemblage of loosely grouped shed-roof boxes. If Kelley had been the modernist in this contest, he would most likely have given the client something like his Bagshaw House, expressing a soft, easygoing, and elegant version of the modern.

The plan of Wurster's *Life* house conveyed a sophisticated approach to the traditional courtyard-oriented dwellings of California (figs. 175, 176). If he had preferred, Wurster could easily have clothed his design in a more traditional and appealing middle-class image, but he chose not to. The woodsy image of the shack was essential to his intent. The cultivated ungainly proportions and detailing of the design successfully hide the presence of the architect in a manner that none of his California contemporaries, north or south, could equal. This aim to hide the presence of the architect within the commonplace is a singular element that separates Wurster's work from that of his California contemporaries. As he wrote of the Bay Region tradition in 1960, "It is therefore a truly popular architecture, in a sense that much of the internationalists' work is not, it is an architecture of everyday use rather than form or intellectual theory. Viewed as sculpture, it may disappoint, but if in a democratic society architecture is a social art, it may have some validity."[79]

175.
Life House, 1938
William Wurster
Elevations

176.
Life House, 1938
William Wurster
Plan

Finally, a factor that emphatically separated Wurster from most of his California contemporaries was his specific use of regional architectural history. Just as the International Style modernists, through the writings of Sigfried Giedion, Nikolaus Pevsner, and Henry-Russell Hitchock, had selectively invented a history to justify the movement, Wurster helped create and then maintain the myth of a Bay Region tradition. But what interested him in this close to make-believe tradition was not the innovative high-art aspects realized in the turn-of-the-century work of Ernest Coxhead, Willis Polk, Bernard Maybeck, and Julia Morgan but rather their use (as he perceived it) of the commonplace.

Notes

1. Other architects represented in the *Pencil Points* series were Royal Barry Wills, Roland E. Coate, Randolph Evans, O'Neil Ford, Don Hatch, John S. Straub, and Alden B. Dow.

2. Kenneth Reid, "The Architect and the House, 3—William Wilson Wurster of California," *Pencil Points* 19, no. 8 (August 1938), pp. 427–94. There were eight architects finally included in the series. Of these, only William Wurster and Roland Coate were from the West Coast.

3. Ibid., p. 473.

4. John Taylor Boyd, Jr., "The Classic Spirit in Our Country Homes," *Arts and Decoration* 31, no. 10 (October 1919), pp. 59–62, 108, 126. In this interview by Taylor, Aldrich presented his views on how an architect should approach the design of country houses.

5. Ibid., p. 108.

6. Ibid., p. 62.

7. Reid, "The Architect and the House," pp. 473, 494.

8. Ibid., p. 472.

9. William Wilson Wurster—4 Houses in California," *Architectural Forum* 64, no. 5 (May 1936), pp. 377–402.

10. "*Life* Presents Eight Houses for Modern Living," "Architects for the Calverts: Kelley and Wurster," *Life* 5 (26 September 1938), pp. 47–48, 52–55.

11. "Exposition Model Homes," *Pencil Points* 20, no. 5 (May 1939), pp. 286–87.

12. Elizabeth Mock, ed., *Built in USA: 1932–1944* (New York: Museum of Modern Art, 1944), pp. 58, 104. The recent architecture of the West Coast was well represented in this exhibition, including work by Gregory Ain, Pietro Belluschi, Burton D. Cairns, Vernon DeMars, Charles H. Franklin, Harwell H. Harris, Ernest J. Kump, Edwin E. Merrill, Richard J. Neutra, John Gerard Raben, Raphael S. Soriano, Harry A. Thompson, Lewis E. Wilson, and John Yeon.

13. "William Wilson Wurster," *Architectural Forum* 79, no. 1 (July 1943), pp. 45–66.

14. Lewis Mumford, "The Skyline: The Status Quo," *The New Yorker* 23, no. 34 (11 October 1947), pp. 94–96, 99.

15. "What Is Happening to Modern Architecture?" *Museum of Modern Art Bulletin* 15, no. 3 (Spring 1948), pp. 3–21.

16. Wayne Andrews, *Architecture, Ambition and Americans* (New York: Harper and Brothers, 1947), pp. 252–87.

17. Ibid., pp. 256, 276.

18. John Burchard and Albert Bush-Brown, *The Architecture of America* (Boston: Little, Brown, 1961), pp 367, 485. Burchard and Bush-Brown were more sympathetic to Wurster's work when he came closer to the norm of International Style modernism, as in his projected housing for San Francisco's Golden Gateway Center Corporation (p. 495).

19. Vincent Scully, *American Architecture and Urbanism* (New York: Praeger, 1969), p. 130.

20. Leland M. Roth, *A Concise History of American Architecture* (New York: Harper & Row, 1979), p. 330.

21. William J. R. Curtis, *Modern Architecture Since 1900* (Englewood Cliffs, N.J.: Prentice-Hall, 1983), p. 334; Kenneth Frampton, *Modern Architecture: A Critical History* (New York and Toronto: Oxford University Press, 1980).

22. The closest match to Wurster among this group would be Lutah Maria Riggs, but even she, in the simplest of woodsy designs, never produced buildings whose goal was to hide the presence of the architect. See David Gebhard, *Lutah Maria Riggs: A Woman in Architecture, 1921–1980* (Santa Barbara: Capra Press, 1992).

23. Elizabeth Church, "Pasatiempo," *California Arts and Architecture* 39, no. 6 (June 1931), p. 54.

24. Clarence Tantau, "Study for a Residence," *Architect and Engineer* 127, no. 1 (October 1936), p. 13; also note in the same issue, p. 11, Tantau's Anglo-Colonial Revival ranch house for Philip Neill, Woodside (1936).

25. "Exposition Model Homes," *Pencil Points* 20, no. 5 (May 1939), pp. 270, 275, 279, 286–87.

26. Gardner A. Dailey, "Is There a Bay Area Style?" *Architectural Record* 105, no. 5 (May 1949), pp. 94–95.

27. Gardner A. Dailey, "Dean S. Arnold House, Hillsborough, California," *California Arts and Architecture* 36, no. 1 (July 1929), p. 44; Delight Ward Merner, "Plan to Bring Beauty into Our Daily Life," *California Arts and Architecture* 41, no. 4 (April 1932), pp. 33–35, 43.

28. Gardner A. Dailey, "Residence of E. M. Manning, Palo Alto, California," *Architect and Engineer* 121, no. 3 (May 1935), p. 32; idem, "Detail of Facade, Residence of E. M. Manning, Palo Alto," *Architect and Engineer* 134, no. 3 (October 1936), p. 15.

29. Dailey received the 1936 first prize from *House Beautiful* for his William Lowe, Jr., House in Woodside and also the 1937 first prize from the same magazine for his William Lowe, Sr., House in Woodside. In 1940 he was awarded first prize for his design of the Hudson House in Monterey. He won the 1937 second prize from *House and Garden* for his Leibs House at Hillsborough. See "Five Prize-Winning Holiday Houses," *House Beautiful* 79, no. 4 (March 1937), pp. 41–48; "*House Beautiful*'s 10th Annual Small House Competition," *House Beautiful* 80, no. 1 (January 1938), pp. 14–23; "*House Beautiful*'s 13th Annual Small House Competition," *House Beautiful* 83, no. 2 (February 1941), pp. 18–19; "*House and Garden* . . . Architects' Competition of 1937," *House and Garden* 72, no. 9 (September 1927), pp. 13–50.

30. Gardner A. Dailey, "Beach Club, Santa Barbara, Calif.," *Architectural Forum* 73, no. 12 (December 1940), pp. 497–500; the William Lowe, Jr., House was illustrated as an example of the modern in James Ford and Katherine Morrow Ford, *The Modern House in America* (New York: Architectural Book Publishing Co., 1940), p. 132. The Lowe House was also published in *Architectural Forum* 66, no. 4 (April 1937), pp. 324–25. Another modern design of the mid-1930s was his "Two Family Roof Terrace Dwelling, Telegraph Hill, San Francisco," illustrated in *Architect and Engineer* 128, no. 4 (March 1937), p. 19.

31. Eugene Neuhaus, *The Art of Treasure Island* (Berkeley: University of California Press, 1939), p. 24.

32. Gardner A. Dailey, "Brazilian Bldg. at San Francisco Fair," *Architectural Forum* 70, no. 6 (June 1938), pp. 492–93; "U.S. of Brazil Pavilion in San Francisco," *Architectural Record* 65, no. 4 (April 1939), p. 45.

33. Gardner A. Dailey, "*Good Housekeeping*" House, "Woodside Hills," *Pencil Points* 20, no. 5 (May 1939), p. 290.

34. "Low Cost House for *Life,* Gardner Dailey, Architect," *Architectural Forum* 72, no. 4 (April 1940), pp. 223–25; "*Life* House No. 2, Menlo Park, Calif., Gardner A. Dailey, Architect," *Architectural Forum* 73, no. 1 (July 1940), p. 6.

35. "Low Cost House for *Life*," p. 223. The "Life" houses were presented for popular consumption in the pages of *Life* magazine. For the professional architect they were illustrated and discussed in *Architectural Forum*.

36. "Houses for $3,000 to $4,000 Income," *Architectural Forum* 69, no. 5 (November 1938), pp. 321–25.

37. Gardner A. Dailey, "Combined Residence and Office for Dr. and Mrs. Bernard

Berliner, San Francisco, Calif.," *Architectural Record* 89, no. 1 (January 1941), pp. 96–98; "A Redwood House, Residence of Dr. and Mrs. B. Berliner, San Francisco, Calif.," *California Arts and Architecture* 26, no. 8 (September 1940), p. 28; "Dr. Bernard Berliner House, San Francisco," *Architect and Engineer* 57, no. 3 (September 1940), p. 26.

38. "A Portfolio of Houses by Gardner A. Dailey," "House in Sausalito," *Architectural Forum* 74, no. 5 (May 1941), pp. 363–65. The Owens House reflected not only the design approach of Dailey but also that of a younger Bay Area figure, Joseph Esherick, who worked in the Dailey office from 1938 to 1943.

39. William W. Wurster, "Office Building for the Schuckl Canning Co.," *Architect and Engineer* 154, no. 2 (August 1943), pp. 12–17; "Country Office Building," *California Arts and Architecture* 61, no. 6 (June 1944), pp. 20–22.

40. Gardner A. Dailey, "Maritime School, West Coast," *Architectural Forum* 78, no. 5 (May 1943), pp. 55–59.

41. Ibid., p. 56.

42. Elizabeth Mock, ed., *Built in USA: 1932–1944,* pp. 78–79; 104–05.

43. Burchard and Bush-Brown, *The Architecture of America,* p. 405; Andrews, *Architecture, Ambition and Americans,* p. 280.

44. Gardner A. Dailey and Joseph Esherick, "House DE-2, Magic Carpet Series," *Architectural Forum* 77, no. 3 (September 1942), p. 133.

45. William Wilson Wurster, "Flexible Space," *Architectural Forum* 77, no. 3 (September 1942), pp. 140–42.

46. Henry-Russell Hitchcock and Arthur Drexler, eds., *Built in USA: Post-war Architecture* (New York: Simon & Schuster, 1953).

47. Ibid., pp. 56–57.

48. James Ford and Katherine Morrow Ford, *The Modern House in America,* p. 123.

49. Dinwiddie studied architecture at the University of Michigan under Eliel Saarinen. He established his own firm in San Francisco in 1931; by the end of the thirties, Henry Hill and Phillip Joseph and the landscape architect Garrett Eckbo were associated with him. During the 1940s he worked on several projects in San Francisco with Erich Mendelsohn. Regrettably, as was the case with several other gifted California designers, including Harwell H. Harris and Gregory Ain, he was lured away from practice in California to be an academic dean; he went to Tulane University in New Orleans in 1953.

50. "Tell Me, What Is Modern Architecture?" *House and Garden* 77, no. 4 (April 1940), pp. 46–47; *House and Garden* 77, no. 5 (May 1940), pp. 50, 60.

51. Ibid., p. 71.

52. Ibid., p. 50.

53. "Prize Winners in Annual Awards in Architecture," *House and Garden* 79, no. 1 (January 1940), pp. 15–23; "*House and Garden* Presents the 1940 Prize Winners," *House and Garden* 79, no. 1 (January 1941), pp. 24–35, 55.

54. John Ekin Dinwiddie, "Second Prize, Class B, Winning Designs in the Home Electric Competition, Sponsored by the General Electric Company," *American Architect* 146, no. 4 (April 1935), p. 39; "General Electric Model Home, Berkeley," *American Architect* 52, no. 10 (October 1937), p. 14.

55. Frederick W. Jones, "Recent Work of John Ekin Dinwiddie, Architect," *Architect and Engineer* 141, no. 4 (April 1940), pp. 23, 42–43.

56. Frederick W. Jones, "Recent Work of John Ekin Dinwiddie, Architect," *Architect and Engineer* 141, no. 4 (April 1940), pp. 17–44.

57. Ibid., pp. 18–19; "House at San Francisco, California," *Progressive Architecture* 27, no. 8 (August 1946), pp. 67–68.

58. *Domestic Architecture of the San Francisco Bay Region* (San Francisco: San Francisco Museum of Art, 1949).

59. Like Dinwiddie, Clark and his partner, John F. Beuttler, were included in the 1949 Bay Region exhibition at the San Francisco Museum of Art. For examples of Clark's pre-World War II work, see "Houses by Hervey Parke Clark," *Architectural Forum* 73, no. 6 (December 1940), pp. 479–91.

60. Hervey Parke Clark, "H. G. de Bivort House, Berkeley," *California Arts and Architecture* 59, no. 3 (March 1942), pp. 28–29.

61. Other important designers who also were exponents of the Bay Region tradition, both before and after World War II, were Warren Callister, Frederick Leroy Confer, Henry Hill, Jack Hillmer, Ernest Kump, Fred Langhorst, Joseph Allen Stein, and Worley K. Wong. A strong case could be made that one of the great monuments of the post–World War II Bay Region tradition was the Russell House (1952) in San Francisco, designed by the expatriate German architect Erich Mendelsohn. In this house Mendelsohn combined his own highly personal version of the International Style, softened through his sensitivity to the urban hillside site, with his use of wood sheathing and details. For a discussion of these and other Bay Area figures, see Sally Woodbridge, ed., *Bay Area Houses* (Salt Lake City: Peregrine Smith, 1988).

62. Elizabeth Mock, ed., *Built in USA: 1932–1944,* cover, pp. 30–31.

63. "House in Modesto, Calif. John Funk, Architect," *Architectural Forum* 74, no. 4 (March 1941), p. 195.

64. Clarence W. W. Mayhew, "House for Harold V. Manor, Soule Tract, Calif.," *Architectural Forum* 71, no. 1 (July 1939), pp. 9–11.

65. Ibid., p. 10.

66. William C. Hays, "A Tribute to the Work of Michael Goodman, Architect," *Architect and Engineer* 139, no. 4 (November 1939), pp. 17–19.

67. Michael Goodman, "Miss Helen L. Crandell House, Berkeley," *Architectural Forum* 66, no. 5 (May 1937), pp. 434–35.

68. "Standard Construction: Modular Design; House of Robert Tryon, Berkeley, Calif., Michael Goodman, Architect," *Architectural Record* 83, no. 5 (May 1938), p. 99.

69. "House Planned Around a Court," *Architectural Record* 88, no. 4 (October 1940), pp. 66–67.

70. "Joseph Esherick and His Use of Form, His Use of Space, His Use of Site," *House and Home* 1, no. 1 (January 1952), p. 125.

71. Born opened his office in San Francisco in 1937, Corbett in 1932, and DeMars in 1937.

72. *Domestic Architecture of the San Francisco Bay Region.*

73. Elizabeth Mock, ed., *Built in USA: 1932–1944,* pp. 60–63; Henry-Russell Hitchcock and Arthur Drexler, eds., *Built in USA: Post-War Architecture,* pp. 54–55.

74. Mario Corbett, "Menlo Park House for H. T. Perry," *Architectural Record* 91, no. 1 (January 1942), pp. 56–57; "House in Menlo Park, Calif.," *Architect and Engineer* 147, no. 6 (December 1941), p. 34.

75. Lloyd Wright, "Ranch House for Raymond Griffith," *Architectural Forum* 68, no. 6 (June 1938), pp. 471–78.

76. Another Southern California architect whose work displays some parallels to Wurster's was the Santa Barbara architect Lutah Maria Riggs. She and Wurster were both trained at the University of California at Berkeley in the teens under John Galen Howard. Like Wurster, she developed a soft version of modernism, though in her case this transformation did not occur until after World War II. The general refinement of her modernist designs places her work closer to Dailey's than to the typical designs of Wurster.

77. Winchton L. Risley, "The Domestic and Other Architecture of H. Roy Kelley," *Architect and Engineer* 106, no. 3 (September 1931), pp. 25–60; H. Roy Kelley, "Three California Houses," *Architect and Engineer* 124, no. 2 (February 1936), pp. 28–31.

78. "*Life* Presents Eight Houses for Modern Living," "Architects for the Calverts: Kelley and Wurster," pp. 47–48, 52–55; "*Life* Houses," *Architectural Forum* 69, no. 5 (November 1938), pp. 321–27.

79. William W. Wurster, "L'Architettura moderna in California," *Casabella continuita,* no. 238 (April 1960), p. 13.

A Partnership: Catherine Bauer and William Wurster

Gwendolyn Wright

The trajectory of individual biography has been viewed from many perspectives, ranging from artistic development to political engagement, from conflicting fragments to holistic synthesis. Biographies of architects' lives usually idealize an innate individual talent, either gradually or suddenly made manifest, which then characterizes all of a person's creative work. I would not counter this romantic schema with poststructuralism's denial of "the author" as a creative force, nor its insistence that "the self" is only an illusion, masking a multitude of roles and self-perceptions that prevail at different moments in life's maelstrom. Yet we do need a more dynamic understanding of architects as individuals. Political actions, intellectual challenges, even the exhilarating impact of love will often produce a dramatic effect—not simply in the background of a person's daily life but at the very core of his or her hopes and ambitions. This is certainly the case with William Wurster, whose personal and professional life first crystallized in one form during his early career, then shifted dramatically, taking on new dimensions, after his marriage to Catherine Bauer in 1940.

During the first, fruitful decade of his career, Wurster focused almost entirely on single-family residences for moderately well-to-do clients. Each dwelling was distinct, though all abided by a deliberate set of architectonic principles. The houses were spare yet emphatically comfortable, casual yet finely composed; each provided an ideal setting for the ordinary yet precious events of daily life, a setting that heightened, but never upstaged, the human events that took place there. Wurster unequivocally considered himself a modernist with these designs, even when he complied with the client's preference for a historic facade. That self-definition, as he later explained in *House and Garden,* meant a fascination with useful new technologies, a comfortable, but never austere, minimalist aesthetic, a concern for functionalism based on varied social and individual uses of the dwelling, and a rejection of categorical rules, whether past or present.[1]

With the onset of the Depression, Wurster, like most architects, thought more seriously about the aesthetics of simplicity and economy, as well as the collective nature of residential design. At Pasatiempo near Santa Cruz and Kent Woodlands in Marin County, he began to explore the relationship between adjacent dwellings. In 1939 came a more defined role as supervising architect for Park Hills, an elite residential enclave facing the Tilden Park golf course at the edge of Berkeley. Here Wurster established design controls, drew up entries for the subdivision, and continued to review proposals for new houses throughout the 1940s, emphasizing a cohesive pattern of setbacks, massing, and facades.

177.
Catherine Bauer Wurster, 1942

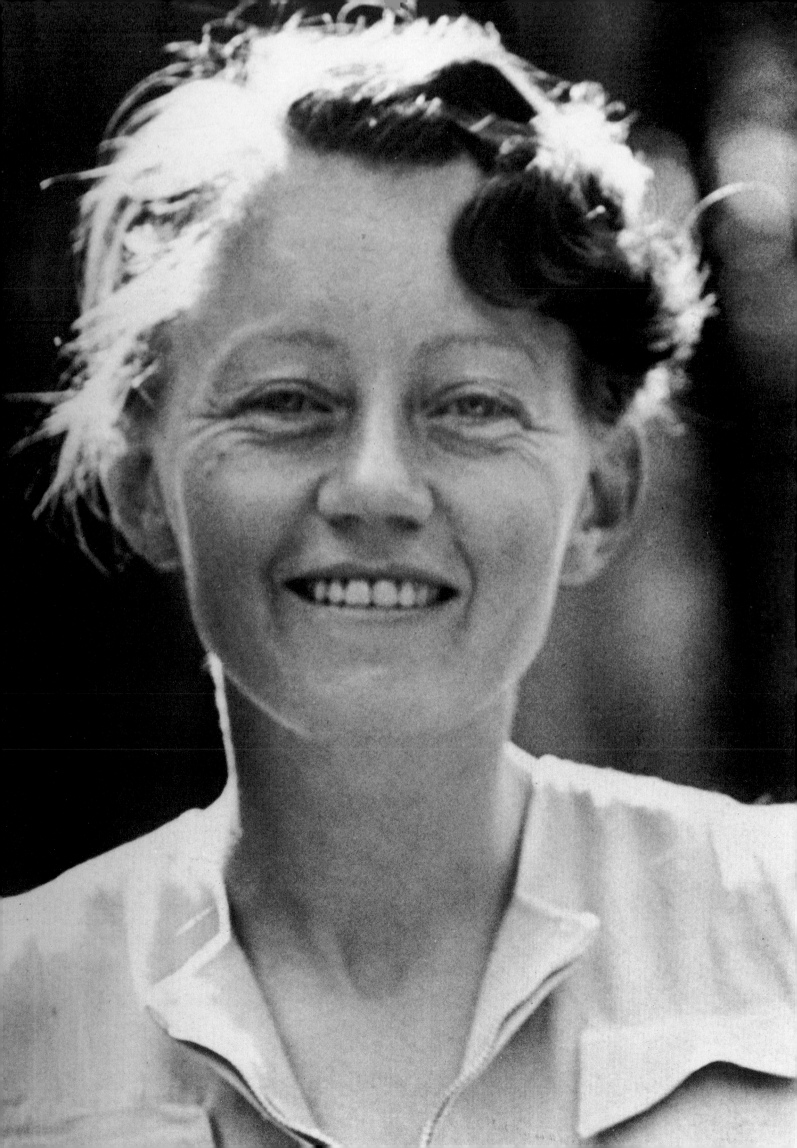

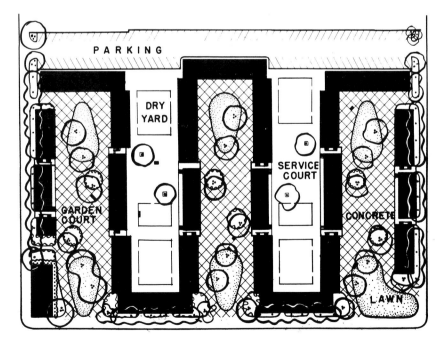

178.
Stern Hall Women's Dormitories, University
of California at Berkeley, 1942–43
William Wurster and Corbett & MacMurray

179.
Valencia Gardens Public Housing,
San Francisco, 1939–43
William Wurster
Plan

He also built a small apartment building in San Francisco, exhibition homes for the 1939 World's Fair, and student dormitories at Berkeley (fig. 178). These suggest more fundamental changes in the kinds of houses he found intriguing. Concretizing the metaphors of inconspicuous consumption he had previously used for upper-middle-class clients, Wurster now began to consider the architectural and political significance of housing that was indeed low cost rather than merely looking that way.

Wurster sought his first social-housing commission simply because he needed work. Early in 1939, he received the commission for Valencia Gardens, located in San Francisco's Mission District, although it was not completed until 1943 because of wartime delays (fig. 179). Ironically, both the federal funds and the guidelines for this project came from the U.S. Housing Authority, which Bauer, then based in Washington, had recently helped launch.

The design assimilates three distinct cultural sources: a close approximation of the efficient unit plans for Ernst May's Frankfurt *Siedlungen;* an appreciation of the lyrical spatial organization in Scandinavian cooperative housing, which Wurster had recently visited; and allusions to the smooth, brightly tinted walls and spacious courtyards of the Mexican vernacular, evoking the heritage of Latino residents in the surrounding neighborhood. Unlike Spanish or Latin American houses, however, the sequence of Wurster's courtyards was not hidden behind a wall but opened directly onto the busy sidewalk, emphasizing a continuity with the people and activities of the street. Moreover, in decided contrast to comparable European housing, Wurster downplayed a strong central axis, preferring "to stress the dignity of the individual . . . family."[2]

Almost simultaneously Wurster also began to explore the parameters of a prefabricated minimalist dwelling, first using steel panels and then, in the 1940s, designing wood-frame model houses for *Life, Pencil Points,* and the *Ladies' Home Journal.* By 1945 he was chosen to build one of the "Case Study Houses" for *Arts and Architecture,* which were intended to demonstrate technology's ability to generate new forms for modern life and design (fig. 180, 182).

With historical distance, such shifts and expansions in an architect's life often seem smooth, even inevitable. In Wurster's case, there is no doubt that the metamorphosis was, in part, a response to the remarkable, vivacious housing reformer, Catherine Bauer, whom he met in early 1940 and married in August of that year. She was thirty-five; he, a decade older. Each had for years challenged conventional notions of sexual propriety and pursued demanding professional careers, never expecting to marry.

To give such prominence to an architect's wife is to challenge the very conventions of architectural biography. The genre has by and large downplayed even the role of clients and office colleagues in favor of a more heroic, autonomous ideal of creative genius. The interpersonal realm seems merely a trivial distraction from higher artistic pursuits. Early upbringing has its formative place, but not adult love, although some feminist writers have speculated about gender biases and desires.[3] Many dimensions still remain virtually unexplored because of such attitudes: the joys and dissonance of intimacy, the counterpoint of understanding another person's difference, a deeper self-knowledge gained through the eyes of a loved one, and ventures beyond the limits of that self, which had once seemed fixed. As Martha Nussbaum writes in *Love's Knowledge: Essays on Philosophy and Literature:*

> And what if it is love one is trying to understand, that strange unmanageable phenomenon or form of life, source at once of illumination and confusion, agony and beauty? Love, in its many varieties, and their tangled relations to the good human life, to aspiration, to general social concern?[4]

All of these questions reverberate in creative work.

180.
Case Study House No. 3, 1945
Wurster and Bernardi
Interior view

Thus we cannot ignore the intellectual, professional, and personal connections between Catherine Bauer and William Wurster during their twenty-four years of married life and collegial relations. Nor is the influence one-sided, even if historical interest might favor one person over another—which should not be the case here. Each of these individuals strengthened certain attributes of the other, opened new dimensions of professional concern, and expanded the sphere of their own commitments.

To understand their lives together, we must first explore Bauer's youth. Born in 1905 in Elizabeth, New Jersey, to a professional family long involved in Republican politics, Catherine graduated from Vassar in 1926.[5] After several adventurous years in Paris and Greenwich Village, crowned by an article on Le Corbusier in the *New York Times Magazine,* Bauer settled into a job at a New York publishing house.[6] Here in 1929 she met the young author Lewis Mumford, who was, like Wurster, a decade her senior. Drawn together by a mutual interest in modern architecture, they soon began a passionate love affair that lasted for several years.

As a couple, they, too, experienced reciprocal growth. With characteristic intensity, Bauer spurred Mumford to take on the grand themes of technology and community, which would become the basis of his best-known books, thus resolving his unique role as a critic.[7] He, in turn, encouraged her to contemplate aspects of design that could not be quantified, to broaden and humanize her definition of housing reform. Mumford introduced Bauer to major architects and critics who would become her lifelong friends: Oscar Stonorov, Frank Lloyd Wright, Frederick Gutheim, Walter Behrendt, and many others. With Mumford, Clarence Stein, the environmentalist Benton MacKaye, and other members of the Regional Planning Association of America (RPAA), she discussed the future of American cities with reference to the legacy of New England towns and planned suburbs in the 1920s. After helping Mumford organize the "Housing" section of the Museum of Modern Art's seminal 1932 exhibition, "Modern Architecture," Bauer became a member of the museum's Committee on Architecture and Industrial Art.[8]

Despite their commonalities, political and aesthetic differences grew sharper. Bauer's enthusiasm for European modernism culminated in an award from *Fortune* magazine in 1931 for her article praising Ernst May's Frankfurt *Siedlungen.*[9] Mumford criticized Bauer's pragmatic belief in such liberal reform, and she became frustrated by his melancholy aestheticism. Quite self-consciously Mumford placed first his wife, then his new lover "on probation," as he sought to determine which relationship would be most beneficial to his writing.[10] By the time he and Bauer set off for Germany in 1932, Mumford expected her to do his research, while she insisted on her own priorities—and even her own sexual liberties. By the spring of 1933, after Mumford had returned to his wife, tensions between them had become irreconcilable. Yet the two (indeed the foursome) would remain lifelong friends and colleagues, with mutual respect and shared goals for American architecture.

Bauer compiled her thoughts, data, and illustrations of European social housing into a book, *Modern Housing*, published in 1934, which *Architectural Forum* hailed as being "to her field what Blackstone's is to law."[11] With its enthusiasm for the "new form . . . [and] joyous, extravagant creative *élan*" of recent European design,[12] this spirited compendium appealed greatly to liberal American architects and New Deal politicians (fig. 183). In contrast to Hitchcock and Johnson's *Modern Architecture* catalogue of 1932, Bauer refused canonical rules of form and ignored sumptuous private houses; her definition of modernism emphasized the multiplicity of approaches in successful low-cost, publicly funded projects. There was no "simple formula"; Bauer astutely analyzed many aspects of community designs and individual unit plans, commending "the innumerable variations, affecting both method and form, which are due to local requirements, habits, limitations or desires."[13] She also insisted that housing reform necessarily involved changes in municipal politics and financing, as well as architectural form.

Modern Housing boldly challenged Americans not to imitate these European examples—for none of them escaped some constructive criticism—but to develop their own indigenous experiments in design, financing, and policy, based on a synthesis of radical innovations and vernacular precedents. In the United States, she declared, the *Neue Sachlichkeit* could become a *"new realism,"* independent of the obsessively rigid standards of Otto Haesler's *Existenzminimum* (which celebrated the spartan beauty of minimal standards) and the overly sculptural forms of Le Corbusier. Americans must instead follow two simultaneous trajectories: "the line of rational investigation" and "the whole broad history of mass emotion and popular desire."[14]

Meanwhile, Bauer went on to help organize the Labor Housing Conference in Philadelphia, then moved to Washington, D.C., where, as a lobbyist for the AFL-CIO Housing Committee, she helped draft and win passage of the Wagner-Steagall housing bills of 1937, then stayed on as a publicist for the U.S. Housing Authority created by that legislation.[15] By 1939, ready to leave Washington politics, Bauer returned to Europe to complete her research on modern housing in Scandinavia and the Soviet Union, funded by the Guggenheim Foundation, but the outbreak of World War II forced her return. Instead, in January 1940 she went to the University of California at Berkeley as the Rosenberg Professor of Public Social Service.

Less than a year later, in choosing to marry Bill Wurster, Bauer found an architect who shared her aesthetic values and her delight in architectural innovation; she expanded the scope of her reform vision and came to cherish the many virtues of the Bay Area. He, in turn, found a "houser" (as such experts and activists called themselves) who shared his philosophical values and his preference for straightforward presentation. Mutual friends agree that she undeniably politicized him; Wurster's projects and pedagogy after 1940 are infused with Bauer's social and political aspirations.

Carquinez Heights was the first example of Wurster's work to suggest this influence: approximately 1,700 units of housing and community buildings, part of an immense federal project to provide for workers at the Vallejo shipyards (figs. 184, 140). Designed in the fall of 1941, this vast complex was built in only seventy-three days. Wurster made "no apology" for the fact that the dwellings were uniform, simple, and cheap.[16] He sought to balance three con-

181.
Catherine Bauer Wurster, no date

182.
Adaptation of Chabot Terrace war housing as a prefabricated "home of the future," 1943
William Wurster

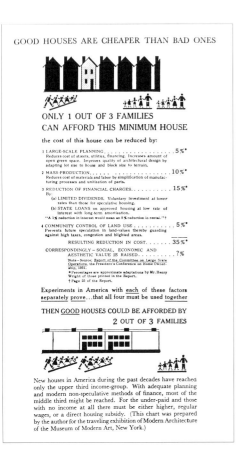

GOOD HOUSES ARE CHEAPER THAN BAD ONES

ONLY 1 OUT OF 3 FAMILIES
CAN AFFORD THIS MINIMUM HOUSE

the cost of this house can be reduced by:

1 LARGE-SCALE PLANNING 5%*
Reduces cost of streets, utilities, financing. Increases amount of
open green space. Improves quality of architectural design by
adapting lot size to house and block size to terrain.

2 MASS-PRODUCTION. 10%*
Reduces cost of materials and labor by simplification of manufacturing processes and unitization of parts.

3 REDUCTION OF FINANCIAL CHARGES. 15%*
By:
  (a) LIMITED DIVIDENDS, Voluntary Investment at lower
      rates than those for speculative housing.
  (b) STATE LOANS on approved housing at low rate of
      interest with long-term amortization.
  "A 1% reduction in interest would mean an 8% reduction in rental."†

4 COMMUNITY CONTROL OF LAND USE 5%*
Prevents future speculation in land-values thereby guarding
against high taxes, congestion and blighted areas.

        RESULTING REDUCTION IN COST. 35%*

CORRESPONDINGLY – SOCIAL, ECONOMIC AND
     AESTHETIC VALUE IS RAISED. . . . .?%
Note—Source: Report of the Committee on Large Scale
Operations, the President's Conference on Home Owner-
ship, 1931.
*Percentages are approximate adaptations by Mr. Henry
Wright of those printed in the Report.
†Page 25 of the Report.

Experiments in America with each of these factors
separately prove...that all four must be used together

THEN GOOD HOUSES COULD BE AFFORDED BY
              2 OUT OF 3 FAMILIES

New houses in America during the past decades have reached
only the upper third income-group. With adequate planning
and modern non-speculative methods of finance, most of the
middle third might be reached. For the under-paid and those
with no income at all there must be either higher, regular
wages, or a direct housing subsidy. (This chart was prepared
by the author for the traveling exhibition of Modern Architecture
of the Museum of Modern Art, New York.)

housing

A MEMORANDUM

TO: DR. REMSEN BIRD AND MR. WILLIAM SCHUCHARDT, REPRE-
SENTING THE CITY OF LOS ANGELES.

FROM: CATHERINE BAUER, VICE-PRESIDENT, CALIFORNIA PLANNING
AND HOUSING ASSOCIATION AND CONSULTANT, FEDERAL
PUBLIC HOUSING AUTHORITY.

SUBJECT: HIGHLIGHTS IN THE HOUSING PICTURE

"Housing" has three different aspects to be considered: (1) As a vital industry in terms of its efficiency,
stability, and effective consumers' market; (2) As a
prime social problem in terms of the removal and
prevention of slums and rehousing of families now
occupying sub-standard dwellings; (3) As the major
element in the physical structure and quality of cities,
hence a determining factor in city and regional planning. Progress in these categories can best be outlined
in terms of three distinct periods.

Back in the 1920's, before the crash, the housing industry was booming, but on a very unstable basis.
Speculative financial practices knew no limits and
costs were so high that the market of potential home

183.
"Good Houses Are Cheaper than Bad Ones"
Chart published in Catherine Bauer's Modern
Housing, 1934

184.
Abstracted site plan of Carquinez Heights.
Published in California Arts and
Architecture, February 1943, accompanying
an article by Catherine Bauer, "Housing: A
Memorandum"

cerns: economical, efficient construction (prefabricated plywood wall panels
and plumbing lines, flat roofs to allow both ceiling and roof to be manufactured at the same time); a familiar typology of forms and materials (lightweight
wood balconies and outdoor stairs); and pleasurable amenities (small enclosed
laundry yards for each unit and the play of bright colors for half the houses—
the rest were in unfinished plywood).

For both economical and ecological reasons, Wurster was determined to
scar the hills as little as possible. The topography supplied animation to the
housing blocks, which were irregularly placed up and down the rolling amber
hills, then wedged into place with concrete footings. The layout was by no
means accidental, for the site plan provided almost every unit with dramatic
views of the bay.

Even under such constraints, Wurster still wanted to push the limits of
existing expectations, echoing Bauer's earlier call for continual, focused experimentation. Arguing that, in every project, "some small portion should attempt
to bring new knowledge," he insisted that the government set aside twenty-
five units where he would have complete freedom, apart from governmental
standards and cost limits, to try three different types of new prefabricated systems—masonry, skeleton frame, and bent frame (figs. 142–146).[17]

In addition, again in line with Bauer's recognition of the pivotal role community buildings could play in a successful housing project, Wurster supervised the placement and design of schools and auditoriums at the core of
Carquinez Heights, together with another group at nearby Chabot Terrace (fig.
185). These structures were envisioned as monumental declarations of a shared
public vision: dynamic architectural statements that would reinforce their role
as social and educational centers for all residents.[18]

Thus Wurster's mode of experimentation did not aim to transgress but
rather to elevate the human experience of a place, even under difficult constraints, through modern technology and sensitive design priorities (fig. 186).
He sought to understand the "feelings of a person who looks at the project. . . .
Don't ask that it be familiar or cozy. But do ask if it fits the site—uses the
view—is gay—is economical—was done on schedule . . . and I hope you can
say, as I do, 'I'd like to live there.'"[19]

Bauer, too, saw war housing as an opportunity for innovation. The speed
of production gave local architects and officials exceptional autonomy vis-à-
vis Washington. She believed that architectural autonomy was directly related
to design of a high quality. Determined to maintain them both, she argued for
imaginative site planning, expansive community services and infrastructure,
public/private financing, and considerable local control as the basis for a comprehensive postwar housing policy for all income groups.[20]

Wurster would carry this concept of community design into one of his
largest postwar commissions: a forty-three-acre complex of community center,
schools, playgrounds, and open space for San Francisco's Sunset District, conceived in 1945 and built in 1952 (figure 187). As coordinating architect, Wurster
developed initial plans for the high school, library, and other units. His master plan of open spaces—interior courts, playgrounds, and generous entry
plazas—defined the whole, connecting activities to one another and to the surrounding streets, trapping sun and creating human scale.[21] The collaboration
of several designers assured stylistic diversity, even within so large a setting.
Today the complex still provides a multivalent focus for the diverse cultural
community in the neighborhood.

A decade later, San Mateo's Woodlake can be seen as Wurster's homage to
Bauer's "philosophy of neighborhood planning" in the aftermath of her accidental death in 1964. This thirty-acre, 944-unit Planned Unit Development
(PUD), completed in 1965, represents a renewed effort to cluster higher-density
row houses in an engaging site plan, setting aside capacious landscaped areas

185.
School, Chabot Terrace, Vallejo, 1942
Franklin and Kump

186.
Carquinez Heights, Vallejo, 1941
William Wurster
Site plan

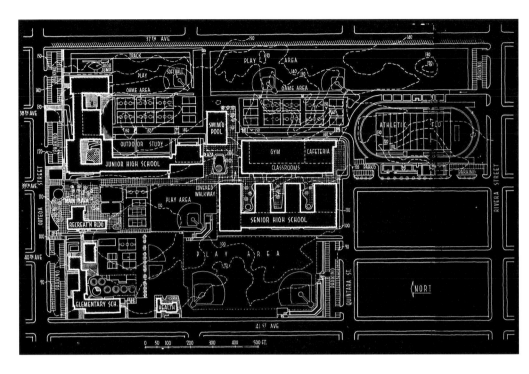

187.
Sunset Community Center, San Francisco,
1950–52
Wurster, Bernardi and Emmons
Site plan

for rest, recreation, and social activities, as well as peripheral areas for parking and neighborhood shops (figures 188, 189). Yet Woodlake's goal of "self-
sufficiency" did not meet a principal aim of Bauer's philosophy—class and
racial integration.[22] Without a concerned advocate, architectural references to
community can easily substitute formal metaphors for social policy.

Certainly it was Bauer who encouraged her husband to recognize and then
publicly insist that housing reform go beyond functional plans and structural
systems. As chairman of the National Housing Agency's advisory committee
in 1942 and again, under President Harry S Truman, in the early 1950s, Wurster
openly criticized the government's failure to address the racial implications of
segregated, overscaled public housing projects and the single-race, single-class
suburbs endorsed by FHA mortgages. As Bauer acerbically pointed out, "The
trend toward segregation is only one example of the kind of question we have
neglected while we argued about cul-de-sacs."[23] Wurster now echoed her con-
tention that it was the *duty* of architects to challenge the status quo—in social
as well as formal terms.[24]

After her marriage and the birth of a daughter, Sadie, in 1945, Bauer continued teaching and writing, consulted in Washington for various federal agencies, and took vocal positions about many local controversies through
organizations she helped found, such as the California Housing and Planning
Association.[25] In an article entitled "Housing's White Knight Is a 'Handsome
Blonde with Brunette Economic Ideas,'" *Architectural Forum* nervously
assured readers that Wurster was "no lap-dog husband, pet of a determined
career woman."[26]

Of course Bauer's marriage to Wurster expanded the scope of her concerns
and her work as well. At least three aspects of the built environment gained
prominence: a call for the preservation of natural environments, a vision of
coordinated urban and suburban development, and a fuller recognition of
architectural aesthetics. In many ways, each of these harks back to her time in
New York with Mumford, but she had now developed the ability to appreciate and synthesize these issues into her own distinctive, politically astute style.
Equally important, Bauer applied herself to a much larger, more truly urban
scale than the garden-city ideal of Mumford and the RPAA. She rejected theirs
as much as any other utopian vision.

It is easy to understand how the natural beauties of the Bay Area, which
Wurster accentuated in his designs, could stir Bauer's passions. Presciently, by

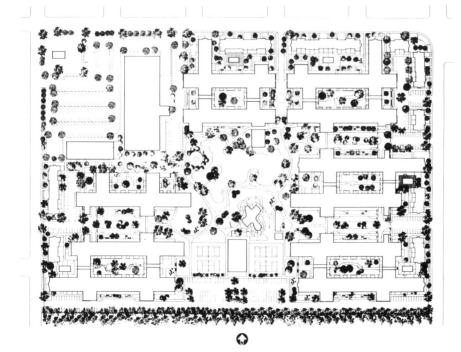

188.
Woodlake Planned Unit Development,
San Mateo, 1963–65
Wurster, Bernardi and Emmons with
Lawrence Halprin, landscape architect
Site plan

189.
Woodlake Planned Unit Development,
San Mateo, 1963–65
Wurster, Bernardi and Emmons with
Lawrence Halprin, landscape architect
View from adjacent Peninsular Avenue

the 1950s she had begun to insist on the need to plan the "fringe" around cities, anticipating the changes that would take place there. She called for the expansion of state and local parklands, kept free from development, and campaigned vigorously against the abuses of agribusiness in California's Central Valley.[27]

If Bauer opened her husband's eyes to the challenge of low-cost housing, he helped her become more aware of the needs of middle-class American families, both in city apartments and suburban homes.[28] She spoke frankly about matters that most architects refused to acknowledge, insisting on the need to understand why so many Americans preferred suburbs. It was not just their moderately priced, familiar-looking homes, good schools, easy access to nature, and automobile mobility, she realized, but another reason—the preference for homogeneous communities.[29] Bauer felt that this honest knowledge could help generate new types of residential settings that balanced comfortable familiarity with necessary reforms.

The same call for diversity, at once socioeconomic and architectural, pertained to urban redevelopment projects. As early as 1943, Bauer had insisted, "Real urbanity and convenience instead of congestion, real distinction other than mere size, are the only qualities that can save the old centers."[30] When actual redevelopment projects took form in the 1950s, Bauer bluntly described them as government subsidies for developers in which local history was demolished for cold, overstandardized architecture, inaccessible in every way to the urban poor and working class who had lost their homes.[31]

Bauer specifically criticized San Francisco's Golden Gateway urban-renewal area. Asking pointedly, "Do Americans Hate Cities?" she denounced the proposed displacement, condemned the segregation, and lamented the isolation of the historic Ferry Building, cut off behind the new Embarcadero Freeway.[32] Wurster's master plan for the site (1960–63) represents an effort to achieve his wife's goal of familiar "meaning and attractiveness" in such settings. Yet no purely architectural resolution, not even his careful balance of small-scale town houses and dense high-rises, could unite the development with its historic surroundings or with the working-class neighbors of Telegraph Hill and the waterfront—largely because the entire complex was carried out above street level with walled "private terraces."[33]

Acknowledging the middle-class abandonment of urban centers, Bauer envisioned a true revitalization that would accentuate the cultural diversity, economic vitality, and historic uniqueness of each city. Simultaneously she hoped to control suburban sprawl, not merely by decrying it but by encouraging a range of residential opportunities that incorporated the appeal of suburbs and yet self-consciously resisted their problems. This approach required regional government to combine the local knowledge of each municipality with a larger social vision; such regional governments could coordinate and assure equity in various overlapping matters, ranging from taxes to public and private transportation.

Bauer idealistically envisioned all residential areas sharing the responsibility to provide employment and housing opportunities for varied income and racial groups. Instead we have come closer to the dichotomy she prophesied, in which city centers "will become solid ghetto for the underprivileged . . . while the newer suburbs remain lily-white and strictly middle-class." By focusing on each project in isolation, architects and planners have, as she warned, inadvertently created "'metropolitan specialization' with a vengeance!"[34]

Most of all, perhaps, Bauer deepened her sense of the power of aesthetics, both for its own sake and for its ability to facilitate or stifle social goals. Together, Wurster and Bauer infused the most essential qualities of local vernaculars into architecture, anticipating our contemporary efforts to achieve good design in affordable housing and enticing public spaces; like today's

"New Urbanism," this drew on historical continuities without imitating previous architecture. For example, Bauer insisted that the American preference
for architectural variety could prevent the feeling of a "project," whether for
public-housing tenants or residents of luxury high-rises.[35] For years she decried
the monotony of monolithic modernist towers, though she was equally
opposed to a focus on the "tailor-made house" or the "artificial juxtaposition
of 'styles.' "[36]

No architecture could be judged solely on the basis of intentions and sym-
bolism; what mattered was how it worked in real circumstances. In 1952 Bauer
caused a stir by championing low-rise row houses for public housing—in specific contrast to Minoru Yamasaki's acclaimed high-rise towers at Pruitt-Igoe
in Saint Louis. Rather than insisting on how "modern man" ought to live, she
recognized the actual practices and preferences of tenants, such as their desire
for proximity to landscapes and children's play areas. Challenging the architectural formulas adopted by the U.S. Housing Authority that she had helped
create, honestly admitting the failure of the European modernist ideal she had
once proclaimed, Bauer denounced the "dreary deadlock" that characterized
American public-housing design—and hence the experience of living there.[37]

Her definition of architectural skill emphasized humility and self-restraint
in the face of complex problems and diverse constituencies. A "capacity for
magnificent self-assertion . . . is *not,* very generally speaking, a desirable quality in the practitioner of architecture," Bauer told her students. "An architect
must primarily have *Tact.* . . . I'm not half as fanatic *for* Neue Sachlichkeit as
I am *against individualism.*"[38] This would have served as an eloquent description of Wurster.

Like Wurster's modern architecture, Bauer's desire to make decent housing universally available did not rely on rigid standards of form or space. Both
were committed to pragmatism: they focused on specific problems over
abstract theories, results over rules. Since we don't really *know* the answers to
many problems that architecture might affect, Bauer insisted that architects
needed social science—the thoughtful, interpretive approach of friends like
Robert Merton, Paul Goodman, and John Dyckman. Like them, she always went
beyond statistics to ask more subjective questions about the "images we carry
around in our minds of the ideal way to live."[39]

Throughout her life, Bauer sought to transcend boundaries, describing the
goals of architectural and urban reformers to the public while explaining the
actuality of social trends to professionals. In her view, architecture and planning were not abstract ideals but flexible goals and expansive responsibilities.
Citizen participation would allow communities to gear local standards to their
own particular cultural habits and economic needs. Yet local autonomy was
never infallible; it could easily support racial segregation and resist innovation. Bauer embodied the professional's obligation to discuss real issues and
options with citizens' groups, listening to their needs and desires while
expanding their concepts of what was needed, what was possible, what was
comely. Such an exchange of knowledge would "give concrete meaning to
these abstract standards."[40]

Others shared those values. In particular, Wurster and later Bauer gave
strong support to a new generation of Bay Area architects, landscape architects, planners, and political activists who formed a group called Telesis.[41]
Telesis had begun informally in 1939 after several members had worked
together on low-income housing and community buildings for the Farm
Security Administration. As modernists with a specifically local focus, they
united around a few basic goals: first, protecting the varied physical landscape
of the Bay Area; second, extending the region's equally distinctive cultural
milieu (which they termed "The More Abundant Life") to a broader range of
people.[42]

Intentionally open-minded and antinomian, Telesis did not even have a name until 1940, when Grace Morley, director of the San Francisco Museum of Art, invited the group to organize an exhibition later that year. (They took the name, of Greek origin, from *Webster's New Words,* which defined "telesis" as "the attainment of desired ends by the application of intelligent human effort to the means.") The museum venue addressed another principal goal: the desire to reach and learn from "the man on the street," or, as they called him, "the cable car conductor." Exhibition panels, some of which suggested possible directions for future growth, pointedly asked open-ended questions: "Is This the Best We Can Do?" and "Do You Like Where You Work?" (fig. 190).

After the initial show, members of Telesis gathered materials for a regional plan, combining the efforts of government agencies, community groups, and artists. In 1942 they organized another exhibition, "Women in the War," which stressed the need to take special account of gender issues (such as child care), not only in defense housing but as a model for all planning deliberations.[43] They deeply admired Bauer and, like her, they wanted to pose questions and frame issues about modern environments for home, work, and leisure rather than assert trends or images that "the people" were bound to follow. Their other mentor, Wurster, was delighted when the youthful radicals soon became "the ones guiding the destinies of one of the most active city planning staffs in the United States. . . . This could not have happened if the Telesis group had all aspired to be in New York."[44]

In 1943 the Wursters moved to Cambridge, Massachusetts, where Bill intended to study for a doctorate in regional planning at Harvard, in order, he explained, "to get an insight into her [Catherine's] world."[45] With Catherine's encouragement, he joined CIAM (Congrès International d'Architecture Moderne), hoping to broaden his own as well as their goals and aesthetics.[46] A year later his fresh ideas had generated such interest that MIT invited the "student" to become dean of its School of Architecture. Catherine became a lecturer on housing and urban development at Harvard while continuing her work in Washington.

As an administrator, Wurster had definite goals and priorities. Even economic policies had their place, and they, too, had to be challenged. "Away with the expense of permanence," Wurster declared:

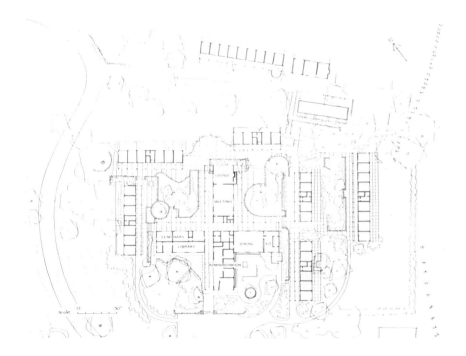

191.
Center for Advanced Study in the Behavioral Sciences, Stanford University, Palo Alto, 1954
Wurster, Bernardi and Emmons with Thomas Church, landscape architect
Plan

Let us have the buildings cost less. . . . [Let us] jump our present local political boundaries and build and plan for a region or metropolitan area. . . [with, he rightly insisted] a uniform tax structure which will grant complete participation.[47]

Was this architecture or planning? critics asked, to which Wurster replied, "[T]o produce inspired architecture, it is necessary to know and interpret, and perhaps to change, the frame in which we live and work."[48] In 1950 Bill Wurster returned to Berkeley as dean of the School of Architecture. Under his leadership, again working closely with Catherine, the school and its various departments were reconfigured to become the College of Environmental Design in 1959.

This name, especially in this setting, raises the issue of regionalism, yet another matter in which Bauer and Wurster helped one another define an appropriate balance. "Regionalism" often conjures up negative connotations: Disneyesque settings evoking an idyllic past, suggestive of a defensive populism, hostile toward anyone who might upset the comfortable status quo. Both Wurster and Bauer recognized the potentially parochial connotations of the term "Bay Area style," fearing that it would suggest a limited affectation. Their modernism consistently invoked a universal set of principles and opportunities, applied appropriately in particular settings, expressed discerningly in each one.

Their regionalism was thus defined in complex terms. Local materials, for example, were appropriate, not just because of sentimental continuity. Familiarity itself encouraged greater opportunities for experimental play with texture, light, and other architectonic qualities. Equally important, local materials supported a regional economy, perhaps even in resistance to a national or global economy. As Wurster insisted:

I am a regionalist to the extent that I believe all buildings are on a specific site, subject to the customs and norms of that site. . . . [They] shouldn't be different just to be different, but they will be different if they solve the problems of the area.[49]

This philosophy had allowed, even encouraged, his engagements with California and Cambridge, Scandinavia and England, and, later in life, with India and Hong Kong.

In other words, the regionalism of Wurster and Bauer, like their modernism, had evolved, not so much from an ideology confined to one place but from the global phenomena of modern architecture and social science. It *also* drew from the specific cultural milieu of the Bay Area, with its emphasis on comfort, the superb natural environment, and rustic vernacular materials. Both personally and professionally, Catherine Bauer and Bill Wurster thrived on this way of life and way of thinking.

This philosophy affected Wurster's 1954 setting for "experimental, . . . serious, humane" research at the Center for Advanced Study in the Behavioral Sciences at Stanford University in Palo Alto. The Center represents a related, yet equally distinctive vision of scholarship enhanced by its environment. The informal low buildings in redwood from the region combined with sensitive site planning that terraced down a slope to create an ideal mix of buildings and open spaces for private reflection and communal discussion[50] (fig. 191).

Unconfined by geographical boundaries, Bauer and Wurster both addressed the urban and architectural problems of Asia late in their careers. In 1957 the family spent seven months traveling around the world, which led them to reflect again on the role of global trends and local particularities for housing and public buildings (fig. 192).[51] Wurster's American consulate in Hong Kong (1957–63) responded to that city's climate with its "contextual" design and environmental controls (fig. 193).

On a larger scale, Bauer's work on developing countries, especially India, focused on land use as a way to maximize economic investment. More vociferously than ever, she criticized the imposition of extravagant modernist schemes on new capitals. This "universal modernism," she contended, only aggravated local social and economic problems and undermined a nation's reliance on its own architectural traditions as a basis for appropriate solutions.[52]

To suggest some of the ways in which Wurster and Bauer affected one another is not to question either one's creativity or independence, just as a focus on the Bay Area did not restrict the scope of their concern or influence. To see these two lives conjointly reminds us of the ways in which significant human choices and the experiences that follow can alter our lives, expanding certain dimensions and foreclosing others. There is still a pattern, unique to an individual's character and creative drive, but the fortuitous role of contingency, intervention, and personal evolution can come into play.

Martin Jay speaks eloquently of a "constellation" of figures in a specific milieu, at once local, national, and transnational. He draws the term from Walter Benjamin and Theodor Adorno to suggest elements (or people) at once juxtaposed and changing; a definite pattern unites them, but it overlaps with other patterns and has no inherent or totalizing "essence."[53] The metaphor is appropriate here. Throughout their lives, Catherine Bauer and William Wurster were luminous stars in many constellations, yet their radiance became more intense and threw its light much farther in one another's presence.

192. (opposite)
William, Catherine, and Sadie Wurster in Macao, 1957, during their trip around the world

193.
United States Consulate Office Building, Hong Kong, 1957–63
Wurster, Bernardi and Emmons

Notes

1. Wurster and Gropius were interviewed in "Tell Me, What Is Modern Architecture?" *House and Garden* 77 (April 1940), pp. 46–53. For an elaboration of this widespread noncanonical definition of modernism, see Gwendolyn Wright, "Inventions and Interventions: American Urban Design in the Twentieth Century," in *Urban Revisions: Current Projects for the Public Realm,* ed. Russell Ferguson (Los Angeles: Museum of Contemporary Art, 1994), pp. 26–37.

2. Wurster and his associated architect, Harry A. Thomsen, Jr., quoted in "Valencia Gardens," *Pencil Points* 25 (January 1944), p. 28.

3. See, for example, Gwendolyn Wright, "On the Fringe of the Profession: Women in American Architecture," in Spiro Kostof, ed., *The Architect: Chapters in the History of*

the Profession (New York: Oxford University Press, 1977), pp. 280–308; and Susana Torre, ed., *Women in American Architecture: A Historic and Contemporary Perspective* (New York: Whitney Library of Design, 1977). Recent forays in this area include Dolores Hayden, *Redesigning the American Dream: The Future of Housing, Work, and Family Life* (New York: W. W. Norton, 1984); "Architecture and the Feminine: Mop-Up Work," special issue of *Any* 4 (January/February 1994); Beatriz Colomina, ed., *Space and Sexuality* (Cambridge: MIT Press, 1994); Robert Twombley, *Louis Sullivan: His Life and Work* (New York: Viking, 1986); and the more voyeuristic discussions about Frank Lloyd Wright and Philip Johnson.

4. Martha C. Nussbaum, *Love's Knowledge: Essays on Philosophy and Literature* (New York: Oxford University Press, 1990), p. 4.

5. Bauer spent her junior year at Cornell University School of Architecture but didn't enjoy the Beaux-Arts focus ("We Present . . . Catherine Bauer in Her Own Words," *Journal of Housing* 1 [November 1944], p. 27). See also Mary Susan Cole, "Catherine Bauer and the Public Housing Movement, 1926–1932," Ph.D. diss., George Washington University, 1975; Eugenie Ladner Birch, "An Urban View: Catherine Bauer's Five Questions," *Journal of Planning Literature* 4 (Summer 1989), pp. 239–58, reprinted in Donald A. Krueckeberg, ed., *The American Planner: Biographies and Recollections* (New Brunswick, N.J.: Rutgers University Center for Urban Policy Research, 1994), pp. 311–44; H. Peter Oberlander and Eva Newbrun, "Catherine Bauer Wurster, CED's First Lady," *CED News* 12 (Spring 1994), pp. 4–9; and Oberlander and Newbrun's forthcoming biography of Bauer.

6. Catherine K. Bauer, "Machine-Age Mansions for Ultra-Moderns: French Builders Apply Ideas of the Steel and Concrete Era in Domestic Architecture," *New York Times Magazine* 10, 15 April 1928, pp. 10, 22.

7. Mumford discusses the affair most vividly and includes some of their correspondence in *My Words and Days: A Personal Chronicle* (New York: Harcourt Brace Jovanovich, 1978), pp. 302–19.

8. See Bauer's insightful comments on the 1932 show: "Are Good Houses Un-American?" *New Republic* 70 (2 March 1932), p. 74, and "Exhibition of Modern Architecture," *Creative Art* 10 (March 1932), pp. 201–06. See also Bauer, "Housing: Paper Plans or a Workers' Movement," in Carol Aronovici, *Americans Can't Have Housing* (New York: Museum of Modern Art, 1934). She later collaborated with Henry-Russell Hitchcock on *Modern Architecture in England* (New York: Museum of Modern Art, 1937). Her sister, Elizabeth Mock (Kassler), was associate curator of architecture and design at the museum from 1940 to 1945 and sought Bauer's and Wurster's advice about exhibitions on modern schools, war housing, and, most notably, her show "Built in USA: 1932–1944" (New York: Museum of Modern Art, 1945).

9. Catherine K. Bauer, "Prize Essay—Art in Industry," which won $1,000 from Pittsburgh's Edgar Kaufmann, was published in *Fortune* 3 (May 1931), pp. 94–99.

10. The affair and its demise are also described in Mumford's *Sketches from Life: The Autobiography of Lewis Mumford, The Early Years* (New York: Dial, 1982), pp. 459–67; the quote "on probation" appears on p. 463. Mumford returned to his wife, Sophia Wittenberg, from whom he had been largely separated during the years with Bauer, in part because the calm of this marriage seemed more conducive to his writing. For a thoughtful account of Mumford's resolution of his sexual and intellectual ambitions during his affair with Bauer, see Thomas Bender, "Lewis Mumford: Young Man and the City," *Skyline* (December 1982), pp. 12–14.

11. "Housing's White Knight Is a 'Handsome Blonde with Brunette Economic Ideas,'" *Architectural Forum* 84 (March 1946), p. 116. In Europe Mumford was working on a series of articles for *Fortune,* which were the basis of his book *Technics and Civilization,* published almost simultaneously with Bauer's *Modern Housing* in the fall of 1934.

12. Catherine K. Bauer, *Modern Housing* (Boston: Houghton Mifflin, 1934), p. 14.

13. Ibid, pp. 148, 157, 141.

14. Ibid., pp. 106–16, 253.

15. Not everyone enjoyed Bauer's intensity; Harold Ickes, secretary of the interior and chief of the Public Works Administration, branded her a "wild eyed female" *(The Secret Diary of Harold Ickes, the First Thousand Days, 1933–1936* [New York: Simon & Schuster, 1953], p. 218).

16. William Wilson Wurster, "Carquinez Heights," *California Arts and Architecture* 57 (November 1941), p. 34; Fred Langhorst, "Experimental Housing, William Wilson Wurster," *California Arts and Architecture* 58 (April 1942), pp. 27–31; and "Industrial Supplement," *California Arts and Architecture* (June 1942), p. 40.

17. Wurster, "Carquinez Heights," p. 34. In the end, all three systems cost less than either the federal allocation or local builders' houses of the same size.

18. "Schools, Chabot Terrace War Housing, Vallejo Calif.," *Pencil Points* 24 (September 1943), pp. 46–49; "Public and Commercial Structures, Chabot Terrace (FPHA)," *Pencil Points* 25 (October 1944), pp. 79–85.

19. Wurster, "Carquinez Heights," p. 34.

20. Catherine Bauer, "Cities in Flux," *American Scholar* 13 (Winter 1943–44), p. 83; idem, "Memorandum on the Experience of California with Defense Housing Agencies," 12 November 1941; Catherine Bauer Wurster Papers, Bancroft Library (hereafter CBW Papers), carton 10; idem, "Housing and Community Development," lecture notes for Arch 5N, 9 November 1953, CBW Papers, carton 2; "Outline of War Housing," *Task* 4 (1943), pp. 5–8; and idem, *War Housing in the United States* (Washington, D.C.: National Housing Agency for the United Nations Conference on International Organization, 1945).

21. The San Francisco Planning Commission, together with several other city agencies, first proposed the plan in 1945. "Sunset Community Center, San Francisco: Forty-Three Acres Cooperatively Planned," *Architectural Record* 111 (March 1952), pp. 121–31, esp. p. 123.

22. "Woodlake: A Small Community Complete Within Itself," *Architectural Record* 139, no. 1 (January 1966), pp. 164–65; Catherine Bauer, "Good Neighborhoods," in Robert B. Mitchell, ed., *Building the Future City: Annals of the American Academy of Political and Social Science* 242 (November 1945), p. 115.

23. Bauer, "Good Neighborhoods," p. 105. In 1944 Bauer helped organize San Francisco's Council for Civic Unity to protest racial segregation. She recognized that local control could reinforce patterns of racial and class segregation. However, the federal government did not take the initiative she expected; indeed, both public housing and FHA mortgage policies actively encouraged segregation policies through the mid-1960s. Also see Bauer "Housing: A Memorandum," *California Arts and Architecture* 60 (February 1943), pp. 18–19, 41–42; and "Housing in the United States: Problems and Policy," *International Labour Review* 52 (July 1945), pp. 1–28.

24. See Wurster's notes of the 3–4 February 1950 advisory committee in carton 14 and various articles from the 1940s and 1950s under "Race Relations" in CBW Papers, carton 25.

25. Bauer was originally secretary, then vice-president, and always the driving force behind this umbrella organization, whose members included Howard Moise, Carey McWilliams, T. J. Kent, and Lloyd Wright. The first annual conference, in September 1941, brought together professionals and citizens from the public and private sectors to discuss major issues, leading to a proposed statewide program. Also see the association's journal, *Agenda,* which began publication in January 1942.

26. "White Knight," p. 117.

27. "CHPA Central Valley Project," CBW Papers, carton 8.

28. See, in particular, Catherine Bauer, "The Middle Class Needs Houses Too," *New Republic* 121 (29 August 1949), pp. 17–20.

29. Catherine Bauer, "Can Cities Compete with Suburbia for Family Living?" *Architectural Record* 136 (December 1964), pp. 149–56.

30. Bauer, "Cities in Flux," p. 79; and idem, "How Do We WANT To Live?" speech in Saint Louis, 15 October 1949, CBW Papers, carton 2.

31. Catherine Bauer, "Redevelopment: A Misfit in the Fifties," in Coleman Woodbury, ed., *The Future of Cities and Redevelopment* (Chicago: University of Chicago Press, 1953), pp. 7–25; and idem, "Architecture and the Cityscape," *Journal of the American Institute of Architects* 27 (March 1961), pp. 36–39.

32. Bauer discussed the example of the Ferry Building, contending that Europeans' "civic imagination" would enhance such distinctive attractions, in "Do Americans Hate Cities?" lecture at the University of California, Berkeley, 27 March 1956, reprinted in *Journal of the American Institute of Planners* 23 (Winter 1956), pp. 2–8, and, more recently, in *Architecture California* 16 (November 1994), pp. 10–17; quote is from p. 11.

33. A cogent critique is Charles W. Moore, "In San Francisco, a Renewal Effort Based on Civic Pride Falls Short of Expectation," *Architectural Forum* 123 (July 1965), pp. 58–63.

34. Bauer, "Do Americans Hate Cities?" p. 16. Also see her much reprinted "Social Questions in Housing and Community Planning," *Journal of Social Issues* 7 (1951), pp. 1–34; idem, "The Case for Regional Planning and Urban Dispersal," in Burnham Kelly, ed., *Housing and Economic Development* (Cambridge: MIT School of Architecture and Planning, 1955), pp. 39–51; and idem, "First Job: Control New-City Sprawl," *Architectural Forum* 105 (September 1956), pp. 43–45.

35. Bauer, "Good Neighborhoods," p. 115.

36. Catherine Bauer, "Housing and the Architect," lecture notes, 5 December 1955, pp. 11–13, CBW Papers, carton 2.

37. "Low Buildings? Catherine Bauer Questions Mr. Yamasaki's Arguments," *Journal of Housing* 9 (July 1952), pp. 227, 232, 246; and Catherine Bauer, "The Dreary Deadlock of Public Housing," *Architectural Forum* 106 (May 1957), pp. 140–42, 219, 221.

38. Catherine Bauer, "On Individualism and Architecture," n.d., manuscript for a lecture, CBW Papers, carton 2.

39. Bauer, "How Do We WANT To Live?" p. 9; Catherine Bauer and Jacob Crane, "What Every Family Should Have," *Survey Graphic* 29 (February 1940), p. 64.

40. Catherine Bauer, "Low-Rent Housing and Home Economics," *Journal of Home Economics* 31 (January 1939), p. 4.

41. On their exhibitions and research, see, in particular, Telesis Environmental Research Group, *Space for Living* (San Francisco: San Francisco Museum of Art, 1940); "Is This the Best We Can Do?" *California Arts and Architecture* 55 (September 1940), pp. 20–21; and Francis Violich, "The Planning Pioneers," *California Living: Magazine of the San Francisco Chronicle,* 26 February 1978, pp. 29–35.

42. Violich, "The Planning Pioneers," p. 29.

43. "Telesis: The Birth of a Group," *Pencil Points* 13 (July 1942), p. 47.

44. William W. Wurster, "Architecture Broadens Its Base," *Journal of the American Institute of Architects* 10 (July 1948), p. 32.

45. *William Wilson Wurster, College of Environmental Design, University of California. Campus Planning and Architectural Practice,* (2 vols.), interview by Suzanne B. Riess (Berkeley: University of California, Regional Cultural History Project [now Regional Oral History Office], 1964), p. 105.

46. I would like to thank my colleague Jos Bosman of Zurich for access to the files on CIAM during these years, now in a private collection in Athens.

47. Wurster, "Architecture Broadens Its Base," pp. 34, 36.

48. Ibid., p. 36.

49. Ibid., p. 36

50. "A Humane Campus for the Study of Man," *Architectural Forum* 102 (January 1955), pp. 130–34; "The Center for Advanced Study in the Behavioral Sciences," *Arts and Architecture* 72 (February 1955), pp. 14–17.

51. See, in particular, William Wurster, "Row House Vernacular and High Style Monument," with photographs by Catherine Bauer, *Architectural Record* 124 (August 1958), pp. 141–50.

52. Catherine Bauer, *Economic Development and Urban Living Conditions: An Argument for Regional Planning to Guide Community Growth* (New York: United Nations Bureau of Social Affairs, 1956); idem, "Urban Living Conditions, Overhead Costs and the Development Pattern," in Roy Turner, ed., *Seminar on Urbanization in India: India's Urban Future* (Berkeley: University of California Press, 1961), pp. 277–98.

53. Martin Jay, *Adorno* (Cambridge: Harvard University Press, 1984), pp. 14–15. Since 1981 Jay has used the term, together with its corollary, "force fields" of ideas, in a semi-annual column for *Salmagundi,* and in a more recent book, *Force Fields: Between Intellectual History and Cultural Critique* (New York and London: Routledge, 1993). See also Richard J. Bernstein, *The New Constellation: The Ethical-Political Horizons of Modernity/Postmodernity* (Cambridge: MIT Press, 1992).

Bernardi, Emmons—and Wurster:
Focus on the Younger Partners

Alan R. Michelson

I n the celebrated architectural partnership of Wurster, Bernardi and Emmons, William Wurster stood first among equals. In a Berkeley hotel room in 1924, Wurster established the independent practice that preceded WBE, and his name still remains first on the door of the office. He was an ambitious and disciplined man—"gentle but tough," in Donn Emmons's estimation—who before World War II spent fourteen hours a day in the office and took only two day-long holidays a year.[1] He had outstanding social skills and sensitivity to diverse points of view. Perhaps most of all he could concentrate on whomever he was with, juggling a schedule filled with consultations while making his clients feel neither rushed nor inconsequential. These interpersonal skills, along with his exceptional design talent, helped make Wurster a star in his profession and memorable to clients.

His fame, however, has served to obscure the achievements of Theodore Bernardi (1903–1990) and Donn Emmons (b. 1910), who joined as partners in 1944 and 1945 respectively. As the partnership's *éminence grise,* Wurster became the focus of postwar writers on architecture, to the exclusion of the younger men.[2] Bernardi and Emmons contributed many widely published designs for residential, commercial, and institutional buildings, yet few surveys of the American architectural scene of the 1950s and 1960s included any biographical or professional information about them. This omission is especially striking considering that the two effectively ran the firm during the years when Wurster headed the school of architecture at the Massachusetts Institute of Technology (1944–50). In Wurster's absence, their influence was crucial, moving the firm solidly toward stylistic modernism while still preserving interest in local building traditions.

Bernardi and Emmons were partly responsible for their own lack of exposure. Both men deeply admired Wurster, whose influence supported them intellectually and financially, and both felt no desire to upstage him. To ensure esprit de corps within the firm, each partner agreed that all published designs would credit "Wurster, Bernardi and Emmons"—not the partner in charge—and that professional award citations (which were numerous) should also carry the corporate name. In addition, neither Bernardi nor Emmons politicked for high office within the American Institute of Architects or academia—positions that could have bolstered their fame. Though personally overlooked in architectural publications, the fact remains that Bernardi and Emmons created some of the firm's finest and most publicized residences.

The Wurster, Bernardi and Emmons office developed efficient collaborative production methods that enabled it to turn out several hundred buildings

194.
Emmons House, Mill Valley, 1947
Wurster, Bernardi and Emmons
Donn Emmons, architect
Interior view (detail)

between 1944 and 1970. At its height during the late 1960s, the office employed more than one hundred people. Partners took on projects as they came in unless a client requested the services of a particular architect. Working with a number of associate-level members of the firm, each partner supervised a small shifting team of drafting personnel.[3] These employees usually followed one job from start to finish, exposing them to all phases of the design and construction process. One draftsperson would sit in on all client meetings to reiterate client preferences at later design sessions. Periodic office tours of recently completed designs afforded these young architects the opportunity to see how their designs actually functioned.[4] At regular office critiques, partners offered suggestions on one another's projects, cross-fertilizing much of the office's output, especially on larger commercial or institutional commissions; one lead partner, however, could plan residences more independently, with less creative input from the other two. For the purposes of this essay, certain houses have been selected to illustrate the design tendencies of Bernardi and Emmons, although the collaboration of other members of the firm may have influenced each final design.

Impact of the Depression and Wurster's Design Philosophy

In interviews, Bernardi and Emmons both made clear the Depression's disastrous impact on architects. Seven years older than Emmons, Bernardi floundered in the job market between 1932 and 1934 during the depths of the Depression. In San Francisco in 1934 he noted, "99 and 99/100ths of architects were out of commissions," and he was among the unemployed when he came to work for Wurster.[5] At the conclusion of each job during his early days in the Wurster office, Bernardi recalled that the four draftsmen would look at one another and wonder who would be fired first.[6] To make ends meet during the mid-1930s, Emmons worked as an oil-refinery worker and a designer of truck bodies; he left Southern California in 1938 when work ran out in the office of the Los Angeles architect Winchton L. Risley. During this tense period survival for architects required intellectual flexibility, a pragmatic ability to synthesize elements of traditional and modern architecture that could satisfy a cross section of middle-class clients. Successful architects such as Wurster knew how to cross-fertilize ideas gleaned from revivalists and avant-gardists alike. Writing in *Architectural Forum* in 1938, Wurster discussed his Neff House, built in Ross two years earlier: "It represents our concept of modernity, for nothing is done as a shock to the neighborhood—nor is anything done as a sentimental or picturesque gesture."[7] Architects interested in producing radical International Style designs could obtain few clients in Northern California.[8] (Few banks would lend scarce mortgage money to borrowers building avant-garde dwellings, which were deemed difficult to resell in case of default.) Beaux-Arts revivalist offices, such as the once mighty San Francisco firm of Bakewell and Brown, also found their work discredited. In conversation, Bernardi scorned Bakewell and Brown as "hacks" and copyists who lacked true intellectual vigor.[9] During this turbulent decade both Bernardi and Emmons learned to avoid being boxed in, confined either by conventions of style or organization.

Wurster's pragmatic regionally based design philosophy, forged during the Depression, deeply influenced Bernardi and Emmons. Wurster mistrusted stylistic and organizational formulas that failed to consider local needs and resources. In 1936 he wrote: "Over and over again I would reiterate that Modern is a point of view not a style. And everyone seems so determined to pin set things to it. Use the site—the money—the local materials—the client—the climate to decide what shall be."[10] Wurster had a deep appreciation for Northern California, its natural environment, customs, and history. In particular, he studied the region's vernacular architecture, passing on this interest

195.
Campbell House, Stockton, 1938
William Wurster
North (front) facade

to Bernardi and Emmons. Before World War II, tours of recent projects for office personnel often stopped at local historic landmarks, and Bernardi and Emmons together made sketching trips to Gold Country destinations in the late 1930s.[11] Wurster, however, was not boxed into a hermetic or sentimental provincialism. Modern transportation and communication enabled him to travel widely, and these trips abroad enriched his vision by providing comparisons and contrasts with his work. In his houses Wurster reconciled an awareness of the local and the international, the immediate and the universal. References to early California adobes or Gold Country cabins were enlivened by his use of glass, concrete block, or various International Style motifs.

Several projects by Bernardi and Emmons underscored the impact of Wurster's interest in California's vernacular architecture. The Campbell House in Stockton (1938), an early design shepherded through the Wurster office by Bernardi, possessed the long single-file arrangement of rooms common to early California adobes (fig. 195). This plan provided thorough cross ventilation in a hot Central Valley location and placed sheltered terraces to the north and south. Similar to the French Consulate in Monterey, an 1848 structure that Bernardi could have seen while working for the Historic American Buildings Survey in the early 1930s, the ends of the north terrace were baffled to provide protection from wind. While the overall conception of the Campbell House suggested adobe models, its light wood-frame construction, crisp form, and long expanses of windows underscored Bernardi's awareness of contemporary modern design.

Wurster pioneered a "cheap" aesthetic—a preference for unpretentious, inexpensive building materials—which he passed on to his partners. Of the firm's perverse preference for utilitarian materials, one partner (probably Bernardi) observed in *Arts and Architecture*, "Although plywood costs more than plaster, we like it better because it looks cheaper."[12] Above all, economic limitations impelled Wurster to improvise, using ordinary building materials. Californians were accustomed to transience and informality and—confirmed by Wurster's experience—did not want to maintain monumental houses with costly finishes. Wurster's second Saxton Pope House in Orinda (1940), a commission on which Bernardi was active, demonstrated Wurster's willingness to test new building materials such as corrugated iron and concrete block. One of Emmons's favorite houses, the Clark House in Aptos (1937), was a more rustic exemplar of this "cheap" aesthetic. Its single-wall construction of redwood boards, sliding barn doors, and patent chimney flue all suggested humble vernacular sources. In 1977 Emmons stated: "I had worked on movie stars' houses [in Los Angeles] where everything had to show, and up here people didn't want

196.
Breinig House, Los Altos Hills, 1952
Wurster, Bernardi and Emmons
Donn Emmons, architect

197.
Breinig House, Los Altos Hills, 1952
Wurster, Bernardi and Emmons
Donn Emmons, architect
Plan

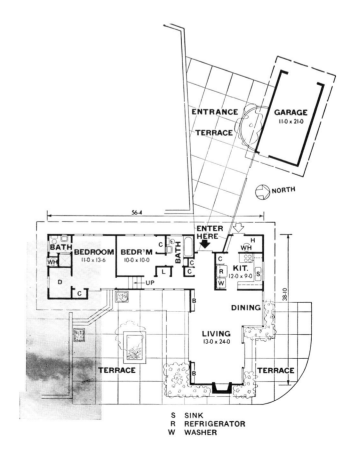

anything to show. . . . The whole climate was to understate things, at least in Northern California, which was just right for Bill."[13] Emmons's own house, as discussed below, possessed this improvisational use of inexpensive materials and framing techniques, down to its windows with barn sliders and patent metal chimney flue.

Wurster resisted being boxed into the traditional boundaries of the house and urged colleagues to take advantage of California's temperate climate whenever possible.[14] The manifold physical and psychological benefits of outdoor living were widely discussed in the popular press during the Depression. New research published in magazines such as *Parents* and *House Beautiful* emphasized that exposure to sunlight aided the proper development of a child's skin and bone structure. The stress induced by work and a rapidly urbanizing environment prompted modern families to conceive of the house as a private sanctum. Emmons echoed Wurster's ideas in an article written in 1949: "What do we want in a house? The average city dweller is a harassed and confused individual. His home is potentially the one place that can possibly be a haven from the hectic pace of making a living. We no longer face the street to greet our neighbors and friends; but we shelter our family from noisy traffic and give them privacy we can in the space available."[15] Automobiles increasingly clogged streets, making them loud, dirty, and unsafe. In response to a busy intersection, Wurster positioned his Lyman House in Atherton (1938) close to the street in order to maximize backyard space. The house served as a curtain wrapping around a central patio/living room. A fence provided further privacy. Here, as in most of his houses, Wurster set aside a variety of shaded, partially covered and open outdoor living rooms; these spaces enlarged floor plans that had become increasingly cramped on smaller lots during the Depression in the 1930s. Emmons's Breinig House in Los Altos Hills (1948) possessed a stylistic vocabulary and an organizational solution similar to that of the Lyman residence (figs. 196, 197). Like the Lyman House, it also minimized the public facade, wrapping in an L-shape around a rear terrace. In contrast to the closed front, the rear fenestration was liberally glazed, linking living areas with the patio. Numerous houses by Bernardi, such as the Jones House in Kent Woodlands (1945), demonstrated the same orientation toward the rear yard.

Wurster's most lasting philosophical lesson for Bernardi and Emmons was his emphasis on allowing clients to lead the design process. Operating in the hinterlands, far from the stylistic centers of New York, London, or Paris, he chose to adapt to regional necessities at a time when Californians needed to feel rooted in their locale, part of its traditions and landscape. In Wurster's view, westerners did not want to be restricted by imported conventions. They led informal lives, employing few servants to clean house or cook dinner, particularly during and after the Depression. As portrayed in the pages of *Sunset* magazine, westerners lived and cooked outside, less fettered than easterners by constraints of tradition and climate. In such a free social atmosphere Wurster urged his clients to articulate their preferences, providing him with clear priorities to interpret. In his office, few preconceptions linked one job to another. As Wurster reflected at the end of his life: "The office has recognized that the work we do is for the client and not in our own image."[16] Works as conceptually varied as the modern industrial second Pope House or the Gerbode House in San Francisco (1939), designed in an updated Regency style, were produced contemporaneously. Each house cannot be understood without knowing something of the owner's tastes and practical requirements. In an era dominated by Wright, Neutra, and other form-givers, this relative absence of the architect's own idiosyncrasies in a finished design was rare.

198.
Minor House, Hillsborough, 1934
William Wurster
Perspective drawing by Theodore Bernardi

Four Houses by Bernardi

Theodore Bernardi was probably the more adventurous designer of the two junior partners, strongly influencing the firm to accept many aspects of modernism. Wurster, who was eight years Bernardi's senior and trained in Beaux-Arts methods in the conservative New York office of Delano and Aldrich, retained in his pre- and postwar houses many overt traces of revivalist architecture—symmetrical entryway compositions, gable roofs, double-hung windows, even adobe walls. Bernardi, in contrast, consistently embraced modern motifs, flat or shed roofs, walls of glass, and the radically open plans promoted by younger International Style designers. Strong in their opinions, Wurster and Bernardi often argued issues of planning and aesthetics in the prewar office. As a result of these debates, Bernardi gained Wurster's respect and by the late 1930s began to wield considerable authority over office design decisions. After the war, with Wurster at MIT, Bernardi set a new, more modern standard for the firm's residential design, as seen in the Smith House and his own residence.

Bernardi received a standard architectural education for the time, but as a student felt some desire to augment his classical training with other, more independent creative influences. Born in Korcula, Dalmatia, in 1903, he came to the United States in 1912. His family settled in West Oakland, and he attended the nearby University of California, where he worked with John Galen Howard, Warren C. Perry, and William Hays, receiving an architectural education modeled on the precepts of the École des Beaux-Arts.[17] In conversation, Bernardi emphasized that he had had more contact with the dour Howard than Wurster did (Howard having been away for much of the time Wurster was at the university). Bernardi took the prescribed undergraduate architecture curriculum, heavily focused on drafting and classical theory, and graduated in 1924. (He also took some master's level classes shortly thereafter.) Despite Howard's presence on the faculty, Bernardi emphasized the formative influence of Bernard Maybeck during his student years. Several times a week he toured Maybeck's houses and commercial buildings in Berkeley and San Francisco.[18] His admiration for Maybeck motivated him to apply for work in the office of the elderly architect, who was then working on the Principia College commission (Elsah, Illinois, 1923–30).[19] Bernardi viewed Maybeck as an energetic, independent designer who, like Wurster, could combine a broad range of sources to produce provocative but practical results suited to the locale.

With his fiery personality, Bernardi bounced around many Bay Area architects' offices until he landed a job with Wurster in 1934. Only two local contemporaries elicited his admiration—Wurster and Timothy Pflueger—because they resisted designing "according to a formula," in the manner of the more conservative firm of Bakewell and Brown.[20] These two architects, in his estimation, "tried to struggle out and figure what was innate."[21] Working for

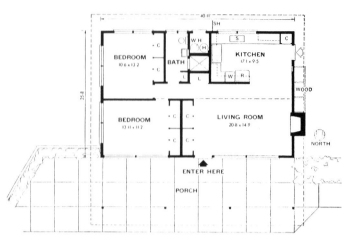

199.
Davison House, Fresno, 1946
Wurster, Bernardi and Emmons
Theodore Bernardi, architect
Exterior view

200.
Davison House, Fresno, 1946
Wurster, Bernardi and Emmons
Theodore Bernardi, architect
Plan

Pflueger, Bernardi helped draft the Paramount Theater (Oakland, 1931), one of the finest Art Deco movie palaces in the United States, and the Mayan Revival Medical-Dental Building (San Francisco, 1931) before being fired, perhaps due to a personality conflict within the office.

Wurster's Gregory Farmhouse (Scotts Valley, 1928) and the Pasatiempo commissions (Santa Cruz, beginning 1930) attracted Bernardi's attention and led him to apply to Wurster for a job. (Wurster was also one of the few local designers who had work during the Depression.) As a university student, Bernardi had known of Wurster, but the two did not establish a friendship until the 1930s. He was Wurster's fourth employee and worked on a number of early jobs as a draftsman. Bernardi's rendering of a house for the real estate developer Richard Minor (1934) illustrates his ability to produce polished presentation drawings (fig. 198). During the late 1930s the outspoken Bernardi became a valuable sounding board for ideas in the Wurster office. As Wurster's workload increased and his travel schedule became more hectic, he began to rely more on assistants. In 1937 he traveled to Scandinavia, leaving the office under the stewardship of Bernardi and another trusted employee, Floyd Comstock. Bernardi and Comstock became the chief draftsmen, overseeing the work of ten to fifteen people.

From 1937 to 1942, influenced in part by Bernardi's ascendance within the office, the work of Wurster's firm became more modern and adventurous. Wurster attracted nearly forty new residential commissions yearly, a volume of work that allowed Bernardi and Wurster to test a variety of new stylistic and organizational ideas. The Campbell House indicated how the two architects updated the early California adobe vernacular, using light wood framing, a shed roof, and glazed walls. The second Saxton Pope House enabled Wurster and Bernardi to test the aesthetic potential of a radically new vocabulary, featuring industrial materials and a circular atrium that was emphatically geometric. The living areas of many house plans of the period opened up, with fewer walls dividing living and dining rooms, as in the 1937 Mendenhall House in Palo Alto. This new spirit of creativity and modernization is aptly illustrated in an unbuilt project, the 1939 Watson House in Sausalito. Here the architects experimented with a flat roof and a sinuous glass wall enclosing a unified stairway, living and dining space. The curving glass wall was a daring Aalto-like touch, unthinkable in Wurster's work five years earlier.

Soon after Wurster and Bernardi incorporated in 1944, Bernardi produced a group of well-publicized houses, each of which underscored both his creative independence and his debt to Wurster. One of these outstanding designs was the Davison House in Fresno (1946), a modernized adaptation of an early California vernacular cabin (figs. 199, 200). The Davison House possessed a rustic "cheap" aesthetic, reminiscent of Wurster's prewar work, with exterior

201.
Smith House, Stockton, 1947
Wurster, Bernardi and Emmons
Theodore Bernardi, architect
Exterior view

202.
Smith House, Stockton, 1947
Wurster, Bernardi and Emmons
Theodore Bernardi, architect
Plan

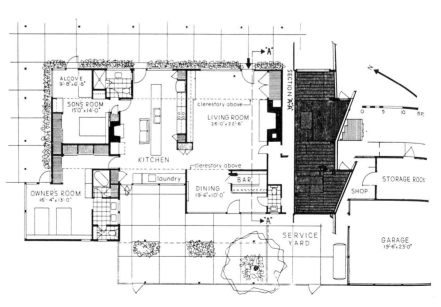

walls clad in redwood board-and-batten siding and interior walls covered by slash grain Douglas fir plywood. Bernardi included a metal chimney stack, used memorably at the second Pope House—a feature that became symbolic of the postwar office's "cheap" aesthetic. Contrary to prewar practice, Bernardi left roof framing exposed in order to cut costs and accentuate the sense of space within a very small plan. The soaring vertical dimension compensated for cramped square footage. He also favored exposed framing, viewing its skeletal aesthetic as a clear, modern expression of structural function.

Bernardi's simple plan for the Davison House was designed to suit the owner's need for economy and comfort in a hot Central Valley location. The economical square plan saved foundation and framing costs, an emphasis on cost-cutting that was crucial because of shortages and inflation just after the war. Its open arrangement of living rooms followed earlier prewar Wurster plans such as that for the Mendenhall House. Unlike the Mendenhall House, however, Bernardi opened the kitchen directly onto the joined living/dining space, a feature Bernardi and Emmons often reused in the 1940s and 1950s. To cope with the warm climate, Bernardi included full-length roof louvers and oriented the large glass patio doors toward the north away from direct sunlight, protected by a deep roof overhang. Discussing this extended porch in the *Architectural Record* in 1948, the writer stated: "There is good local precedent in the loggia-like porch, first brought to this vicinity by Italian viticulturists, which is admirably suited to informal outdoor living."[22] Wurster, who had earlier noted high loggias in the dwellings of Italian immigrants in and near his hometown of Stockton, used the motif on another Central Valley commission well known to Bernardi, the 1941 Turner House in Modesto (fig. 134).[23]

Despite its rusticity, Bernardi managed to give the Davison House taut modern lines. Its simple form, lacking any decorative elements, included wide expanses of glass. He made the battens unusually thick, creating deep cast shadows and bold visual rhythms that gave the wood exterior the look of corrugated metal (reminiscent of the second Pope House). These serially repeated patterns appealed to the modern eye. The nonintersecting halves of the gable roof emphasized the flatness and planarity of each half and provided a louvered clerestory for ventilation, also giving the house a striking and original silhouette. The long clerestories would reappear later in several important commissions, making it a distinctive Bernardi motif.

One of Bernardi's most intriguing houses, the Smith House in Stockton (1947), possessed a synthetic rustic/industrial aesthetic, unlike anything produced in the prewar office (figs. 201, 202). Working for a client who owned a lumber planing mill, Bernardi lined interior and exterior walls with vertical boards of California incense cedar, creating a rustic effect similar to a weekend cabin in the Sierra. Clear finishes on both inside and outside enhanced the wood's natural grain. The strong aroma of the cedar surfaces accentuated the house's rustic qualities. Bernardi again exposed the house's structural beams, reinforcing the dwelling's sense of informality. Trees, in close proximity to the house, provided shade. In the manner of Frank Lloyd Wright, one tree was allowed to poke through the roof of the western porch.

This rusticity was merged with many elements drawn from modern architecture. The house was composed of hard-edged geometric forms. Flat roofs covered much of the dwelling, creating strong rectangular volumes, especially in the garage, and a rectangular frame pergola—a favorite motif of California modernists—hung cantilevered above the service yard. A stark rectangular chimney stack projected above the living room; in the kitchen many built-in seats and cabinets had sharply defined contours. Bernardi used glass more extensively in the Smith residence than in Wurster houses of the 1930s, creating a varied fenestration of sliding and awning windows. Tall porch roofs sheltered walls of glass on the east and west facades. Bernardi utilized clerestories

203.
Bernardi House, Sausalito, 1950
Wurster, Bernardi and Emmons
Theodore Bernardi, architect
Exterior view

204.
Bernardi House, Sausalito, 1950
Wurster, Bernardi and Emmons
Theodore Bernardi, architect
Living room

to break open boxy, confining interiors. Here he included monitor roofs, an element derived from factory architecture to illuminate the wide living and dining rooms. On the exterior and interior the monitors provided the house with its strongest formal element. In the monitors and throughout the house the architect employed blue-green tinted glass—another idea appropriated from contemporary industrial design—to cool the light entering the house. A subtle colorist, Bernardi enlivened this living room with the blue-green filtered light, a red fireplace, and a green cement floor.

Bernardi organized the Smith House into three spacious zones—sleeping, kitchen, and living—the last two meant to accommodate a three-person family who entertained frequently. The kitchen was remarkable, both in its centrality and its size. The house literally revolved around this huge multipurpose space, which at 26 by 16 feet was only slightly narrower than the living room. In 1946 Wurster began to advocate the return of what he called the "old farm kitchen." He wrote of this room:

> It gives a place for the children to eat in, a place for the person who cooks to rest in, a place where the family can gather informally. Connected to it by one door only, have a large living room where you can also eat when occasion demands. Formerly one had to have three areas: kitchen, dining, and living; now rearrange this to be two areas: kitchen and living with dining in either one.[24]

Although Wurster designed virtually no houses from 1944 to 1950, Bernardi implemented the idea of a multipurpose "farm kitchen" here. In addition to ample space for cooking, the Smith kitchen also provided a laundry area, a place for eating, and an informal sitting room. Guests could relax on a built-in couch and watch their meals being prepared on a built-in brick grill. Linked to the kitchen by one door, the living and dining rooms formed essentially one space, large enough for big groups and expandable by handling the overflow of guests on east or west terraces. In subsequent houses Bernardi and Emmons used this new conception of the kitchen as an informal, central, multipurpose space, a clear change from prewar notions of kitchen planning.

Bernardi's widely published design for his own hillside house in Sausalito (1950), which won a 1956 American Institute of Architects Award of Merit, rephrased many of his favorite features of the Smith residence (figs. 203–205). On the first floor he reused the trizonal plan of the Smith House. (The lower floor was conceived as a separate unit, housing a studio, workshop, and guest rooms, and was not connected to the first floor by an internal stairway.) Bernardi joined his dining room to the kitchen, making it an even more versatile multipurpose space. Two walls of the house were almost entirely glazed, with outdoor living areas on either end to extend useful living space. Bernardi frequently lined the exteriors of hillside houses with wraparound walkways, which functioned both as terraces and as additional circulation spaces. California incense cedar, a costly wood obtained through connections with his Stockton client, sheathed the inside and outside walls. A clerestory illuminated the middle of an interior sheltered by trees. Particularly inside the living room, Bernardi highlighted the roof's joists and beams in a manner reminiscent of Bernard Maybeck. The interlocking network of roof members and the clerestory became decorative elements—features that also emphasized the interior's roominess. Finally, the house demonstrated the customary Wurster, Bernardi and Emmons understatement, the "cheap" aesthetic, in which simple materials—unpainted tongue-and-groove cedar boards, concrete floors, and a patent chimney flue—combined to produce spare refined effects.

Bernardi developed a vocabulary of motifs that he reassembled in various ways to suit the particular circumstances of client and site. The Azevedo House in Tiburon (1964) had the familiar tripartite plan of earlier work, yet its stylistic character was completely different (fig. 206). Here Bernardi interconnected three hexagonal pavilions, one containing bedrooms, the second, family

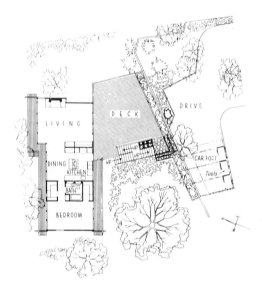

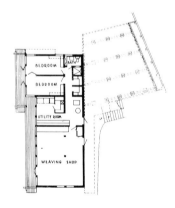

205.
Bernardi House, Sausalito, 1950
Wurster, Bernardi and Emmons
Theodore Bernardi, architect
Plans

room/kitchen, and the third, a living room. Again, the kitchen occupied the central location, serving as a versatile nexus point for the other wings. As at Bernardi's Sausalito house, balcony walkways extended around the dwelling. The architect used a hexagonal plan to satisfy a client who did not want bay views to overwhelm the interior through panoramic windows. Instead, he framed views through tall thin windows located at the multiple corners of each hexagon. The resulting aesthetic was far different from any house previously designed by the firm, underscoring Bernardi's insistence on creative growth and independence.

Four Houses by Emmons

The youngest partner, Donn Emmons, in over forty years of practice, proved to be an excellent draftsman and administrator, capable of maintaining the high design standards of Wurster and Bernardi. A less adventurous designer than Bernardi, Emmons was more like Wurster in his preference for simple horizontal forms, uncomplicated roof lines, and less structural exposure. As a result, Emmons's houses generally had a slightly more traditional flavor than those of Bernardi. Like Wurster, he displayed a flair for understatement and creating elegant effects using very simple means. Throughout a very active career he designed many of the firm's smaller meat-and-potatoes houses, including the Breinig House, the Allen House in San Francisco (1949), and the house for *Better Homes and Gardens* (1955). These residences were published extensively in the popular press and portrayed by magazines as important models for tract-house builders. At the same time, Emmons also created larger country houses set on extensive sites, some of which retained the early California flavor of Wurster's early work but were undertaken in a modernized vocabulary.

Emmons was born in Olean, New York, in 1910. His father, a high school principal, had earned a Ph.D. in education from Columbia University and moved the family to Elizabeth, New Jersey, when Emmons was a boy. He attended architecture school at Cornell from 1929 to 1933, following a course of study patterned on conventional Beaux-Arts teaching. (Emmons's brother, Frederick, three years older, also went to Cornell and became an architect). At Cornell the younger Emmons met Frederick Langhorst, a talented architect who would join Wurster's office in the late 1930s. After graduating, Emmons entered the merchant marine and sailed on a steamship operated by the Dollar Line to Germany and other countries around the world. (In his early twenties Wurster also had joined the merchant marine in order to see the world.) Upon arriving in California, Emmons took a class in rendering at the University of Southern California and worked at odd jobs until he could land employment in an architectural office.

During his five or so years in Los Angeles, Emmons worked for four architects: H. Roy Kelley, Roland E. Coate, Edgar Bissantz, and Winchton Leamon Risley. In later conversations Emmons had little to say about the revivalists Kelley and Coate. Operating a prolific practice, Kelley won many design awards from the architectural and popular press before modernism became a strong influence in California in the mid-1930s. In Emmons's opinion, Kelley designed in an uninspired piecemeal fashion, selecting and recombining details from architectural books. Emmons had fonder memories of Bissantz and Risley. He worked on Bissantz's best-known house, the Drake House in Pasadena (ca. 1936), a sort of Japanese ranch house, and a number of jobs for Risley, including the Saeta House in Los Angeles (ca. 1934). Risley, whom Emmons regarded as "by far the best of the four," worked in a pared-down traditional manner, which in some ways resembled Wurster's work of the mid-1930s.[25] While working for Risley, Emmons met Wurster, who visited the office in the mid-1930s. He accompanied Wurster on a tour of Los Angeles architec-

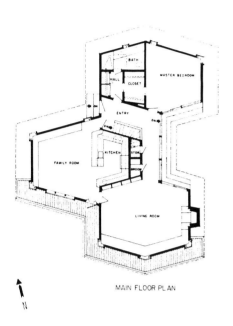

MAIN FLOOR PLAN

206.
Azevedo House, Tiburon, 1964
Wurster, Bernardi and Emmons
Theodore Bernardi, architect
Plan

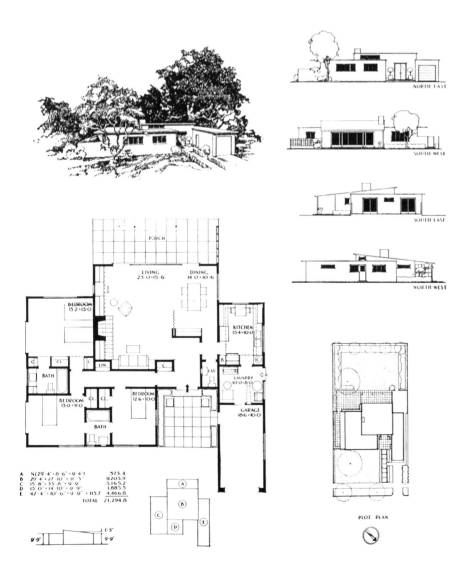

ture, which pointedly did not include the avant-garde work of Richard Neutra or Rudolph Schindler, whose designs did not appeal to Wurster.

In 1938, while still living in Los Angeles, Emmons and his brother, Frederick, entered the American Gas Association Small House Competition and won a $200 award (fig. 207). The house emphasized the strong distinction between front and rear, public and private realms of the house, characteristic of Donn Emmons's later work. The living and dining rooms were joined to create a single space that flowed outward to a rear porch. Floor-to-ceiling windows opened the living areas to this porch, sheltered by an extension of the modern shed roof. In contrast, the fenestration of the front facade was quite limited. No windows surrounded the main entryway. In a traditional touch, symmetrical planters framed paired front doors. A fence integral with the northeast wall shielded family activities in the backyard. A garage projected in front, serving as a sound barrier for the rear living areas. The Emmonses' entry, with its minimal front fenestration, open rear plan, entry court, and projecting garage anticipated later residential designs, such as the influential subdivision houses done for the Palo Alto developer Joseph Eichler in the late 1940s and 1950s.[26]

When he was unable to find employment in Los Angeles, Emmons headed north to work for Wurster, whose reputation was rapidly growing in California and also nationally. By the late 1930s Wurster, along with Gardner Dailey, John Ekin Dinwiddie, Henry Hill, Phillip Joseph, Clarence Mayhew, and others, began to attract architects from across the country. Many young architects viewed San Francisco as the center for innovative domestic design from 1937 to 1942. Once in Wurster's employ, Emmons worked as a draftsman on a num-

207.
Entry for the American Gas Association Small House Competition, 1938
Donn Emmons and Frederick Emmons
Elevation and plan of project

208.
Emmons House, Mill Valley, 1947
Wurster, Bernardi and Emmons
Donn Emmons, architect
Interior view

ber of varied commissions, receiving a comprehensive introduction to the design and construction processes. He participated in the design of Yerba Buena Gardens in San Francisco, his first project for Wurster (1939–40), Sugar Bowl Ski Lodge in Placer County (1939), the Schuckl Canning Company Building in Sunnyvale (1942), the Gerbode House, the Reynolds House in Gilroy (1940), and many other domestic commissions. Emmons recalled this formative training: "As a project progressed, each draftsman, according to his ability, made presentation drawings, working drawings, wrote specifications, and supervised construction. It was a learning experience the likes of which I haven't seen before or since."[27] During World War II Emmons worked on informational exhibitions in the Navy's Special Devices Office with photographer Edward Steichen, returning to the Wurster and Bernardi office for work after the war ended. Bernardi, who managed the overworked office in Wurster's absence, was the first to suggest the possibility of a partnership to Emmons in 1945.

One of Emmons's most engaging and unconventional efforts was his own residence in Mill Valley (1947), set on a hillside overlooking San Francisco Bay (figs. 208, 209).[28] The Emmons House and its two identical neighbors, built for friends, reflected the architect's skill at improvisation. This house was "cheap" in the best Wursterian sense of the word. Emmons originally hoped to build a house from Quonset-hut surplus, aiming to maximize the amount of usable space his meager finances would allow. A Quonset hut, however, would not have provided the two-floor height he wanted in order to increase living space on a very small plot. To cut framing and foundation costs to the bone, Emmons composed the simplest form—a rectangular box covered by a shed roof. This elemental composition resembled that of the Owens House in nearby Sausalito (1939), designed by his friend Joseph Esherick when he was working in Gardner Dailey's office. Seen from the rear, the Owens House shared the full height glazing of Emmons's house and had a similar loft-type spatial arrangement (fig. 155). Both houses also had a vernacular metal flue instead of a full brick stack. Emmons located the totemic flue in a central position on the front facade to make it eye-catching. On the interior he sandwiched the fireplace between two full-height windows, creating a bold contrast of glass and brick, mass and transparency.

The floor plan reflected Emmons's restricted economical program. Roughly dividing the first floor in half lengthwise, he designed a single living/dining area that occupied a two-floor space on one side, while a study, an extra bedroom, and a kitchen took up the other half of the first floor. Above the latter half, a loft containing three bedrooms extended fourteen feet. To save money and allow views of the bay, walls enclosed only one loft bedroom. The plan required no corridors to link rooms, maximizing space and reducing cost. Plumbing stacks for each floor's bathroom were aligned to save money on pipes. A steep ship's ladder, much like the one Wurster used to reach the sunroof of the Mendenhall House, led to the second floor, thereby cutting the substantial cost of framing a stairway.

With its loft and simple wall detailing, the house had an informal barnlike character. Tall posts supported a network of thin beams and diagonal braces, creating a distinctive linear ceiling pattern. The diagonal members were needed to reinforce the house's light frame against seismic forces and strong winds blowing off San Francisco Bay.[29] Rear windows lacked the usual double-hung or casement framing details; for budgetary and aesthetic reasons, Emmons employed sliding windows set on wooden runners nailed to the exterior, similar to the barn doors of Wurster's Clark House. Sliding windows trimmed by these horizontal wooden strips became a trademark on many of Emmons's houses thereafter.

In the late 1940s and 1950s Emmons designed a number of distinguished country houses in the rapidly expanding suburbs of the San Francisco peninsula. Many of these were for well-to-do clients who did not need to economize but for whom ostentation was anathema. The Schuman House in Woodside (1949), built for a real estate developer and his wife, had a traditional western ranch-house plan (figs. 210, 211), in many ways comparable to the layout of Wurster's archetypal Gregory Farmhouse. (The firm kept a file of photographs of previous houses to show clients, and many were shown the Gregory residence as an initial stimulus for discussion.) Both houses had L-shaped, one-story configurations designed to suit clients who did not employ servants and who requested informal surroundings; each plan was anchored around a mature oak tree. Intended for year-round habitation, the Schuman House had some refinements of plan not found in Wurster's earlier weekend dwelling. Entry, for example, was gained directly into the living room of the Gregory Farmhouse, whereas Emmons provided a more formal entry hall for the Schuman House. A large living room dominated both plans, and both architects elevated the ceiling of this main room to provide a greater sense of spaciousness and importance. The kitchen stood just off the living room in both plans; again Emmons adopted a unified living, dining, and kitchen arrangement. The configuration of the bedroom wings in both plans was parallel, although Emmons dispensed with the extra bedroom porch in favor of a dressing room and added a bath for the Schumans. The location of the Schuman House study mirrored the bedroom off the sleeping porch of the Gregory Farmhouse. Emmons transformed this porch into a service yard but kept the walk-in tool shed just off the garage.

Wurster and Emmons sought to merge interior and exterior spaces as much as possible in the Schuman and Gregory houses, but differences were required in the former residence because of its more densely populated suburban context. Emmons worked with landscape architect Lawrence Halprin, the Schumans' son-in-law, to plan the three-and-a-half-acre property. Emmons eliminated the covered gallery lining the front of the Gregory Farmhouse, perhaps in part because of its cost and also because he usually designed subur-

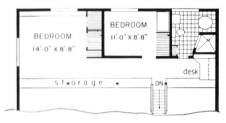

MEZZANINE

FIRST FLOOR

209.
Emmons House, Mill Valley, 1947
Wurster, Bernardi and Emmons
Donn Emmons, architect
Plans

210.
Schuman House, Woodside, 1949
Wurster, Bernardi and Emmons
Donn Emmons, architect, with Lawrence
Halprin, landscape architect
Exterior view

211.
Schuman House, Woodside, 1949
Wurster, Bernardi and Emmons
Donn Emmons, architect
Plan

(Photo by Morley Baer)

212.
Schuman House, Woodside, 1949
Wurster, Bernardi and Emmons
Donn Emmons, architect
View of living room fireplace

ban houses to open to the private rear yard rather than the public facade. Aside from the main entrance and doors to service rooms, no entries led outside on the front facade. Doors from all major rooms led out to covered spaces in the rear. In lieu of a covered gallery, the eaves of the Schuman House projected outward, providing shelter from sun or rain for those seated near the house. The extended eaves also shaded walls of glass on the rear facade, which, according to the owners, offered "the feeling of being outdoors in every room of the house."[30] Both Wurster and Emmons used a porch to add space to the living room. Emmons screened his porch to make it insect-proof and more habitable for guests. Off the porch was a round terrace encircling the living room.

Seen vis-à-vis the Gregory Farmhouse, the Schuman House, though informal, possessed stylistic refinements reflective of well-to-do clients during an affluent era. Emmons's dwelling had decidedly contemporary elevations, with transparent walls, clean lines free from period ornamentation, and an emphatic flat roof. The living room's added height produced an elegant spatial effect, providing strong contrast to the lower, more utilitarian kitchen and bedrooms. Unlike the living room in Bernardi's own house, Emmons hid the living room's roof framing to create a more finished appearance. The walls and ceiling of tongue-and-groove Douglas fir boards and flush ceiling lights gave this space crisp, precise lines without seeming sterile. Emmons carefully framed the fireplace for effect, balancing it between two paneled wall sections (fig. 212). Within such a muted interior, the irregular texture and shapes of the native fieldstone chimney contrasted markedly with the smooth, uniform wood boards on either side. The transparency of the glass on either side of the wood walls, in turn, emphasized the solidity of the wall mass. Emmons included other refinements, such as custom-made door hardware and drawer pulls, lighting fixtures, and built-in cabinets. Provided with a fairly generous budget, the architect could also include costly copper gutters, downspouts, and roof flashing. Compared to the Gregory Farmhouse, the Schuman House retained a familiar ranch-house plan that provided for informal living on backyard terraces, yet its woodsiness and rusticity were tempered by modern styling and numerous refinements of detail.

In 1955 Emmons executed a house plan for *Better Homes and Gardens* magazine—a design inspired by Wurster's rambling early California houses of the 1930s, which were enlarged to satisfy affluent middle-class families of the 1950s[31] (figs. 213). The plan was antithetical to designs for the inexpensive Davidson and Emmons houses. Its T-shaped arrangement occupied 1,690 square feet and, according to an advertisement, contained "that 'extra' space that's so necessary to graceful living."[32] The T-plan, observed the ad, "affords more outside wall, resulting in better view, lighting and ventilation."[33] Emmons located bedrooms and baths in the long tail of the plan on a double-loaded corridor, while living room, kitchen, and family room occupied the head of the T. Emmons's plan provided for the separation of adults and children in different living zones: a quiet living room for adult reading and entertaining stood apart from a family room set up for children's activities. To foster the illusion of endless space, Emmons included four outdoor living areas. The formal living room was extended by a covered terrace comparable to the porches of the Davidson and Smith houses. A screened porch accommodated an additional eating space for the informal family room. Additional paved terraces were provided off the master bedroom and entrance court.

The *Better Homes and Gardens* house not only had to look spacious but also had to appear private as well. Public and private areas were carefully demarcated. The entrance court served as a large external foyer, highlighting the approach of visitors. The interior foyer served as an additional filter, dissuading guests from penetrating internal spaces. Few windows revealed views of the interior from the street or entry-court facades, although Emmons glazed

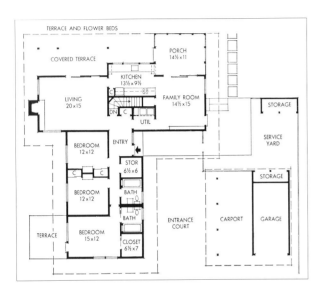

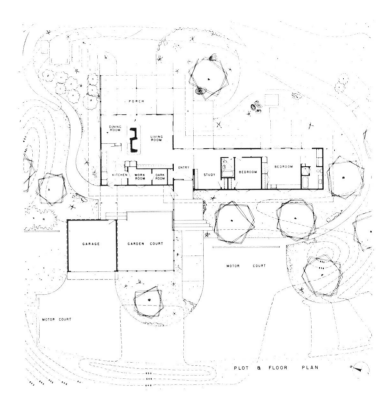

213.
House for **Better Homes and Gardens**, 1955
Wurster, Bernardi and Emmons
Donn Emmons, architect
Plan (built for varous sites)

214.
Williams House, Portola Valley, 1956
Wurster, Bernardi and Emmons
Donn Emmons, architect
Plan

fenestrations liberally along the rear terrace. While the master bedroom's terrace was exposed to the street, the extension of the living room's chimney wall blocked views of the rear terrace from the street. Finally, by placing the house's long axis perpendicular to the street, Emmons maximized the distance of the backyard from intrusions of the street. In short, the *Better Homes and Gardens* house provided the expanded space and privacy desired by families fleeing what they felt were crowded, crime-ridden urban areas of the 1950s.

The editors of *Better Homes and Gardens* hoped to build seventy-one copies of this model house in the United States. To attract a wide audience, the styling had to be fairly traditional. No walls of glass revealed the interior on the front facade; standard wood siding clad the exterior. A familiar gable roof with a low pitch and spreading form communicated to the neighborhood this dwelling's sprawling interior. The house proved popular with readers, and at least seventy-eight identical model houses were erected across the United States and Canada.

Further evidence of Emmons's traditionalist approach is the Williams residence in Portola Valley (1956), a ranch house with rustic but contemporary styling (figs. 214, 215). Like the Schuman House, it had a long, low silhouette configured in an L-shape on one floor. Exterior siding of vertical redwood boards stained dark brown and the gable roof's cedar shingles contributed to its rustic appearance. Like the *Better Homes and Gardens* house, a photogenic gable roof dominated the exterior view of the dwelling. The gable's extensive eaves, shallow pitch, and thin supports recalled 1930s ranch houses by Wurster, as well as Pietro Belluschi's Menafee House in Yamhill, Oregon (1948). Reflective of Wurster's influence, Emmons shaved the fascia boards of the Williams eaves to a razor thinness, giving a traditional form a precise, up-to-date look. Also contemporary was the manner in which he glazed the gable end wall (one of his favorite motifs in the 1950s), revealing its light skeleton of posts and beams. This glass wall admitted sweeping views of nearby Stanford University and the San Francisco Bay.

215.
Williams House, Portola Valley, 1956
Wurster, Bernardi and Emmons
Donn Emmons, architect
Exterior view

Emmons laid out a plan that extended horizontally, serving as a screen for the rear outdoor living spaces. Again, few windows along the front opened the interior to public view. The entryway was located between the linear bedroom wing to the south and the square living areas to the north. A single loaded corridor, with an open study, was faced in floor-to-ceiling glass, and it adjoined a long rear terrace. The corridor recalled Wurster's trademark glazed galleries of the 1930s—circulation spaces that were widened to become sitting rooms. The Williams corridor, however, lacked the width or transitional indoor/outdoor character Wurster gave to his glazed galleries. (Wurster frequently tiled or bricked the floors of his glazed galleries. Spanish tile or brick served as a durable, transitional surface from outdoor terraces to clean carpeted interiors.) In general, Emmons and Bernardi discontinued use of the glazed gallery after 1947, although Wurster continued to experiment with this element well into the 1960s. Emmons chose to divide kitchen, dining, and living rooms in a traditional manner, but did so by using a fireplace wall, consistent with modern designs by Marcel Breuer and others. The fireplace wall provided a visual anchor, its imposing mass underscored by the light surrounding post-and-beam wall members and the plate-glass windows.

These houses demonstrated the ability of Bernardi and Emmons to keep pace with changes in planning and design. Their houses became confidently modern after World War II, yet still maintained the regional vernacular characteristics of Wurster's prewar work. Bernardi's role was especially catalytic within the firm, helping to test new ideas of roof design, materials, and space planning. Emmons was more of a traditionalist, who retained many of Wurster's tendencies but subtly updated them. Emmons and Bernardi produced the lion's share of residential work in the office after 1945, owing to Wurster's full-time academic duties.[34] One might say that Wurster had to meet the high design standards set by Bernardi and Emmons after World War II.

Notes

1. Donn Emmons, interview by the author, Sausalito, 9 July 1992.

2. Ian McCallum, for example, in his 1959 book, *Architecture U.S.A.,* published a photograph of Wurster, Emmons, and Bernardi but discussed only Wurster's biography and recent projects. See Ian McCallum, *Architecture U.S.A.* (New York: Reinhold, 1959), pp. 71–73. An important early article in *Casabella* by Richard Peters also concentrated on Wurster without mentioning Bernardi or Emmons. Richard Peters, "L'architetto William Wurster," *Casabella continuita,* no. 238 (April 1960), pp. 14–17.

3. In 1964 the firm had six associates: James D. Wickenden (one of Wurster's earliest and most talented draftsmen, hired in the early 1930s), Albert Aronson, Willard D. Rand (Rand was Wurster's right-hand man within the office during the 1950s), George R. Kennaday, Don E. Stover, and Ralph O. Butterfield. Prior to the war, Wurster hired only men for drafting positions. Women in the office were viewed as distractions; Wurster took this so seriously that the female office secretary, Faye Hogue, occupied an office two floors below the drafting room. Materials to be typed were lowered to her by use of a pulley system. It was after the war, and under urging from Wurster's wife, Catherine Bauer, that women were hired to draft and design.

4. While working in Delano and Aldrich's office in 1923–24, Wurster organized office tours of recent country houses to demonstrate to drafting personnel how their paper designs satisfied the client's practical demands. His organization of these tours strongly impressed William Adams Delano, who subsequently gave Wurster personal tours of recent houses. The organization of seasonal tours of recent work became a fixture of the Wurster office in the 1930s and 1940s. Extensive maps of the Bay Area showing recent houses by Wurster and other local designers (plus Frank Lloyd Wright) were kept in the office to guide employees and visiting architects. Bernardi and Emmons continued the practices of office tours and mapmaking well into the 1950s.

5. Theodore Bernardi, interview by the author, San Francisco, 31 October 1985.

6. Ibid.

7. "House for Mitchell T. Neff, Ross, Ca.," *Architectural Forum* 66, no. 4 (April 1938), p. 346.

8. Northern California did not sustain architects who worked in the vein of Richard Neutra or Rudolph Schindler during the 1930s; the few San Franciscans who wanted high International Style designs traveled to Los Angeles to commission work from one of the two designers, usually Neutra. Neutra built only a half dozen or so houses in and around San Francisco at this time.

9. Bernardi, interview by the author, 31 October 1985.

10. "1936 Convention in Retrospect," *Architect and Engineer* 127, no. 2 (November 1936), p. 52.

11. Watercolors of these Gold Country buildings were still displayed on the walls of Emmons's Sausalito house when the author visited 9 July 1992.

12. "Case Study House No. 3," *Arts and Architecture* 62, no. 6 (June 1945), p. 30. Bernardi was in full charge of the office at this time, as Emmons was still in the Navy and Wurster was at MIT. Most magazine correspondence between 1944 and 1946 was handled by Bernardi.

13. Donn Emmons, "Two Architects and a Photographer Recall the Hard Work and the Good Times with Church and Wurster, 1930s, 1940s," interview by Suzanne B. Riess, 19 April 1977, in *Thomas D. Church, Landscape Architect,* vol. 1 (Berkeley: University of California, Regional Oral History Office, The Bancroft Library, 1978), pp. 96–97.

14. In 1949 Wurster wrote: "Every architect who is designing places for living must keep in mind the common quality which can and should in some measure be possessed by every house—be it apartment, row house, or free-standing cottage—and that is out-of-door space, usable, and private." See William Wurster, "The Outdoors in Residential Design," *Architectural Forum* 91, no. 3 (September 1949), p. 68.

15. Donn Emmons, "Frontiers in the Design of Houses," *Journal of Home Economics* 41, no. 9 (November 1949), p. 491.

16. William Wurster, "A Third Generation of Clients," *AIA Journal* (September 1969), p. 77.

17. Bernardi became a fiercely loyal citizen of California, rarely traveling outside its borders. He waited until the summer of 1947 to take his first trip to the East Coast of the United States.

18. Bernardi, interview by the author, 31 October 1985. Bernardi noted his special admiration for Maybeck's Christian Science church (Berkeley, 1910) and later paid homage to it in his own Unitarian church (Berkeley, 1961).

19. Ibid. Bernardi was not hired by Maybeck for the Principia College project.

20. Ibid.

21. Ibid.

22. "A Befitting Setting for a Way of Life," *Architectural Record* 104, no. 3 (September 1948), p. 88.

23. Wurster mentioned these Italian loggias in a press release dated August 1945. Turner House file, William Wurster Archive, College of Environmental Design, Documents Collection, University of California, Berkeley.

24. William Wurster, "From Log Cabin to Modern House," *New York Times Magazine*, 20 January 1946, p. 77.

25. Donn Emmons, interview by the author, 7 July 1992. For reviews of Bissantz's Drake House, see "Distinction with Restraint. The Pasadena Home of Miss Jeanette M. Drake," *California Arts and Architecture* 51 (March 1937), pp. 22–23; and *"House Beautiful's* Tenth Annual Small House Competition, Weekend Houses," *House Beautiful* 80 (March 1938), pp. 50–52. For more on Risley's Saeta House, see "House of Maurice Saeta, Los Angeles," *Architectural Record* 77 (January 1935), p. 30, and "House for Maurice Saeta, Los Angeles, Ca., Winchton L. Risley, Architect," *Architectural Forum* 70 (February 1939), p. 114–15.

26. Frederick Emmons, who also worked for Wurster in the late 1930s and early 1940s, incorporated with A. Quincy Jones after World War II to form a successful architectural firm in Los Angeles, well known for its designs for the real estate developer Joseph Eichler. This 1938 design had a number of features in common with a courtyard house done for Eichler in the late 1950s by Jones and Emmons. See "Separate Worlds for Parents and Children," *Sunset* 123, no. 5 (November 1959), p. 86.

27. Donn Emmons, "A Unique Architectural Practice," in R. Thomas Hille, ed., *Inside the Large Small House: The Residential Legacy of William W. Wurster* (Princeton, N.J.: Princeton Architectural Press, 1994), p. 8.

28. Emmons's own house also proved to be one of his most popular; it was published in at least ten books and magazines on domestic design from 1952 to 1956. At least two other houses by Emmons—the Schmidt House at Stinson Beach (1950) and the Carpenter House in Los Gatos (1959)—were directly patterned on the first three Mill Valley copies.

29. Emmons liked the thin, elegant framing pattern of the ceiling enough to reuse it in the living room of the house for landscape architect Lawrence Halprin (Kentwoodlands, 1951).

30. Thomas Creighton and Katherine Morrow Ford, *Contemporary Houses Evaluated by Their Owners* (New York: Reinhold, 1961), p. 141.

31. See "Idea House for 1957," *Better Homes and Gardens* 36, no. 1 (September 1957), pp. 49–63, 138–40, 142. In 1956 Emmons proposed to the editors of *Better Homes and Gardens* plan variations for northeastern, southeastern, and southwestern regions to suit climatic differences. To the best of my knowledge, these plans were never published.

32. Advertisement in *House and Home* 11, no. 4 (April 1957), p. 30.

33. Ibid.

34. Theodore Bernardi continued to work on projects for the firm until his death in 1990 at the age of eighty-six. His role within the firm became less active, however, during the late 1970s. Donn Emmons retired from the firm in the mid-1980s. Today, Wurster, Bernardi and Emmons is run by Ralph Butterfield, who joined the firm in 1956.

William Wurster Chronology

Alan R. Michelson

1895
William Wilson Wilson Wurster is born to Frederick and Maude Wurster 20 October 1895 in Stockton, California.

1912
Graduates from Stockton Public High School.

1913–14
Enters the School of Architecture at the University of California at Berkeley in August 1913. Attends classes for a year and a half until an illness forces him to recuperate at home.

1915–16
Works as surveyor in Stockton while recuperating.

1917
Attempts to enlist in the armed forces during World War I, but is rejected for health reasons. Returns to the University of California to study naval architecture and maritime engineering for one year.

1918
Joins the merchant marine. Sails to Hawaii and the Philippines, working as the ship's engineer on a freighter.

1919

A Public Library, student project, 1919

Returns to University of California School of Architecture to finish course work; graduates with honors in the fall.

1919–20
Enters the office of architect John Reid, Jr., 1 Montgomery Street, San Francisco; works on the designs of elementary and high school buildings for the city of San Francisco.

1912–22
Charles Gilman Hyde, professor of engineering at the University of California, assists Wurster in obtaining employment in the Sacramento office of Charles Dean, where he works on designs for the city of Sacramento's water-treatment facility. Hyde is instrumental in referring several other water-treatment-plant commissions to Wurster.

1921–22
Moonlights as designer of two houses in Sacramento, a residence in Stockton, and a small office building in Merced. Becomes a licensed architect in April 1922.

1922–23
Travels in Europe from May 1922 to May 1923.

1923–24
Works for the New York architectural firm Delano and Aldrich. In the summer of 1924 William Adams Delano asks Wurster to live at the Delano country house in Syosset, New York, and tutor his son William Richard Potter Delano, later a student of architecture at the École des Beaux-Arts and Yale University.

1924
Returns to Berkeley in the fall; establishes a practice in the Hotel Whitecotton on Allston Way.

1925
Completes his first house as a licensed architect, the Wright House in the Oakland Hills (destroyed by fire 1991).

1926
Moves his practice to the eighth floor of the Newhall Building, 260 California Street, San Francisco. Occupies various offices in this building for seventeen years.

Begins to make frequent visits to Santa Barbara (until 1930), touring the area with his friend landscape architect Lockwood de Forest.

1927
Works on the Warren and Sadie Gregory Farmhouse, completed in 1928.

1928
Becomes a member of the American Institute of Architects, sponsored by William Adams Delano.

1929
Wins his first Honor Award from the Northern California Chapter of the American Institute of Architects, 8 July 1929.

Begins association with Marion Hollins and her Pasatiempo country-club development.

1930
Hires his first long-term employee, Floyd Comstock.

1931

Church House, 1931

House Beautiful awards the Gregory Farmhouse the top prize in its Small House Competition.

1932

Hires James Donald Wickenden, from Clarence Tantau's office, who becomes an associate of the firm after World War II.

Wurster's designs for the Howes, Church, and Hollins houses at Pasatiempo are displayed in the Northern California American Institute of Architects Biennial Exhibition held at the De Young Museum in San Francisco. Wins achievement awards for these projects and also the Cherney water-filtration plant.

Selected as one of four delegates to represent the Northern California Chapter at the American Institute of Architects' national convention in Washington, D.C.

Sails for Honolulu to undertake two residential commissions, 30 May–24 June.

Meets the Los Angeles architect Reginald Johnson at Pasatiempo. Johnson's son, Joseph, enters Wurster's office in the late 1930s.

1933

Moves to 1078 Green Street in San Francisco after residing in Berkeley since 1924. Typical of Wurster, he relocates near close friends, including Donald Gregory, whose residence is one block away.

Elected to the Allied Arts Committee of Standing and Special Committees of the American Institute of Architects.

Attends the "Century of Progress" exposition in Chicago, 9–16 October.

1934

Hires Theodore Bernardi, who had recently worked on the Historic American Buildings Survey. His office at this time has four draftsmen: Comstock, Wickenden, Bernardi, and Horn.

Wurster's work is displayed at the Building Material Exhibit Building, San Francisco, in March, sponsored by the Association of California Architects.

1935

Appointed one of nine members of committee to take charge of Honor Awards for the Northern California Chapter of the American Institute of Architects' biennial exhibition. Wins Honor Awards for three projects: the Converse House (Carmel, 1933), the Robbins House (Hillsborough, 1932), and the Donald Gregory House (Scotts Valley, 1933).

Wurster's Colby House (Berkeley, 1931) is included in the "New Architecture from California" exhibition presented at the Museum of Modern Art, New York. His work continues to be featured in the museum's catalogues and exhibitions until approximately 1950.

Moves his residence to a small apartment at 1730 Jones Street, San Francisco.

1936

First major article on Wurster appears in May issue of *Architectural Forum.*

1937

Travels in Europe for six weeks during August and September, accompanied part of the time by Thomas and Elizabeth Church. Meets Alvar Aalto and sees work by Le Corbusier, Tecton, and Jacobsen. Wurster receives the Médaille de Bronze at the Exposition Internationale des Arts et Techniques, Paris.

Wins second prize for the Seebe House (Ross, 1936) in *House and Garden*'s architects' competition.

Wurster's office now has eight to ten draftsmen.

1938–41

Voss House (Big Sur, 1931) is included in a traveling show, "Modern Houses in America," organized by the Department of Circulating Exhibitions at the Museum of Modern Art and presented at twenty-four venues throughout the United States.

1938

Clark House, 1937

The Clark House (Aptos, 1937) is included in the survey of American architecture staged by the Architectural League of New York in April.

Occupies the choice rooftop offices (twelfth floor) of the Newhall Building.

When Alvar Aalto visits the Bay Area, Wurster takes him to see Frank Lloyd Wright's Hanna House (Stanford, 1937) and the Gregory farmhouses (Scotts Valley, 1928 and 1933).

Hires Donn Emmons, who had worked previously for Winchton L. Risley in Los Angeles.

1939

Designs the Yerba Buena Pavilion at the Golden Gate International Exposition and two houses that are added to the tour of model homes set up to coincide with the San Francisco's World's Fair. The Sullivan House (Saratoga, 1939) is part of an exhibition at the Homes and Gardens Building at the fair. Travels to see Aalto's Finnish Pavilion at the New York World's Fair.

Moves into an apartment at 1015 Vallejo Street, San Francisco, designed by Willis Polk.

1940

In April tours Los Angeles work by Frank Lloyd Wright and Harwell Harris.

Wurster's office creates model-city drawings for the city of Richmond, Calif., which are exhibited at the city hall in April.

Marries the noted urban-planning and housing expert Catherine Bauer in Seattle, 12 August; Berkeley architect Vernon DeMars and his wife, Elizabeth, are witnesses.

Wurster and Bauer visit New York from late December to 13 January 1941.

1941

"Experimental" Housing, Carquinez Heights, 1941

Makes at least three trips to Washington for the defense-housing project at Vallejo.

Wurster and Bauer move into an apartment at 2632B Hyde Street, San Francisco. Wurster's friend the landscape architect Thomas Church, and his wife, Elizabeth, live at 2626 Hyde Street.

The Reynolds House (Gilroy, 1940) is added to one version of the Museum of Modern Art's traveling exhibition "What Is Modern Architecture?" The Reynolds House is included in another MoMA exhibition that year, "Regional Building in America."

The Green House (Mount Diablo, 1941) is included in an exhibition of Bay Area work, "Architecture Around San Francisco Bay, 1941," shown at the Architectural League of New York during the spring and at the San Francisco Museum of Art, 17 June–6 July.

1942

Named chairman of the Architects' Advisory Committee for the National Housing Agency overseeing war-housing commissions. Spends a week in Washington, D.C., in February.

1942–43

The Sullivan House (Saratoga, 1939) is shown in the exhibition "Western Living: Five Houses under $7,500," presented at the San Francisco Museum of Art, 7–27 April 1942. Other architects represented are Frank Llyod Wright, Harwell Harris, Richard Neutra, John Ekin Dinwiddie, and Hervey Parke Clark. The show is repackaged as "Five Houses under $7,500" and presented later at the Museum of Modern Art, New York, in March–April 1943.

1943

Moves to Cambridge, Massachusetts, to undertake graduate study in urban planning at Harvard. Plans to obtain a Ph.D. working with John Gaus, but never finishes the degree.

Architectural Forum features Wurster's work in its July issue.

While at Harvard, serves as a visiting design critic at Yale School of Architecture for one semester.

Wurster employees Theodore Bernardi, John Funk, James Wickenden, and Fred Langhorst open a shared practice at 402 Jackson Street.

1944

Visits Frank Lloyd Wright's houses in Oak Park, Illinois.

His Schuckl Canning Company office building (Sunnyvale, 1942) and other designs are displayed in the "Built in USA, 1932–1944" exhibition at the Museum of Modern Art, New York.

Appointed dean of the School of Architecture at the Massachusetts Institute of Technology.

Incorporates with his onetime employee Theodore Bernardi, opening an office at 402 Jackson Street. This third-floor office is directly above that of the landscape architect Thomas Church.

The Prebilt House designed by Wurster and Bernardi, collaborating with Ernest Kump, is included in the Museum of Modern Art's exhibition "Tomorrow's Small House" in New York.

Documentation of Wurster's defense workers' housing at Vallejo is added to MoMA's exhibition "Housing: Recent Developments in Europe and America, 1940–44."

1945

William, Catherine, and Sadie Wurster in Macao, 1957

A daughter, Sadie, is born to Wurster and Catherine Bauer in Boston, 24 August. Their only child, she is named for Wurster's friend and early client Sarah (Sadie) Gregory.

Wurster and Bernardi invite former employee Donn Emmons to rejoin the office as a partner. Firm becomes known as Wurster, Bernardi and Emmons.

Selected to be a Fellow of the American Academy of Arts and Sciences.

1947

Named an affiliate of the American Institute of Planners.

Called a leading practitioner of the "Bay Region style" in Lewis Mumford's column, "The Skyline: Status Quo," published in *The New Yorker,* 11 October.

1948

Appointed by President Harry Truman to the National Capital Park and Planning Commission, 9 July. Serves three years overseeing the planning of Washington, D.C.

As committee chairman, supervises the selection of Eero Saarinen's "Gateway Arch" entry in the Jefferson National Expansion Memorial Competition in Saint Louis.

1949

The work of Wurster, Bernardi and Emmons is displayed in the exhibition "Domestic Architecture of the San Francisco Bay Area," presented at the San Francisco Museum of Art, 15 August–21 September.

Receives Honor Award from the American Institute of Architects for the Nowell House (Carmel, 1947).

1950

Heller House, 1950

Returns to the University of California at Berkeley as dean of the School of Architecture after the resignation, in December 1949, of Warren C. Perry.

Receives the San Francisco Art Commission Award.

1952

Moves into the old Warren Gregory House at 1459 Greenwood Terrace in the Berkeley hills.

1953

Receives Honor Award from the American Institute of Architects for the Schuckl Cannery office building (Sunnyvale, 1942) and Stern Hall dormitory at the University of California at Berkeley (1938).

Named consulting architect for building on the University of California campus at Berkeley. Holds the post until 1967. Also consults on the design of a number of other campus planning projects at MIT (1944–50); Trinity University, San Antonio, Texas (1951); Brigham Young University, Provo, Utah (1953, 1958, 1960); the University of Washington, Seattle (1959–60); Victoria University, British Columbia (1961–66); and the University of British Columbia, Vancouver (1962–64).

1954

Selected as a Fellow of the American Institute of Architects, along with twenty others, including Ludwig Mies van der Rohe, Royal Barry Wills, and Marion Sims Wyeth, at the group's eighty-sixth annual convention in Boston in July. Serves as an active participant on the Design and Architectural Education panels.

Named a Fellow of the Royal Danish Academy of Fine Arts, Copenhagen.

Named an Honorary Corresponding Member of the Royal Institute of British Architects.

Travels to Hong Kong during the summer to oversee the design of the U.S. Consulate.

Wurster, Bernardi and Emmons moves to 202 Green Street, San Francisco.

1955

Develops the Greenwood Common Property in Berkeley; invites architects John Funk, Joseph Esherick, and Howard Moise, among others, to design single-family homes on land below his Greenwood Terrace house.

1956

George Pope House, 1956

Wurster, Bernardi and Emmons wins three American Institute of Architects awards: for the Center for Advanced Study in the Behavioral Sciences (Palo Alto, 1954), the Bernardi House (Sausalito, 1950), and the Nowell House (Stockton, 1953).

1957

Receives an Honor Award from the American Institute of Architects for the Bissinger House, Kent Woodlands.

Takes a trip to Asia and Europe with his wife and daughter while on sabbatical, 28 January–27 August.

1958–64

Appointed to the Architectural Advisory Panel for the U.S. State Department overseeing construction overseas.

1959

Facing some resistance, integrates the University of California's Department of Architecture, Landscape Architecture, and Urban Planning to create the new College of Environmental Design.

Named a member of the Capitol Building and Planning Commission of Sacramento.

1960

Wurster, Bernardi and Emmons moves to 1620 Montgomery Street, San Francisco.

1962

Serves as chairman of the Awards Jury for the Boston City Hall competition.

Symptoms of Parkinson's disease detected.

1963

Retires as dean of the College of Environmental Design at Berkeley.

Wins an Honor Award from the American Institute of Architects for the Capitol Towers redevelopment design (Sacramento, 1958–63).

1964

Catherine Bauer Wurster dies in a hiking accident on Mount Tamalpais in Marin County, 22 November.

Awarded an honorary Doctor of Laws degree from the University of California.

Receives a California Council of the American Institute of Architects Certificate for Distinguished Service, 9 October.

1965

Named an Extraordinary Member of the German Akademie der Kunst.

Wurster, Bernardi and Emmons receives a Special Award for Distinguished Service from the American Institute of Architects, September.

1966

The new building housing the College of Environmental Design is named Wurster Hall.

Receives a Collaborative Achievement in Architecture Award from the American Institute of Architects for Ghirardelli Square, San Francisco.

1968

Named a charter member of the Berkeley Fellows, University of California at Berkeley.

1969

The American Institute of Architects awards Wurster the Gold Medal, its highest honor for lifetime achievement, in Chicago, 26 June.

1973

Wurster dies at his Greenwood Terrace house, 19 September.

The Twentieth-Century Architect

William Wilson Wurster

PUBLISHED IN **ARCHITECTURE:
A PROFESSION AND A CAREER**
(WASHINGTON, D.C.: AIA PRESS, 1945)

The task of the true architect has always included more than structural dimensions. There has never been a time when a building was an isolated phenomenon shorn of its relationship with the community's social and economic needs. It is true this broad concept has not always been fulfilled and at times it has even been obscured as the goal. The difference between the twentieth-century architect and his predecessor is possibly the very attempt by today's group to keep this goal in sight. Even acknowledging this difference, it is presumptuous to imply an overwhelming change in architectural viewpoint simply because we are writing of our own period. And, too, before we proceed further let me give assurance that it may be architect, engineer, or builder who meets the basic needs, and of course this does not affect the efficacy of the solution. I mention this, for often the goal is obscured by the shoptalk which swirls around allocation and credit for work performed, and is not clarified by discussion of the solution itself.

Architecture does truly mirror change, and changing conditions force upon us a recognition of their presence. Architecture, the art and science of building, offers solutions that must meet these changing conditions and satisfy them. This immediately implies that there is no honesty in attempting to bring into being a *blend* of the familiar and the strange. If there is a *blend* it is the result of forces, materials, and decisions which are related to basic factors, and is not a matter for choice. Failure to recognize this is the cause of much professional and lay confusion. This is all well illustrated by the success of free contemporary architecture on the West Coast, which has frequently been attributed to the notion that here is a "blend" of the old and the new which attracted clients. This just isn't true. There are numerous architects who have not consciously used an eclectic form for many years. It was fortunate that the climate, the new taste for outdoor living, and an informal society freed clients from rigid preconceptions. It was sensible to base the design on the kind of life people wanted, and *not* on the basis of theoretical modernism. Few of the people who live in these houses have ever said to themselves, "This is modern." The approach was not sophisticated or stylistic; so out of it has come—not individual masterpieces—but the nearest thing to a contemporary vernacular that this country has yet produced. There is much to be said for this common or garden variety of things which fits the new conditions as the Colonial houses of New England fitted theirs when they were built two hundred years ago.

A good example of an effective contemporary approach to the placing and the surrounding of urban structures is the Rockefeller Center group in New York. In the case of most office buildings you look at them, possibly go to the top for a view, call on a business acquaintance, and you are through. At Rockefeller Center you do these things and in addition skate, drink, eat, shop, go to the theater (in fact, two theaters) or a museum, and loiter on the gardened terraces.

Now let us take the simpler case of a house. All too often in the past one watched the leveling of hills and pleasant slopes to make the design, as previously drawn, fit this achieved plateau. But now the matter of tree location, orientation, and earth-slope information has become of increasing concern. The first thing an architect requests of an owner is an accurate survey. If the architect and surveyor are on their toes this will indicate contours, utilities, trees and their spread, and the direction and extent of any view. This gives an accurate knowledge of outside space for living and tends to avoid the placing of a block of a house on the ground with no sheltered corners in the yard—where each door and every inch of garden space is exposed to the white glare of publicity.

Possibly the greatest resistance to contemporary architecture comes in the visual aspect of the work. There is one small sentimental survival that perhaps reflects this resistance as well as anything else. Does anyone object to the convenience of electricity? Does anyone long for the danger and work of filling coal oil lamps? Does anyone long for the inconvenience of candles? Yet the lamp and candle forms persist with us, even though they negate reality and are inefficient and inconvenient. Just look about you and see the dripping-covered cardboard cylinders with bulbs emerging, all a distorted recollection of a candle. I have long sought a reason for this type of completely irrational hangover and have come to the conclusion that it springs from the fact that the imitative is the most powerful of all shaping factors and is most easily accepted by the unthinking. Of course, a really deep and analytical longing for the familiar would demand not only the form of the lamp or candle but the reality itself in place of the sham.

Window glass, in the early years of its making, came in small pieces; so the divided (muntined) sash was a familiar sight. This, like the candle form, has persisted. More work is necessary in the fabricating and in the washing, and this last is a recurring, never-ending process; so by any measurable standard the large panes of glass should be desired by all.

Heating systems and insulation have brought about an enormous possibility of change. We certainly accept their convenience, but often we refuse the freedom they offer and cling to the spotty under-windowing of rooms. Perhaps, to some, solid walls symbolize protection from Indians and cold weather, but the advent of double insulating glass and modern heating makes protection from cold as obsolete a function as shelter from Indians.

Thus we could review the entire list of modern developments. For instance, we no longer need a basement, with its dangerous stairs and added work. We can enjoy the freedom a flat roof gives to a plan without the restrictions set up by sloping roof forms. Another illustration is plumbing. Would anyone of choice return to the privy in the back yard? There are probably few remaining sentiments for tin tubs.

All of these things are easy to understand once they are expressed in words, and facing reality is part of the modern architect's training. This training extends into non-visual things, including social, economic, and technical matters, and the truthful solution of all these will produce an architecture that is indigenous to our life and times.

Architecture, including all its techniques and aesthetics, has been called a "social art," which implies that it should not be solely the self-expression of the architect. It is not an easel painting. It is a part of the life of the client and all those who use and look at it. A test of the true architect is whether he is serving the best interests of the client, and not imposing whims of his own.

This frame for living which we call architecture is not life itself, but encourages freedom for the growth of the occupants. We should encourage the lonely innovator, often martyr to the future—particularly at a time when false architectural ideals have been so long entrenched, and in a period of general crisis when the simple truth is often hard to come by. But in the long run no architecture can be much better than, or greatly at variance with, the life that it shelters.

All of this sums up to the fact that when buildings are built which boldly meet the needs—physical, economic, and social, as well as aesthetic—we then have a great period. Such can never come when we follow the forms of the past and try to fit them to the content of today. Our twentieth-century architect is prepared to meet the challenge of these human needs. In this talent and this kind of thinking lies the hope of a truly great period of our own.

The Outdoors in Residential Design

William Wilson Wurster

Digest of a talk before the Baltimore and Washington chapters of the American Institute of Architects

PUBLISHED IN **ARCHITECTURAL FORUM** (SEPTEMBER 1949)

Here is a very specific and concrete proposal: that private outdoor space, with a large glass area overlooking it, be considered a minimum standard for modern homes, whether single dwellings, row houses, flats or tall apartments.

In discussing this proposal it is important to start with the fundamental question of *how people actually want to live and carry on their family and social life,* in specific, tangible terms of shelter, space and equipment. What are some of the broad facts and trends which must be thought through in their bearing on the design of homes?

First and foremost, we are becoming more and more an urban nation. During the period 1910–40 the U.S. as a whole increased 41 per cent in population, but in urban areas the increase was 76 per cent while in rural non-farm areas (mostly in metropolitan sections) the increase was only 42 per cent and there was a drop of 6 per cent in rural farm areas. These comparisons substantiate the view that the problems we face today are not in any way identical with those of 40 years ago.

Urbanization under any setup, but particularly with our present pattern of location of industry and commerce, brings an ever-increasing separation between home and work, home and recreation. Knotty problems of the "journey to work," automobile traffic on the roads and parking at journey's end are inevitably raised. Urbanization also puts stress on the intensity of land use. The more people who wish to live near a given point the less land each person can have. (We are very prone to act in America as if we had no land problem. We act as if the waste lands of the Rocky Mountains could help our metropolitan areas, but such is not so.)

All these problems raise their heads in every modern urban industrial society. But in our own society in America there is one special angle which makes these problems particularly acute: Most of us are tied to cities. We make our living in cities, and we demand the kinds of schools, shops, entertainment and intense and varied social life which are the recognized "urban advantages."

Unlike many of our European cousins, however, we still like to *live,* by and large, in a rural kind of way. Perhaps it is a sentimental heritage from the frontier, an innate desire for elbow room. Perhaps it is our well-known "individualism." Perhaps it's our national addiction to sun, air, exercise and general hygiene, or just our restlessness. Perhaps it comes from the way we bring up our children. Whatever the cause, we *don't* like congested living conditions; we do like space and freedom.

So we move out of the crowded city districts as fast as we can find something that we can afford. Unfortunately, this is not a universally available solution. Ownership is not always possible and is not always sensible, considering the family cycle.

It is not merely ownership, but also the physical form of the free-standing house, which has been coming into serious question as a universal pattern or ideal. Free-standing houses, particularly the rambling one-story type that has recently come into fashion, take up a lot of land. If they are set too close together they are self-defeating. But the more they are spread out the longer the distance, by and large to the places where people work.

Controlled outdoor space . . .

It is important to determine what people are really seeking, specifically, when they ask for free-standing cottages, and to figure out ways to provide these benefits in closer kinds of communities. Privacy and quiet could well be persuading factors for this. But probably the predominant single desire is for personally controlled out-of-door space, where the family can have a flower or vegetable garden at its door, where the baby can be put out in a play pen or the younger children can make mud pies. This is what people want most, I think, when they vote overwhelmingly for the individual house, even though all these qualities are not necessarily confined to this type of dwelling. Every architect who is designing places for living must keep in mind the common quality which can and should in some measure be possessed by *every* home—be it apartment, row house or free-standing cottage—and that is out-of-door space, usable and private.

. . . in detached houses

Even the free-standing house itself is rarely ideal in this respect: it provides "space," but not necessarily the right kind of space for garden, play area and for private eating and sunning. For maximum use and control over the space, a yard should have a fence or wall. Here the mother can leave her baby in the sun and air and feel that no harm can come to it. It gives passive recreation for the adults and active play space for the young children up to school age. If the space be quite small, then care in the design of the fence will permit the maximum light and air—perhaps a wire mesh fence with vines, or open pickets.

. . . in row houses

But it is not necessary to have a free-standing house to secure many, if not most of these advantages. They may be given to the row house or the so called "garden apartment." This has been done to some extent by the Metropolitan Life Insurance Co. in San Francisco and by the John Hancock Insurance Co. in Brookline, Mass. One constructive solution is having the door on the street front be the one through which everything enters and leaves the house—family, guests, groceries and garbage. This leaves the inner space for garden living with control over the young child and with no danger from gates left open by delivery men. The system also permits greater density with corresponding savings in utilities and transportation. Very much that has been said above about the plot of the free-standing house holds for the row house.

Far too many housing projects, private as well as public, have merely set down their row houses carelessly in a flat and featureless open field, with no real effort to enclose some *private* space or to relate it properly to interior living room and kitchen. In a Danish project by Kay Fisker, which has much greater density than we would usually permit for row houses, a real outdoor living room was provided for each dwelling by means of a high curving wall or hedge. This in turn made the walks interesting and attractive, with changing views and that sense of not seeing *everything* all at once, as one does perforce in a military camp or baseball diamond.

Garages are a special problem in this kind of scheme, but one of the few things we have really learned in the past 20 years—since Sunnyside and Chatham Village, to be exact—is that people will walk quite a distance to a garage compound in order to save their quiet gardens and courts from desecration. And I've always thought that even the typical San Francisco row-house plan, with the garage on the street-front under the house, had something to commend it as an idea, if not in actual execution.

. . . in apartments

Most of the European countries have accepted urbanization with greater grace than we have. One always feels that apartment life in the Italian cities in some way has become a goal and not something from which all desire to escape. Scandinavia is always to be viewed with praise in this regard, for it has developed some community facilities within the apartments which do much to simplify living.

But almost every apartment house built in Europe in the past 20–30 years has one thing which is very, very rare in the U.S.—a balcony. Now, at long last, we should face the fact that the demand for private outdoor space (above all in America!) requires balconies for multi-family dwellings if we are to make them anything but makeshifts or mere way-stations for the rich on their way from Maine to Florida. Not balconies put on for esthetic reasons but usable, well-located places with high nonclimbable railings for the safety of children. And each apartment should have for those who wish it a small allotment of garden space. The restlessness of apartment living has much of its root in the fact that we have never regarded a balcony on a par with the bathroom. Everyone resents the fact that there can be no simple out-of-door lounging in our present apartments; instead, their occupants must dress for the street or to go down via the elevator to the garden—if there is one—or to a public park. (No harm in going to a park, of course, although it does not per-mit the momentary, casual touch with the outdoors that stepping out of one's door provides.)

The need for apartment balconies is not new. Holland, Scandinavia, England, and Switzerland have acted upon this knowledge for years. The much-used fire escapes of the New York tenement have proved the desire for a balcony—if we would but observe it. But no, we are prone to follow blindly that more modern slum, Park Avenue, where apartments have neither view nor out-of-doors so the only hope is to use them for as short a period as possible. I would feel greater hope if some of the new apartments in New York realized how wrong they are—Stuyvesant Town and Fresh Meadows, for instance.

To become *positively* good, apartments must take full advantage of their compact form to make life simpler and easier. They must encourage the kind of cooperative living and highly developed social life they make possible. Again, the Scandinavian models—with their restaurants that send up cooked dinners, their 24-hour nurseries and whatnot—point the way. With the trend toward weekend and vacation shacks in real country, where people can satisfy all their most "individual" desires and enjoy complete solitude, there may be more people, even in America, who would like the impersonal ease of living in a really modern apartment during work and school days.

Varying regional, climatic, and cultural demands will enter this picture in wide variety, but one basic human wish is clear; to be able to enjoy the out-of-doors if and when it is wanted.

. . . through big windows

Also necessary is a large glass area in at least one of the rooms—controlled from glare. With this all can enjoy the changing sky and season no matter what the weather conditions are. (Years ago I moved into an office with continuous windows, and the whole day became richer.) Without expenditure of effort in a busy life or money in a frugal one, the day expands. This I would term controlled out-of-door space with a real importance to the lives of the people. This would help us achieve the new minimum standard for modern houses: private green space which may be enjoyed inside as well as out-of-doors.

California Architecture for Living

William Wilson Wurster

PUBLISHED IN **CALIFORNIA MONTHLY**
(APRIL 1954)

M an-made environment plays an increasingly important role in each of our lives. With the industrial-
ization of the world's work and the increase in
population, more of us live in cities or in the suburbs as a
part of the city. At the turn of the century, 39.7 per cent of
the United States population lived in cities; by 1950, however, this number had increased to 64 per cent. And in
California, 80.7 per cent of the population lived in cities in
1950. Since this tendency will increase, it is most important
to train people whose business it is to shape the surroundings in which we live and work so closely together.

We shall hear from the city planners who deal with the
large framework which must be based on social, economic,
political and civic design aspects. We shall hear also from
the landscape architects whose scale approaches planning
but whose stress is properly on the growing things, gardens,
green belts and open spaces.

Architects team up with city planners and landscape
architects to bring about the design of the physical aspects
of all that lies about you. It is the architect who is responsible for the actual structures and siting.

What is architecture? Who are the architects?

Architecture is a social art. Social because it must ever
deal with man's shelter needs, and an art since it is called
upon to put these needs together in a way that will provide
pleasure and pride. Architecture strives to find successful
solutions to three problems: the use (Does it work for its
function? Is it efficient and economical?); the strength (Will
it survive an earthquake? Do its materials stand up under
wear?); the beauty (Does it adorn our environment? Does it
express spiritual value?)

Writers have said this in many ways—a poetic one is: "A
building must have firmness, commodity and delight,"
which is restating safety, function and beauty. These values
interweave in all structures—varying of course in proportion. All seem to share the need of firmness, but in the case
of a monument you have the use (function) actually becoming beauty and symbolic expression.

Who are the architects? Let me quote from *Sunset
Magazine:*

*Every house has an architect. Sometimes it's the contractor,
sometimes it's the owner, sometimes it's your mother-in-law.
Maybe it is a handful of magazine clippings. But in every
structure there are a certain number of decisions to be made
and somebody has to make them. Somebody has to decide
on details like the kitchen counter height and the big things
like the orientation and the relationship of rooms. Somebody
has to resolve the inevitable conflict between what you want
and what you can reasonably afford. Every owner will cost
himself more than the architectural fee if he makes these
decisions himself.*

Historians have used architecture as a tool to trace the
course of civilization. Life is immeasurably enriched for
the traveler if he has some knowledge of the history of buildings and the life they express. I recall so well how I was
equipped with guide books when I first went out to look at
the world, and how these were gradually pushed into the
background by the history books which told the "why" of
what I was seeing.

All this may become more real to you if you list the
famous landmarks so well known to all travelers: the tem-
ples of Egypt, the Acropolis at Athens, the great fora of
Rome, the medieval Cathedral of Chartres, the Renaissance
palaces in Italy and through the centuries to the civic grace
of that city of cities, Paris. Even in our own country we find
all our civic architecture deeply and constantly influenced
by historical precedent. Think of the Georgian precedent of
Independence Hall in Philadelphia. Think of the Greek
revival which went further than architecture and set the
names of our college fraternal organizations. For Gothic
revival I have only to mention most of the churches whose
pointed windows and steep spires have become synony-
mous in most minds with spiritual meaning.

Only gradually did social consciousness, cultural independence and economic necessity make it become apparent, however, that slavish copy of the old is a hollow affair.
Buildings cannot and should not conjure up life in any
terms but those of their own era—only thus can we pull
together all the factors which surround the decisions and
express them adequately for contemporary life. This brings

us head on into what should guide the decisions of the architect, be he professional or amateur.

The Influence of Climate

First of all there are the conditions and possibilities of the place itself. California has an "eastern" winter at the high altitudes and a mild winter climate at the low levels, and these low levels have summer variety also. Our state has three major geographic divisions: Los Angles and its coastal plain extending from Santa Barbara to San Diego; the San Francisco Bay area; and the central valleys of the Sacramento and the San Joaquin which share the same dry heat as the area east and north of Los Angeles. Let me speak first of the Bay Area and the great central valley, for it is those I know so well.

In California, what we lack in sharp seasonal differentiations we make up for in our change by the hour, particularly in San Francisco, and also by the infinite variety of climates which takes place in a comparatively small area. For example, in San Francisco you want the sun at all times but if you are over on the west slope in the sun there is often too much wind. In other parts of the United States one goes many hundreds of miles before there is a comparable degree of change.

San Francisco is in the same latitude as Washington, D.C., but has two great factors that change the climate. First there is the ocean that warms the air so that sea level has no snow or freezing weather. Second, San Francisco Bay is the only low-level inlet for the air to the great central valleys of the San Joaquin and Sacramento. In this valley area the climate is hot and dry in summer, sometimes reaching over 100 degrees. As the hot air rises the air is pulled in at water level and places San Francisco in a great air-conditioning duct. The exact topography of each section in turn determines how much it is affected by this draft and you have the reason for my statement of the great variance—even block by block. The great draft also draws in swirling fog to further confuse the situation. San Francisco can be truly said to have no summer. We can wear an overcoat almost any evening, and have a fire in the fireplace 350 days of the 365. As the winds are westerly (except during rain) and these come from over the ocean, there is no dust. Since the temperature is not high there is little need to open windows in San Francisco and this encourages row houses and close living. There is never the problem of the warm summer nights and the raucous radio.

This condition is somewhat modified as you commute in any of three directions—north over the Golden Gate bridge to Marin County, south down the Peninsula toward Palo Alto and Stanford, and east over the Bay bridge to Berkeley, Oakland and Alameda—and on further over the hills to Orinda, Lafayette and Walnut Creek.

As a result of the cool climate we find no insects (mosquitoes or flies) in San Francisco, which holds good for Berkeley and Oakland also. But as we go a few miles into warmer summer weather, the need for screens appears, which alters the design of outdoor sitting places. In addition to all this general change within a few miles you have local changes due to hilly terrain and wind. On one side it will

be cold—on the lee side warm and sheltered. In midsummer one can quickly go from 60 degrees in San Francisco to 80 and higher in the suburbs. Think how this affects architectural designs. No insulation is needed on one slope—some is needed on another only a few hundred feet away. Heating systems have the same variance in need.

In the great Sacramento and San Joaquin valleys the whole situation changes, for one must seek protection from the summer sun. In early days a wonderful custom had developed which built a wooden awning over all side-walks in the shopping districts; this was somehow lost for a fifty-year period and is only now reappearing in the new shopping centers. The lovely valley evenings, made so by the cool breeze which comes after sunset, are lacking in Bay Area climate.

In the central valleys large glass areas must be placed under deep overhangs lest you roast the occupants, although less than 100 miles away in San Francisco you are trying to coax the sun into every nook and cranny. This accounts for the lack of trees and gardens in San Francisco—you don't want shade for you need the sun, and both trees and gardens are more valuable to look at than to live in. Add to all of this the hills and blue water and streets which cut down from the hills to the Bay and it becomes clearer that what you look at often counts more than what you live in. Even bad weather—and there is a great deal of it—has a dramatic quality; violent storms in winter, fog morning and evening in summer. I stress all of this because I lived in Massachusetts for seven years.

Los Angeles and that general area have contrasts less harsh than does the Bay Area. This holds good for both winter and summer and gives particular emphasis to out-of-door winter living where there is a much milder climate. But here, too, there are variances in summer as one goes east inland to the dry warmer places and west to the beaches with fresh ocean breezes.

Out-of-door living makes for a delightful life but brings the need for more land for each house to give desired privacy. Thus Los Angeles is the most open city in the world, the first major city wholly dependent upon the automobile for transportation.

Let me mention three other factors of nature which shape our architecture.

First: We have no summer rain. The hills grow brown and all gardens must be watered. This, of course, forces us into terraces in the Spanish garden tradition unless we are lavish with water, and water is expensive, for it is often brought from storage in the Sierra hundreds of miles away. In Massachusetts they have 36 inches of water a year (in the form of snow in winter) falling at about 3 inches each month.

Second: We have had several earthquakes, the bad ones in 1906 and another in the early thirties. This makes us cling to wood frame homes and to steel or reinforced concrete for our commercial structures. If masonry is used at all it must be reinforced, with the result that brick is not the natural building material so extensively used elsewhere.

Third: We have no good building stone (sandstone does not weather well and granite is too expensive); this, combined with the earthquake hazard, has made us turn more and more to concrete. Fortunately our cities are clean for the fuel is gas and, having no freezing weather, we can expose concrete or plaster with no difficulty.

Social Factors

Next, let us turn to the social aspects of California, for these—like climate—are dominant factors in design. Our west coast is still adventuresome—pioneering—and is still willing to take a chance. My clients, like those of many other architects, do not think of architecture as coming in alternative "styles"—they want it to live well and work well in their own terms. None of them, when they come in, say anything about a "modern" house—they assume that it will be of today. Anything else is unthinkable.

For a great many years there has been a shortage of domestic servants in California so we began long ago to design homes that could be kept up by the owners. This means that all sorts of labor saving devices have been incorporated from the start. It is inconceivable that anyone would have the old Boston system of kitchen in the basement, a floor below the dining room! I have designed houses with a three-car garage and no servant's room. All of this goes toward informality and we have a way of life which does not use, nor want to stimulate, service. In fact the reverse is true and people pride themselves on the food they cook and serve and the gardens they cultivate. The out-of-doors is used tremendously in our part of the world. Perhaps the climate permitted its start but it has gone far beyond this to become something in its own right everywhere. It complements the informal atmosphere which I have mentioned. I have only to note the articles in home designing magazines to emphasize my point.

Again on the social side, we have a cosmopolitan population. The first immigrants were Spanish; then came the world-wide publicity of the Gold Rush; and finally there is the geographical fact that the West Coast is the end of the line—French, Germans, Italians, Russians, English and Yankees could go no further so their itching feet were stayed and we have their heritage in their descendants, restaurants and foreign newspapers. From the other direction came Chinese and Japanese. For such a varied group—mixed from the start—there was no single "traditional" style to cling to or to impose on newcomers.

The economy has been as mixed and shifting as the population, and has prevented our society from being jelled into any rigid, settled pattern. The great ranches are a speculative business, not a way of life, and the *Okies* and *Arkies* of one era are the business and civic leaders of the next. Movies, then airplanes, now sport clothes, develop mainly because of the climate. We're still experimenting.

This experimentation extends from a way of living to the methods of building and speculative builders in California turned to architects for leadership. The tract houses here have set the highest standards in the country for economical, efficient and advanced design. This interest in the economical aspect has produced better value for the client than in other places.

Add to this the great number of people who, when freed from economic pressures, choose to live in this particular coastal area because of its lack of extreme heat or cold the year round. These people not only bring capital for the purchase of their original land and house, but continuing income for the service trades. They have leisure and want houses to enjoy it in. I think of the family from Chicago who are now in their fourth generation in California with income still from Chicago real estate. There are also old couples who want a simple one-story cottage to relax in.

Our Architectural Heritage

What is the historical architectural heritage? Spanish monks came up the coast, building missions, at about the time the settlers on the Atlantic seaboard were writing the Declaration of Independence. These buildings you know well in fable and photograph by their adobe walls, cloisters and tile roofs. The great ranchos adopted this same style, later translating it into light wood structures which replaced cloisters with porches. In Monterey the Spanish motif was urbanized in about 1800 and the houses came close to the street, with the garden at the rear and the balcony at the second floor. It is quite Latin in feeling and very different from the old New England towns and the later universal pattern with each house set in the center of its garden. The same urbane, almost French, feeling, was felt in the mining towns in the eighteen-fifties. The patio comes from Spain and Italy and finds itself at home in California.

Then came the riotous architecture of the Victorian era. Wood could be cut and carved and painted in many colors. San Francisco still has many exuberant examples of the bay windows and jig-saw decoration that once filled every street.

What kind of a training can be given at the University to recognize and interpret such a vast list of factors? They must all be assimilated, understood and properly related to each other in the resulting experience.

This is not the time or place to give the details of our curriculum but it is appropriate to mention two major qualities we hope to impart to our students.

First there is skill in drawing, because design is the language of our profession. This proficiency must become second nature. But it must not outrun the analytical context: the *why* of what he is to produce for you. Second, the architect must have knowledge in many fields and he must know where to obtain additional knowledge when he needs it.

Along with all other students, architects must have a good general education to equip them for life as intelligent human beings and responsible citizens. Certain phases of specialization are essential in our complicated modern world, but can go too far in limiting the outlook and capacities of the individual.

Even in terms of strictly professional leadership, it is now clear that highly specialized technical and creative skills are by no means the only requirement. There is therefore a strong trend in American universities, of which our recent change to a broader five-year curriculum in architecture is an example, toward providing a broader general basis for professional and technical training.

Bibliography

Compiled by Marc Petr and Sabrina Owen

Archival Materials

William Wurster Archive. Documents Collection, College of Environmental Design, University of California at Berkeley.

Articles

"Architecture and the Feminine: Mop-Up Work." *Any* 4 (January/February 1994), special issue.

Barr, Alfred H., Jr. "What Is Happening to Modern Architecture?" *Museum of Modern Art Bulletin* 15, no. 3 (Spring 1948), pp. 5–8.

Bauer, Catherine. "Architecture and the Cityscape." *AIA Journal* 27, no. 3 (March 1961), pp. 36-39.

——. "Are Good Houses Un-American?" *New Republic* 70
(2 March 1932), p. 74.

——. "Can Cities Compete with Suburbia for Family Living?" *Architectural Record* 136, no. 12 (December 1964), pp. 149–56.

——. "Cities in Flux." *American Scholar* 13 (Winter 1943–44),
p. 83.

——. "The Dreary Deadlock of Public Housing." *Architectural Forum* 106, no. 5 (May 1957), pp. 140–42, 219, 221.

——. "Exhibition of Modern Architecture." *Creative Art* 10 (March 1932), pp. 201–06.

——. "First Job: Control New-City Sprawl." *Architectural Forum* 105, no. 9 (September 1956), pp. 43–45.

——. "Good Neighborhoods." In *Building the Future City: Annals of the American Academy of Political and Social Science,* 242,
no. 11 (November 1945), edited by Robert B. Mitchell.

——. "Housing: A Memorandum." *California Arts and Architecture* 60, no. 2 (February 1943), pp. 18–19, 41–42.

——. "Housing in the United States: Problems and Policy." *International Labour Review* 52, no. 7 (July 1945), pp. 1–28.

——. "Low-Rent Housing and Home Economics." *Journal of Home Economics* 31, no. 1 (January 1939), p. 4.

——. "The Middle Class Needs Houses Too." *New Republic* 121 (29 August 1949), pp. 17–20.

——. "Outline of War Housing." *Task* 4 (1943), pp. 5–8.

——. "Prize Essay—Art in Industry." *Fortune* 3 (May 1931), pp. 94–99.

——. "Social Questions in Housing and Community Planning." *Journal of Social Issues* 7 (1951), pp. 1–34.

——. "Town Meeting of the Air." *Architect and Engineer* (October 1942), p. 33.

Bauer, Catherine, and Jacob Crane. "What Every Family Should Have." *Survey Graphic* 29, no. 2 (February 1940), p. 64.

Bender, Thomas. "Lewis Mumford: Young Man and the City." *Skyline* (December 1982), pp. 12–14.

"A Befitting Setting for a Way of Life." *Architectural Record* 104, no. 3 (September 1948), pp. 88–91.

Birch, Eugenie Ladner. "An Urban View: Catherine Bauer's Five Questions." *Journal of Planning Literature* 4 (Summer 1989), pp. 239–58. Reprinted in *The American Planner: Biographies and Recollections,* edited by Donald A. Krueckeberg. New Brunswick, N.J.: Rutgers University Center for Urban Policy Research, 1994.

Boyd, John Taylor, Jr. "The Classic Spirit in Our Country Homes." *Arts and Decoration* 31 (October 1919), pp. 59–62.

Carrighar, Sally. "Dormitories in Transition." *Architect and Engineer* (February 1943), pp. 15–25.

"Case Study House No. 3." *Arts and Architecture* 62, no. 4 (April 1945), pp. 36–38.

"Case Study House No. 3." *Arts and Architecture* 62, no. 6 (June 1945), pp. 26–30, 39.

"Case Study House No. 3." *Arts and Architecture* 62, no. 7 (July 1945), pp. 35–38.

"Case Study House No. 3." *Arts and Architecture* 66, no. 3 (March 1949), pp. 34–41.

"The Center for Advanced Study in the Behavioral Sciences." *Arts and Architecture* 71, no. 2 (February 1955), pp. 14–17.

"Chabot Terrace: Public and Commercial Structures." *Pencil Points* 25 (October 1944), p. 30.

Church, Elizabeth. "Pasatiempo." *California Arts and Architecture* 39 (June 1931), pp. 40–42.

Church, Thomas. "Architectural Pattern Can Take the Place of Flowers." *House Beautiful* 90 (January 1948), p. 41.

Clark, Hervey Parke. "H. G. de Bivort House, Berkeley." *California Arts and Architecture* 59 (March 1942), pp. 28–29.

Corbett, Mario. "Menlo Park House for H. T. Perry." *Architectural Record* 91 (January 1942), pp. 56–57.

"Country Office Building." *California Arts and Architecture* 61 (June 1944), pp. 20–22.

Dailey, Gardner A. "Woodside Hills." *Pencil Points* 20, no. 5 (May 1939), p. 290.

———. "Maritime School, West Coast." *Architectural Forum* 78, no. 5 (May 1943), pp. 55–59.

———. "Is There a Bay Area Style?" *Architectural Record* 105, no. 5 (May 1949), pp. 94–95.

———. "Residence of E. M. Manning, Palo Alto, California." *Architect and Engineer* 121, no. 3 (May 1935), p. 32.

———. "Brazilian Bldg. at San Francisco Fair." *Architectural Forum* 70, no. 6 (June 1938), pp. 492–93.

———. "Detail of Facade, Residence of E. M. Manning, Palo Alto." *Architect and Engineer* 134, no. 3 (October 1936), p. 15.

———. "Dean S. Arnold House, Hillsborough, California." *California Arts and Architecture* 36, no. 1 (July 1929), p. 44.

———. "Beach Club, Santa Barbara, California." *Architectural Forum* 73, no. 12 (December 1940), pp. 497–500.

———. "Combined Residence and Office for Dr. and Mrs. Bernard Berliner, San Francisco, Calif." *Architectural Record* 89, no. 1 (January 1941), pp. 96–98.

Dailey, Gardner A., and Joseph Esherick. "House DE-2, Magic Carpet Series." *Architectural Forum* 77, no. 3 (September 1942), p. 133.

Dinwiddie, John Ekin. "Second Prize, Class B, Winning Designs in the Home Electric Competition, Sponsored by the General Electric Company." *American Architect* 146, no. 4 (April 1935), p. 39.

"Distinction with Restraint: The Pasadena Home of Miss Jeanette M. Drake." *California Arts and Architecture* 51, no. 3 (March 1941), pp. 22–23.

"Dr. Bernard Berliner House, San Francisco." *Architect and Engineer* 57, no. 3 (September 1940), p. 26.

Esherick, Joseph. "Image and Reality." *Places* 7, no. 1 (Fall 1990), p. 86.

"Exposition Model Homes." *Pencil Points* 20, no. 5 (May 1939), pp. 286–87.

"Farm House of Mrs. Warren Gregory, Santa Cruz Mountains, California." *Architecture* 72, no. 2 (August 1935), p. 91.

"Fitting the Garden to the House: Exhibit in San Francisco Shows the Best in Gardens." *Christian Science Monitor* (17 February 1937).

"Five Prize-Winning Holiday Houses." *House Beautiful* 79, no. 4 (March 1937), pp. 41–48.

Foster, Richard H., Jr. "Wartime Trailer Housing in the San Francisco Bay Area." *Geographical Review* 70, no. 3 (July 1980), pp. 276–90.

Frampton, Kenneth. "Towards a Critical Regionalism: Six Points for an Architecture of Resistance." In *The Anti-Aesthetic: Essays in Postmodern Culture,* edited by Hal Foster. Port Townsend, Washington: Bay Press, 1983.

Garren, William I. "There Must Be Romance in the Home You Build." *Sunset* 65, no. 1 (July 1930), pp. 22–24.

"General Electric Model Home, Berkeley." *American Architect* 52, no. 10 (October 1937), p. 14.

Goodman, Michael. "Miss Helen L. Crandell House, Berkeley." *Architectural Forum* 66, no. 5 (May 1937), pp. 434–35.

Gregory, Daniel P. "An Indigenous Thing: The Story of William Wurster and the Gregory Farmhouse." *Places* 7, no. 1 (Fall 1990), pp. 78–93.

———. "Pasatiempo." In *Sidewalk Companion to Santa Cruz,* edited by John Chase. Santa Cruz, Calif.: Paper Vision Press, 1979.

Hamlin, Talbot Faulkner. "What Makes It American: American Architecture of the Southwest and West." *Pencil Points* 20 (December 1939), pp. 774–75.

———. "Of Houses as Places to Live." *Pencil Points* 19, no. 8 (August 1938), pp. 487–89.

Hays, William C. "A Tribute to the Work of Michael Goodman, Architect." *Architect and Engineer* 139, no. 4 (November 1939), pp. 17–19.

Hise, Greg. "Home Building and Industrial Decentralization in Los Angeles: The Roots of the Postwar Urban Region." *Journal of Urban History* 19, no. 2 (February 1993), pp. 95–125.

"House and Garden Presents the 1940 Prize Winners." *House and Garden* 79, no. 1 (January 1941), pp. 24–35, 55.

"House Beautiful's 10th Annual Small House Competition." *House Beautiful* 80, no.1 (January 1938), pp. 14–23.

"House Beautiful's 10th Annual Small House Competition, Weekend Houses." *House Beautiful* 80, no. 3 (March 1938), pp. 50–52.

"House Beautiful's 13th Annual Small House Competition." *House Beautiful* 83, no. 2 (February 1941), pp. 18–19.

"House and Garden...Architects' Competition of 1937." *House and Garden* 72 (September 1927), pp. 13–50.

"House at San Francisco, California." *Progressive Architecture* 27, no. 8 (August 1946), pp. 67–68.

"House for Maurice Saeta, Los Angeles, Ca., Winchton L. Risley, Architect." *Architectural Forum* 70, no. 2 (February 1939), pp. 114–15.

"House for Mitchell T. Neff, Ross, Ca." *Architectural Forum* 66, no. 4 (April 1938), p. 346.

"House in Menlo Park, Calif." *Architect and Engineer* 147, no. 6 (December 1941), p. 34.

"House in Modesto, Calif. John Funk, Architect." *Architectural Forum* 74, no. 4 (March 1941), p. 195.

"House of Maurice Saeta, Los Angeles." *Architectural Record* 77, no. 1 (January 1935), p. 30.

"Houses by Hervey Parke Clark." *Architectural Forum* 73, no. 6 (December 1940), pp. 479–91.

"Houses for $3,000 to $4,000 Income." *Architectural Forum* 69, no. 5 (November 1938), pp. 321–25.

"A Humane Campus for the Study of Man." *Architectural Forum* 102, no. 1 (January 1955), pp. 130–34.

"Idea House for 1957." *Better Homes and Gardens* 36, no. 1 (September 1957), pp. 49–63, 138–40, 142.

"Industrial Supplement." *California Arts and Architecture* 58, no. 6 (June 1942), p. 40.

"Is This the Best We Can Do?" *California Arts and Architecture* 55, no. 9 (September 1940), pp. 20–21.

Jones, Frederick W. "Recent Work of John Ekin Dinwiddie, Architect." *Architect and Engineer* 141, no. 4 (April 1940), pp. 17–44.

Jones, Robert T. "Omitting the Cellar to Cut Building Costs," *Small Home* (January/February 1926).

Kelley, H. Roy. "Three California Houses." *Architect and Engineer* 124, no. 2 (February 1936), pp. 28–31.

Klein, Alexander. "Judging the Small Home." *Architectural Forum* 55 (August 1931), pp. 166–72.

Langhorst, Fred. "A New Approach to Large Scale Housing: The Office of William Wilson Wurster Attacks the Problem of Mass Housing." *California Arts and Architecture* 59 (April 1942), pp. 27–31.

———. "Experimental Housing, William Wilson Wurster." *California Arts and Architecture* 59, no. 4 (April 1942), pp. 27–31.

Lee, Marcia. "Utility Use of Aluminum in Attractive Residence, Mandeville Canyon, Los Angeles County." *Architect and Engineer* 184 (January 1951), pp. 24–27.

"Life Houses." *Architectural Forum* 69, no. 5 (November 1938), pp. 321–27.

"Life House No. 2, Menlo Park, Calif., Gardner A. Dailey, Architect." *Architectural Forum* 73, no. 1 (July 1940), p. 6.

"Life Presents Eight Houses for Modern Living." *Life* 5 (26 September 1938), pp. 47–48.

"Low Cost House for Life, Gardner Dailey, Architect." *Architectural Forum* 72, no. 4 (April 1940), pp. 223–25.

Mayhew, Clarence W. W. "House for Harold V. Manor, Soule Tract, Calif." *Architectural Forum* 71, no. 1 (July 1939), pp. 9–11.

Merner, Delight Ward. "Plan to Bring Beauty into Our Daily Life." *California Arts and Architecture* 41, no. 4 (April 1932), pp. 33–35, 43.

Moore, Charles W. "In San Francisco, a renewal effort based on civic pride falls short of expectation." *Architectural Forum* 123, no. 7 (July 1965), pp. 58–63.

Moses, Robert. "Mr. Moses Dissects the 'Long-Haired Planners.'" *New York Times Magazine* (25 June 1944). Reprinted in Joan Ockman, *Architecture Culture 1943–1968.* New York: Rizzoli International, 1993.

Mumford, Lewis. "The Skyline: The Status Quo." *The New Yorker* 23, no. 43 (11 October 1947), pp. 94–96. Reprinted in *Museum of Modern Art Bulletin* (Spring 1948), p. 4.

"1936 Convention in Retrospect." *Architect and Engineer* 127, no. 2 (November 1936), p. 52.

"Our First Prize House." *House Beautiful* 69 no. 3 (March 1931), p. 239.

Peters, Richard. "L'architetto William Wurster." *Casabella continuita,* no. 238 (April 1960), pp. 14–17.

Polyzoides, Stephanos. "Schindler, Lovell and the Newport Beach House, Los Angeles, 1921–26." *Oppositions,* no. 18 (Fall 1979), pp. 60–73.

"A Portfolio of Houses by Gardner A. Dailey." *Architectural Forum* 74, no. 5 (May 1941), pp. 363–65.

[A portfolio of Wurster's work.] *Architecture d'Aujourd'hui.* Reprinted in *Architectural Forum* (January 1938), pp. 29–30.

"Prefabrication for Flexible Planning." *Architectural Record.* (August 1954), pp. 96–98.

"Prize Winners in Annual Awards in Architecture." *House and Garden* 77, no. 1 (January 1940), pp. 15–23.

"Public and Commercial Structures, Chabot Terrace (FPHA)." *Pencil Points* 25, no. 8 (October. 1944), pp. 79–85.

"Quoting Mr. Wurster." *Architectural Forum* (May 1936), pp. 36–37.

"A Redwood House, Residence of Dr. and Mrs. B. Berliner, San Francisco, Calif." *California Arts and Architecture* 26, no. 8 (September 1940), p. 28.

Reid, Kenneth. "The Architect and the House: William Wurster of California." *Pencil Points* 19, no. 8 (August 1938), pp. 472–74.

Risley, Winchton L. "The Domestic and Other Architecture of H. Roy Kelley." *Architect and Engineer* 106, no. 3 (September 1931), pp. 25–60.

"Schools, Chabot Terrace War Housing, Vallejo, Calif." *Pencil Points* 24 (September 1943), pp. 46–49.

"Separate Worlds for Parents and Children." *Sunset* 123, no. 5 (November 1959), p. 86.

"Standard Engineering Corporation Shows New Type Manufactured Home at San Anselmo Preview." *Daily Pacific Builder* (13 March 1945), p. 1.

Stein, Clarence S., and Catherine. Bauer. "Store Buildings and Neighborhood Shopping Centers." *Architectural Record* 75 (February 1934), pp. 174–87.

"Sunset Community Center, San Francisco: Forty-three Acres Cooperatively Planned." *Architectural Record* 111, no. 3 (March 1952), pp. 121–32.

Tantau, Clarence. "Study for a Residence." *Architect and Engineer* 127, no. 1 (October 1936), p. 13.

Tunnard, Christopher. "Modern Gardens for Modern Homes: Reflections on Current Trends in Landscape Design." *Landscape Architecture* (January 1942).

"Two Family Roof Terrace Dwelling, Telegraph Hill, San Francisco." *Architect and Engineer* 128, no. 3 (March 1937), p. 19.

"Two Houses: A Formal House in an Informal Setting." *Architectural Record* 127, no. 4 (April 1960), p. 190.

"Unit No. 1 of the 'Prebilt' House." *Architectural Record* (September 1945), pp. 82–85.

Upton, Dell. "Pattern Books and Professionalism: Aspects of the Transformation of Domestic Architecture in America, 1800–1860." *Winterthur Portfolio* 19, no. 2–3 (Summer/Autumn), pp. 107–50.

"U.S. of Brazil Pavilion in San Francisco." *Architectural Record* 65, no. 4 (April 1939), p. 45.

"Vallejo War Housing." *California Arts and Architecture* 59 (December 1942), pp. 22–25.

Violich, Francis. " The Planning Pioneers." *California Living: Magazine of the San Francisco Chronicle* (26 February 1978), pp. 29–35.

"We Present...Catherine Bauer in Her Own Words." *Journal of Housing* 1, no. 11 (November 1944), p. 27.

"William Lowe, Jr. House, Santa Barbara, Calif." *Architectural Forum* 66, no. 4 (April 1927), pp. 324–25.

"William Wilson Wurster — 4 Houses in California." *Architectural Forum* 64, no. 5 (May 1936), pp. 377–402.

"William Wilson Wurster." *Architectural Forum* 79, no. 1 (July 1943), pp. 45–66.

"Woodlake: 'A Small Community Complete Within Itself.'" *Architectural Record* 139, no. 1 (January 1966), pp. 164–65.

Wright, Frank Lloyd. "Ranch House for Raymond Griffith." *Architectural Forum* 68, no. 6 (June 1938), pp. 471–78.

Wurster, William Wilson. "L'Architettura moderna in California." *Casabella continuita*, no. 238 (April 1960), p. 13.

———. "Architectural Education." *AIA Journal* 9, no. 1 (January 1948), p. 36.

———. "Architecture Broadens Its Base." *AIA Journal* 10, no. 7 (July 1948), pp. 30–32.

———. "Building Now." *House and Garden* 89, no. 5 (May 1946), pp. 74–77.

———. "California Architecture for Living." *California Monthly* 44, no. 8 (August 1954), pp. 14–15.

———. "Carquinez Heights." *California Arts and Architecture* 57 (November 1941), p. 34.

———. "Competition for U.S. Chancery Building, London." *Architectural Record* 119 (April 1956), p. 222.

———. "Flexible Space." *Architectural Forum* 77, no. 3 (September 1942), pp. 140–42.

———. "From Log Cabin to Modern House: An Architect Urges a Return to Simple Fundamentals in Planning Our New Homes." *New York Times Magazine* (20 January 1946).

———. "My Favorite Small Home." *Our Home* (ca. 1942).

———. "Office Building for the Schuckl Canning Co." *Architect and Engineer* 154, no. 2 (August 1943), pp. 12–17.

———. "The Outdoors in Residential Design of Houses." *Architectural Forum* 91, no. 3 (September 1949), p. 68.

———. "Planned for Prefabrication." *Architectural Record* (January 1944), pp. 79–84.

———. "Row House Vernacular and High Style Monument." *Architectural Record* 124, no. 8, pp. 141–50.

———. "San Francisco Bay Portfolio" *Magazine of Art* 77, no. 4 (April 1940), p. 301.

———. "Tell Me, What Is Modern Architecture?" *House and Garden* 77, no. 4 (April 1940), pp. 46–47, 71; *House and Garden* 77, no. 5 (May 1940), pp. 50, 60.

———. "Toward Urban Redevelopment." *Architect and Engineer* (July 1944), pp. 25–28.

———. "When Is a Small House Large?" *House and Garden* 92, no. 2 (August 1947), pp. 72–75.

Books

American Public Health Association, Committee on the Hygiene of Housing. *Basic Principles of Healthful Housing.* New York: The Committee, 1939.

Andrews, Wayne. *Architecture, Ambition and Americans.* New York: Harper & Brothers, 1947.

Aronovici, Carol, ed. *America Can't Have Housing.* New York: Museum of Modern Art, 1934.

Bauer, Catherine. *Modern Housing.* Boston: Houghton Mifflin, 1934.

———. *Economic Development and Urban Living Conditions: An Argument for Regional Planning to Guide Community Growth.* New York: United Nations Bureau of Social Affairs, 1956.

———. *War Housing in the United States.* Washington, D.C.: National Housing Agency for the United Nations Conference on International Organizations, 1945.

Bauer, Catherine, and Henry-Russell Hitchcock. *Modern Architecture in England.* New York: Museum of Modern Art, 1937.

Blake, Peter. *Marcel Breuer: Architect and Designer.* New York: Museum of Modern Art, 1949.

Bunting, Bainbridge. *John Gaw Meem: Southwestern Architect.* Albuquerque: University of New Mexico Press, 1983.

Burchard, John, and Albert Bush-Brown. *The Architecture of America: A Social and Cultural History.* Boston: Little, Brown, 1961.

Cardwell, Kenneth. *Bernard Maybeck: Artisan, Architect, Artist.* Santa Barbara: Peregrine Smith, 1977.

Church, Thomas. *Gardens Are for People.* New York: Reinhold, 1955.

———. *Your Private World.* San Francisco: Chronicle Books, 1969.

———. "A Study of Mediterranean Gardens and Their Adaptability to California Conditions." M.S. thesis, Harvard University, 1927.

Cole, Mary Susan. "Catherine Bauer and the Public Housing Movement, 1926–1932." Ph.D. diss., George Washington University, 1975.

Contemporary Architecture. San Francisco: San Francisco Museum of Art, 1937.

Creighton, Thomas, and Katherine Morrow Ford. *Contemporary Houses Evaluated by Their Owners.* New York: Reinhold, 1961.

De Zurko, Edward. *Origins of Functionalist Theory.* New York: Columbia University Press, 1957.

Domestic Architecture of the San Francisco Bay Region. San Francisco: San Francisco Museum of Modern Art, 1949.

Eckbo, Garrett. *Landscape for Living.* New York: F. W. Dodge, 1950.

Eichler, Ned. *The Merchant Builders.* Cambridge: MIT Press, 1982.

Ford, James, and Katherine Morrow Ford. *The Modern House in America.* New York: Architectural Book Publishing Co., 1940.

Fortune Magazine. *Housing America.* New York: Harcourt Brace, 1932.

Freudenheim, Leslie, and Elizabeth Sussman. *Building with Nature: Roots of the San Francisco Bay Region Tradition.* Santa Barbara: Peregrine Smith, 1974.

Gebhard, David. *Lutah Maria Riggs: A Woman in Architecture, 1921-1980.* Santa Barbara: Capra Press, 1992.

———. *Rudolph Schindler.* New York: Viking Press, 1971.

George, Mary Carolyn Hollers. *O'Neil Ford, Architect.* College Station, Texas: Texas A&M University Press, 1992.

Goldsmith, Margaret Olthof. *Designs for Outdoor Living.* New York: George W. Stewart, 1941.

Graham, John, Jr. *Housing in Scandinavia.* Chapel Hill: University of North Carolina Press, 1940.

Hanson, A. E. *An Arcadian Landscape: The Californian Gardens of A. E. Hanson, 1920–1932.* Edited by David Gebhard and Sheila Lynds. Los Angeles: Hennessey & Ingalls, 1985.

Hayden, Dolores. *Redesigning the American Dream: The Future of Housing, Work, and Family Life.* New York: W. W. Norton, 1984.

Hille, R. Thomas. *Inside the Large Small House: The Residential Design Legacy of William W. Wurster.* Princeton, N.J.: Princeton Architectural Press, 1994.

Hines, Thomas S. *Richard Neutra and the Search for a Modern Architecture.* New York: Oxford University Press, 1982.

Hise, Greg. "The Roots of the Postwar Urban Region: Mass Housing and Community Planning in California, 1920-1950." Ph.D. diss., University of California, Berkeley, 1992.

Hitchcock, Henry-Russell. *The International Style.* New York: W. W. Norton, 1932.

Hitchcock, Henry-Russell, and Arthur Drexler. *Built in USA: Post-war Architecture.* New York: Simon & Schuster, 1953.

Howard, Ebenezer. *The Garden Cities of Tomorrow.* London: Faber & Faber, 1902.

Imbert, Dorothée. *The Modernist Garden in France.* New Haven: Yale University Press, 1993.

Jay, Martin. *Force Fields: Between Intellectual History and Cultural Critique.* New York and London: Routledge, 1993.

Keeler, Charles. *The Simple House.* Santa Barbara: Peregrine Smith, 1904, reprint 1979.

Landscape Design. San Francisco: San Francisco Museum of Art and Association of Landscape Architects, San Francisco Region, 1948.

Le Corbusier. *Vers une architecture.* Paris: Editions Crès, 1923. Translated by Frederick Etchells under the title *Towards a New Architecture.* London: John Rodker, 1927; London: Architectural Press, 1965.

Lotchin, Roger. *Fortress California, 1910–1961: From Warfare to Welfare.* New York: Oxford University Press, 1992.

Longstreth, Richard. *On the Edge of the World: Four Architects in San Francisco at the Turn of the Century.* New York: Architectural History Foundation, 1983.

Lynes, Russell. *The Tastemakers: The Shaping of American Popular Taste.* New York: Dover, 1980.

McAndrews, John. *Guide to Modern Architecture: Northeast States.* New York: Museum of Modern Art, 1940.

McCallum, Ian. *Architecture U.S.A.* New York: Reinhold, 1959.

McWilliams, Carey. *Southern California: An Island on the Land.* Salt Lake City: Peregrine Smith, 1990.

Mitchell, Lucy Sprague. *Two Lives: The Story of Wesley Claire Mitchell and Myself.* New York: Simon & Schuster, 1953.

Mock, Elizabeth. *The Architecture of Bridges.* New York: Museum of Modern Art, 1949.

———. *Built in the USA: 1932–1944.* New York: Museum of Modern Art, 1944.

———. *If You Want to Build a House.* New York: Museum of Modern Art, 1946.

———. *Modern Gardens in the Landscape.* New York: Museum of Modern Art, 1964.

———. *What Is Modern Architecture?* New York: Museum of Modern Art, 1942.

Mumford, Lewis. *Sketches from Life: The Autobiography of Lewis Mumford, The Early Years.* New York: Dial, 1982.

———. *My Words and Days: A Personal Chronicle.* New York: Harcourt Brace Jovanovich, 1978.

Nash, Gerald. *The American West Transformed: The Impact of the Second World War.* Bloomington: Indiana University Press, 1985.

Nelson, George, and Henry Wright. *Tomorrow's House.* New York: Simon & Schuster, 1945.

O'Malley, Therese, and Marc Treib, eds. *The Regional Garden in the United States.* Washington, D.C.: Dumbarton Oaks, 1995.

Partridge, Loren W. *John Galen Howard and the Berkeley Campus: Beaux-Arts Architecture in the "Athens of the West."* Berkeley: Berkeley Architectural Heritage Association, 1978.

Perry, Clarence Arthur. *Housing for the Machine Age.* New York: Russell Sage Foundation, 1939.

Repton, Humphry. *Sketches and Hints on Landscape Gardening.* London: 1794. Reprinted in *The Landscape Gardening and Landscape Architecture of the Late Humphry Repton, Esq.* London: J. C. Loudon, 1840. Reprint, Westmead, Farnborough, England: Gregg International Publishers, 1969.

Richards, J.M., and Elizabeth Mock. *Introduction to Modern Architecture.* Revised American edition. New York: Penguin Books, 1947.

Roth, Leland M. *A Concise History of American Architecture.* New York: Harper & Row, 1979 and 1980.

Schildt, Göran. *Alvar Aalto: The Mature Years.* New York: Rizzoli International, 1991.

Scully, Vincent. *American Architecture and Urbanism.* New York: Praeger, 1969.

Smith, Elizabeth, ed. *Blueprints for Modern Living: History and Legacy of the Case Study Houses.* Los Angeles: Museum of Contemporary Art, 1989.

Solano County Chamber of Commerce. *Solano County Greets You.* 1939.

Stubblebine, Jo, ed. *The Northwest Architecture of Pietro Belluschi.* New York: F. W. Dodge, 1953.

Sunset Magazine and Books. *Western Ranch Houses by Cliff May.* Menlo Park, Calif.: Lane, 1958.

Telesis Environmental Research Group. *Space for Living.* San Francisco: San Francisco Museum of Art, 1940.

Thomas D. Church, Landscape Architect (2 vols.). Interviews by Suzanne B. Riess. Berkeley: University of California, Regional Oral History Office, 1978.

Treib, Marc, ed. *Modern Landscape Architecture: A Critical Review.* Cambridge: MIT Press, 1993.

Tunnard, Christopher. *Gardens in the Modern Landscape.* 2nd edition. London: Architectural Press; New York: Charles Scribner's Sons, 1948.

Weiss, Marc E. *The Rise of the Community Builders: The American Real Estate Industry and Urban Land Planning.* New York: Columbia University Press, 1987.

William Wilson Wurster: College of Environmental Design, University of California, Campus Planning, and Architectural Practice (2 vols.). Interview by Suzanne B. Riess. Berkeley: University of California, Regional Cultural History Project (now Regional Oral History Office), 1964).

Wills, Royal Barry. *Houses for Good Living.* New York: Architectural Book Publishing Co., 1940.

———. *Better Houses for Budgeteers.* New York: Architectural Book Publishing Co., 1941.

Woodbridge, Sally. *Bernard Maybeck: Visionary Architect.* New York: Abbeville, 1992.

———, ed. *Bay Area Houses.* Salt Lake City: Peregrine Smith, 1988.

Woodbury, Coleman, ed. *The Future of Cities and Redevelopment.* Chicago: University of Chicago Press, 1953.

Wurster, William Wilson. "The Twentieth-Century Architect." In *Architecture—A Profession and a Career.* Washington, D.C.: American Institute of Architects Press, 1945.

Illustration Credits

All photographs by Roger Sturtevant are copyright the Roger Sturtevant Collection, The City of Oakland, The Oakland Museum.

Originally published in *Architect and Engineer:*
figure 182 (July 1943)

Courtesy Architectural Drawing Collection/University Art Museum, University of California, Santa Barbara:
figures 124, 156–57, 159, 169

Courtesy The Architectural Drawings Collection, Architecture and Planning Library, the General Libraries at the University of Texas at Austin:
figures 34–35

Originally published in *Architectural Forum:*
figures 111 (May 1936), 171–72 (July 1939), 173–76 (November 1938), 202 (September 1950), 207 (July 1938)

Permission for use granted by *Architectural Record:*
figures 158 (February 1934), 200 (September 1948)

Originally published in *Architecture:*
figure 106 (August 1935)

Originally published in *Arts and Architecture:*
figures 160 (April 1930), 184 (February 1943)

Courtesy Avery Architectural and Fine Arts Library, Columbia University in the City of New York:
figures 4, 7

Originally published in *Better Houses for Budgeteers* (Architectural Book Publishing Company, Inc., 1941):
figure 31

Originally published in *California Arts and Architecture:*
figure 211 (December 1954)

Courtesy Center for Southwest Research, University of New Mexico:
figure 32

Courtesy Thomas Church and Associates:
figures 119, 127

Courtesy College of Environmental Design Documents Collection, University of California at Berkeley:
figures 2–3, 5–6, 10, 14–16, 19–21, 38, 44, 48 (drawing by Norman Thompson), 52, 55, 61–63, 69–71, 73–74, 77, 86 (drawing by Russell Quacchia), 87 (photo by Morley Baer), 95 (photo by Moss Photography), 96–98, 107, 120 (drawing by Norman Thompson), 122, 136–39, 193 (photo by Rondal Partridge), 198, and frontispiece. Roger Sturtevant photographs: figures 24, 26, 39, 41, 45, 53, 60, 78, 85, 117, 121, 135, 151–52, 161, 163, 165

Courtesy Dean's Office, College of Environmental Design, University of California at Berkeley:
figures 177 (photo by Thomas Church), 181 (photo by Roger Sturtevant)

Courtesy Garrett Eckbo:
figure 123

Originally published in *Gardens Are for People,* 1955 (reprinted by University of California Press, ©1983, Elizabeth R. Church):
figure 132

Courtesy David Gebhard:
figure 166

Courtesy M. C. H. George:
figures 36 (©1986 Eugene George), 37, 40 (©1986 Eugene George)

Originally published in *Good Housekeeping:*
figure 197 (August 1952)

Courtesy Daniel Gregory:
figures 99, 100 (photo by Thomas Church), 104 (photo by William Wurster), 105, 109 (photo by Thomas Church), 110 (photo by Thomas Church), 113 (photo by Daniel Gregory), 115, 192

Courtesy of Lawrence Halprin:
figures 80, 82

Originally published in *House and Home:*
figure 209 (February 1952)

Originally published in *Houses for Good Living* (Architectural Book Publishing Company, Inc., 1940):
figures 11–12

Courtesy Dorothée Imbert:
figure 116

Courtesy Elizabeth Gregory Kent:
figure 101

Originally published in *Landscape Design* (San Francisco Museum of Art, 1948):
figures 129–30, 179

Originally published in *Modern Housing* (Houghton Mifflin, 1934):
figure 183

Courtesy Oregon Historical Society:
figure 33 (# CN 020342)

Courtesy Rondal Partridge:
figures 114, 128, 193

Courtesy San Francisco Museum of Modern Art: Accessions Committee Fund:
figure 49 (photo by Ben Blackwell)

Courtesy San Francisco Museum of Modern Art: gift of Walter A. and Evelyn Haas, Jr., and Mr. and Mrs. Brooks Walker, Jr.:
figures 8–9 (photos by Ben Blackwell)

Courtesy Roger Sturtevant Collection, The City of Oakland, The Oakland Museum. Gift of the Artist:
figures 1, 13, 17, 22–23, 25, 42–43, 46–47, 50–51, 54, 58–59, 64–68, 72, 75–76, 79, 90, 92–94, 102–3, 118, 125, 134, 142, 145, 149–50, 153, 155, 162, 164, 167–68, 170, 178, 189, 195–96, 199, 201, and cover (all photos by Roger Sturtevant)

Courtesy Sunset Publishing Company:
figure 108

Courtesy Marc Treib:
figures 27–30, 56–57, 84, 91, 131, 133

Courtesy Wurster, Bernardi and Emmons:
figures 18 (photo by Roger Sturtevant), 80, 88, 112 (photo by Roger Sturtevant), 140–41, 143, 144, 146–47, 154, 180 (drawing by Arne Korwalt), 185–86, 191, 194 (photo by Roger Sturtevant), 200, 203–6, 208 (photo by Roger Sturtevant), 212–14

Index